KT-382-535

The Penguin Dictionary of Proverbs

Rosalind Fergusson was born in Liverpool in 1953 and obtained her degree in French from Exeter University. From here she took a teaching certificate and became an assistant teacher at a school in West Sussex. From 1978 to 1984 she worked for Market House Books where she trained as an assistant editor and rose to the position of Senior Editor. During this time she worked on a range of reference books. Since leaving Market House Books she has worked as a freelance editor.

Her other publications include *The Penguin Rhyming Dictionary* (1985), *Choose your Baby's Name* (1987), *The Hamlyn Dictionary of Quotations* (1989), *The Penguin Dictionary of English Synonyms and Antonyms* (1992), *Chambers Dictionary of Foreign Words and Phrases* (1995) and *The New Penguin Dictionary of Abbreviations* (2000). Rosalind Fergusson has also edited and co-edited a number of dictionaries and reference books, and has contributed to *The Bloomsbury Good Word Guide* (1988) and *Brewer's Dictionary of 20th-Century Phrase and Fable* (1991), among others.

Rosalind Fergusson is married and lives in Kent. Her leisure interests include walking, sailing and music.

Jonathan Law was born in rural Somerset in 1961 and educated at Oxford University, where he obtained a degree in English. After postgraduate and teaching work he spent several years helping to research a major biography of T. E. Lawrence. Since 1989 he has worked as an editor at Market House Books, where he has contributed to numerous reference works, including successive editions of the *Collins English Dictionary* and the *Macmillan Encyclopedia*. He is the editor of *European Culture: A Contemporary Companion* (1993) and *The Cassell Companion to Cinema* (1995). The books he has co-edited include *The Penguin Biographical Dictionary of Women* (1998) and *Who's Who in the Twentieth Century* (1999). Jonathan Law is married and lives in Buckinghamshire. As the father of two small children he has no leisure interests of any kind.

The Penguin Dictionary of

Proverbs

Market House Books Ltd

PENGUIN BOOKS

Editors for Market House Books Ltd

Rosalind Fergusson (first edition)
Jonathan Law (second edition)

PENGUIN BOOKS

Published by the Penguin Group
Penguin Books Ltd, 80 Strand, London WC2R 0RL, England
Penguin Putnam Inc., 375 Hudson Street, New York, New York 10014, USA
Penguin Books Australia Ltd, 250 Camberwell Road, Camberwell, Victoria 3124, Australia
Penguin Books Canada Ltd, 10 Alcorn Avenue, Toronto, Ontario, Canada M4V 3B2
Penguin Books India (P) Ltd, 11 Community Centre, Panchsheel Park, New Delhi – 110 017, India
Penguin Books (NZ) Ltd, Cnr Rosedale and Airborne Roads, Albany, Auckland, New Zealand
Penguin Books (South Africa) (Pty) Ltd, 24 Sturdee Avenue, Rosebank 2196, South Africa

Penguin Books Ltd, Registered Offices: 80 Strand, London WC2R 0RL, England

www.penguin.com

First published 1983
Published simultaneously by Allen Lane
This revised and enlarged edition published 2000
5

Typeset in ITC Stone
Typeset by Market House Books Ltd
Printed in England by Clays Ltd, St Ives plc

This collection of over 6,000 proverbs, from all nations and all ages, ranges from the classical wisdom of *Familiarity breeds contempt* to the 20th-century cynicism of *Those who can, do: those who can't, teach.* For the purposes of this dictionary a proverb is defined as a succinct and memorable statement that contains advice (*First thrive and then wive*), a warning or prediction (*Marry in haste and repent at leisure*), or an analytical observation (*A maid marries to please her parents, a widow to please herself*). Idiomatic phrases, such as *between the devil and the deep blue sea*, and similes, such as *like a bat out of hell*, are not included.

The proverbs are arranged in the book in categories, such as ABSENCE, LOVE, and WEATHER, and are divided within each category into groups that express various aspects of the main theme. This arrangement draws attention to the less common variants of familiar proverbs, and also reveals some interesting contradictions. The categories themselves are arranged in alphabetical order.

Some proverbs are simple folk sayings (*An apple a day keeps the doctor away*); these have only their literal meaning. Some, broader and more philosophical, aspire to deal with the great mysteries and paradoxes of life (*Opportunity seldom knocks twice*). Others are metaphorical: while apparently belonging to the first class they really belong to the second. *There is more than one way to skin a cat* has no more to do with cats than *Don't count your chickens before they are hatched* has to do with chickens. In this book these metaphorical proverbs are sorted into categories that refer to their metaphorical rather than their literal meanings; thus *Every cloud has a silver lining* appears under OPTIMISM (not WEATHER).

This system greatly reduces the need to explain the meaning of the proverbs; however, a short explanation is provided in the notes where the meaning or implication is not obvious. Many proverbs have become obscure because they presume a familiarity with activities and pursuits that were almost universal in the preindustrial world but no longer form part of the daily experience of most people. For this reason, brief explanatory notes have been added to some of the numerous proverbs that allude to e.g. agriculture, animal husbandry, and traditional handicrafts. These notes provide a glimpse into the daily lives of our ancestors that can be fascinating in its own right. By the same token archaic and dialect words are also explained or translated if their meaning is not apparent from the context.

In many cases notes have also been used to supply attribution. A surprising number of proverbs are in fact direct quotations (or misquotations) from the Bible, from Shakespeare, or from some other literary source, while a still larger group are based more loosely on biblical or classical texts. These sources (with dates) have been indicated wherever it seemed useful or interesting to do so. Owing to their oral and traditional character, few other proverbs can be dated with any degree of accuracy (especially as so many have variants in more than one language). In most cases, therefore, such information has only been ventured where the proverb is clearly very ancient or unusually recent. As most of the proverbs in this collection have been handed down by word of mouth from generation to generation, it is inevitable that slight variations in the wording will exist. In general, the proverbs have been entered in their most familiar form, with the most common or intriguing variants mentioned in the notes.

A number of foreign proverbs in translation have been included in this collection. The Chinese, in particular, are renowned for their cogent and picturesque idiom (*Wise is the man who has two loaves, and sells one to buy a lily*); the origin of such proverbs is given with some measure of certainty. However, proverbs from Spain, France, and other European countries have not generally been acknowledged, as a variant of the same proverb often exists in several countries and it is usually impossible to pinpoint its origin. In the case of Latin proverbs the English version is given first, even when the Latin form is better known (*Caveat emptor*, for example, will be found under *Let the buyer beware*).

Finally, a word about the wisdom of proverbs. Proverbs have to be short, they have to be memorable, and they must not be mere platitudes: but they do not have to be true. Folk wisdom is often contradictory. *A fair face cannot have a crabbed heart* and *Fair face, foul heart* cannot both be correct. While proverbs can often be astute, down-to-earth, and even inspiring, a reader of this collection will find others that seem small-minded, superstitious, or plain wrong. At the same time, *A proverb comes not from nothing*. If it is a mistake to put too much faith in proverbs as a source of accumulated wisdom, perhaps they are better seen as a collection of tags that enable thoughts to be communicated and exchanged, without the effort of formulation. An English dictionary lists words with which to formulate ideas. This *Dictionary of Proverbs* lists a selection of preformulated ideas, ready for instant use in the appropriate situation.

ROSALIND FERGUSSON
JONATHAN LAW
2000.

Using the Index

The index is an important part of this dictionary. Each proverb is indexed under its first keyword and the index entry gives either the complete proverb or the opening phrase. This is followed by the category number and the number of the proverb within that category. Thus *Look before you leap* and *A stitch in time saves nine* are indexed as:

Look L. before you leap 85:33
Stitch A s. in time... 52:21

Contents

1 Absence

Its effect on love

1 Absence makes the heart grow fonder.
First used in precisely this form by the British poet and playwright Thomas Haynes Bayly, in his song "Isle of Beauty" (c. 1850). The sentiment can be traced back to the Roman poet Propertius (1st century BC).

2 Men are best loved furthest off.

3 Absence diminishes little passions and increases great ones.
In the more elaborate form "Absence to love is like wind to a fire, it diminishes..." this is a quotation from the French libertine Roger de Bussy-Rabutin.

4 Absence sharpens love, presence strengthens it.

5 Far from eye, far from heart.

6 Salt water and absence wash away love.
"Salt water" here refers to the sea, or more precisely the separation caused by a long sea voyage. Cited by Horatio Nelson in a letter (1790s) to his mistress, Lady Hamilton.

Its effect on friendship

7 Friends agree best at a distance.

8 Separation secures manifest friendship.
Indian proverb.

9 Long absence changes a friend.

10 To dead men and absent there are no friends left.

Its effect on discipline

11 When the cat's away, the mice will play.
For other proverbs on this theme see DISCIPLINE: *The watchful master*.

12 Well kens the mouse when the cat's out of the house.

13 If the dog is not at home, he barks not.
African proverb.

14 He that fears you present will hate you absent.

Its dangers

15 The absent are always in the wrong.

16 The absent are never without fault, nor the present without excuse.
The earliest known citation in this form is by Benjamin Franklin (1736); however, there are many older variants.

17 The absent party is always to blame.

18 Never were the absent in the right.

19 If a person is away, his right is away.
Moorish proverb.

20 He is guilty who is not at home.
Ukrainian proverb.

Other disadvantages

21 Out of sight, out of mind.
First recorded in English in the 15th century, when "mind" had the specific sense "memory, recollection" rather than the more general "consciousness".

22 Present to the eye, present to the mind.
Chinese proverb.

23 Unminded, unmoaned.
"Unmoaned" means "unlamented".

24 Unseen, unrued.

25 Long absent, soon forgotten.

26 Seldom seen, soon forgotten.

27 The absent get farther off every day.
Japanese proverb.

28 Absence is the mother of disillusion.

29 The absent saint gets no candle.
Even the most virtuous find no one to praise or thank them when they are absent. The reference is to the (mainly Roman Catholic) practice of lighting votive candles at the shrine of a saint.

Other advantages

30 Far folk fare best.
Like proverb 31 below, this implies that people are always willing to praise their far-off friends or relations (presumably because they are not around to cause trouble or irritation).

31 They are aye good that are away.

32 Far from court, far from care.

2 Adversity

Its sources

1 Misfortunes come of themselves.

2 An ill marriage is a spring of ill fortune.

Its effects

3 Adversity makes a man wise, not rich.

4 Trouble brings experience and experience brings wisdom.

5 The wind in one's face makes one wise.
"The wind in one's face" implies adversity or difficulty.

6 Misfortunes hasten age.

7 Adversity makes strange bedfellows.
Like proverb 8 below, this implies that unlikely alliances are formed through common

misfortune. The saying's first recorded use (with "misery" substituted for "adversity") is in Shakespeare's *The Tempest* (1611). Other writers have substituted "poverty" or "politics" for "adversity".

8 Woes unite foes.

9 Misfortune makes foes of friends.
   For other proverbs on this theme see FRIENDS: *Their disloyalty*.

10 It is easy to bear the misfortunes of others.
   Variants appear in works by Pope, Goldsmith, and La Rochefoucauld.

Its value

11 Adversity is the touchstone of virtue.

12 Adversity comes with instruction in its hand.

13 Misfortunes tell us what fortune is.
   Like proverb 14 below, this implies that good fortune can be better appreciated when one has experienced misfortune.

14 No man better knows what good is than he who has endured evil.

15 He that is down needs fear no fall.
   A quotation from the shepherd boy's song in Bunyan's *Pilgrim's Progress* (1684).

16 Ill luck is good for something.

17 Sweet are the uses of adversity.
   A quotation from Shakespeare's *As You Like It* (c. 1600).

Its undesirability

18 What is worse than ill luck?

19 He gains enough whom fortune loses.
   "Fortune" here means "misfortune".

Its inevitability

20 Misfortunes find their way even on the darkest night.

21 Misfortune comes to all men and most women.
   Chinese proverb.

22 There is a crook in the lot of every one.
   "Crook" here means "trial, affliction".

23 Misfortune is not that which can be avoided, but that which cannot.
   Chinese proverb.

Its method of attack

24 Misfortune arrives on horseback but departs on foot.

25 Mischief comes by the pound and goes away by the ounce.

26 Ill comes in by ells, and goes out by inches.
   An "ell" was a former unit of length, used mainly to measure cloth; originally calculated from the length of a man's forearm (about 18 inches), it was later standardized at 45 inches in England and 37 in Scotland.

27 Misfortunes never come singly.

28 It never rains but it pours.

29 Of one ill come many.

30 Ill comes often on the back of worse.

31 An unhappy man's cart is eith to tumble.
"Unhappy" means "unlucky" and "eith to tumble" means "easy to overturn". The implication is that an unfortunate person is most susceptible to further misfortune.
32 Lightning never strikes twice in the same place.

3 Advice

Its value

1 Good counsel has no price.
2 Good counsel never comes too late.
3 Good counsel never comes amiss.
4 Good take heed does surely speed.
Take heed" here means "willingness to heed advice".
5 Take heed is a fair thing.

Its limitations

6 Advice is a stranger; if welcome he stays for the night; if not welcome he returns home the same day.
African proverb.
7 Counsel is irksome, when the matter is past remedy.
8 When a thing is done, advice comes too late.
9 We may give advice, but we cannot give conduct.
10 Counsel is no command.
11 Take counsel only of your own head.
12 Though thou hast never so many counsellors, yet do not forsake the counsel of thy own soul.
13 A good scare is worth more to a man than good advice.

Its dangers

14 Counsel will make a man stick his own mare.
Advice can make a man more determined to go his own way. "Stick his own mare" means "spur on his own horse", i.e. forge determinedly ahead.
15 Ill counsel mars all.

The importance of seeking advice

16 While the discreet advise, the fool does his business.
Here, as in proverbs 17 and 18 below, "advise" means "seek advice".
17 Though old and wise, yet still advise.
18 There never came ill of good advisement.
19 He that will not be counselled, cannot be helped.

The importance of following advice

20 Counsel must be followed, not praised.
21 In vain he craves advice that will not follow it.
22 He was slain that had warning, not he that took it.
23 Advice when most needed is least heeded.
24 The first degree of folly is to hold one's self wise, the second to profess it, the third to despise counsel.

25 Who will not be ruled by the rudder, must be ruled by the rock.
Implies that those who will not be guided by advice and warning must learn from disaster. A nautical saying.

26 Write down the advice of him who loves you, though you like it not at present.

27 In wiving and thriving a man should take counsel of all the world.
That is, you cannot take too much advice in matters of marriage or commerce.

The need to be selective

28 Steer not after every mariner's direction.

29 Too much consulting confounds.

30 He that speers all opinions, comes ill speed.
He that seeks ("speers") everybody's opinion will come to grief (because the advice is sure to conflict).

31 Like counsellor, like counsel.

Good sources of advice

32 If you wish good advice, consult an old man.

33 Night is the mother of counsel.
Both this and proverb 34 below are ways of saying "sleep on it". Variants of the expression are found in Menander, Spenser, and Dryden.

34 The best advice is found on the pillow.

35 Counsel is to be given by the wise, the remedy by the rich.

36 The healthful man can give counsel to the sick.

37 An enemy may chance to give good counsel.

38 If the counsel be good, no matter who gave it.

39 A fool may give a wise man counsel.

40 The egg shows the hen the place where to hatch.
African proverb. The implication is that the advice of the young should not be despised.

41 A woman's advice is no great thing, but he who won't take it is a fool.

Bad sources of advice

42 Counsels in wine seldom prosper.

43 Counsel over cups is crazy.

44 Advice whispered in the ear is not worth a tare.
"Tare" was a name for the wild vetch and particularly for its tiny seeds, which became a byword for worthlessness.

45 Advice whispered is worthless.

46 Take the first advice of a woman and not the second.
Implies that the first advice, based on intuition, will be more reliable than the second, based on inferior reasoning.

47 Women's counsel is cold.
An old Icelandic saying. "Cold" here means "deadly, fatal".

Giving advice

48 It is safer to hear and take counsel, than to give it.

49 It is as hard to follow good advice as to give it.

50 Give neither counsel nor salt till you are asked for it.

51 Come not to counsel uncalled.

52 Don't teach your grandmother to suck eggs.
Don't attempt to teach someone what he or she may reasonably be expected to know better than you. Variants of this curious expression include "...to spin eggs", "...to grope ducks", and "...to sup sour milk".

53 Overhasty counsels are rarely prosperous.

54 Anger and haste hinder good counsel.

55 The counsel thou wouldst have another keep, first keep it thyself.

56 We have better counsel to give than to take.

57 Nothing is given so freely as advice.

58 The land is never void of counsellors.

59 He that thatches his house with turds shall have more teachers than reachers.
Implies that someone who puts himself in an unpleasant situation through his own folly must expect people to be more ready with advice than practical assistance.

60 Bachelors' wives and maids' children are well taught.
Like proverbs 61–63 below, this implies that those who have no experience of a situation are only too eager to offer advice.

61 He that has no children brings them up well.

62 Every man can rule a shrew save he that has her.

63 He that has no wife, beats her oft.

4 Ambition

Its value

1 Ambition makes people diligent.

2 Poor by condition, rich by ambition.
Chinese proverb.

3 He who aims at the moon may hit the top of a tree; he who aims at the top of a tree is unlikely to get off the ground.

4 He that stays in the valley, shall never get over the hill.

5 Nothing crave, nothing have.

6 Nothing seek, nothing find.

7 Seek and ye shall find.
A quotation from the Sermon on the Mount (Matthew 7:7).

8 Seek mickle, and get something; seek little, and get nothing.
"Mickle" means "much".

9 Look to a gown of gold, and you will at least get a sleeve of it.

10 Bode a robe, and wear it; bode a sack, and bear it.
"Bode" here means "expect".

11 He begins to die that quits his desires.

12 Hitch your wagon to a star.
A quotation from Ralph Waldo Emerson's essay "Civilization", published in *Society and Solitude* (1870). Although Emerson's injunction was meant in the most idealistic sense, the phrase is now often used quite cynically, to suggest that an ambitious person should attach his or her fortunes to those of a rising star in politics, business, etc.

13 There's always room at the top.
Attributed to the US statesman Daniel Webster (1782–1852), who is said to have replied thus when advised not to become a lawyer because the profession was overcrowded.

The phrase remains well known as the title of John Braine's novel *Room at the Top* (1957) and the subsequent film (1958).

Its dangers

14 Ambition loses many a man.

15 He who opens his heart to ambition closes it to repose.

16 Every ambitious man is a captive and every covetous one a pauper.
Arabic proverb.

17 Desire has no rest.

18 The best is the enemy of the good.
Implies that by continually striving for the best one may waste good opportunities. The earliest recorded use is by Voltaire (1772) but the expression is probably of older origin. The saying is sometimes reversed to give the opposite meaning: see GOODNESS: 32.

19 Better sit still than rise and fall.

20 Hasty climbers have sudden falls.

21 High places have their precipices.

22 The higher the mountain the greater descent.

23 Hew not too high lest the chips fall in thine eye.
The allusion is to chopping down a tree; if blows are struck above head height, chips may blind the hewer, with potentially dangerous consequences.

24 In a great river, great fish are found; but take heed lest you be drowned.

25 The ant had wings to her hurt.
A warning against aspiring to higher positions than one is equipped to cope with.

Against over-ambition

26 Better be first in a village than second at Rome.
A saying attributed to Julius Caesar in Plutarch's *Lives* (1st century AD).

27 Better be the head of a dog than the tail of a lion.
Variants substitute "fox", "mouse", or "lizard" for "dog". Others substitute "ass...horse", "pike...sturgeon", or "yeomanry...gentry" for "dog...lion".

28 Better ride on an ass that carries me than a horse that throws me.

29 Seek that which may be found.

See also GREATNESS: *Its dangers*

5 Anger

Its undesirability

1 He that is angry is seldom at ease.

2 An angry man never wants woe.

3 Anger makes a rich man hated, and a poor man scorned.

Its dangers

4 Anger and haste hinder good counsel.

5 Anger punishes itself.

6 Wrath killeth the foolish man.
A biblical quotation: Job 5:2.

7 Wrath often consumes what goodness husbands.
Icelandic proverb.

8 Anger ends in cruelty.
Indian proverb.

9 Take heed of the wrath of a mighty man, and the tumult of the people.
A more elaborate version continues "...from a widow that has thrice married, from a wind that comes in at a hole, and from a reconciled enemy."

10 From a choleric man withdraw a little; from him that says nothing for ever.
Implies that silent anger is more lasting and dangerous than noisy ill-temper.

Its irrationality

11 Anger has no eyes.
Hindi proverb.

12 When a man grows angry, his reason rides out.

13 When wrath speaks, wisdom veils her face.

14 Anger begins with folly, and ends with repentance.

15 When a man is angry, he cannot be in the right.
Chinese proverb.

Its causes

16 As fire is kindled by bellows, so is anger by words.

17 A hungry man is an angry man.

18 Patience provoked turns to fury.

19 Short folk are soon angry.
For other expressions of this common folk belief see SMALL THINGS: 42–43.

Its duration

20 Anger dies quickly with a good man.

21 Anger is a short madness.

22 The anger is not warrantable that has seen two suns.

23 He who slowly gets angry keeps his anger longer.

Its remedies

24 When angry, count a hundred.
A variant suggests "...recite the alphabet".

25 Delay is the antidote of anger.

26 If you be angry, you may turn the buckle of your belt behind you.
The aim of turning one's belt is apparently to provide a harmless outlet for one's anger.

27 When meat is in, anger is out.

28 A soft answer turneth away wrath.
A biblical quotation: Proverbs 15:1.

Controlling one's anger

29 Anger restrained is wisdom gained.

30 When you enter into a house, leave the anger ever at the door.

31 He has wisdom at will, that with an angry heart can hold him still.

32 Let not the sun go down upon your wrath.
A biblical quotation: Ephesians 4:26.

Needless anger

33 Two things a man should never be angry at; what he can help, and what he cannot help.
Implies that *all* anger is futile.

34 He that is angry without a cause, shall be pleased without amends.

6 Anticipation

Its effects

1 Expectation is better than realization.

2 Prospect is often better than possession.

3 Fear of death is worse than death itself.

4 Easter so longed for is gone in a day.

5 It is better to travel hopefully than to arrive.
A quotation from Robert Louis Stevenson's *Virginibus Puerisque* (1881).

Its inadvisability

6 Don't count your chickens before they are hatched.
The moral of "The Milkmaid and her Pail", one of the fables attributed to Aesop (6th century BC).

7 Don't sell the skin till you have caught the bear.
The moral of La Fontaine's fable "The Bear and the Two Companions" (late 17th century). This is probably the origin of the stock-market term "bear", meaning a dealer who exploits a falling market by selling securities, etc., that he does not have in the expectation of buying them in at a lower rate.

8 First catch your hare.
Commonly believed to be the first direction in a recipe for jugged hare in either Mrs Beeton's *Book of Household Management* (1851) or Mrs Glasse's *Art of Cookery* (1747); however, no such phrase appears in either work and the saying is clearly much older, being a variant of proverb 7 above.

9 Never spend your money before you have it.

10 Count not four, except you have them in a wallet.
Don't enumerate your expectations until you have them safely in the bag.

11 Don't bargain for fish which are still in the water.
Indian proverb.

12 It is ill fishing before the net.
That is, before the net is drawn in.

13 Don't build the sty before the litter comes.

14 Boil not the pap before the child is born.
"Pap" was a mixture of breadcrumbs and boiled milk formerly fed to infants.

15 Don't spread the cloth till the pot begins to boil.

16 Gut no fish till you get them.

17 Make not your sauce, before you have caught the fish.

18 Don't eat the calf in the cow's belly.

19 It is ill prizing of green barley.

20 Do not halloo till you are out of the wood.
Don't rejoice at extricating yourself from a difficult situation until you are sure that there

are no further problems ahead; now mainly familiar from the idiom "we're not out of the woods yet."

21 Do not triumph before the victory.

22 The opera isn't over till the fat lady sings.
A modern US proverb implying that something can't be considered over until an appropriate climax has been reached. It has been attributed to a Texan sports editor, Dan Cook (1970s).

23 He laughs best who laughs last.

24 He who laughs last, laughs longest.
A 20th-century variant of proverb 23 above.

25 There's many a slip 'twixt the cup and the lip.
A very ancient proverb, cited by several classical authors. It apparently originates from the legend of Ancaeus, king of Ionia. In mockery of a prophecy that he would not live to taste the wine from his vineyards, Ancaeus raised a goblet of the new wine to his lips. However, before he could drink a drop he received a message that a wild boar was tearing up the vineyard; he immediately went to drive it away and was killed in the attempt.

26 Blessed is he who expects nothing, for he shall never be disappointed.
Cited as "the ninth beatitude" by Alexander Pope in a letter of 1725.

27 He that hopes not for good, fears not evil.

The unexpected

28 The unexpected always happens.

29 Nothing is certain but the unforeseen.

See also WORRY: *Against worrying about the future*

7 Appearance

Misleading appearance

1 Appearances are deceptive.

2 Things are not always what they seem.

3 All that glitters is not gold.
Variants appear in Chaucer, Shakespeare, and Gray.

4 All are not maidens that wear bare hair.
A reference to the former fashion of virgins to go without hats.

5 It is not the beard that makes the philosopher.

6 If the beard were all, the goat might preach.

7 It is not the gay coat that makes the gentleman.

8 The cowl does not make the monk.
A cowl is the hooded garment distinctive to monks.

9 The face is no index to the heart.
Another common proverb states the opposite: "The face is index to the heart (or mind)."

10 He that looks in a man's face knows not what money is in his purse.

11 All are not merry that dance lightly.

12 They that are booted are not always ready.

13 All Stuarts are not sib to the king.
"Sib" means "related"; the Stuarts were the ruling dynasty in Scotland from 1371 to 1714

and in England from 1603 to 1714. A saying directed at those with pretensions to greatness.

The need for caution

14 The bait hides the hook.
15 Bees that have honey in their mouths have stings in their tails.
16 Cats hide their claws.
17 The still sow eats up all the draff.
    "Draff" means "scraps". A saying directed at an innocuous-seeming person judged to be slyly self-seeking.
18 Fair face, foul heart.
19 Fair without, false within.
20 There is many a fair thing full false.
21 Straight trees have crooked roots.
22 Vice is often clothed in virtue's habit.
23 What is sweet in the mouth is oft bitter in the stomach.
24 Poison is poison though it comes in a golden cup.
25 The fowler's pipe sounds sweet till the bird is caught.
26 Distance lends enchantment to the view.
    A quotation from Thomas Campbell's once widely read poem *The Pleasures of Hope* (1799). Like proverbs 27 and 28 below, this implies that things that appear attractive at a distance may be disappointing when viewed at close quarters.
27 Blue are the faraway hills.
28 Far fowls have fair feathers.

Against judging by appearances

29 Never judge from appearances.
    Oscar Wilde's riposte is well known: "It is only shallow people who do not judge by appearances" (1891).
30 All clouds bring not rain.
31 None can guess the jewel by the casket.
32 You can't tell a book by its cover.
    Of 20th-century US origin.
33 You cannot know the wine by the barrel.
34 Still waters run deep.
    An example of a proverb that has completely changed its meaning. Before the 19th century it was used to point out that a fair appearance can be dangerously deceptive; since then, it has been used in a mainly favourable sense, to suggest that a person with a placid manner may have hidden depths.
35 Truth has a good face, but bad clothes.
36 There's many a good cock come out of a tattered bag.
    A proverb originating in the sport of cockfighting.
37 Crooked logs make straight fires.
38 A straight stick is crooked in the water.
39 A black plum is as sweet as a white.
40 A black hen lays a white egg.
41 In the coldest flint there is hot fire.
42 All are not thieves that dogs bark at.

The inadequacy of disguise

43 An ape's an ape, a varlet's a varlet, though they be clad in silk or scarlet.
    "Scarlet" here signifies the ceremonial robe of a judge or other dignitary. Variants of the
    saying can be traced back to Lucan (1st century AD).
44 The filth under the white snow the sun discovers.
45 Fine dressing is a foul house swept before the doors.
46 A whore in a fine dress is like a clean entry to a dirty house.
47 A holy habit cleanses not a foul soul.

8 Asking

Its importance

1 He that cannot ask, cannot live.
2 A man may lose his goods for want of demanding them.
3 Bashfulness is an enemy to poverty.
   That is, bashfulness is a great disadvantage to a poor man.
4 Better to ask the way than go astray.

Its effects

5 Ask and it shall be given you.
   A biblical quotation: Matthew 7:7.
6 Speak and speed, ask and have.
7 He that demands misses not, unless his demands be foolish.

Questions

8 Question for question is all fair.
9 Like question, like answer.
10 Ask a silly question and you'll get a silly answer.
    In this form a 20th-century saying, although the sentiment is much older (see e.g.
    Proverbs 26:5).
11 Never answer a question until it is asked.
12 Ask no questions and hear no lies.
    Variants of this common saying appear in works by Goldsmith, Scott, and Kipling.
13 It is not every question that deserves an answer.
14 Every why has a wherefore.
    "Wherefore" here means "because of which"; the phrase as a whole therefore means
    "every question has an answer" or "there's an explanation for everything".

Refusal

15 He that asks faintly begs a denial.
16 Shameful craving must have shameful nay.
17 A civil denial is better than a rude grant.
18 Delays are not denials.
19 Don't say 'No' till you are asked.
20 If you always say 'No', you'll never be married.
21 'No, thank you', has lost many a good butter-cake.
    An old Lancashire saying.

22 Never refuse a good offer.
23 The money you refuse will never do you good.
24 Money refused loses its brightness.

9 Authority

Its advantages

1 Better to rule than be ruled by the rout.
2 It is better to be the hammer than the anvil.
3 He who has the frying-pan in his hand turns it at will.
4 He who holds the thread holds the ball.

Its dangers

5 Mickle power makes many enemies.
   "Mickle" means "much".
6 Out of office, out of danger.
7 It is ill putting a sword in a madman's hand.
8 Power corrupts.
   A proverb based on the words of the British historian Lord Acton: "Power tends to corrupt and absolute power corrupts absolutely" (from a letter of 1887). Acton continued "Great men are almost always bad men."

Its effects

9 If you wish to know a man, give him authority.
10 Authority shows the man.
11 Mastery mows the meadows down.
   That is, those in authority get things done.
12 Where MacGregor sits is the head of the table.
   Sometimes attributed to Robert MacGregor of Campbell, the notorious outlaw "Rob Roy" (1671–1734); the name of any other important person may be substituted for MacGregor.
13 He that puts on a public gown, must put off a private person.
   Implies that those in authority must not be influenced by private interests and affairs.
14 Caesar's wife must be above suspicion.
   "Caesar's wife" refers to any relative or close friend of a person in authority. The saying originates from Julius Caesar's action in divorcing his second wife Pompeia, whose name had been dragged into a scandalous court case. Although he accepted that she had done nothing wrong, Caesar considered his position compromised and insisted on a divorce. The story is told in Plutarch's *Lives* (1st century AD).

Qualities of leadership

15 An army of stags led by a lion would be more formidable than one of lions led by a stag.
   The saying, which implies that the strength of the leader is far more important than the strength of the army, can be traced back to Plutarch (1st century AD). Compare the well-known description of Britain's World War I armies as "lions led by donkeys" (sometimes attributed to the German general Erich Ludendorf).
16 No man can be a good ruler, unless he has first been ruled.

17 One must be a servant before one can be a master.

18 Servants make the worst masters.

19 He is not fit to command others, that cannot command himself.

20 He that is master of himself, will soon be master of others.

21 Every man cannot be a master.

22 He is the best general who makes the fewest mistakes.

A saying of Sir Ian Hamilton (1853–1947), commander in chief of the ill-fated Gallipoli Campaign (1915).

The dangers of shared authority

23 Where every man is master, the world goes to wrack.

"Wrack" means "collapse, destruction", as in "rack and ruin".

24 One master in a house is enough.

25 There is no good accord, where every man would be a lord.

26 That voyage never has luck where each one has a vote.

27 Where grooms and householders are all alike great, very disastrous will it be for the houses and all that dwell in them.

28 Every man's man had a man, and that made the Treve fall.

"The Treve" was a Scottish castle whose capture was attributed to the negligence of a substitute deputy governor. The warning is of the danger of delegating authority.

29 He that has a fellow-ruler, has an over-ruler.

10 Badness

Its sources

1 Covetousness is the root of all evil.
   Variants substitute "money", "riches", or "idleness" for "covetousness"; the saying is based on 1 Timothy 6:10. See WEALTH: 29.
2 No mischief but a woman or a priest is at the bottom of it.
3 Mischief comes without calling for.
4 Weeds want no sowing.
5 He who does no good, does evil enough.
6 When the weasel and the cat make a marriage, it is a very ill presage.
   Implies that no good can come of an alliance between two bad characters who were formerly enemies.

Its effects

7 He that does ill, hates the light.
   An adaptation of John 3:20.
8 He that lives not well one year, sorrows seven after.
9 Sin is the root of sorrow.
   Chinese proverb.
10 Who swims in sin shall sink in sorrow.
11 Sin plucks on sin.
   That is, one sin leads to another.
12 He that has done ill once, will do it again.
13 One might as well be hanged for a sheep as for a lamb.
   An excuse for further or greater wrongdoing once one has committed (or decided to commit) a minor offence. Before the criminal law reforms of the 1820s theft of goods worth more than one shilling could incur the death penalty in Britain.
14 He that mischief hatches, mischief catches.
15 They that sow the wind shall reap the whirlwind.
   Based on Hosea 8:7.
16 Vice is its own punishment, and sometimes its own cure.
   Compare GOODNESS: 14 and note.
17 A wicked man is his own hell.
18 An ill life, an ill end.
19 He that lives wickedly can hardly die honestly.

20 He that does evil, never weens good.
"Weens" means "expects".

Its value

21 The more mischief, the better sport.
22 The more wicked, the more lucky.
23 The more knave, the better luck.
24 Thieves and rogues have the best luck, if they do but scape hanging.
25 The greater the sinner, the greater the saint.

Its dangers

26 Wickedness with beauty is the devil's hook baited.
27 Never open the door to a little vice, lest a great one enter with it.
28 The wages of sin is death.
A biblical quotation: Romans 6:23.
29 Every sin brings its punishment with it.
30 Where vice is, vengeance follows.
31 Fear nothing but sin.

Its universality

32 It is a good world, but they are ill that are on it.
33 It is a wicked world, and we make part of it.
34 The world is full of knaves.
35 To fall into sin is human, to remain in sin is devilish.

Characteristics of the bad

36 A bad penny always turns up.
A bad coin circulates fast because each new owner hastens to get rid of it; similarly, a disreputable person is likely to turn up again when least wanted.
37 Some do amend when they cannot grow worse.
38 A knave and a fool never take thought.
39 The love of the wicked is more dangerous than their hatred.
40 Show a good man his error, and he turns it to a virtue; but an ill, it doubles his fault.
41 Two false knaves need no broker.
42 Ill weeds grow apace.
43 The weeds overgrow the corn.
Implies that the bad outnumber the good.
44 Evil doers are evil dreaders.
Implies that bad people are always the first to suspect others.

Handling bad people

45 The best remedy against an ill man, is much ground between.
46 He who sups with the devil should have a long spoon.
Cited by Chaucer and Shakespeare.
47 One hates not the person, but the vice.
The variant "Hate the sin, not the sinner" is common in Christian moral teaching.
48 Give a thief enough rope and he'll hang himself.

A variant substitutes "fool" for "thief". The implication is that given enough freedom, a bad or troublesome person will eventually bring about his own downfall.

Wrong and right

49 The end justifies the means.
   Implies that a worthy result may justify doubtful means of achieving it. Proverbs 50 and 51 below support the opposite view.
50 Never do evil that good may come of it.
51 Wrong has no warrant.
52 Wrong never comes right.
53 Two wrongs do not make a right.
   Used to answer those who excuse wrongdoing on the grounds that others have done similarly or worse. The cynical variant "If two wrongs don't make a right, try three" has been attributed to President Richard M. Nixon (1970s).
54 Two blacks do not make a white.

See also DEEDS: *Bad deeds*; GOODNESS: *Good and evil*

11 Beauty

Its superficiality

1 Beauty is only skin-deep.
2 Beauty is only one layer.
   Japanese proverb.
3 Beauty may have fair leaves, yet bitter fruit.
4 Fair face, foul heart.
5 The peacock has fair feathers, but foul feet.
6 There is many a fair thing full false.
7 Fair without, false within.
8 Beauty and honesty seldom agree.
   Implies that a beautiful woman is rarely virtuous. Variations substitute "chastity" or "wisdom" for "honesty".
9 Beauty and folly go often in company.
10 White silver draws black lines.

Its influence

11 Beauty draws more than oxen.
   A more elaborate variant has "One hair of a woman draws more than a hundred yoke of oxen."
12 Beauty opens locked doors.
13 Beauty is eloquent even when silent.
14 A good face is a letter of recommendation.
15 A fair face is half a portion.
   "Portion" here means "wedding portion, dowry".

Its unimportance

16 The fair and the foul, by dark are like store.
   "Like store" means "similar (farm) animals".

17 All cats are grey in the dark.

18 Goodness is better than beauty.

19 Good fame is better than a good face.

20 Handsome is as handsome does.
   Originally a proverb about good breeding rather than good looks: "handsome" formerly had the sense of "courteous" or "genteel".

Its inadequacy

21 Beauty without bounty avails nought.

22 A fair woman without virtue is like palled wine.
   "Palled" is an obsolete term describing wine that has become stale from exposure to the
   air.

23 Beauty won't make the pot boil.

24 No one can live on beauty, but they can die for it.

25 Prettiness makes no pottage.
   "Pottage" is an old word for soup or stew.

26 A poor beauty finds more lovers than husbands.

27 Beauty is no inheritance.

28 Beauty is potent but money is omnipotent.

Its ephemerality

29 Beauty fades like a flower.
   Like proverbs 30–32 below, a commonplace of lyrical and elegaic poetry with innumer-
   able variants.

30 Beauty is but a blossom.

31 The fairest flowers soonest fade.

32 The fairest rose at last is withered.

33 Grace will last, beauty will blast.

34 Prettiness dies first.

Its subjectivity

35 Beauty is in the eye of the beholder.
   A sentiment that has been traced back to the Greek poet Theocritus (3rd century BC).

36 Fair is not fair, but that which pleases.

37 A ship under sail, a man in complete armour, a woman with a great belly are
   three of the handsomest sights.

38 If Jack's in love, he's no judge of Jill's beauty.

39 The owl thinks her own young fairest.
   An allusion to one of the fables attributed to Aesop (6th century BC).

Its sources

40 Health and gaiety foster beauty.

41 Health and wealth create beauty.

42 A blithe heart makes a blooming visage.

43 The joy of the heart makes the face fair.

Its disadvantages

44 The fairest silk is soonest stained.

This, like proverbs 45 and 46 below, implies that beauty shows up by contrast even the smallest fault.

45 In an ermine spots are soon discovered.
"Ermine" is the winter fur of the stoat, prized for its pure whiteness.

46 The fairer the paper, the fouler the blot.

47 The smaller the peas, the more to the pot; the fairer the woman, the more the giglot.
"Giglot" means "wanton".

48 Who has a fair wife needs more than two eyes.

49 Please your eye and plague your heart.

50 A fair wife and a frontier castle breed quarrels.

51 Pretty face, poor fate.
Chinese proverb.

52 Beauty's sister is vanity, and its daughter lust.

53 A woman and a cherry are painted for their own harm.
As the attractive colour of a cherry leads to its destruction, so does beauty (or make-up) on a woman.

Its value

54 A bonny bride is soon buskit, and a short horse is soon wispit.
"Buskit" means "adorned", "wispit" means "rubbed down".

55 A good face needs no band, and a bad one deserves none.
"Band" here means "adornment".

56 Who is born fair is born married.

57 A fair face cannot have a crabbed heart.

58 An enemy to beauty is a foe to nature.

59 A thing of beauty is a joy forever.
The first line of Keats's poem *Endymion* (1818).

12 Beginnings

Their importance

1 Everything must have a beginning.

2 Everything has its seed.

3 No root, no fruit.

4 Rivers need a spring.

5 First impressions are the most lasting.

6 The first blow is half the battle.

Their difficulty

7 Every beginning is hard.

8 The first step is the hardest.
Also known in the form "The distance doesn't matter: it is only the first step that is difficult." This was the celebrated retort of the Marquise du Deffand (1697–1780), on hearing an admiring description of the miracle of St Denys, who supposedly carried his head for six miles after being decapitated.

9 The greatest step is that out of doors.

The importance of beginning well

10 If the beginning is good, the end must be perfect.
    Burmese proverb.

11 A good beginning makes a good ending.
    Contrast PERSEVERANCE: 8 and 9.

12 An ill beginning, an ill ending.

13 Such beginning, such end.

14 Well begun is half done.
    A very old saying, cited by Plato and Horace among others. In a letter (1817) Keats described the proverb as "a bad one", suggesting the alternative "Not begun at all until half done."

15 A beard well lathered is half shaved.

16 No good building without a good foundation.

13 Believing

Its sources

1 We soon believe what we desire.

2 Seeing is believing.

3 That which is easily done, is soon believed.

4 Men have greater faith in those things which they do not understand.

Its value

5 Believe well and have well.

6 He can who believes he can.

7 Faith will move mountains.
   An adaptation of Matthew 17:20.

8 Belief is better than investigation.

The need for caution

9 He that believes all, misses; he that believes nothing, misses.

10 Believe nothing of what you hear, and only half of what you see.

11 Of money, wit, and virtue, believe one-fourth of what you hear.

12 Believe no tales from an enemy's tongue.

13 Thinking is very far from knowing.

The gullible

14 They that think none ill, are soonest beguiled.

15 No man so wise but he may be deceived.

16 A fool believes everything.
    An adaptation of Proverbs 14:15.

17 A fool and his money are soon parted.

18 If fools went not to market, bad wares would not be sold.

Doubt

19 The more one knows, the less one believes.

20 He that knows nothing, doubts nothing.

21 Doubt is the key of knowledge.
   Persian proverb.
22 He that nothing questions, nothing learns.
23 The persuasion of the fortunate sways the doubtful.

14 Borrowing

Against borrowing

1 Better buy than borrow.
2 Better to pay and have little than have much and be in debt.
3 Better go to bed supperless than to rise in debt.
4 Debt is the worst poverty.
5 He who has good health is young; and he is rich who owes nothing.
6 He may well be contented who needs neither borrow nor flatter.
7 Not so good to borrow, as to be able to lend.
8 Neither a borrower nor a lender be.
   A quotation from Polonius's speech of advice to his son in Shakespeare's *Hamlet* (c. 1600); the speech continues "For loan oft loses both itself and friend."
9 The world still he keeps at his staff's end that needs not to borrow and never will lend.

Its disadvantages

10 Borrowed garments never fit well.
11 He that trusts to borrowed ploughs, will have his land lie fallow.
12 He that borrows binds himself with his neighbour's rope.
13 A man in debt is caught in a net.
14 Shame fades in the morning, but debts remain from day to day.
   Chinese proverb.
15 Debt is an evil conscience.
16 Let him that sleeps too sound, borrow the debtor's pillow.
17 He that goes a borrowing, goes a sorrowing.
18 Woe's to them that have the cat's dish, and she aye mewing.
   Implies that those who borrow something will be subjected to constant nagging and complaints until it is returned.
19 Creditors have better memories than debtors.
20 He that borrows must pay again with shame or loss.

Debtors

21 The borrower is servant to the lender.
   A biblical quotation: Proverbs 22:7.
22 He who owes, is in all the wrong.
23 Debtors are liars.
24 Lying rides upon debt's back.

Repayment of debts

25 Borrowed thing will home again.
26 A borrowed loan should come laughing home.

27 A pound of care will not pay an ounce of debt.

28 An hundred pounds of sorrow pays not one ounce of debt.

29 Sorrow will pay no debt.

30 Old thanks pay not for a new debt.

31 Unpaid debts are unforgiven sins.

32 He has but a short Lent, that must pay money at Easter.
Implies that, for a borrower, the day of repayment always comes around too soon.

33 Pay what you owe and you'll know what you're worth.

34 Pay with the same dish you borrow.

35 Out of debt, out of danger.

36 Once paid, never craved.
That is, pay what you owe and you'll never again be pestered for it.

37 Short reckonings make long friends.
"Short reckonings" here means "prompt repayment of debts".

38 Death pays all debts.
Combines the idea of death as repaying "the debt to nature" with the general principle that debts cannot be inherited.

39 Of ill debtors, men take oats.
Implies that one must take what one can in repayment of a bad debt.

See also LENDING: *Usurers*

15 Breeding

Its importance

1 Better unborn than unbred.

2 The best bred have the best portion.
"Portion" here means "inheritance".

3 Birth is much, but breeding is more.

4 Nurture is above nature.
Implies that breeding is of more importance than inherited qualities. The formulation "nature...nurture" is still common in debates about the relative importance of hereditary or environmental factors.

5 Nurture and good manners maketh man.
See note on proverb 9 below.

Manners

6 Civility costs nothing.
Some versions add "...and is worth much" or "...but buys everything". Variants of this and of proverb 7 below substitute "politeness" or "courtesy" for "civility".

7 There is nothing lost by civility.

8 Courtesy is the inseparable companion of virtue.

9 Manners maketh man.
A saying associated with the English churchman William of Wykeham (1324–1404). It is the motto of Winchester School and New College, Oxford, both of which he founded.

10 Manners make often fortunes.

11 Manners and money make a gentleman.

12 Meat is much, but manners is better.

13 Leave is light.
   Implies that it is easy enough to ask "leave", or permission, before doing something.
14 'After you' is good manners.
15 It is not good manners to show your learning before ladies.
   It was formerly considered impolite to use Latin or Greek in mixed company, as very few
   women had been educated in these languages.
16 Speak when you are spoken to.
   An admonition to servants or children.
17 A well-bred youth neither speaks of himself, nor, being spoken to, is silent.
18 Curiosity is ill manners in another house.
19 Do on the hill as you would do in the hall.

The ill-bred

20 It is an ill-bred dog that will beat a bitch.
21 The higher the ape goes, the more he shows his tail.
   Less genteel versions substitute "arse" for "tail". The proverb implies that the higher ill-
   bred people are promoted, the more obvious their inadequacies become.
22 Courtesy is cumbersome to them that ken it not.
   That is, good manners don't come naturally to those who are not used to polite society.
   A sarcastic "excuse" for someone who behaves discourteously.
23 Dogs bark as they are bred.
24 Beware of breed.
   "Breed" here refers to the ill-bred.
25 Do not cast your pearls before swine.
   A slight rephrasing of Matthew 7:6.

The gentry

26 Gentility is but ancient riches.
27 Gentility without ability is worse than plain beggary.
28 Gentry sent to market will not buy one bushel of corn.
   Implies that noble blood alone is of no material value.
29 Good blood makes bad puddings without groats or suet.
   Alludes to the making of black pudding from pigs' blood and suet, etc. "Groats" were
   both fragments of crushed grain and coins worth four pennies; for the implied meaning
   see proverbs 30 and 39 below.
30 Nobility, without ability, is like a pudding wanting suet.
31 Great birth is a very poor dish at table.
32 The more noble, the more humble.
33 Kind hearts are more than coronets.
   A quotation from Tennyson's "Lady Clara Vere de Vere" (1848). The phrase provided the
   title of the Ealing film *Kind Hearts and Coronets* (1949).
34 Better a good cow than a cow of good kind.
35 Virtue is the only true nobility.
36 He is noble that has noble conditions.
37 He is a gentleman that has gentle conditions.
38 A gentleman will do like a gentleman.
   Compare BEAUTY: 20.
39 A gentleman without an estate is like a pudding without suet.
   Compare proverbs 29 and 30 above.

40 A thief passes for a gentleman when stealing has made him rich.
41 Jack would be a gentleman if he had money.
42 Jack would be a gentleman if he could speak French.
43 It is not the gay coat that makes the gentleman.
44 It takes three generations to make a gentleman.
45 The king can make a knight, but not a gentleman.
46 The Peerage is the Englishman's Bible.
   A reference to *Burke's Peerage* (1826), a directory of peers and their genealogy.

16 Building

Its expense

1 Building is a thief.
   Like proverbs 2–7 below, this alludes to the still common experience of finding that, once started, building work incurs large unforeseen expenses.
2 Building is a sweet impoverishing.
3 Building and borrowing, a sack full of sorrowing.
4 Building and marrying of children are great wasters.
5 The charges of building, and making of gardens are unknown.
6 Fools build houses, and wise men buy them.
7 Who borrows to build, builds to sell.
   Chinese proverb.

17 Change

Its value

1 A change is as good as a rest.
The earliest recorded use is by Conan Doyle (1890), who attributed the saying to an unidentified "great statesman".

2 Change brings life.

3 Change your dwelling-place often, for the sweetness of life consists in variety.
Arabic proverb.

4 Variety is the spice of life.
Adapted from Cowper's lines in *The Task* (1785): "Variety's the very spice of life/ That gives it all its flavour."

5 Variety takes away satiety.

6 Variety is charming.

7 Changing of works is lighting of hearts.

8 Change of pasture makes fat calves.

9 New meat begets a new appetite.

Its inadvisability

10 Better the devil you know than the devil you don't know.

11 Better rue sit than rue flit.
That is, better to stay as you are and regret it than uproot yourself and regret that.

12 A tree often transplanted, bears not much fruit.

13 Three removals are as bad as a fire.
Refers to the damage done to furniture, etc., in moving house (with a more general implication that those who frequently uproot themselves cannot expect to thrive).

14 Don't change horses in midstream.
A variant substitutes "swap" for "change". The first recorded use is in a speech by Abraham Lincoln (1864), where it forms the punchline of a jocular story about two Dutch settlers fording a river.

15 As a tree falls, so shall it lie.
Sometimes accompanied by the rhyming line "As a man lives, so shall he die"; the proverb implies that there is no point in attempting to change the habits of a lifetime (as in a deathbed conversion, etc.). It is an abridged version of a fatalistic passage in Ecclesiastes 11:3.

Its effects

16 A rolling stone gathers no moss.
   The proverb gave rise to the Muddy Waters blues song "Rolling Stone" (1940s), which in turn gave its name to the rock group (formed 1962).

17 A new broom sweeps clean.
   A saying now generally shortened to the phrase "new broom", meaning a newly appointed person who makes radical changes to procedures (often, it is implied, for the sake of change).

18 Of a new prince, new bondage.

19 New lords, new laws.

Its inevitability

20 Times change and we with them.
   An old Latin proverb, sometimes attributed to Ovid (1st century BC).

21 One cannot put back the clock.
   It was C. S. Lewis (1898–1963) who observed that one always can and often ought to.

22 Paul's will not always stand.
   A reference to St Paul's Cathedral in London. The first recorded use dates from 1659, only seven years before the original St Paul's was destroyed in the Fire of London.

23 The world will not last alway.

24 There is nothing permanent except change.

Conservatism

25 Nature hates all sudden changes.

26 When a new book appears, read an old one.
   Sometimes attributed to the writer Charles Lamb (1775–1834), who was known for his antiquarian tastes.

27 Who leaves the old way for the new, will find himself deceived.

28 Old chains gall less than new.

29 Old shoes are easiest.

30 Old fish, old oil, and an old friend are the best.

31 Old friends and old wine and old gold are best.

32 Old wood is best to burn, old horse to ride, and old books to read, and old wine to drink.
   Sometimes attributed to Alfonso I the Magnanimous (1385–1458), king of Aragon, Sicily, and Naples.

33 Old customs are best.

34 Preserve the old, but know the new.
   Chinese proverb.

Novelty

35 Novelty always appears handsome.

36 New things are fair.

37 Everything new is fine.

38 It is a sairy brewing that is not good in the newing.
   "Sairy" means "poor"; "in the newing" means "when it is new".

39 Yule is young in Yule even, and as old in Saint Stephen.
   "Yule even" is Christmas Eve and St Stephen's Day is December 26th. Like proverbs 35–38 above, this implies that the initial attraction of new things does not last.

40 There is nothing new under the sun.
    A biblical quotation: Ecclesiastes 1:9.
41 What is new cannot be true.
42 Newer is truer.
43 You can't put new wine into old bottles.
    Adapted from Matthew 9:17. The biblical text explains that the result of putting young
    wine into old (leather) bottles is that the bottles burst and the wine is wasted.

18 Character

Hereditary influences

1 We may not expect a good whelp from an ill dog.
2 The tod's bairns are ill to tame.
   "Tod" means "fox".
3 Eagles do not breed doves.
4 Of an evil crow, an evil egg.
5 He that comes of a hen, must scrape.
6 How can the foal amble if the horse and mare trot?
7 The litter is like to the sire and dam.
8 The apple never falls far from the tree.
9 Of a thorn springs not a fig.
   Like proverbs 10 and 11 below, this is based on Matthew 7:16–18.
10 One cannot gather grapes of thorns or figs of thistles.
11 No good apple on a sour stock.
12 Of evil grain, no good seed can come.
13 What is bred in the bone will come out in the flesh.
    Until the 20th century the usual form of this proverb was "What is bred in the bone
    will *not* out *of* the flesh". While earlier version stressed the difficulty of eradicating deep-
    rooted characteristics, the modern form implies that hereditary qualities will always
    reveal themselves.
14 Blood will tell.
15 A wise man commonly has foolish children.
    Like proverb 16 below, this contradicts proverbs 11–14 above, all of which imply that the
    character of the offspring must match that of its parents.
16 Many a good cow has an evil calf.

Other influences

17 Names and natures do often agree.
    Implies that people come to possess the character traits suggested by their name. Com-
    pare NAMES: 3.
18 A man's studies pass into his character.
19 The cask savours of the first fill.
    Emphasizes the influence of childhood experience on the formation of character.

The inability to change or conceal a person's character

20 He that is born a fool is never cured.
21 Send a fool to the market, and a fool he will return again.
    Variants substitute "to France" or "abroad" for "to the market".

22 If an ass goes a-travelling, he'll not come home a horse.
See TRAVEL: 8–12 for variants of this proverb.

23 Travellers change climates, not conditions.
"Conditions" here means "character". The observation can be traced back to Horace's *Epistles* (1st century BC).

24 It is harder to change human nature than to change rivers and mountains.

25 You can drive out nature with a pitchfork, but she keeps on coming back.
A quotation from Horace's *Epistles* (1st century BC).

26 Cut off a dog's tail and he will be a dog still.

27 Reek comes aye down again however high it flees.
"Reek" means "smoke".

28 Once a knave, always a knave.
Variants of this proverb substitute "bishop", "devil", "parson", "priest", "thief", or "whore" for "knave". The versions referring to ecclesiastical offices allude to the doctrine that holy orders are indelible.

29 The fox may grow grey, but never good.

30 The wolf may lose his teeth, but never his nature.

31 The leopard cannot change his spots.
Adapted from Jeremiah 13:23.

32 Black will take no other hue.

33 A carrion kite will never be a good hawk.

34 You cannot make a silk purse out of a sow's ear.

35 There comes nought out of the sack but what was there.

36 Bring a cow to the hall and she'll run to the byre.

37 The frog cannot out of her bog.

38 You cannot make a crab walk straight.

39 What can you expect from a pig but a grunt?
Used of rude or boorish behaviour.

40 A kindly aver will never make a good horse.
A "kindly aver" is a horse that is naturally suited to being a work animal. The implication is that someone born and bred to being a labourer will not succeed in a higher position.

41 An ape's an ape, a varlet's a varlet, though they be clad in silk or scarlet.
"Scarlet" here signifies the ceremonial robe of a judge or other dignitary. Variants of the saying can be traced back to Lucan (1st century AD).

42 Fire cannot be hidden in flax.

43 Nature and the sin of Adam can ill be concealed by fig-leaves.
An allusion to Adam and Eve's attempt to hide their nakedness after their fall (Genesis 3:7).

19 Children

Their value

1 He that has no children knows not what is love.

2 The best smell is bread, the best savour salt, the best love that of children.

3 If you live without being a father you will die without being a human being.
Russian proverb.

4 Children are poor men's riches.

5 Happy is he that is happy in his children.

6 A son is a son till he gets him a wife, but a daughter's a daughter all the days of her life.

7 A child's service is little, yet he is no little fool that despises it.

Their disadvantages

8 He that has children, all his morsels are not his own.

9 Children suck the mother when they are young, and the father when they are old.

10 Wife and children are bills of charges.

11 Small birds must have meat.

12 The first service a child does his father is to make him foolish.

13 Children when they are little make their parents fools, when they are great they make them mad.

14 A little child weighs on your knee, a big one on your heart.

15 Children are certain cares, but uncertain comforts.

Their shortcomings

16 Children are to be deceived with comfits and men with oaths.
That is, adults are bought off with promises as easily as children are bribed with sweets.

17 Kindness is lost that's bestowed on children and old folk.
Implies that children forget former kindnesses when they grow up, and old men die before they can repay them.

18 Woe to the kingdom whose king is a child.

Their appetite

19 Children and chicken must be always picking.

20 A growing youth has a wolf in his belly.

Their honesty

21 Children and fools cannot lie.
Some versions add "drunkards" to the list of truth-tellers.

22 The child says nothing, but what it heard by the fire.
Like proverbs 23–25 below, this warns against discussing private affairs in front of one's children.

23 What children hear at home, soon flies abroad.

24 Children pick up words as pigeons peas, and utter them again as God shall please.

25 Little pitchers have great ears.
The "ear" of a pitcher (jug) is its handle.

Their impressionability

26 Raw leather will stretch.

27 Soft wax will take any impression.

28 Youth and white paper take any impression.

29 As the twig is bent, so is the tree inclined.

30 Thraw the wand while it is green.
"Thraw" means "twist"; the reference is to making baskets, etc., from willow wands.

31 Train up a child in the way he should go.

Their behaviour

32 Boys will be boys.
   Like proverbs 33–35 below, this may be used to excuse unruly behaviour in the young.

33 God's lambs will play.

34 Young colts will canter.

35 Youth will have its course.

36 You cannot put an old head on young shoulders.

37 Children should be seen and not heard.
   Until the 19th century this saying was applied more often to young women than to children. See WOMEN: 62.

38 When children stand quiet, they have done some ill.

Care of children

39 Let not a child sleep upon bones.
   The advice here is that a child should not be allowed to sleep on a person's lap.

40 Shod in the cradle, barefoot in the stubble.
   Implies that over-protected children will not thrive as adults.

The child and the man

41 The child is father of the man.
   A quotation from Wordsworth's short poem "My Heart Leaps Up" (1802). Like proverbs 42–45 below, this suggest that one may see in a child a model of the future adult. The remaining proverbs in this section contradict this belief.

42 Boys will be men.

43 It early pricks that will be a thorn.

44 The fine pullet shows its excellence from the egg.
   Arabic proverb. A pullet is a hen.

45 Timely crooks the tree, that will good cammock be.
   A "cammock" is a crooked piece of wood used for a staff or crook, etc.

46 A man at five may be a fool at fifteen.

47 Young saint, old devil.

48 Royet lads make sober men.
   "Royet" means "wild".

49 Wanton kittens make sober cats.

50 Naughty boys sometimes make good men.

51 A ragged colt may make a good horse.

Precocity

52 Soon ripe, soon rotten.

53 Old young, young old.
   Implies that a precocious child may compensate for his lost youth by being childish in his old age.

54 A man at sixteen will prove a child at sixty.

55 He that would be old long, must be old betimes.
   "Betimes" means "early".

The recklessness of youth

56 Youth never casts for peril.
   "Casts for" means "takes account of".

57 Reckless youth makes rueful age.

58 An idle youth, a needy age.

59 If you lie upon roses when young, you'll lie upon thorns when old.

60 He sups ill who eats all at dinner.

Implies that he who uses up all his resources in his youth will have nothing left for his old age ("dinner" here is a midday meal).

61 If youth knew what age would crave, it would both get and save.

62 Spare when you're young, and spend when you're old.

63 Diligent youth makes easy age.

64 Young men's knocks old men feel.

65 Who that in youth no virtue uses, in age all honour him refuses.

See also DEATH: *Its choice of victims*; DISCIPLINE: *Disciplining children, The spoilt child*; OLD PEOPLE: *The generation gap*

20 Choosing

Its necessity

1 You cannot have it both ways.

2 You cannot have your cake and eat it.

3 You cannot sell the cow and sup the milk.

4 A door must either be shut or open.

5 You cannot serve God and Mammon.

A quotation from Matthew 6:24. "Mammon", an Aramaic word meaning "wealth" or "riches", was taken by many later commentators on the Gospels to be the proper name of the devil of avarice; in either case, the choice here is between piety and worldliness.

Making one's choice

6 Choose neither women nor linen by candlelight.

7 Of two evils choose the less.

Advice that can be traced back to the *Nicomachean Ethics* of Aristotle (4th century BC).

8 Where bad's the best, bad must be the choice.

9 There's small choice in rotten apples.

The earliest recorded use is in Shakespeare's *The Taming of the Shrew* (c. 1594) but the saying is probably older.

10 No choice amongst stinking fish.

11 You pays your money and you takes your choice.

Generally used in situations where one is obliged to choose at random. The more grammatical variant, substituting "pay...take" for "pays...takes", is less common.

12 A maiden with many wooers often chooses the worst.

See also MARRIAGE: *Choosing a partner*

21 Cleanliness

Its value

1 Cleanliness is next to godliness.
  The earliest known citation is in John Wesley's sermon "On Dress" (1791) but the saying is almost certainly much older. In the late 19th century it was used as an advertising slogan for Pears soap.

2 For washing his hands, none sells his lands.
  Time taken to be clean and neat rarely harms a person's livelihood.

3 Clean and whole makes poor clothes shine.

Dirtiness

4 The clartier the cosier.
  "Clartier" is a Scots word meaning "dirtier".

5 Where there's muck there's brass.
  A variant substitutes "luck" for "brass", which here refers to money. Like proverb 6 below, this implies that the most lucrative occupations are not necessarily the cleanest, physically or morally.

6 Muck and money go together.

7 We must eat a peck of dirt before we die.
  Frequently quoted as a jocular excuse for unwashed crockery or food. It may also be used metaphorically to imply that we must all put up with a certain amount of unpleasantness in this life. A "peck" was a former unit of dry measure equal to eight quarts.

22 Commerce

Its tactics

1 Ask but enough, and you may lower the price as you list.

2 Ask much to have a little.

3 When you go to buy, don't show your silver.
  Chinese proverb.

4 He praises who wishes to sell.

5 He that blames would buy.
  Like proverbs 6–9 below, this refers to the practice of criticizing the goods one wishes to buy, in order to obtain them at a lower price.

6 Many men lack what they would fain have in their pack.
  "Lack" here means "criticize".

7 He that speaks ill of the mare would buy her.

8 Never cheapen unless you mean to buy.
  "Cheapen" means "haggle".

9 There is a difference between 'Will you buy?' and 'Will you sell?'
  Implies that over-eagerness to sell may discourage prospective buyers, just as over-eagerness to buy may encourage sellers to raise their prices.

The need for caution

10 Let the buyer beware.
  A legal saying equally familiar in its Latin form, *caveat emptor*. This common-law maxim warns that it is the buyer's responsibility to check the nature and quality of goods before

the transaction is concluded (or to obtain any necessary guarantees). Under modern English statute law it is an implied condition of most contracts of sale that the goods be of a satisfactory quality; however, there are certain areas in which the principle of *caveat emptor* still very much applies, notably property sales and the buying of second-hand goods from private vendors.

11 Keep your eyes open: a sale is a sale.

12 The buyer needs a hundred eyes, the seller but one.

13 There are more foolish buyers than foolish sellers.

14 At a good bargain, think twice.

Sound business sense

15 The best payment is on the peck bottom.
A "peck" was a vessel used for measuring grain. The proverb implies that it is best to receive immediate payment for one's wares.

16 Ell and tell is good merchandise.
An "ell" was a stick used to measure lengths of cloth, etc., while "tell" here refers to counting out money. The sense is therefore the same as proverb 15 above: insist on payment straight after measuring out the goods.

17 While the dust is on your feet, sell what you have bought.
Like proverb 18 below, this implies that rapid turnover may be more important than holding out for a high profit.

18 Quick returns make rich merchants.

19 A man must sell his ware after the rates of the market.

20 He that desires to make a market of his ware, must watch an opportunity to open his shop.

21 Look to the main chance.
Keep an eye out for the most likely source of gain. The saying derives from the once-popular game of hazard, in which the first and most important throw of the dice was known as the "main" or "main chance".

22 Drive your business, do not let it drive you.

23 Business is business.

24 Business before pleasure.

25 Who buys dear and takes up on credit, shall ever sell to his loss.

26 Buy in the cheapest market and sell in the dearest.

27 A merchant that gains not, loses.

28 He that buys and sells is called a merchant.
Jewish proverb. It implies that to buy and sell without profit brings one nothing but the title of "merchant".

29 Never open your pack, and sell no wares.

30 Buy at a fair, but sell at home.

31 He that could know what would be dear, need be a merchant but one year.
Implies that if one could predict future shortages of a particular commodity, one could buy it cheaply while it was plentiful and sell it at a high profit when it was in short supply.

32 The customer is always right.
A business axiom often attributed to the US-born retail pioneer H. Gordon Selfridge (1856–1947), who founded the London department store that still bears his name in the 1930s.

Honest dealings

33 The blind man's peck should be well measured.
A "peck" was a former measure for grain, etc., equal to eight quarts.

34 Weight and measure take away strife.

35 It is no sin to sell dear, but a sin to give ill measure.

36 Weigh justly and sell dearly.

Bad bargains

37 A thing you don't want is dear at any price.

38 Light cheap, lither yield.
A medieval saying that may be translated as "Low price, poor reward".

39 Many have been ruined by buying good pennyworths.

40 A good bargain is a pick-purse.

41 Good cheap is dear.
"Good cheap" means "a bargain".

42 Best is best cheap.
The best quality goods are the best bargain (whatever their price). A later variant of this saying is "Best is cheapest."

43 Ill ware is never cheap.

Prices and quality

44 To buy dear is not bounty.

45 He will never have a good thing cheap that is afraid to ask the price.

46 The dearer it is the cheaper.
The retort of someone who refuses to buy a particular commodity: "the more money you ask for it, the more I shall save by not buying."

47 They buy good cheap that bring nothing home.
A sarcastic retort to someone who objects that you have paid too much for something.

48 Good ware makes quick markets.

49 Pleasing ware is half sold.

50 Good wine needs no bush.
A reference to the bunch of ivy that wine-merchants used to hang outside their shops as a sign of their trade. The implication is that goods of a high quality should not need advertising.

23 Company

Its sources

1 Two is company, three is none.
The proverb was formerly used to make the point that three can be an awkward number socially (too many for confidential talk but too few for conviviality). It is now mainly used (especially in the modern variant "...but three's a crowd") to imply that the third person is "playing gooseberry".

2 A crowd is not company.

The value of good company

3 Keep good men company, and you shall be of the number.

  4 Choose thy company before thy drink.
  5 The company makes the feast.
  6 Good company upon the road is the shortest cut.
  7 A merry companion is a wagon in the way. Implies that to have good company when travelling on foot makes the journey seem as easy as if one were riding in a wagon.

The undesirability of bad company
  8 Better be alone than in bad company.
  9 Better to be beaten than be in bad company.
  10 He keeps his road well enough who gets rid of bad company.

The influence of one's companions
  11 A man is known by the company he keeps.
  12 A man is known by his friends.
  13 As a man is, so is his company.
  14 Sike a man as thou wald be, draw thee to sike company.
    "Sike" means "such"; "wald" means "would".
  15 Tell me with whom thou goest, and I'll tell thee what thou doest.
  16 Keep company with good men, and good men you'll imitate; keep company with beggars, and sleep outside some gate.
    Chinese proverb.

See also CORRUPTION: *Its causes*

24 Conceit

Its universality
  1 Men love to hear well of themselves.
  2 Every bird loves to hear himself sing.
  3 Every sprat now-a-days calls itself a herring.
  4 There is one good wife in the country, and every man thinks he has her.
  5 There is no such flatterer as a man's self.

Its inadequacy
  6 Vainglory blossoms but never bears.
  7 Brag is a good dog but dares not bite.
    A variant has "…but Holdfast is better" (implying that a barking dog cannot keep hold of anything).

Its dangers
  8 An ounce of vanity spoils a hundredweight of merit.
  9 The more women look in their glass, the less they look to their house.
  10 Do not triumph before the victory.
  11 Never be boastful; someone may pass who knew you as a child.
    Chinese proverb.

Characteristics of the boastful

12 A vaunter and a liar are near akin.

13 They can do least who boast loudest.

14 Great braggers, little doers.

15 Great boast, small roast.

Modesty

16 Modesty sets off one newly come to honour.

17 Though modesty be a virtue, yet bashfulness is a vice.

18 No man cries stinking fish.
That is, no hawker cries out that he has bad fish for sale. The implication is that one should not disparage oneself or one's wares through excessive modesty.

19 Don't hide your light under a bushel.
A "bushel" is a measure or container for corn. The proverb is based on Matthew 5:15.

20 What is the good of a sundial in the shade?
A further warning against excessive modesty.

See also PRAISE: *Self-praise*

25 Conformity

Its necessity

1 When in Rome, do as the Romans do.
This well-known saying derives from an incident (late 4th century AD) in the lives of St Ambrose and St Augustine of Hippo. The young Augustine, who was troubled by the diverse practices he found within the Church, asked Ambrose, bishop of Milan, whether it was correct to fast on Saturday, as the Romans did, or to eat normally, as the Milanese did. St Ambrose replied that when in each city he followed the local custom.

2 If you see a town worshipping a calf, mow grass and feed him.
Egyptian proverb.

3 One must howl with the wolves.
Cynical advice to join in the public outcry of the moment if you don't wish to be attacked yourself.

4 It is ill sitting at Rome and striving against the Pope.

5 It is ill shaving against the wool.

6 It is ill striving against the stream.

7 Piss not against the wind.
A polite variant substitutes "puff" for "piss".

8 If you can't beat 'em, join 'em.
Not recorded before the mid-20th century; the saying seems to have originated in the USA (where "lick 'em" is usually substituted for "beat 'em").

9 Better bend than break.

10 Better be out of the world than out of the fashion.

11 Say as men say, but think to yourself.

12 Do as most men do, then most men will speak well of you.

26 Conscience

The effects of a guilty conscience

1 A guilty conscience needs no accuser.
  Sometimes attributed to Cato the Elder (3rd–2nd centuries BC).

2 Conscience is a cut-throat.

3 Conscience is a thousand witnesses.

4 A guilty conscience feels continual fear.

5 The faulty stands on his guard.

6 He that lives ill, fear follows him.

7 Who has skirts of straw, needs fear the fire.

8 The thief doth fear each bush an officer.
  Cited by Shakespeare in 3 Henry VI (c. 1591).

9 Conscience does make cowards of us all.
  A quotation from Shakespeare's *Hamlet* (c. 1600).

10 Whose conscience is cumbered and stands not clean, of another man's deeds the worse will he deem.

11 Who is in fault suspects everybody.

12 He that commits a fault, thinks everyone speaks of it.

13 The truest jests sound worst in guilty ears.

The value of a clear conscience

14 A clear conscience fears not false accusations.

15 Men whose consciences are clear, of a knock at midnight have no fear.
  Chinese proverb.

16 Do right and fear no man.

17 Preserve a clear conscience, and sleep without fear in the desert.
  Arabic proverb.

18 A quiet conscience sleeps in thunder.

19 A good conscience makes an easy couch.

20 A good conscience is a soft pillow.

21 A good conscience is the best divinity.
  "Divinity" here means "theology".

22 A good conscience is a continual feast.
  Adapted from Proverbs 15:15.

23 A clear conscience is like a coat of mail.

Innocence

24 No protection is as sure as innocence.

25 Innocent actions carry their warrant with them.
  "Warrant" here means "guarantee".

26 Every one is held to be innocent until he is proved guilty.
  It is a well-known principle of English law that a defendant must be aquitted unless the prosecution proves its case "beyond reasonable doubt"; although the principle is long-established, this form of words is no older than the early 20th century.

27 Innocence is no protection.

27 Contempt

Its sources

1 Familiarity breeds contempt.
Cited by St Augustine of Hippo as "a common proverb" (early 5th century AD).

2 A maid oft seen, and a gown oft worn, are disesteemed and held in scorn.

3 Scorn comes commonly with scathe.
"Scathe" means "harm, injury".

4 Where the demand is a jest, the fittest answer is a scoff.

5 To be too busy, gets contempt.
"Busy" here has the sense of "meddlesome".

Its effects

6 Contempt will sooner kill an injury than revenge.
Compare REVENGE: 4–5 and 7–8. Scorn for those who injure you is a more effective remedy than revenge.

7 Contempt is the sharpest reproof.

8 Some evils are cured by contempt.
The sense is similar to that of proverb 6 above.

9 Scorn at first makes after-love the more.

10 Contempt pierces even through the shell of the tortoise.

11 Many can bear adversity, but few contempt.

12 Never was a scornful person well received.

The value of respect

13 If the laird slight the lady, so will all the kitchen boys.

14 He that respects not is not respected.

15 Respect a man, he will do the more.

16 He is a silly man that can neither do good nor ill.
"Silly" here means "sorry, poor". The implication is that one should treat even the meanest person with respect, since he or she may well have the power to help or hurt you.

17 Better to have a dog fawn on you than bite you.

28 Contentment

Its value

1 Content is all.

2 He has nothing, that is not contented.

3 Content is more than a kingdom.

4 Content is happiness.

5 Content is the philosopher's stone, that turns all it touches into gold.

6 He who is content in his poverty, is wonderfully rich.

7 He is not rich that possesses much, but he that is content with what he has.

8 A contented mind is a continual feast.
Adapted from Proverbs 15:15.

9 Who is contented, enjoys.

Its sources

10 Content lodges oftener in cottages than palaces.
11 He may well be contented who needs neither borrow nor flatter.
12 A little with quiet is the only diet.

Having enough

13 He is at ease who has enough.
14 Enough is as good as a feast.
15 More than enough is too much.
16 Of enough, men leave.
   Like proverb 17 below, this implies that only when something is left over (from a meal, etc.), can we be sure that there was enough to start with.
17 There was never enough where nothing was left.
18 That which suffices, is not little.
19 Women, priests, and poultry, have never enough.

Humble desires

20 He that desires but little has no need of much.
21 He has enough who is contented with little.
22 Humble hearts have humble desires.
23 Little things please little minds.
   First cited in approximately this form in Disraeli's *Sybil* (1845), although the thought can be traced back to Ovid (1st century BC). It is generally used to imply pettiness rather than an admirable humility.
24 Little things are great to little men.
25 A little bird is content with a little nest.
26 A little wood will heat a little oven.
27 The greatest wealth is contentment with a little.
28 Nature is content with a little.
29 A wise man cares not for what he cannot have.

Discontent

30 Discontent is the first step in progress.
31 A man's discontent is his worst evil.
32 A discontented man knows not where to sit easy.
33 He that has nothing, is not contented.
34 He that studies his content, wants it.
   The same thought is expressed in J. S. Mill's conclusion (1873), "Ask yourself whether you are happy, and you cease to be so."
35 No man is content with his lot.
36 None says his garner is full.
37 Though stone were changed to gold, the heart of man would not be satisfied.
   Chinese proverb.
38 Vast chasms can be filled, but the heart of man never.
   Chinese proverb.
39 Man's heart is never satisfied, the snake would swallow the elephant.
   Chinese proverb.
40 The grass is always greener on the other side of the fence.

Not recorded in this form until the mid-20th century, although the thought appears as early as Ovid (1st century BC).

41 The apples on the other side of the wall are the sweetest.

42 Our neighbour's ground yields better corn than ours.

43 Acorns were good till bread was found.

Accepting one's lot

44 Worse things happen at sea.

45 Let every man be content with his own kevel.
   "Kevel" means "lot".

46 Gnaw the bone which is fallen to thy lot.

47 When you are an anvil, hold you still; when you are a hammer, strike your fill.

48 If thou hast not a capon, feed on an onion.
   A "capon" is a fattened cock fowl.

49 He that may not do as he would, must do as he may.

50 The goat must browse where she is tied.

51 We must not look for a golden life in an iron age.

52 A man must plough with such oxen as he has.

29 Corruption

Its causes

1 Evil communications corrupt good manners.
   A biblical quotation: 1 Corinthians 15:33. Although St Paul's meaning here was "false teachings lead to immoral behaviour", the saying is now mainly used to warn of the ill-effects of bad company or example.

2 The unrighteous penny corrupts the righteous pound.

3 The rotten apple injures its neighbours.

4 One ill weed mars a whole pot of pottage.
   "Pottage" is stew or soup. A variant substitutes "turd" for "ill weed".

5 One drop of poison infects the whole tun of wine.

6 One scabbed sheep will mar a whole flock.
   The saying can be traced back to the *Satires* of Juvenal (1st–2nd centuries AD).

7 Near vermilion one gets stained pink.
   Chinese proverb.

8 He who squeezes in between the onion and the peel, picks up its stink.
   Arabic proverb.

9 A hog that's bemired endeavours to bemire others.

10 He that deals in dirt has aye foul fingers.

11 He that touches pitch shall be defiled.
   Adapted from the apocryphal book of Ecclesiasticus (13:1).

12 He that has to do with what is foul, never comes away clean.

13 Keep not ill men company, lest you increase the number.

14 Who keeps company with the wolf, will learn to howl.

15 He that dwells next door to a cripple, will learn to halt.
   "Halt" here means "limp".

16 If you lie down with dogs, you will get up with fleas.

17 He who lives with cats will get a taste for mice.

18 He who goes into a mill comes out powdered.

19 Power corrupts.
A proverb based on the words of the British historian Lord Acton: "Power tends to corrupt and absolute power corrupts absolutely" (from a letter of 1887).

20 Fish begins to stink at the head.
The freshness of fish is, indeed, best judged by examining the head. The proverb implies that corruption begins in the highest ranks of an organization.

21 No man ever became thoroughly bad all at once.
A quotation from the *Satires* of Juvenal (1st–2nd centuries AD).

Its effects

22 The corruption of one thing is the generation of another.
Among the numerous variants of this proverb are Dryden's "the corruption of a poet is the generation of a critic" (1693) and Swift's "the corruption of pipes is the generation of stoppers" (1738).

23 Corruption of the best becomes the worst.

24 Who trusts to rotten boughs, may fall.

25 One is not smelt where all stink.

Bribery

26 Neither bribe, nor lose thy right.

27 A bribe will enter without knocking.

28 Gifts enter everywhere without a wimble.
A "wimble" is a gimlet.

29 Gold goes in at any gate except heaven's.

30 What cannot gold do?

31 No lock will hold against the power of gold.

32 Every man has his price.
A cynical maxim attributed to Sir Robert Walpole, whose long period as prime minister (1721–42) owed much to his shrewd use of patronage.

33 There is no wool so white but a dyer can make it black.

34 Gifts blind the eyes.

35 Who greases his way travels easily.

Religious corruption

36 The devil gets up to the belfry by the vicar's skirts.

37 No penny, no pardon.
Like proverb 38 below, this implies that without payment, the priest will not perform the duties and services expected of him (such as absolving penitents).

38 No penny, no paternoster.
The "paternoster" is the Lord's Prayer.

Corruption at law

39 Law is a flag, and gold is the wind that makes it wave.
Russian proverb.

40 A pocketful of right needs a pocketful of gold.

41 A golden handshake is better than ten witnesses.

42 The devil makes his Christmas-pies of lawyer's tongues and clerk's fingers.
   Some versions add "...and the third thing you may guess" (implying women's genitals).

43 Home is home, as the devil said when he found himself in the Court of Session.
   The Court of Session is the supreme civil court in Scotland.

44 A basket-justice will do justice right or wrong.
   A "basket-justice" was a judge who could be bribed with a basket of game, etc.

45 He whose father is judge, goes safe to his trial.

46 Show me the man, and I'll show you the law.
   A reference to biased judges.

47 Little thieves are hanged, but great ones escape.
   According to more subversive variants, the great thieves "rob" or "hang" the little ones.

30 Country lore

Agriculture

1 A field requires three things; fair weather, sound seed, and a good husbandman.

2 Lime makes a rich father and a poor son.
   Implies that liming the soil will provide improved crops in the short term, but in the long term will damage the soil.

3 He who marls sand, may buy the land.
   "Marl" is a mixture of clay and lime, a valuable fertilizer for sandy soil.

4 It is time to cock your hay and corn, when the old donkey blows his horn.
   The braying of a donkey was thought to presage heavy rain.

5 Corn and horn go together.
   A reference to the market prices of corn and cattle, suggesting that they generally rise and fall together. Another proverb, "Up corn, down horn", suggests the opposite.

6 When the corn is in the shock, the fish are on the rock.
   This refers to the coincidence of the harvest and the fishing season.

7 If you cut oats green, you get both king and queen.
   Advises the farmer to cut oats before they are fully ripe, so as not to lose the largest grains at the top of the heads.

8 Oats will mow themselves.

9 A famine in England begins at the horse-manger.
   Implies that a shortage of oats is generally followed by a shortage of other crops, and that a lack of animal feed will lead to a more general famine. See also HUNGER: 1.

10 Hops make or break.
   A reference to the unreliability of this expensive crop.

11 Plenty of ladybirds, plenty of hops.

12 Sow wheat in dirt, and rye in dust.

13 Sow in the slop, 'twill be heavy at top.
   The advice here is to sow wheat in wet ground for maximum yield.

14 This rule in gardening never forget, to sow dry and to set wet.
   To "set" is to transplant seedlings, etc.

15 Sow beans in the mud, and they'll grow like a wood.

16 One for the mouse, one for the crow, one to rot and one to grow.

A reference to the mishaps that commonly befall a crop of beans, suggesting that only a 25% yield may be expected.

17 Sow peas and beans in the wane of the moon; who soweth them sooner, he soweth too soon.

The usual country superstition was that plants grew best when the moon was waxing. Peas and beans are here made an exception to the rule, probably because their tendrils are unusual in growing anticlockwise around their supporting sticks.

18 A crooked man should sow beans, and a wud man peas.

"Crooked" here means "lame"; "wud" means "mad". The implication is that beans may be thickly sown, whereas peas should be sown more thinly.

19 Turnips like a dry bed but a wet head.

Dairy produce

20 Butter is once a year in the cow's horn.

A reference to the time of year when a cow gives no milk.

21 Butter is mad twice a year.

Refers to the summer, when butter is too soft to spread, and to the winter, when it is too hard.

22 If you will have a good cheese and hav'n old, you must turn'n seven times before he is cold.

23 Cheese and money should always sleep together one night.

A saying of farmers, who insisted that payment for cheese should be received before the goods were dispatched.

24 A red cow gives good milk.

Animals

25 A leap year is never a good sheep year.

26 He that has sheep, swine, and bees, sleep he, wake he, he may thrive.

27 Pigs see the wind.

An allusion to the restlessness of pigs when a storm is brewing.

28 Look to the cow, and the sow, and the wheat mow, and all will be well enow.

29 Roast meat does cattle.

"Meat" here means "food"; "does" means "fattens". The implication is that the burnt grass of a dry season is more fattening than the grass of a wet season.

30 The ox is never woe, till he to the harrow go.

Refers to the comparative discomfort of pulling a harrow (used to break up hard soil) rather than a plough.

31 Quey calves are dear veal.

"Quey" means "heifer".

32 You may beat a horse till he be sad, and a cow till she be mad.

Birds

33 He who will have a full flock, must have an old stag and a young cock.

"Stag" here means "gander".

34 He that will have his farm full, must keep an old cock and a young bull.

35 When the cuckoo comes to the bare thorn, sell your cow and buy you corn: but when she comes to the full bit, sell your corn and buy you sheep.

The blossoming of the hawthorn is still considered a reliable indication that summer is at hand.

36 When the pigeons go a benting, then the farmers lie lamenting.
"Benting" is feeding on the seeds of grasses—a food that pigeons only resort to when nothing better is growing.

37 The pigeon never knows woe, but when she does a-benting go.

38 If the partridge had the woodcock's thigh, it would be the best bird that ever did fly.

Trees and plants

39 He that plants a tree plants for posterity.

40 Set trees poor and they will grow rich, set them rich and they will grow poor.
The advice is to transplant trees from a barren soil into a fertile soil, rather than vice versa.

41 Red wood makes gude spindles.
"Red wood" here refers to the hard wood found at the heart of trees.

42 Every elm has its man.
A reference to the sinister reputation of the elm, which was commonly regarded as a malevolent and murderous tree. Elms can be dangerous as they are frequently uprooted and shed their branches easily in a storm. There may also be an allusion to the fact that coffins were traditionally made of elm wood.

43 The willow will buy a horse before the oak will pay for a saddle.
A reference to the fast speed at which a willow grows.

44 A cherry year, a merry year; a plum year, a dumb year; a pear year, a dear year.

45 Plant pears for your heirs.

46 He who plants a walnut-tree, expects not to eat of the fruit.

47 If you would fruit have, you must bring the leaf to the grave.
The advice here is to transplant trees as the leaves are falling, so that they have time to take root before the frosts of winter. To move them earlier would disturb the motion of the sap.

48 Short boughs, long vintage.
Like proverb 49 below, this refers to the advantages of pruning vines.

49 Make the vine poor, and it will make you rich.

50 When elder's white, brew and bake a peck; when elder's black, brew and bake a sack.
Elder has white blossoms and black berries. A "peck" is a measure of grain equal to eight quarts.

51 When the sloe tree is as white as a sheet, sow your barley whether it be dry or wet.

52 When the gorse is out of bloom, kissing's out of fashion.
An excuse for kissing at any time of the year, as gorse is never out of bloom.

53 When the fern is as high as a spoon, you may sleep an hour at noon.

54 Parsley seed goes nine times to the devil.
A reference to the slow germination of parsley seeds, which were said to go down to hell and back nine times before they began to grow upwards.

See also MONTHS; SEASONS; WEATHER

31 Courage

Its value

1 Courage and resolution are the spirit and soul of virtue.
2 Courage and perseverance conquer all before them.
3 Valour is the nobleness of the mind.
4 Fear can keep a man out of danger, but courage can support him in it.
5 Great things are done more through courage than through wisdom.
6 Fortune favours the bold.
   The saying can be traced back to the Roman playwright Terence (2nd century BC).
7 A bold heart is half the battle.

Its necessity

8 Faint heart never won fair lady.
9 None but the brave deserves the fair.
   A quotation from Dryden's *Alexander's Feast* (1697), where it refers to the supposed love affair between Alexander the Great and the courtesan Thaïs.
10 Put a stout heart to a stey brae.
   The advice here is to face difficulties with courage. "Stey brae" means "steep slope".

Its sources

11 Valour is born with us, not acquired.
12 Despair gives courage to a coward.
13 Necessity and opportunity may make a coward valiant.

Characteristics of the brave

14 A valiant man's look is more than a coward's sword.
15 The weapon of the brave is in his heart.
16 A man of courage never wants weapons.
17 A brave arm makes a short sword long.
18 A brave man's wounds are seldom on his back.
19 A brave man may fall, but he cannot yield.
20 Bold men have generous hearts.
21 To the real hero life is a mere straw.
   Indian proverb.
22 Valour delights in the test.
23 Calamity is the touchstone of a brave mind.
   Implies that bravery can only truly be assessed in time of danger.
24 To a brave and faithful man nothing is difficult.

False courage

25 Hares may pull dead lions by the beard.
26 Who takes a lion when he is absent, fears a mouse present.
27 Every cock will crow upon his own dung-hill.
   This contemptuous saying derives from a phrase in Seneca's *Apocolocyntosis* (c. 54 AD), a satire on the deification of the emperor Claudius.
28 Every dog is valiant at his own door.
29 Every dog is a lion at home.

Foolhardiness

30 It is a bold mouse that breeds in the cat's ear.

31 Nothing so bold as a blind mare.

32 Discretion is the better part of valour.
A quotation (slightly altered) from Shakespeare's *1 Henry IV* (c. 1597), where Falstaff uses it as an excuse for self-preservation. Like proverb 33 below it implies that what appears to be cowardice may be wise caution, and that what appears to be valour may be foolish rashness.

33 Valour would fight, but discretion would run away.

32 Cowardice

Its effects

1 Cowards run the greatest danger of any man in a battle.
A reference to the danger of turning one's back on one's enemy.

2 Cowards die often.
Like proverbs 3 and 4 below, this implies that to the coward the mere prospect of danger is as bad as death.

3 Cowards die many times before their deaths.
A quotation from Shakespeare's *Julius Caesar* (c. 1599).

4 To fazarts, hard hazards are death ere they come there.
"Fazarts" means "cowards".

5 He that forecasts all perils, will never sail the sea.

6 The mother of the coward does not worry about him.
Arabic proverb.

7 Faint heart never won fair lady.

Its shame

8 Cowardice is afraid to be known or seen.

9 Better die with honour than live with shame.
A modern variant, sometimes attributed to the Spanish Republican heroine La Pasionaria (1895–1989), is "Better die on your feet than live on your knees."

10 Of cowards no history is written.

11 He that forecasts all perils, will win no worship.

Its value

12 It is better to be a coward for a minute than dead for the rest of your life.

13 It is good sleeping in a whole skin.

14 One pair of heels is often worth two pairs of hands.

15 He that fights and runs away, may live to fight another day.
This is sometimes completed with the addition "But he that is in battle slain, will never rise to fight again." The thought is sometimes attributed to Demosthenes (4th century BC), who used his oratory to urge continuing Athenian resistance to Macedonian power.

Characteristics of the cowardly

16 Cowards are cruel.

17 A bully is always a coward.

18 Many would be cowards, if they had courage enough.
Like proverb 19 below, this implies that in some situations it may be more difficult to run away than to stay and fight. Both probably derive from a line in Rochester's *Satire Against Mankind* (1693): "All men would be cowards if they durst."

19 Some have been thought brave because they were afraid to run away.

20 Put a coward to his mettle, and he'll fight the devil.
Like proverbs 21 and 22 below, this implies that in desperate situations even the cowardly can be brave.

21 Despair gives courage to a coward.

22 Necessity and opportunity may make a coward valiant.

23 The virtue of a coward is suspicion.

24 Who has not a heart, let him have legs.
"Heart" is used here in the sense of "courage".

33 Crime

Its causes

1 Poverty is the mother of crime.
The French satirist Jean La Bruyère added "…and stupidity is its father" (1688).

2 He that brings up his son to nothing, breeds a thief.

3 It is a hard task to be poor and leal.
"Leal" means "honest".

4 It is hard for a greedy eye to have a leal heart.

5 The postern door makes thief and whore.
Implies that the back door of a house provides the necessary concealment for dishonest servants and unfaithful wives.

6 The back door robs the house.

7 Two daughters and a back door are three arrant thieves.
"Two daughters" refers to the expense of bringing up daughters.

8 A careless hussy makes many thieves.
"Hussy" here means "housewife".

9 He that is suffered to do more than is fitting, will do more than is lawful.

10 The more laws, the more offenders.
Adapted from an aphorism in Tacitus's *Annals* (2nd century AD). The saying can be used to make two different points: that the existence of many laws in a country points to the badness of the national character; or that an over-regulated society tends to encourage, rather than deter, law-breaking.

Its effects

11 He that does what he should not, shall feel what he would not.

12 Crimes are made secure by greater crimes.
Compare BADNESS: 11–12.

13 The law grows of sin, and chastises it.

14 Stolen waters are sweet.
A biblical quotation: Proverbs 9:17. Variants substitute "pleasures" or "fruit" for "waters". When "fruit" is used the allusion is generally to the temptation of Eve in the Garden of Eden (Genesis 3:6).

Its dangers

15 Frost and fraud both end in foul.
Just as a frost leads to foul conditions, dishonesty will come to a bad end.

16 He that steals honey should beware of the sting.

17 He that eats the king's goose shall be choked with the feathers.
"Eating the king's goose" may imply theft or, more probably, living corruptly on royal favour. Several variants stress the delayed or long-lasting nature of the consequences by adding "...for seven years after" or "...after 100 years".

18 Murder will out.
Variants are cited by Chaucer and Shakespeare.

19 If you steal for others, you shall be hanged yourself.

Its unprofitability

20 Crime does not pay.

21 Ill-gotten goods never prosper.
A very old saying that can be traced as far back as Hesiod (8th century BC).

22 Stolen goods never thrive.

23 The devil's meal is all bran.
"Bran" was formerly the staple diet of the very poor. Some variants have "half bran".

24 Ill gotten, ill spent.

25 Come with the wind, go with the water.
This reiterates the sentiments of proverbs 21–24 above.

Criminals

26 He that will steal a pin, will steal a better thing.
Children were often taught the rhyming tag "It's a sin to steal a pin."

27 He that will steal an egg, will steal an ox.

28 Hang a thief when he's young, and he'll no steal when he's old.
A favourite saying of the notorious Scottish hanging judge Lord Braxfield (1722–99).

29 Set a thief to catch a thief.

30 An old poacher makes the best gamekeeper.
The phrase "poacher turned gamekeeper" is now frequently applied to anyone who switches from one career to another possibly conflicting one (e.g. businessman to industry watchdog, etc.)

31 The wolf knows what the ill beast thinks.

32 A true man and a thief think not the same.

33 Show me a liar, and I will show thee a thief.

34 A tale-bearer is worse than a thief.

35 The receiver is as bad as the thief.

36 If there were no receivers, there would be no thieves.

37 One thief robs another.
Also current in the form "...does *not* rob another." Compare LOYALTY: 4.

38 A thief knows a thief as a wolf knows a wolf.

39 The thief is sorry he is to be hanged, but not that he is a thief.
Implies that the thief does not repent his misdeeds, he merely regrets their consequences.

40 Thieves' handsel ever unlucky.
"Handsel" means "gift".

41 A cut-purse is a sure trade, for he has ready money when his work is done.

See also TEMPTATION: *Its sources*

34 Criticism

Its effects

1 Hard words break no bones.
2 Lacking breeds laziness, praise breeds pith.
   "Lacking" here means "censure"; "pith" means "effort".
3 Judge not, that ye be not judged.
   A biblical quotation: Matthew 7:1.

Against criticizing others

4 Live and let live.
5 Those who live in glass houses should not throw stones.
   Some early citations use the form "Those who have glass heads..." Like proverbs 6–21 below, this implies that people should not be too eager to criticize in others faults they possess themselves.
6 Every man's censure is first moulded in his own nature.
7 The pot calls the kettle black.
8 The kettle calls the pot burnt-arse.
9 Ill may the kiln call the oven burnt-tail.
10 The frying-pan said to the kettle, 'Avaunt, black brows!'
   "Avaunt" is an archaic term meaning "go away!"
11 The snite need not the woodcock betwite.
   "Snite" means "snipe"; "betwite" means "criticize". The proverb refers to the long bills of these birds.
12 He should have a hale pow, that calls his neighbour nitty know.
   "Pow" means "head"; "know" means "hillock". To call a person "nitty know" would imply that he or she was stupid.
13 The camel never sees its own hump, but that of its brother is always before its eyes.
   Arabic proverb.
14 The hunchback does not see his own hump, but sees his companion's.
15 The eye that sees all things else sees not itself.
   Like proverbs 16–21 below, this implies that those who criticize others are often blind to their own faults.
16 We see not what is in the wallet behind.
   A reference to Aesop's idea that everyone carries two packs, one hanging in front of him and one behind. Into the first, which is always before his eyes, he puts the faults of others, but he hides his own faults in the one behind his back.
17 You can see a mote in another's eye but cannot see a beam in your own.
   A "mote" is a particle of dust. The metaphor is taken from Matthew 7:3.
18 Point not at others' spots with a foul finger.
19 Physician, heal thyself.
   A biblical quotation: Luke 4:23.

20 Every one's faults are not written in their foreheads.
    A retort made to those who criticize, implying that their faults, though less obvious, are
    as bad.

21 If every man would sweep before his own door, the city would soon be clean.

The critical

22 He may find fault that cannot mend.
    It is easier to carp at faults than to correct them.

23 One mend-fault is worth twenty spy-faults.

24 The most high God sees, and bears: my neighbour knows nothing, and yet is
    always finding fault.

Handling criticism

25 When all men say you are an ass, it is time to bray.

26 If one, two, or three tell you you are an ass, put on a bridle.

27 Fling at the brod was ne'er a good ox.
    "Brod" means "goad"; "fling" here means "kick". The implication is that those who
    spurn criticism will never improve themselves.

28 If the cap fits, wear it.
    The original allusion was to a dunce's or fool's cap.

35 Cruelty

Its evil

1 A man of cruelty is God's enemy.

2 Cruelty deserves no mercy.

3 Cruelty is the first attribute of the devil.

4 Cruelty is the strength of the wicked.

Its value

5 Sometimes severity is better than gentleness.

6 Sometimes clemency is cruelty, and cruelty clemency.

7 Knock a carle, and ding a carle, and that's the way to win a carle.
   "Ding" means "beat"; "carle" means "fellow". The proverb implies that some people re-
   spond best to rough or harsh treatment.

Its effects

8 He that hurts another hurts himself.

9 Malice hurts itself most.

10 He threatens many that hurts any.

11 Tramp on a snail, and she'll shoot out her horns.
    Implies that not even the most lowly will tolerate cruelty without retaliation. Compare
    ENDURANCE: 6.

Cruelty and fear

12 Cruelty is a tyrant that's always attended with fear.

13 Cowards are cruel.
    Like proverb 14 below, this implies that the cruellest people are generally the least brave.

14 A bully is always a coward.

See also TALKING: *The tongue as a weapon*

36 Cunning

Its value

1 Cunning surpasses strength.
2 Wiles help weak folk.
3 If the lion's skin cannot, the fox's shall.
   Implies that what cannot be gained by strength must be gained by cunning. The saying has been attributed to Lysander, the Spartan naval commander in the Peloponnesian War (5th century BC).

Its limitations

4 Too much cunning undoes.
5 At length the fox is brought to the furrier.
6 Though the fox run, the chicken has wings.

Characteristics of the cunning

7 A crafty knave needs no broker.
8 Full of courtesy, full of craft.
   Like proverbs 9 and 10 below, this refers to the hypocrisy of the cunning.
9 When the fox preaches, then beware your geese.
10 It is an ill sign to see a fox lick a lamb.
11 The fox preys farthest from his home.
   Some versions substitute "wolf" for "fox".

Handling the cunning

12 The fox knows much, but more he that catcheth him.
13 To a crafty man, a crafty and a half.
   Implies that a crafty person will only be caught by one more crafty than he.
14 An old fox is not easily snared.
15 If you deal with a fox, think of his tricks.
16 He that will deceive the fox must rise betimes.
   "Betimes" means "early".

D

37 Danger

Its sources

1 Far from home, near thy harm.
2 A man far from his good is near his harm.
   "Good" here means "property".
3 When we have gold, we are in fear; when we have none we are in danger.
4 Love and pease-pottage are two dangerous things.
   The implication is that one attacks the heart and the other the stomach ("pease-pottage" is a dish of boiled peas notorious for causing flatulence). A variant states that both "…will make their way".
5 No safe wading in an unknown water.
6 What is not wisdom, is danger.
7 He that is not in the wars, is not out of danger.
8 There is a scorpion under every stone.
   The earliest known occurrence of this very old saying is in a fragment by Sophocles (5th century BC).
9 The post of honour is the post of danger.
10 He lives unsafely that looks too near on things.
11 A running horse is an open grave.
12 When you ride a young colt, see your saddle be well girt.

Its effects

13 Any port in a storm.
    In time of danger, any refuge (literal or metaphorical) is better than none.
14 While the thunder lasted, two bad men were friends.
    Like proverbs 15–17 below, this implies that danger may have good effects, which unfortunately do not last once the danger is past.
15 When it thunders, the thief becomes honest.
16 Danger makes men devout.
17 Vows made in storms are forgotten in calms.
18 Calamity is the touchstone of a brave mind.
    Both this and proverb 19 below imply that bravery can only be assessed in time of danger.
19 In a calm sea, every man is a pilot.
20 He that dallies with his enemy, dies by his own hand.
    "Dallies with" here means "trifles with, underestimates".

21 He that brings himself into needless dangers, dies the devil's martyr.

22 They that bourd wi' cats, maun count on scarts.
"Bourd" means "jest"; "maun" means "must"; "scarts" means "scratches".

23 The fly that plays too long in the candle, singes his wings at last.

24 You may play with a bull till you get his horn in your eye.

25 He that steals honey, should beware of the sting.

26 Dear bought is the honey that is licked from the thorn.

27 He that handles thorns shall prick his fingers.

28 Who remove stones, bruise their fingers.

Its importance

29 The more danger, the more honour.

30 Danger is next neighbour to security.
Implies that the person who thinks himself most secure is actually in the most danger (because he or she may not take proper precautions). Compare SAFETY: 9–10.

31 Danger itself is the best remedy for danger.
Both this and proverb 32 below imply that perilous action is often the only means of avoiding greater peril.

32 Without danger we cannot get beyond danger.

The dangers of the sea

33 He that would sail without danger, must never come on the main sea.
"Main" here means "open".

34 He who travels not by sea, knows not what the fear of God is.

35 He that will learn to pray, let him go to sea.

Taking a risk

36 Nothing ventured, nothing gained.
Variants of this proverb substitute "venture" for "ventured" and "gain", "have", or "win" for "gained".

37 Nothing stake, nothing draw.

38 Nought lay down, nought take up.

39 Adventures are to the adventurous.
"Adventures" here has the sense of "good fortune, luck". The earliest recorded use is in Disraeli's *Coningsby* (1844).

40 He that is afraid to shake the dice will never throw a six.
Chinese proverb.

41 Take your venture, as many a good ship has done.

42 If you do not enter a tiger's den, you cannot get his cubs.
Chinese proverb.

Against taking risks

43 Don't go near the water until you learn how to swim.
Of 20th-century origin.

44 Children and fools must not play with edged tools.

45 It is ill jesting with edged tools.

46 It is ill contending with the master of thirty legions.
The alleged response of the philosopher Favorinus (2nd century BC), when he was accused of giving in too easily during a philosophical debate with the emperor Hadrian.

47 Be not too bold with your biggers or betters.

48 If you play with fire you get burnt.

49 Bourd not with Bawty, lest he bite you.
"Bourd" means "jest"; "Bawty" is a watch-dog.

50 Though the mastiff be gentle, yet bite him not by the lip.

51 Three things are not to be trusted: a cow's horn, a dog's tooth, and a horse's hoof.

38 Days

Popular rhymes

1 Monday for wealth, Tuesday for health, Wednesday the best day of all; Thursday for crosses, Friday for losses, Saturday no luck at all.
A reference to the good or ill fortune associated with the day of one's wedding.

2 Monday's child is fair of face, Tuesday's child is full of grace; Wednesday's child is full of woe, Thursday's child has far to go; Friday's child is loving and giving, Saturday's child works hard for its living; and the child that's born on the Sabbath day, is fair and wise and good and gay.
This familiar jingle was first recorded in the mid-19th century.

3 Monday is Sunday's brother, Tuesday is such another; Wednesday you must go to church and pray, Thursday is half-holiday; on Friday it is too late to begin to spin, then Saturday is half-holiday agen.
An ironic excuse for being idle all week.

Particular days

4 Thursday come, and the week is gone.

5 Friday and the week is seldom alike.
The reference is mainly to the weather. Another proverb states "Friday will be either king or underling", i.e. will be either the best or the worst day of the week.

6 Friday night's dream on the Saturday told, is sure to come true be it never so old.

7 Friday's hair, and Saturday's horn, goes to the devil on Monday morn.
Implies that it is unlucky to cut one's hair on Friday and to cut one's nails on Saturday. However, according to another old rhyme Sunday, Monday, Thursday, and Saturday are the unlucky days for cutting one's hair "and best of all is Friday". See also RELIGION: 65.

8 Friday's moon, come when it will, comes too soon.
"Moon" here means a new moon; the reference, again, is mainly to the weather. (A variant states "A Friday moon brings foul weather.")

9 There is never a Saturday without some sunshine.

10 Saturday's servants never stay, Sunday servants run away.
A proverb with a similar meaning is "Saturday's flittings, light sittings" ("flittings" here means a change of job or home). It was once widely believed that starting a new job on a Saturday was unlucky.

11 A Saturday's moon, if it comes once in seven years, it comes too soon.
"Moon" here means a new moon.

12 Saturday's new, and Sunday's full, was never fine and never wool.
"New" and "full" refer to phases of the moon; "wool" means "will be".

See also RELIGION: *Sunday*

39 Death

Its inevitability

1 All men are mortal.
2 Grass and hay, we are all mortal.
A saying based on 1 Peter 1:23–24: "For all flesh is as grass...the grass withereth, and the flower thereof falleth away."
3 All men must die.
4 Charon waits for all.
In Greek mythology, Charon was the ferryman who conveyed the souls of the dead across the river Styx to Hades.
5 Death is sure to all.
6 Nothing is certain but death and taxes.
The earliest known citation is by Defoe (1726) but the saying is certainly older.
7 Nothing so certain as death.
8 Death is the black camel that kneels before every door.
Arabic proverb.
9 Every door may be shut but death's door.
10 Arthur himself had but his time.
A reference to the mortality of great men such as King Arthur.
11 Dying is as natural as living.
12 It is as natural to die as to be born.
A quotation from Francis Bacon's essay "Of Death" (1625). Bacon continues "...and to a little infant, perhaps, the one is as painful as the other." See also proverb 83 below.
13 As soon as man is born he begins to die.
14 The first breath is the beginning of death.
15 He that is once born, once must die.
16 No man has a lease of his life.
17 When thou dost hear a toll or knell, then think upon thy passing bell.
This echoes the famous words from Donne's *Devotions* (1624): "never send to know for whom the bell tolls; it tolls for thee."
18 Death defies the doctor.
19 Death is deaf to our wailings.
20 Death does not recognize strength.
African proverb.

Its unpredictability

21 Death keeps no calendar.
22 At every hour death is near.
23 Death surprises us in the midst of our hopes.
24 Men know where they were born, not where they shall die.
25 No man knows when he shall die, although he knows he must die.
26 Today a man, tomorrow none.

Its finality

27 Death is the end of all.

28 Stone-dead has no fellow.
   Compare proverbs 94–97 below.

29 A dead bee makes no honey.

30 There is a remedy for all things but death.

31 There is hope from the mouth of the sea, but none from the mouth of the grave.

32 The evening crowns the day.
   This, like proverbs 33–36 below, implies that only at the end of his life can a man be truly judged.

33 Praise a fair day at night.

34 Praise no man till he is dead.

35 Call no man happy till he dies.
   The Athenian sage Solon (6th century BC) is said to have used these words to rebuke Croesus, the fabulously wealthy king of Lydia, when he claimed to be the happiest of mankind. According to legend, when Croesus was finally defeated by Cyrus, king of Persia, and sentenced to be burnt alive, he cried out "Solon! Solon!" as he was led to the stake. Cyrus asked him the reason for this outburst and was so moved by the reply that he reprieved Croesus and the two men became friends.

36 Death's day is doom's day.

Its consolations

37 A dead mouse feels no cold.

38 Death is a remedy for all ills.

39 A ground sweat cures all disorders.
   Induced sweating was formerly used as something of a cure-all by the medical profession; hence a "ground sweat" is a facetious way of referring to the universal cure of being dead and buried.

40 Death is the poor man's best physician.

41 Death rather frees us from ills, than robs us of our goods.

42 Death pays all debts.

43 A man can die but once.

44 Our birth made us mortal, our death will make us immortal.

45 Death is a dying man's friend.

46 Look upon death as a going home.
   Chinese proverb.

47 Earth is the best shelter.

Its advantages

48 Dead dogs bark not.

49 Dead men don't bite.
   In Plutarch's *Lives* (1st century AD) these words are attributed to the men who murdered and then decapitated Pompey the Great.

50 Dead men tell no tales.
   Now a cliché of crime films, etc., in which it is generally used by the villains to justify the murder of a potential informant. It has therefore come to have an opposite meaning to CRIME: 18. A US variant is "Dead men don't sing."

51 The death of a young wolf never comes too soon.

52 The death of the wolves is the safety of the sheep.

Its causes

53 There is but one way to enter this life, but the gates of death are without number.
54 One funeral makes many.
This superstition may be based on the unhealthy practice of mourners standing around a grave in a cold churchyard.
55 Old men, when they marry young women, make much of death.
Implies that when an old man embraces his young wife he embraces death, for she will bring him to an early grave.
56 A green Yule makes a fat churchyard.
Like proverb 57 below, this comments on the unhealthy effects of mild weather at certain times of the year.
57 A hot May makes a fat churchyard.
58 A young physician fattens the churchyard.
59 War is death's feast.

Its effects

60 Dying men speak true.
There was formerly a widespread belief that the words of the dying were inspired or prophetic.
61 When death is on the tongue, repentance is not difficult.

Its choice of victims

62 The best go first.
63 Whom the gods love dies young.
The earliest known use is in a fragment by Menander (4th century BC).
64 The good die young.
65 Death is the only master who takes his servants without a character.
66 In Golgotha are skulls of all sizes.
Like proverbs 67–70 below, this implies that none are too young to die. "Golgotha", the Hebrew name for the site of the Crucifixion, meant "skull"; in Britain it was sometimes used to mean a burial place.
67 Graves are of all sizes.
68 Death devours lambs as well as sheep.
69 As soon goes the young sheep to the pot as the old.
70 As soon goes the young lamb's skin to the market as the old ewe's.

Equality in death

71 Death is the great leveller.
The phrasing can be traced back to the Roman poet Claudian (4th century AD), although the thought is doubtless older.
72 A piece of churchyard fits everybody.
73 We shall lie all alike in our graves.
74 All our pomp the earth covers.
75 Six feet of earth make all men equal.
76 On the turf all men are equal – and under it.
A 19th-century saying from the world of horse racing ("the turf"). It implies that in bet-

ting on something as unpredictable as a horse race men are as equal as they will be in death.

77 The end makes all equal.

78 Death makes us equal in the grave and unequal in eternity.

79 Death combs us all with the same comb.

80 Death carries a fat tsar on his shoulders as easily as a lean beggar.
    Russian proverb.

Fear of death

81 Fear of death is worse than death itself.

82 He that fears death lives not.

83 Men fear death as children fear to go in the dark.
    A quotation from Francis Bacon's essay "Of Death" (1625). See also proverb 12 above.

84 Death hath not so ghastly a face at a distance, as it hath at hand.

The manner of death

85 A good life makes a good death.

86 They die well that live well.

87 An ill life, an ill end.

88 He dies like a beast who has done no good while he lived.

89 Such a life, such a death.

90 Let all live as they would die.

91 A fair death honours the whole life.

Our attitude to the dead

92 Never speak ill of the dead.
    A maxim attributed to the Spartan philosopher Chilo (6th century BC).

93 Speak only what is true of the living and what is honourable of the dead.

94 Dead men are of no family, and are akin to none.
    Like proverbs 95–97 below, this implies that the dead have no one to defend them.

95 To dead men and absent there are no friends left.

96 Dead men have no friends.

97 The dead are always wrong.

98 Let the dead bury their dead.
    A biblical quotation: Matthew 8:22. The literal meaning is that the living have more important things to do than to attend to the needs of the dead; more generally, the saying implies that the truly vital should not allow themselves to be held back by the dead past.

99 We must live by the living, not by the dead.

100 To lament the dead avails not and revenge vents hatred.

See also OLD PEOPLE: *Old age and death*

40 Deceit

Its sources

1 Believe no tales from an enemy's tongue.

2 A false tongue will hardly speak truth.

3 There is falsehood in fellowship.
Implies that friendship involves an element of flattery and often proves insubstantial.
Variants substitute "flattery" or "fraud" for "falsehood".

4 Trust is the mother of deceit.

5 Debtors are liars.

6 Lying rides upon debt's back.
Implies that debt will lead people to make false excuses for not paying back what they owe.

7 Half the truth is often a whole lie.

8 Where there is whispering there is lying.

9 In many words a lie or two may escape.
Compare TALK: 68.

Its dangers

10 A liar can go round the world but cannot come back.
Implies that the liar dare not return to those people he has previously deceived.

11 The liar is sooner caught than the cripple.

12 A blister will rise upon one's tongue that tells a lie.

13 One lie makes many.

14 Oh, what a tangled web we weave, when first we practise to deceive!
A quotation from Scott's poem *Marmion* (1808).

15 A liar is not believed when he speaks the truth.

16 He that once deceives, is ever suspected.

17 Liars begin by imposing upon others, but end by deceiving themselves.

18 Falsehood never made a fair hinder end.

19 Women and wine, game and deceit, make the wealth small, and the wants great.

20 Cheats never prosper.

Its sinfulness

21 Deceiving those that trust us, is more than a sin.

22 A lie is the curse of God.
The words (1951) of the US statesman Adlai Stevenson are also well known: "A lie is an abomination unto the Lord and a very present help in trouble."

23 The liar and the murderer are children of the same village.

24 A liar is worse than a thief.

Its permissibility

25 To deceive a deceiver is no deceit.

26 No law for lying.
Points out that lying is not generally against the law.

27 Old men and travellers may lie by authority.
Variants add "soldiers" and "physicians" to the list of confirmed liars.

28 Painters and poets have leave to lie.
Adapted from Horace's *Ars Poetica* (1st century BC).

29 Better a lie that heals than a truth that wounds.

Concealing lies

30 Though a lie be well drest, it is ever overcome.

31 Almost and well nigh saves many a lie.
Implies that tactful or crafty phrasing may serve much the same purpose as a bare lie, e.g. by saying a task is "almost" completed when it is scarcely begun.

Self-deception

32 Who thinks to deceive God has already deceived himself.

33 To deceive oneself is very easy.

Characteristics of the deceitful

34 A liar should have a good memory.
Although sometimes attributed to Montaigne (16th century), the saying is much older, having been traced back to the Roman rhetorician Quintilian (1st century AD).

35 He that will lie, will steal.

36 He that will swear, will lie.

37 He that will cheat at play, will cheat you anyway.

38 False with one can be false with two.

39 Deceivers have full mouths and empty hands.
That is, they have nothing to offer but words.

40 You can't kid a kidder.

41 Deeds

Their value

1 'Tis action makes the hero.

2 Our own actions are our security, not others' judgments.

3 Well is, that well does.

4 By his deeds we know a man.
African proverb.

5 Action is the proper fruit of knowledge.

Words and deeds

6 Actions speak louder than words.
First recorded in the American colonies (mid-18th century).

7 The effect speaks, the tongue needs not.

8 Deeds are fruits, words are but leaves.

9 Words are mere bubbles of water, but deeds are drops of gold.
Chinese proverb.

10 A man of words and not of deeds, is like a garden full of weeds.

11 Deeds will show themselves, and words will pass away.

12 Doing is better than saying.

13 It is better to do well than to say well.

14 A little help is worth a deal of pity.

15 Say well, and do well, end with one letter; say well is good, but do well is better.

16 Good words without deeds are rushes and reeds.

17 The shortest answer is doing.

18 The greatest talkers are the least doers.

19 There is great difference between word and deed.

20 Saying and doing are two things.

21 Saying is one thing, and doing another.

22 From word to deed is a great space.

23 Easier said than done.
"Sooner" is sometimes substituted for "easier".

24 Fair words and foul deeds cheat wise men as well as fools.

25 Fair words and foul play cheat both young and old.

26 Good words and ill deeds deceive wise men and fools.

Action and intention

27 The good intention excuses the bad action.

28 Every deed is to be judged by the doer's intention.

29 Take the will for the deed.
Implies that where something has been inadvertently left undone, the intention or will to do it is all that matters. Although originally a reflection of the Christian belief that God rewards or punishes intentions as much as deeds (see proverb 30 below), the saying now mainly functions as a jocular excuse.

30 Man punishes the action, but God the intention.

Good deeds

31 One good deed atones for a thousand bad ones.
Chinese proverb.

32 A good deed is never lost.

33 To see a man do a good deed is to forget all his faults.
Chinese proverb.

34 Do good: thou doest it for thyself.

35 Do well and have well.

36 He that does well, wearies not himself.

37 One never loses by doing a good turn.

38 One good turn deserves another.
Variants substitute "requires" or "meets with" for "deserves".

39 Never be weary of well doing.
A near-quotation from Galatians 6:9.

Bad deeds

40 An ill deed cannot bring honour.

41 Better suffer ill than do ill.

42 An evil deed remains with the evil-doer.
Japanese proverb.

43 An ill turn is soon done.

44 Who would do ill, ne'er wants occasion.

45 If you do no ill, do no ill like.
Like proverb 46 below, this implies that to be sure of doing no evil, one must avoid all occasions and appearances of evil.

46 Whoso will no evil do, should do nothing that belongs thereto.

47 Evil deeds are like perfume, difficult to hide.
African proverb.

48 Do wrong once and you'll never hear the end of it.

49 Ten good turns lie dead and one ill deed report abroad does spread.
Like proverbs 50–53 below, this implies that while good deeds are soon forgotten, the memory of bad deeds and past injuries can never be effaced.

50 Old sins cast long shadows.

51 Injuries are written in brass.
Some variants add "...and good turns are written in dust (*or* sand *or* water)."

52 Injuries don't use to be written on ice.

53 The evil that men do lives after them, the good is oft interred with their bones.
A quotation from Shakespeare's *Julius Caesar* (*c.* 1599).

See also PROMISES: *Promise and performance*; TALKING: *Its inadequacy*

42 Defamation

Its effects

1 Throw dirt enough, and some will stick.

2 If the ball does not stick to the wall, it will at least leave a mark.

3 Slander leaves a score behind it.
"Score" here means "mark". (Some versions substitute "slur" or "scar").

4 Slander is a shipwreck by a dry tempest.

5 Slander cannot make a good man bad; when the water recedes the stone is still there.
Chinese proverb.

6 He that falls into the dirt, the longer he stays there the fouler he is.
The advice here is to clear oneself of defamatory accusations as soon as possible.

7 Give a dog a bad name and hang him.
Like proverbs 8 and 9 below, this implies that once a person's reputation is ruined, he or she is in a hopeless position (however unjust the accusations).

8 He that has an ill name is half hanged.

9 An ill wound is cured, not an ill name.

10 The fox fares best when he is cursed.
The fox is most severely "cursed" by the farmer when its forays have been most successful; usually said as an answer to envious criticism.

11 He that flings dirt at another, dirtieth himself most.

12 Slander flings stones at itself.

13 The slanderer kills a thousand times, the assassin but once.
Chinese proverb.

14 The devil is not so black as he is painted.
Usually said to extenuate an unpopular or heavily censured person.

Handling insults

15 The more you tramp on a turd, the broader it grows.
Implies that to make a great fuss about an undeserved insult serves only to draw further attention to it.

16 The wise forget insults, as the ungrateful a kindness.
Chinese proverb.

17 Neglect will kill an injury sooner than revenge.
Compare CONTEMPT: 6.

18 No reply is best.

19 The remedy for injuries, is not to remember them.

20 There were no ill language, if it were not ill taken.
Said in self-defence by someone whose remarks have inadvertently caused offence.

21 It was never ill said that was not ill taken.

22 Patience under old injuries invites new ones.

See also GOSSIP; TALKING: *Speaking ill*

43 Delay

Its dangers

1 Delays are dangerous.

2 While the grass grows, the horse starves.

3 While men go after a leech, the body is buried.

4 'Time enough' lost the ducks.
Refers to the danger of putting off such precautionary measures as locking up the ducks to protect them from the fox.

5 Time lost cannot be recalled.
Variants include "Lost time is not found again."

Its advantages

6 That delay is good which makes the way the safer.

7 Desires are nourished by delays.

8 If today will not, tomorrow may.

9 Put off the evil hour as long as you can.

10 Delay is the antidote of anger.

Its effects

11 Cruelty is more cruel, if we defer the pain.

12 Hope deferred maketh the heart sick.
A biblical quotation: Proverbs 13:12.

13 Long tarrying takes all the thanks away.
A favour granted too long after it was first sought is not received with gratitude. For proverbs with a similar implication see GIVING: 19–22.

14 He loses his thanks who promises and delays.

15 Tarry-long brings little home.

16 After a delay comes a let.
"Let" here means "hindrance".

17 What is deferred is not abandoned.
Both this and proverb 18 below warn that delay neither releases one from an obligation nor spares one from punishment.

18 The thing that's fristed is not forgiven.
"Fristed" means "delayed".

Against procrastination

19 Procrastination is the thief of time.
A quotation from Edward Young's once widely read poem *Night Thoughts* (1742–45).

20 Never put off till tomorrow what you can do today.
Now often humorously reversed.

21 One hour today is worth two tomorrow.

22 One today is worth two tomorrows.

23 Tomorrow never comes.

24 One of these days is none of these days.

25 Sooner begun, sooner done.

26 No time like the present.

See also OPPORTUNITY

44 Deserving

Rightful reward

1 A good dog deserves a good bone.

2 One good turn deserves another.

3 He that blows best, bears away the horn.

4 He that serves well, needs not ask his wages.
A variant has "…need not be afraid to ask his wages."

5 Desert and reward seldom keep company.

6 The labourer is worthy of his hire.
A biblical quotation: Luke 10:7. Like proverbs 7 and 8 below, this implies that everybody deserves to be paid for work done or services rendered.

7 Good hand, good hire.
"Hire" here and in the preceding proverb means "payment, reward".

8 It is an ill dog that deserves not a crust.

Just deserts

9 He that sows thistles shall reap prickles.

10 The deed comes back upon the doer.

11 The biter is sometimes bit.
Frequently shortened to "the biter bit."

12 An arrow shot upright falls on the shooter's head.

13 Who spits against the wind, it falls in his face.
Variants substitute "heaven" for "the wind" to suggest hubris or blasphemy.

14 Curses, like chickens, come home to roost.

15 After your fling, watch for the sting.

16 Sweet meat will have sour sauce.

17 Like fault, like punishment.

18 Such answer as man gives, such will he get.

19 One ill word asks another.

20 If you give a jest, you must take a jest.

21 Punishment is lame, but it comes.

The undeserving

22 He deserves not the sweet that will not taste the sour.

23 He that cannot abide a bad market, deserves not a good one.

24 He is worth no weal that can bide no woe.
"Weal" is an archaic word meaning "prosperity, well-being".

25 Into the mouth of a bad dog, often falls a good bone.

26 The worst hog often gets the best pear.

See also GOD: *Divine retribution*

45 Destiny

Its inescapability

1 Destiny has four feet, eight hands, and sixteen eyes; how then shall the ill-doer with only two of each hope to escape?
Chinese proverb.

2 No flying from fate.

3 Flee never so fast you cannot flee your fortune.

4 Do what you ought, and come what can.

5 What must be, must be.
Variants substitute "will" or "shall" for "must". The proverb is also familiar in its Italian form, *Che serà, serà*.

6 Fate leads the willing, but drives the stubborn.
A saying attributed to the stoic philosopher Cleanthes (3rd century BC).

7 He that is born to be hanged, shall never be drowned.
Variants appear in works by Shakespeare, Defoe, and Swift.

8 Every bullet has its billet.

9 There's a divinity that shapes our ends, rough-hew them how we will.
A quotation from Shakespeare's *Hamlet* (c. 1600).

Its mystery

10 A man's destiny is always dark.
Implies that nobody knows what fate has in store.

11 She is an old wife that wats her weird.
"Wats" means "knows"; "weird" means "fortune".

46 Devil

His trickery

1 The devil is subtle, yet weaves a coarse web.
"Coarse" here implies "strong".

2 The devil can cite Scripture for his purpose.
In this form a quotation from Shakespeare's *The Merchant of Venice* (c. 1597), although the thought is older. The saying alludes to the temptation of Christ in the wilderness (Matthew 4:6), where the devil cites scripture to support his arguments.

3 When the devil prays, he has a booty in his eye.

4 The devil sometimes speaks the truth.

His evil

5 The devil always leaves a stink behind him.
6 It is an ill battle where the devil carries the colours.
   "Colours" here refers to military banners.
7 When rogues go in procession, the devil holds the cross.

His power

8 He that the devil drives, feels no lead at his heels.
   That is, he moves fast.
9 The devil knows many things because he is old.
10 There is no redemption from hell.

His persistence

11 Where the devil cannot come, he will send.
   Implies that the devil's influence extends everywhere (even the holiest places) because
   of his numerous human agents.
12 The devil will play small game before he will sit out.
   That is, he will play for low stakes rather than abstain from the game. The implication is
   that the devil is keen to tempt ordinary people in small matters as well as the great and
   influential.

His omnipresence

13 The devil is a busy bishop in his own diocese.
   Implies that the devil is never out of his own diocese, for it has no boundaries.
14 The devil is at home.
   A reminder that not even at home can one escape the temptations of the devil.
15 The devil lurks behind the cross.

Handling the devil

16 The devil loves no holy water.
17 They that deal wi' the devil, get a dear pennyworth.
18 He is fond of barter that niffers with Old Nick.
   "Niffers" means "bargains".
19 He must rise betimes that will cozen the devil.
   "Betimes" means "early"; "cozen" means "cheat".

See also GOD: *God and the devil*

47 Differences

Their existence

1 It takes all sorts to make a world.
   First cited in this form in the 1840s, although variants can be traced back to the early 17th
   century.
2 There's nowt so queer as folk.
   An old north-country saying. "Nowt" means "nothing".

3 All feet tread not in one shoe.
4 Every shoe fits not every foot.
5 All things fit not all persons.
6 There may be blue and better blue.
   That is, there may be differences in quality between things (or people) of the same kind.
7 Every couple is not a pair.
8 Every man after his fashion.
9 Every man buckles his belt his ain gate.
   "His ain gate" means "his own way".
10 So many men, so many opinions.
   The saying has been traced back to Terence (2nd century BC). Variants substitute "heads" for "men" and "minds" or "wits" for "opinions".

Different tastes

11 There is no accounting for tastes.
   Like proverb 12 below, this derives from the common Latin tag *De gustibus non est disputandum*, meaning that there is no point in disputing about differences in taste.
12 There is no disputing about tastes.
13 Every one to his taste.
14 One man's meat is another man's poison.
   The saying can be traced back to Lucretius's *De rerum natura* (1st century BC).
15 All meat pleases not all mouths.
16 No dish pleases all palates alike.
17 All meats to be eaten, and all maids to be wed.
   Like proverb 18 below, this implies that what is rejected by one person will be taken up by another.
18 If one will not, another will.
19 If minds were alike goods would age in the shops.
   Arabic proverb.
20 Every man as he loves, quoth the good man when he kissed his cow.

Different needs

21 You can't please everyone.
22 He that would please all and himself too, undertakes what he cannot do.
23 He had need rise betimes that would please everybody.
   "Betimes" means "early".
24 He that all men will please shall never find ease.
25 Not God above gets all men's love.
   Implies that since not even God can please everybody simultaneously it is futile for a mere mortal to try.

Different methods

26 There are more ways to the wood than one.
27 There is more than one way to skin a cat.
28 There are more ways to kill a cat than choking it with cream.
   A variant substitutes "dog...butter" for "cat...cream".
29 There are more ways to kill a dog than hanging it.
30 All roads lead to Rome.
   In medieval Europe, where this saying originated, the road system was still essentially

that of the Roman Empire, in which roads from the provinces all converged in the capital.

48 Diligence

Its value

1 If a job's worth doing, it's worth doing well.
   A common variant substitutes "thing" for "job". The earliest recorded use is in Lord Chesterfield's letters of advice to his son (1774).
2 Diligence is the mother of good fortune.
3 Care and diligence bring luck.
4 Diligence makes an expert workman.
5 Diligence is a great teacher.
   Arabic proverb.
6 Lice do not bite busy men.
7 Better wear out shoes than sheets.
   To "wear out sheets" may imply sloth, debauchery, or sickness.
8 Without business, debauchery.
   In this and proverb 9 below "business" means "being busy".
9 Business is the salt of life.
10 Labour overcomes all things.
11 A diligent scholar, and the master's paid.
12 Better to wear out than to rust out.
13 Elbow grease gives the best polish.
   "Elbow grease" is a jocular expression for the physical effort required in cleaning or polishing, etc.
14 The gear that is gifted is never so sweet as the gear that is won.
   Implies that goods that have been earned by honest hard work are valued more than gifts.
15 A little labour, much health.
16 Where bees are, there is honey.
   Like proverbs 17–25 below, this refers to the material gains of hard work.
17 No bees, no honey; no work, no money.
18 Keep your shop and your shop will keep you.
19 The mill gets by going.
20 A going foot is aye getting.
   Some more cynical variants add "...if it were but a thorn."
21 He that labours and thrives, spins gold.
22 Industry is fortune's right hand, and frugality her left.
23 Plough deep, while sluggards sleep; and you shall have corn to sell and to keep.
24 The diligent spinner has a large shift.
25 Win gold and wear gold.
   A variant substitutes "purple" for "gold".
26 That which is well done is twice done.
   Implies that a thing done well is done for ever, whereas a thing done badly must be done again.

Its necessity

27 It is good to work wisely lest a man be prevented.
"Prevented" here means outstripped by events or circumstances.

28 Labour as long lived, pray as ever dying.

29 God gives the milk, but not the pail.
Implies that hard work is needed to make the most of nature's benefits. Compare GOD: 38–40.

30 Footprints on the sands of time are not made by sitting down.

31 No sweet without sweat.

32 Ninety per cent of inspiration is perspiration.
Usually attributed (in various forms) to the US inventor Thomas Edison (c. 1903).

33 Genius is an infinite capacity for taking pains.
Probably derived ultimately from a remark by the French naturalist the Comte de Buffon (1707–88), claiming that genius "is only a greater aptitude for patience"; Carlyle later defined genius as "transcendent capacity of taking trouble, first of all" in his *Frederick the Great* (1858).

34 Without diligence, no prize.

35 No pains, no gains.
Now best known (with both nouns in the singular) as a slogan of the aerobics exercise craze of the 1980s. However, it has been recorded as early as the 17th century and there are much older variants.

36 You don't get something for nothing.
Also well known in its north-country variant "You don't get owt for nowt."

37 He that will eat the kernel, must crack the nut.

38 He that would have the fruit, must climb the tree.

39 If you put nothing into your purse, you can take nothing out.

40 It is not with saying 'Honey, honey', that sweetness will come into the mouth.

41 If you won't work you shan't eat.
A near-quotation from St Paul (2 Thessalonians 3:10).

42 He that will not endure labour in this world, let him not be born.

43 The race is got by running.

44 Think of ease, but work on.

Its effects

45 Busiest men find the most leisure time.
The earliest recorded expression of this thought is in Samuel Smiles's *Self-Help* (1859).

46 Those that make the best use of their time, have none to spare.
A direct contradiction of proverb 45 above.

47 Work expands to fill the time available.
This facetious notion was formulated by C. Northcote Parkinson (1909–93) and is known as Parkinson's Law.

The dangers of working too hard

48 To be too busy, gets contempt.

49 Ever busy, ever bare.
Implies that the busiest people do not have the most wealth and possessions.

50 All work and no play makes Jack a dull boy.

51 Mix work with leisure and you will never go mad.
Russian proverb.

52 There are only twenty-four hours in the day.

53 Many irons in the fire, some must cool.
That is, if you undertake too many tasks or roles at once some will be neglected. Note, however, that the phrase "to have several irons in the fire" is generally used to make the opposite point – that it is always prudent to have more than one plan or project. In both cases the allusion is to work in a blacksmith's forge.

54 He who begins many things, finishes but few.

55 If you run after two hares, you will catch neither.

56 He that does most at once, does least.

57 One thing at a time, and that done well, is a very good thing, as many can tell.

Diligent people

58 For the diligent the week has seven todays, for the slothful seven tomorrows.

59 Not a long day, but a good heart rids work.

60 The workman is known by his work.

Making an effort

61 You never know what you can do till you try.

62 If the mountain will not come to Mahomet, Mahomet must go to the mountain.
According to a folk tradition, certain Arabs once asked Mohammed to give proof of his God-given mission by performing a miracle. He accordingly called on Mount Safa to up-root itself and come before him; when it did no such thing, the Prophet immediately gave thanks to God for His mercy, on the grounds that had the mountain obeyed they would all have been killed in the upheaval. The saying implies that it is wise to bow to the inevitable.

49 Discipline

Its importance

1 Reward and punishment are the walls of a city.

2 Corn is cleansed with wind, and the soul with chastenings.

3 He that corrects not small faults, will not control great ones.

4 The best horse needs breaking, and the aptest child needs teaching.

5 It is the bridle and spur that makes a good horse.

6 A boisterous horse must have a rough bridle.

7 The plough goes not well if the ploughman hold it not.

8 He that chastens one, chastens twenty.
Because of the power of example.

9 He that chastises one, amends many.

Disciplining children

10 Better children weep than old men.
Implies that it is better to punish children, however cruel it may seem, than to let them develop faults that will cause more sorrow in later life.

11 Rule youth well, and age will rule itself.

12 Give me a child for the first seven years, and you may do what you like with him afterwards.

A maxim often attributed to Jesuit educators, with the implication that their teaching has an indelible effect on young minds.

13 The kick of the dam hurts not the colt.

14 Time is the rider that breaks youth.

15 She spins well that breeds her children.

The spoilt child

16 A child may have too much of his mother's blessing.

17 He that cockers his child, provides for his enemy.

"Cockers" means "spoils".

18 Give a child while he craves, and a dog while his tail doth wave, and you'll have a fair dog, but a foul knave.

19 A pitiful mother makes a scabby daughter.

"Scabby" here means "nasty".

20 Dawted daughters make daidling wives.

"Dawted" means "spoilt"; "daidling" means "lazy".

21 A blate cat makes a proud mouse.

"Blate" means "bashful". The implication is that a lenient parent or master makes impertinent children or servants.

Corporal punishment

22 Spare the rod and spoil the child.

First used in precisely this form in Samuel Butler's *Hudibras* (1664), although the saying derives ultimately from Proverbs 13:24.

23 A whip for a fool, and a rod for a school, is always in good season.

24 The rod breaks no bones.

25 Birchen twigs break no ribs.

26 A woman, a dog, and a walnut-tree, the more you beat them the better they be.

It was formerly believed that beating a walnut tree would increase its yield.

27 Spaniels that fawn when beaten, will never forsake their masters.

28 He that is sick of a fever lurden, must be cured by the hazel gelding.

"Fever lurden" means "lazy fever"; a "gelding" here means a young tree (whose branches will serve well for a whip).

29 You may ding the devil into a wife, but you'll never ding him out of her.

"Ding" means "beat".

30 Never take the tawse when a word will do the turn.

The "tawse" is a leather strap with a split end, formerly used in Scotland for corporal punishment.

Self-discipline

31 Happy is he that chastens himself.

32 He that is master of himself, will soon be master of others.

33 He is not fit to command others, that cannot command himself.

34 He gets a double victory, who conquers himself.

The watchful master

35 The eye of the master will do more work than both his hands.
Like proverbs 36–39 below, this implies that discipline in a household can only be maintained when the master is present to supervise and inspect.

36 One eye of the master sees more than ten of the servants.

37 The master's eye makes the horse fat.
A reference to the need for supervision of stable-hands. The saying can be traced back to Plutarch's *Moral Essays* (1st–2nd century AD).

38 The master's footsteps fatten the soil, and his foot the ground.
A variant has "The master's foot is the best manure."

39 A sleepy master makes his servant a lout.

See also ABSENCE: *Its effect on discipline*

50 Dress

Its effects

1 Clothes make people, priests make brides.

2 God makes and apparel shapes.
Variants substitute "man" or "the tailor" for "apparel".

3 Apparel makes the man.

4 The tailor makes the man.
Clearly related to the old (and somewhat obscure) saying that "Nine tailors make a man". One meaning of this is that a truly well-dressed man will choose his clothes from at least nine specialist suppliers. However, the saying also seems to allude to the proverbial puniness of tailors, many of whom developed a stunted physique owing to their sedentary trade and poor working conditions. It has also been suggested that "tailors" is in fact a corruption of "tellers" (strokes of a bell): a funeral bell was tolled nine times for a man, as compared to six for a woman and three for a child.

5 Good clothes open all doors.

6 Fine feathers make fine birds.
This reverses the moral of "The Jay and the Peacock", a fable attributed to Aesop (6th century BC): "It is not only fine feathers that make fine birds."

7 Dress up a stick and it does not appear to be a stick.

8 Fine dressing is a foul house swept before the doors.

9 Ugly women, finely dressed, are the uglier for it.

10 Clothes do not make the man.
A direct contradiction of proverbs 1 and 3 above.

Fashion

11 The present fashion is always handsome.

12 Fools may invent fashions that wise men will wear.

13 What has been the fashion will come into fashion again.
Japanese proverb.

14 Better be out of the world than out of the fashion.

Sunday best

15 Alike every day makes a clout on Sunday.

Wear your Sunday best everyday and you'll soon have only a rag ("clout") to wear on Sunday itself. The same point is made by proverb 16 below.

16 Every day braw makes Sunday a daw.
"Braw" means "fine"; "daw" means "drab".

51 Drinking

Drunkenness

1 When the wine is in, the wit is out.
A variant substitutes "truth" for "wit".

2 Ale will make a cat speak.

3 Drunkards and fools cannot lie.
Compare CHILDREN: 21.

4 There is truth in wine.
Equally familiar in its Latin form, *In vino veritas*, which is sometimes attributed to Pliny the Elder (1st century AD). A Greek version has been attributed to the semilegendary poet Alcaeus (7th century BC).

5 What soberness conceals, drunkenness reveals.

6 Drunkenness does not produce faults, it discovers them.
Chinese proverb.

7 Wine wears no breeches.
Implies that drink reveals a man's failings.

8 Wine is the glass of the mind.
That is, drink presents a true reflection of someone's mind or character.

9 When wine sinks, words swim.

10 Wine does not intoxicate men: men intoxicate themselves.
Chinese proverb.

11 Drunken days have all their tomorrows.
That is, there is always a morning after.

12 Let but the drunkard alone, and he will fall of himself.

13 A drunkard's purse is a bottle.

14 You cannot make people sober by Act of Parliament.
Often used in reference to laws restricting the sale of alcohol. "Honest" is sometimes substituted for "sober".

15 The best cure for drunkenness is while sober to see a drunken man.
Chinese proverb.

Its advantages

16 Drunken folks seldom take harm.

17 There are more old drunkards than old doctors.

18 Wine is the best broom for troubles.
Japanese proverb.

19 A cask of wine works more miracles than a church full of saints.
Italian proverb.

20 A good drink makes the old young.

21 Wine makes old wives wenches.

22 Wine and youth increase love.

23 A spur in the head is worth two in the heel.

Implies that a drunken man rides faster; some versions add "A cup in the pate is a mile in the gait (going)."

24 Wine is a whetstone to wit.

Its dangers

25 Bacchus has drowned more men than Neptune.
Bacchus is the god of wine, Neptune the god of the sea.

26 There is a devil in every berry of the grape.
A saying that is sometimes attributed to the Prophet Mohammed (alcoholic liquor being forbidden by Islam).

27 He that kills a man when he is drunk shall be hanged when he is sober.

28 Wine and wealth change wise men's manners.

29 The first glass for thirst, the second for nourishment, the third for pleasure, and the fourth for madness.

30 Dicing, drabbing and drinking bring men to destruction.
A "drab" is a prostitute.

31 Gaming, women, and wine, while they laugh, they make men pine.

32 Play, women, and wine undo men laughing.

33 Wine and wenches empty men's purses.

34 Women and wine, game and deceit, make the wealth small, and the wants great.

Beer

35 Good ale is meat, drink, and cloth.

36 He that buys land buys many stones; he that buys flesh buys many bones; he that buys eggs buys many shells; but he that buys good ale buys nothing else.

37 Heresy and beer came into England both in a year.
Beer (flavoured with hops) began to replace ale (a stronger drink brewed without hops) as the staple drink of the English at about the same time that Protestant doctrines were first introduced (the 1520s). For a more elaborate version see RELIGION: 46.

38 Every one has a penny to spend at a new ale-house.

39 He goes not out of his way that goes to a good inn.

Wine

40 The vine brings forth three grapes: the first of pleasure, the second of drunkenness, the third of sorrow.
Sometimes attributed to the Scythian philosopher Anacharsis (7th century BC), who was known for his temperance.

41 Wine is a turncoat.
Implies that although wine is pleasant to drink, it has unpleasant after-effects.

42 Wine is old men's milk.

43 Wine makes all sorts of creatures at table.

44 It is a good wind that blows a man to the wine.

45 The wine is the master's, the goodness is the butler's.
Implies that the credit for a good wine should go to the butler, who selects and serves it, rather than to the master, who merely pays for it.

46 Of wine the middle, of oil the top, and of honey the bottom, is the best.
The saying can be traced back to the Latin writer Macrobius (4th century AD).

47 Fish must swim thrice.
Implies that fish should first swim in the water, then in the sauce in which it is cooked, and finally in the wine with which it is drunk.

48 The peach will have wine and the fig water.

49 After melon, wine is a felon.

50 Drink wine in winter for cold, and in summer for heat.

Water

51 Water is the king of food.
African proverb.

52 Adam's ale is the best brew.
"Adam's ale" is water.

53 Drinking water neither makes a man sick, nor in debt, nor his wife a widow.

54 Those who drink but water will have no liquor to buy.

55 Drink only with the duck.
That is, drink only water.

56 Water drinkers bring forth nothing good.

Healthy drinking habits

57 Drink less, and go home by daylight.

58 Eat at pleasure, drink by measure.

59 Clothe thee warm, eat little, drink enough, and thou shalt live.

60 Of all victuals, drink digests the quickest.
An excuse for drinking after a meal.

61 Never mix your liquor.
May be taken to mean either that one should not mix different types of liquor or, facetiously, that one should not mix liquor with water to dilute it.

62 Our fathers which were wondrous wise, did wash their throats before their eyes.
That is, they preferred to drink and rejoice rather than to weep and lament.

63 Do not drink between meals.

64 Drink as much after an egg as after an ox.
Implies that one should drink as much with a small meal as with a large.

65 Good wine engenders good blood.

66 If you would live ever, you must wash milk from your liver.
This and proverb 67 below refer to the belief that wine should be drunk after milk.

67 Milk says to wine, Welcome friend.

Unhealthy drinking habits

68 He who drinks a little too much drinks much too much.

69 If you drink in your pottage, you'll cough in your grave.
An ironic warning against drinking with soup.

70 Drink wine, and have the gout; drink no wine, and have the gout too.
An excuse for drinking wine.

71 He that drinks not wine after salad is in danger of being sick.

Thirst

72 He who is master of his thirst is master of his health.

73 He is not thirsty who doesn't drink water.

74 Many words would have much drink.
75 Salt beef draws down drink apace.
   "Apace" means quickly.
76 A drunken man is always dry.
77 Ever drunk, ever dry.
78 He that goes to bed thirsty, rises healthy.

52 Earliness

Its advantages

1 The early bird catches the worm.
2 The sleepy fox has seldom feathered breakfasts.
3 The cow that's first up, gets the first of the dew.
4 He that comes first to the hill, may sit where he will.
   "Dunghill" or "midden" is sometimes substituted for "hill", in which case the saying is clearly ironic.
5 First come, first served.
6 He that rises first, is first dressed.
7 Early to bed and early to rise, makes a man healthy, wealthy and wise.
   James Thurber's humorous reversal is well known: "Early to rise and early to bed, makes a man healthy and wealthy and dead" (mid-20th century).
8 He that will thrive, must rise at five; he that has thriven, may lie till seven; but he that will never thrive may lie till eleven.
9 Go to bed with the lamb, and rise with the lark.
10 Some work in the morning may trimly be done, that all the day after may hardly be won.
   "Trimly" here means "efficiently" or "thoroughly".
11 An hour in the morning is worth two in the evening.
12 He who works before dawn will soon be his own master.
13 The early man never borrows from the late man.
14 Early sow, early mow.
15 Sooner begun, sooner done.

Its necessity

16 He that will deceive the fox must rise betimes.
   "Betimes" means "early". As in proverbs 17 and 18 below, the "must rise betimes" formulation is ironic, implying that the activity in question is impossible.
17 He must rise betimes that will cozen the devil.
   "Cozen" means "cheat".
18 He had need rise betimes that would please everybody.
19 A green wound is soon healed.
   Like proverb 20 below, this implies that a wound (physical or psychological) is best healed if treated early, before it can fester.
20 It is ill healing of an old sore.

21 A stitch in time saves nine.
Like proverbs 22–24 below, this illustrates the value of prompt action in avoiding future trouble.

22 Who repairs not his gutter, repairs his whole house.

23 He that repairs not a part, builds all.

24 Destroy the lion while he is yet but a whelp.

Its inadequacy

25 God's health is better than early rising.

26 Though you rise early, yet the day comes at his time, and not till then.

27 In vain they rise early that used to rise late.

The importance of punctuality

28 Punctuality is the politeness of princes.
Attributed to Louis XVIII of France (1755–1824).

29 Punctuality is the soul of business.

53 Eating

Its importance

1 Bread is the staff of life.

2 An army marches on its stomach.
A maxim sometimes attributed to Napoleon and sometimes to Frederick the Great of Prussia (1712–86).

3 The belly carries the legs.

4 Stuffing holds out storm.
The advice here is that one should eat a good meal before setting off on a journey in bad weather.

5 The guts uphold the heart, and not the heart the guts.

6 The way to an Englishman's heart is through his stomach.
A common variant substitutes "man" for "Englishman". First noted in the mid-19th century.

7 Without Ceres and Bacchus, Venus grows cold.
A quotation from the Roman playwright Terence (2nd century BC). Ceres is the goddess of agriculture, Bacchus the god of wine, and Venus the goddess of love; the implication is that without food and wine a man loses his desire to make love.

8 If it wasn't for meat and good drink, the women might gnaw the sheets.
The implication here is the same as that of proverb 7 above.

9 When meat is in, anger is out.

10 Spread the table, and contention will cease.

11 All griefs with bread are less.

12 Meat and mass never hindered any man.
Implies that one's business is never harmed by making the time to eat or pray.

13 The mouth is the executioner and the doctor of the body.
Implies that a bad or good diet may either kill or cure.

14 He was an ingenious man that first found out eating and drinking.

Its unimportance

15 Man cannot live by bread alone.
   Adapted from Deuteronomy 8:3: the biblical text continues "but by every word that pro-
   ceedeth out of the mouth of the Lord doth man live."

16 Meat is much, but manners is more.

17 It is better to want meat than guests or company.

Appetite

18 All things require skill but an appetite.

19 The eye is bigger than the belly.
   Often (with "my" substituted for "the") used as a jocular excuse for failing to eat the
   whole of one's portion.

20 Better fill a man's belly than his eye.

21 One shoulder of mutton draws down another.
   This saying, contrary to proverb 22 below, suggests that appetite increases with eating.

22 Eating and drinking takes away one's stomach.

23 The first dish is aye best eaten.

24 The first dish pleases all.
   Like proverb 23 above, this implies that the first course of a meal will always be the best
   appreciated because it takes the edge off one's appetite.

25 A growing youth has a wolf in his belly.

Desirable foods

26 The best food is that which fills the belly.
   Arabic proverb.

27 The best smell is bread, the best savour salt, the best love that of children.

28 Salt seasons all things.

29 Good kail is half a meal.
   "Kail" is a Scottish word meaning "broth".

30 Kail spares bread.

31 Of soup and love, the first is the best.

32 Milk is white, and lies not in the dyke, but all men know it good meat.
   That is, milk may not be water but it is still good to drink; a response to someone who
   implies that there is only one way of doing something.

33 Tripe's good meat if it be well wiped.

34 A meal without flesh is like feeding on grass.
   Indian proverb.

35 He that has breams in his pond is able to bid his friend welcome.
   According to Walton's *The Compleat Angler* (1653) this proverb originated in France,
   where bream were highly valued as food.

36 The wholesomest meat is at another man's cost.

37 It is good beef that costs nothing.

Undesirable foods

38 He was a bold man that first ate an oyster.
   Sometimes attributed to James I and VI.

39 Oysters are ungodly, because they are eaten without grace; uncharitable

because we leave nought but shells; and unprofitable because they must swim in wine.

40 Garlic makes a man wink, drink, and stink.

"Wink" here means "sleep".

41 There is no such thing as good small beer, good brown bread, or a good old woman.

"Small beer" was weak or inferior beer and brown (i.e. rye) bread the cheapest kind.

42 Hare is melancholy meat.

According to medieval naturalists, the hare was a melancholy animal owing to an excess of black bile in its constitution; the same disposition would be passed on to anyone who ate its flesh.

43 Parsley fried will bring a man to his saddle, and a woman to her grave.

44 Every pease has its veaze, and a bean fifteen.

"Veaze" literally means "a sudden rush", here referring to flatulence. The implication is that although peas are flatulent, beans are many times more so.

45 Raw pulleyn, veal, and fish, make the churchyards fat.

"Pulleyn" means "poultry".

46 Sweet things are bad for the teeth.

47 In a shoulder of veal, there are twenty and two good bits.

A cynical or jocular saying implying *not* that there are 22 good bits in a shoulder of veal, but rather that there are twenty indifferent bits and just two good ones. Used of anything that seems a very mixed blessing.

Cheese

48 After cheese comes nothing.

Cheese is traditionally the last course of a meal.

49 Cheese digests everything but itself.

50 An apple-pie without some cheese is like a kiss without a squeeze.

Healthy eating habits

51 After dinner sit awhile, after supper walk a mile.

52 When the belly is full, the bones would be at rest.

53 Clothe thee warm, eat little, drink enough, and thou shalt live.

54 Feed by measure and defy the physician.

55 He that eats least eats most.

Implies that eating sparingly enables one to live longer, and thus eat more.

56 Eat to live and not live to eat.

57 Eat at pleasure, drink by measure.

58 Eat an apple going to bed, make the doctor beg his bread.

59 An apple a day keeps the doctor away.

Variants are recorded from the mid-19th century onwards. Apples are rich in amino acids, vitamins, and mineral salts.

60 Eat leeks in Lide and ramsins in May, and all the year after physicians may play.

"Lide" is a dialect word for "March"; "ramsins" means "garlic".

61 He that would live for aye, must eat sage in May.

Sage was an ingredient in many early medicines and is still valued as a tonic and aid to digestion.

62 If they would drink nettles in March, and eat mugwort in May, so many fine maidens wouldn't go to the clay.

Nettle juice and mugwort are still used as herbal remedies, the former as a diuretic and general tonic and the latter for menstrual problems.

63 Oysters are only in season in the R months.

The "R months" are those that have the letter R in their name. Implies that oysters should not be eaten in the summer months, namely May, June, July, and August.

Unhealthy eating habits

64 Whatsoever was the father of a disease, an ill diet was the mother.

65 Many dishes make many diseases.

The warning here is against overelaborate cuisine rather than simple overeating.

66 Much meat, much malady.

67 Often and little eating makes a man fat.

Table manners and superstitions

68 Fingers were made before forks, and hands before knives.

An apology for picking food up in one's fingers.

69 None but fools and fiddlers sing at their meat.

70 He loved mutton well that licked where the ewe lay.

Like proverbs 71 and 72 below, this is said as a reproach to those who scrape or lick their dish after a good meal.

71 He loves bacon well that licks the swinesty door.

72 He loves roast meat well that licks the spit.

73 Never be ashamed to eat your meat.

That is, don't hide your enthusiasm for a good meal out of misplaced refinement.

74 Speak not of a dead man at the table.

75 To speak of a usurer at the table mars the wine.

76 Help you to salt, help you to sorrow.

Cooks

77 If you want your dinner, don't offend the cook.

Chinese proverb.

78 God sends meat and the devil sends cooks.

See also GLUTTONY; HUNGER

54 Education

Its importance

1 Education polishes good natures, and correcteth bad ones.

2 Learn not and know not.

3 The best horse needs breaking, and the aptest child needs teaching.

4 Better unborn than untaught.

A severer variant substitutes "unbeaten" for "untaught".

The process of learning

5 Knowledge has bitter roots but sweet fruits.
This, like proverbs 6 and 7 below, refers to the suffering involved in learning, and its final reward.

6 The rain of tears is necessary to the harvest of learning.
Indian proverb.

7 Learn weeping, and you shall gain laughing.

8 There is no royal road to learning.
Based on the reply given by Euclid (c. 300 BC) to Ptolemy I, when he asked if there was a quick and easy way to master the science of geometry.

9 Soon learnt, soon forgotten.

The ideal time

10 Learn young, learn fair.

11 Whoso learns young, forgets not when he is old.

12 Learning in one's youth is engraving in stone.

13 What's learnt in the cradle lasts till the tomb.

14 What youth is used to, age remembers.

15 What we first learn, we best can.

16 Never too late to learn.
"Old" is often substituted for "late".

17 A man may learn wit every day.

Teachers and pupils

18 Teaching of others, teacheth the teacher.

19 In every art, it is good to have a master.

20 He teaches ill, who teaches all.
There are two possible implications: that a good teacher takes care to instil the basics of a subject before attempting to explain its more sophisticated points; or that he will always leave something for his pupils to work out for themselves.

21 Better untaught than ill taught.

22 Those who can, do; those who can't, teach.
Adapted from one of George Bernard Shaw's *Maxims for Revolutionists* (1903): "He who can, does. He who cannot, teaches." Modern variations substitute "manages" or "attends conferences" for "teaches".

23 He that teaches himself, has a fool for his master.

24 Every good scholar is not a good schoolmaster.

25 He can ill be master that never was scholar.

26 A good master, a good scholar.

27 An ill master, an ill scholar.

28 The scholar may waur the master.
"Waur" means "be better than".

29 Silly child is soon ylered.
"Silly" here means "good"; "ylered" means "taught".

See also EXPERIENCE: *Learning by experience*

55 Endings

Their importance

1 The end crowns the work.
"All" is sometimes substituted for "the work".

2 Think on the end before you begin.

3 Look to the end.

4 At the game's end, we shall see who gains.

5 All's well that ends well.
Already a long-established proverb by the time Shakespeare wrote his play of this title (c. 1602).

Their inevitability

6 Everything has an end.

7 All good things must come to an end.
The word "good" is a 20th-century addition to a much older proverb.

8 The best of friends must part.

The end result

9 Garbage in, garbage out.
A 20th-century proverb originating in computer science but now frequently applied to other fields; it implies that, however sophisticated the system, the output can still only be as good as the input. The acronym GIGO is also used.

10 If better were within, better would come out.

11 Such beef, such broth.

12 Whether you boil snow or pound it, you can have but water of it.

See also BEGINNINGS: *The importance of beginning well*; OPTIMISM: *Nothing is permanent*

56 Endurance

Its value

1 He conquers who endures.

2 He that endures is not overcome.

Its necessity

3 What can't be cured, must be endured.

4 Bear and forbear.
The "golden rule" of the Stoic philosopher Epictetus (1st century AD).

5 He that will not endure to itch, must endure to smart.
Implies that some discomforts have to be endured because any attempt to relieve them (such as scratching an itch) will make them worse.

Its limitations

6 Even a worm will turn.
Implies that even the most lowly will tolerate only a limited amount of abuse.

7 The orange that is too hard squeezed yields a bitter juice.

8 An ass endures his burden, but not more than his burden.

9 A man may bear till his back break.

10 It is not the burden, but the over-burden that kills the beast.

11 Too long burden makes weary bones.

12 Bind the sack before it be full.
Because otherwise it may burst and you will lose your labour. Like proverbs 13–22 below this is a warning against pushing any person or thing to the limit.

13 Double charge will rive a cannon.
"Charge" here means "explosive" and "rive" means "burst". The proverb implies that an excess of anything, whether it be food, drink, or work, may have disastrous results.

14 Too-too will in two.

15 A bow long bent at last waxes weak.

16 The pitcher goes so often to the well that it is broken at last.

17 Put not the bucket too often in the well.

18 Strings high stretched either soon crack or quickly grow out of tune.

19 When the well is full, it will run over.

20 The last drop makes the cup run over.

21 The last straw breaks the camel's back.
Frequently alluded to in the short phrase "the last straw".

22 The cord breaks at last by the weakest pull.

Its dangers

23 All lay load on the willing horse.

24 If thou suffer a calf to be laid on thee, within a little they'll clap on the cow.

25 The submitting to one wrong brings on another.
The moral of Aesop's fable of the snake who failed to bite the first man to tread on him (6th century BC).

26 He that makes himself a sheep, shall be eaten by the wolf.
The implication is that those who meekly endure insults and injuries will only receive more.

57 Enemies

Their value

1 An enemy may chance to give good counsel.
The saying can be traced back to Aristophanes's *The Birds* (5th century BC).

2 If you have no enemies, it's a sign fortune has forgot you.
That is, all fortunate or prominent people must expect to have enemies.

Their danger

3 There is no little enemy.

4 One enemy can do more hurt than ten friends can do good.

5 One enemy is too many; and a hundred friends too few.

6 An enemy's mouth seldom speaks well.

7 No friend to a bosom friend; no enemy to a bosom enemy.
Implies that just as there is no better friend than a bosom friend, there is no worse enemy than an intimate or familiar one.

8 Nothing worse than a familiar enemy.
"Familiar" here means "of one's own household".

9 Better a thousand enemies outside the house than one inside.
Arabic proverb.

10 A secret foe gives a sudden blow.

11 Better go by your enemy's grave than by his gate.

Handling one's enemies

12 Make your enemy your friend.

13 For a flying enemy make a golden bridge.
The advice here is to leave an easy retreat or way out for one's enemy, thereby discouraging him from fighting on. In Plutarch's *Lives* (1st century AD) the saying is attributed to the Athenian commander Aristides, who advised Themistocles not to destroy the bridge of boats across the Hellespont by which Xerxes hoped to retreat from Greece after his defeat at Salamis (480 BC).

14 Speak well of your friend, of your enemy say nothing.

Words of caution

15 Believe no tales from an enemy's tongue.

16 Though thy enemy seem a mouse, yet watch him like a lion.

17 If we are bound to forgive an enemy, we are not bound to trust him.
"Always forgive your enemies – but never forget their names" was a maxim of the US politician Robert Kennedy (1960s).

18 Fear the Greeks bearing gifts.
A quotation from Virgil's *Aeneid* (1st century BC); the allusion is to the wooden horse, a treacherous "gift" that enabled the Greeks to gain access to Troy and destroy it. When the phrase is used proverbially, "the Greeks" refers to any enemy.

19 He that gives honour to his enemy, is like to an ass.

20 The only good Indian is a dead Indian.
Adapted from a saying of the US general Philip H. Sheridan (1831–88): "The only good Indians I ever saw were dead." There are now many variants, the word "Indian" being replaced by the nationality of the enemy concerned.

21 Take heed of reconciled enemies.
Some versions add "...and of meat twice boiled".

22 Take heed of wind that comes in at a hole, and a reconciled enemy.
The machinations of a false friend are compared to the unperceived danger of sitting in a draught.

23 Trust not a new friend nor an old enemy.

58 England

Attitudes to England

1 England is a good land, and a bad people.
French proverb.

2 England is the paradise of women, the hell of horses, and the purgatory of servants.
Adapted (16th century) from an earlier saying about Paris.

3 England is the ringing island.
   A reference to the large number of church bells in the country.

4 With all the world have war, but with England do not jar.
   A 16th-century Spanish proverb.

5 England is a little garden full of very sour weeds.

6 Shoulder of mutton and English beer, make the Flemings tarry here.
   An allusion to the many Flemish traders to be found in London and other English ports in the 17th century.

7 There is more good victuals in England, than in seven other kingdoms.

8 The English are a nation of shopkeepers.
   Generally attributed to Napoleon, although the saying appeared earlier in Adam Smith's *The Wealth of Nations* (1766).

Characteristics of the English

9 Gluttony is the sin of England.

10 The way to an Englishman's heart is through his stomach.

11 The English have one hundred religions, but only one sauce.
   Attributed to Domenico Caracciolo, an 18th-century governor of Sicily; the saying refers to England's numerous Protestant sects and somewhat unvaried cuisine. Compare PEOPLE AND PLACES: 5.

12 An Englishman's word is his bond.

13 The English are the swearing nation.

14 Every English archer beareth under his girdle twenty-four Scots.
   A medieval Scottish saying referring to the deadliness of the English longbow.

15 One Englishman can beat three Frenchmen.

16 The English never know when they are beaten.
   Sometimes attributed to Napoleon.

17 A right Englishman knows not when a thing is well.

18 An Englishman loves a lord.
   First recorded in the early 20th century.

19 It is an Englishman's privilege to grumble.

20 An Englishman's home is his castle.
   The saying, which is sometimes attributed to the jurist Sir Edward Coke (1552–1634), reflects the common-law principle that a person has the right to be unmolested in his or her own home. It is now mainly used to emphasize the Englishman's love of privacy and independence. Variants substitute "man" for "Englishman" or "house" for "home".

21 Long beards heartless; painted hoods witless; gay coats graceless; makes England thriftless.
   A contemptuous Scottish proverb, dating from the 14th-century wars with England.

Regions and counties

22 Blessed is the eye, that is betwixt Severn and Wye.
   This refers to the pleasant countryside of Herefordshire and Worcestershire.

23 What Lancashire thinks today, all England will think tomorrow.
   Coined in the days of the Anti-Corn Law League, an influential movement for free trade that originated in Lancashire in 1839. See also proverb 55 below.

24 He that would take a Lancashire man at any time or tide, must bait his hook with a good egg-pie, or an apple with a red side.

25 When all the world shall be aloft, then Hallamshire shall be God's croft.

"Hallamshire" was a former name for the hilly country to the west of Sheffield, which was notorious for its poor agricultural land.

26 When Sheffield Park is ploughed and sown, then little England hold thine own.
The reference is once again to the poor farming country around Sheffield.

27 Yorkshire born and Yorkshire bred, strong in the arm and weak in the head.
Variants substitute other northern counties or towns for Yorkshire.

28 Give a Yorkshireman a halter, and he'll find a horse.
Like proverb 29 below, this refers to the Yorkshireman's supposed love of riding.

29 Shake a bridle over a Yorkshire tike's grave, and he'll rise again.
A "tyke" or "tike" was a derogatory term for a Yorkshire person.

30 Shake a Leicestershire man by the collar, and you shall hear the beans rattle in his belly.

31 Suffolk is the land of churches.
The county is noted for its many splendid churches, built with money from the medieval wool trade.

32 Essex stiles, Kentish miles, Norfolk wiles, many a man beguiles.

33 Some places of Kent have health and no wealth, some wealth and no health, some health and wealth, some have neither health nor wealth.

34 Sussex won't be druv.
"Druv" means "driven". The proverb implies that the people of Sussex cannot be forced to do anything against their will.

35 Hampshire ground requires every day in the week a shower of rain and on Sunday twain.
The soil of Hampshire is mainly chalky or sandy. See also proverb 39 below.

36 The Isle of Wight has no monks, lawyers, or foxes.
A former boast, probably without foundation, of the inhabitants of the Isle of Wight. Monks, lawyers, and foxes were all considered undesirable characters.

37 All Cornish gentlemen are cousins.
Implies that the Cornish upper classes generally intermarry.

38 The devil will not come into Cornwall, for fear of being put into a pie.
A reference to the Cornish tendency to make pies (the famous Cornish pasties) of anything edible.

39 Cornwall will bear a shower every day, and two on Sunday.
The soil of Cornwall is generally poor and stony. See also proverb 35 above.

40 There are more saints in Cornwall than in heaven.
A reference to the numerous Cornish places named after (and churches dedicated to) obscure saints of the Celtic Church.

41 The north of England for an ox, the south for a sheep, and the middle part for a man.

42 The north for greatness, the east for health; the south for neatness, the west for wealth.

43 Out of the north, all ill comes forth.
Many long-established superstitions associate the north with evil and ill-luck.

44 Three ills come from the north, a cold wind, a shrinking cloth, and a dissembling man.
Yorkshire cloth was notorious for shrinking when wet and Yorkshire people had a reputation for craftiness.

45 Cold weather and knaves come out of the north.

Rivers and mountains

46 Hengsten Down well wrought is worth London town dear bought.
Hengston (or Hingston) Down in Cornwall was once a valuable source of tin.

47 Ingleborough, Pendle, and Penyghent, are the highest hills between Scotland and Trent.
Pendle Hill is in Lancashire, Ingleborough and Pen-y-Ghent are in Yorkshire. The proverb is inaccurate, as there are several higher peaks than these in the Lake District and the northern part of the Pennines.

48 Kent and Keer have parted many a good man and his mare.
A reference to the dangers of fording the rivers Kent and Keer, which flow into the treacherous sands of Morecambe Bay.

49 River of Dart! O river of Dart! every year thou claimest a heart.
This refers to the fast-flowing river Dart in Devon, which was said to claim the life of at least one person every year.

50 Witham pike: England has none like.
The river Witham is in Lincolnshire.

51 Salisbury Plain is seldom without a thief or twain.

Towns and villages

52 Oxford is the home of lost causes.
Adapted from a passage in Matthew Arnold's *Essays in Criticism* (1865): "Home of lost causes, and forsaken beliefs, and unpopular names, and impossible loyalties!" Arnold was thinking primarily of Oxford's support for the king in the Civil War and the 19th-century Oxford Movement in the Anglican Church.

53 When Oxford draws knife, England's soon at strife.
During the middle ages many outbreaks of ecclesiastical or political strife were heralded by rioting in Oxford.

54 Oxford for learning, London for wit, Hull for women, and York for a tit.
"Tit" here means "horse".

55 What Manchester says today, the rest of England says tomorrow.
A variant of proverb 23 above; Manchester was the centre of the free-trade movement in the 19th century.

56 From hell, Hull, and Halifax, good Lord deliver us.
This proverb is also known as "the thieves' litany". Hull was apparently to be avoided because of the strict administration of justice there and Halifax because (until 1650) thieves were summarily beheaded at the Halifax Gibbet for stealing cloth. It has been suggested that "hell" is a corruption of Elland, another cloth-trading town in the area.

57 Said the devil when flying o'er Harrogate Wells, I think I am getting near home by the smells.
A reference to the sulphur springs at Harrogate.

58 Northampton stands on other men's legs.
Northampton was a centre of the shoemaking trade.

59 The Mayor of Northampton opens oysters with his dagger.
A reference to the distance of Northampton from the sea. Oysters and other seafood would be rather stale by the time they reached the town.

60 If Poole was a fish-pool, and the men of Poole fish, there'd be a pool for the devil and fish for his dish.

61 When Plymouth was a vuzzy down, Plympton was a borough town.
"Vuzzy" means "covered in gorse". The proverb gives evidence of local rivalry between
the smaller but more ancient town of Plympton and the larger town of Plymouth. Variants substitute Dartmouth and Kingswear, or Exon (Exeter) and Kirton (Crediton), for
Plymouth and Plympton. All are places in Devon.

62 Salisbury Cathedral was built upon wool-packs.
Implies that the funds for building the cathedral were obtained from the revenue from
the wool trade. The same observation was sometimes made of London Bridge.

63 A Royston horse and a Cambridge master of arts will give way to nobody.
Royston is in Cambridgeshire.

64 Sutton for mutton, Carshalton for beeves; Epsom for whores, and Ewell for
thieves.
Like proverb 65 below, this refers to towns in Surrey. "Beeves" is an archaic word for
cattle.

65 Sutton for good mutton, Cheam for juicy beef, Croydon for a pretty girl, and
Mitcham for a thief.

66 Tring, Wing, and Ivinghoe, three dirty villages all in a row, and never without a rogue or two. Would you know the reason why? Leighton Buzzard is
hard by.
Tring is in Hertfordshire, Wing and Ivinghoe in Buckinghamshire, and Leighton Buzzard
in Bedfordshire.

67 The Mayor of Altrincham lies in bed while his breeches are mending.
Altrincham, in Cheshire, was reputed to be so poor that the mayor could only afford one
pair of breeches.

68 Through the pass of Alton, poverty might pass without peril of robbing.
The pass of Alton, on the Hampshire–Surrey border, was heavily wooded and therefore
an ideal place for outlaws to ambush travellers.

69 It is written upon a wall in Rome, Ribchester was as rich as any town in
Christendom.
The village of Ribchester, in Lancashire, was the site of an important Roman town.

70 Rising was, Lynn is, and Downham shall be, the greatest seaport of the three.
A reference to Castle Rising, King's Lynn, and Downham Market, in Norfolk.

71 Rising was a seaport town, and Lynn it was a wash, but now Lynne is a seaport town, and Rising fares the worst.

72 Gimmingham, Trimmingham, Knapton and Trunch, North Repps and South
Repps are all of a bunch.
This refers to six Norfolk villages which lie close together.

73 The stoutest beggar that goes by the way, can't beg through Long on an midsummer's day.
A reference to the straggling village of Longdon in Staffordshire.

74 All the maids in Wanswell may dance in an eggshell.
The girls of Wanswell, in Gloucestershire, were notorious for unchastity (apparently because the holy well there provided a trysting place for young men and women).

London

75 When a man is tired of London, he is tired of life.
A quotation from Samuel Johnson, recorded in Boswell's *Life* (1791).

76 Who goes to Westminster for a wife, to Paul's for a man, and to Smithfield
for a horse, may meet a whore, a knave, and a jade.

77 The streets of London are paved with gold.
   The implication is that it is easy to make one's fortune in London. The inaccuracy of the proverb has been found out by many to their cost.

78 London Bridge was made for wise men to go over, and fools to go under.
   Implies that it was considered safer to go across the bridge than under it.

English names

79 In 'ford', in 'ham', in 'ley', and 'ton', the most of English surnames run.

80 By Tre, Pol, and Pen, you shall know the Cornish men.
   A reference to three common prefixes of Cornish surnames.

81 In Cheshire there are Lees as plenty as fleas, and as many Davenports as dogs' tails.

82 The people of Clent are all Hills, Waldrons, or devils.
   Clent is near Birmingham. "Hill" and "Waldron" were common surnames in the area.

59 Envy

Its dangers

1 Envy eats nothing but its own heart.
   The origin of the mainly 20th-century expression "to eat one's heart out", meaning to be sick with envy.

2 Envy shoots at others, and wounds herself.

3 Envy never dies.

4 Envy and covetousness are never satisfied.

5 The envious man shall never want woe.

6 An envious man waxes lean with the fatness of his neighbour.
   That is, he pines away to see the prosperity of another.

Its effects

7 Envy and idleness married together begot curiosity.

8 Nothing sharpens sight like envy.

9 Envy envies itself.

10 He who envies admits his inferiority.

11 Envy never enriched any man.

Its universality

12 If envy were a fever, all mankind would be ill.

13 One potter envies another.
   Implies that every man envies potential rivals within his own field. The saying can be traced back to Hesiod (8th century BC).

60 Equality

Its effects

1 When Greek meets Greek, then comes the tug of war.
   A reference to any contest between two sides of equal strength. The proverb is based on

a line from *The Rival Queens* (1677), a once-popular tragedy by Nathaniel Lee, where it refers to the stout resistance of the Greek city states to the Macedonian conquerors Philip and Alexander the Great (4th century BC).

2 At a round table, there's no dispute of place.

3 If all were equal, if all were rich, and if all were at table, who would lay the cloth?

4 You a lady, I a lady, who will milk the cow?
Variants of this proverb exist in many languages throughout the world.

Basic equality

5 We are all Adam's children.

6 Homo is a common name to all men.

7 Before God and the bus-conductor we are all equal.

8 In church, in an inn, and in a coffin, all men are equal.

9 Human blood is all of a colour.

10 All blood is alike ancient.

11 There is no difference of bloods in a basin.

12 The sun shines upon all alike.
Adapted from Matthew 5:45.

13 The rain falls on every roof.
African proverb.

Equality of the great and the lowly

14 A cat may look at a king.

15 Every ass thinks himself worthy to stand with the king's horses.

16 As good horses draw in carts, as coaches.

17 The lower millstone grinds as well as the upper.

18 Every groom is a king at home.

19 It is as hard to please a knave as a knight.
A "knave" here is a male servant.

20 When Adam delved and Eve span, who was then a gentleman?
This was the rallying cry of John Ball, the ideological leader of the Peasants' Revolt of 1381.

21 Every beggar is descended from some king, and every king is descended from some beggar.

22 Jack is as good as his master.
"Jack" is here used as a generic name for a serving man.

23 At the end of the game the king and pawn go into the same bag.

24 Put the poor man's penny and the rich man's penny in ae purse, and they'll come out alike.
"Ae" means "one".

25 Joan is as good as my lady in the dark.
"Joan" is used here as a generic name for a serving woman.

26 The balance distinguishes not between gold and lead.

See also AUTHORITY: *The dangers of shared authority*; DEATH: *Equality in death*

61 Example

Example and precept

1 Practise what you preach.

2 Example is better than precept.

3 Precepts may lead but examples draw.

4 Precept begins, example accomplishes.

5 A good example is the best sermon.

6 He preaches well that lives well.

7 Do as I say, not as I do.
Based ultimately on Matthew 23:3. Now most familiar as the retort of exasperated parents to their disobedient (but observant) children.

8 Do as the friar says, not as he does.

9 We live by laws not by examples.

Setting an example

10 Do as you would be done by.
A saying based on the same New Testament injunction as proverb 11 below. Mrs Doasyouwouldbedoneby and Mrs Bedonebyasyoudid are characters in Kingsley's *The Water Babies* (1863).

11 Do unto others as you would they should do unto you.
Adapted from Luke 6:31.

12 Law makers should not be law breakers.

13 Where the dam leaps over, the kid follows.

14 One sheep follows another.
Sheep have long been (and still are) proverbial for unthinking conformity.

15 If one sheep leap o'er the dyke, all the rest will follow.

16 No marvel if the imps follow when the devil goes before.

62 Experience

Its value

1 Experience is the mother of wisdom.
Some variants add "…and memory the father."

2 Trouble brings experience and experience brings wisdom.

3 Experience is good, if not bought too dear.

4 Experience without learning is better than learning without experience.

5 Knowledge without practice makes but half an artist.

6 Experience is a precious gift, only given a man when his hair is gone.
Turkish proverb.

7 The tongue of experience has most truth.
Arabic proverb.

8 An ounce of practice is worth a pound of precept.

9 Practice makes perfect.

10 Custom makes all things easy.

11 Use makes mastery.

12 Use is all.

Learning by experience

13 Experience is the best teacher.
   A modern variant has been coined by the US baseball player Vernon Law (1960s): "Experience is the worst teacher – she gives the test first and the lesson afterwards."

14 Live and learn.

15 In doing we learn.

16 By writing you learn to write.

17 Failure teaches success.

18 Experience must be bought.

19 Experience is the mistress of fools.

20 Experience keeps a dear school, but fools learn in no other.

21 Once bitten, twice shy.
   Not recorded before the mid-19th century; the allusion is to a horse shying at a snake.

22 The burnt child dreads the fire.

23 Wherever an ass falls, there will he never fall again.

24 Though the wound be healed, yet a scar remains.

25 Birds once snared fear all bushes.

26 He that has been bitten by a serpent, is afraid of a rope.
   Jewish saying.

27 Whom a serpent has bitten, a lizard alarms.

28 A scalded cat fears hot water.
   Some variants substitute "cold water".

29 The escaped mouse ever feels the taste of the bait.

30 He complains wrongfully on the sea that twice suffers shipwreck.
   That is, if you fail to learn from experience you have only yourself to blame.

31 He that deceives me once, shame fall him; if he deceives me twice, shame fall me.

32 It is a silly fish that is caught twice with the same bait.

33 He that stumbles twice over one stone, deserves to break his shins.

34 In war, it is not permitted twice to err.
   First said of the general Lamachus (5th century BC), a leader of the Athenians' ill-fated expedition against Sicily.

35 Better learn by your neighbour's skaith than by your own.
   "Skaith" means "harm".

36 Wise men learn by other men's harms, fools, by their own.

37 It is good to beware by other men's harms.

38 It is good to learn at other men's cost.

39 Let another's shipwreck be your sea-mark.

See also OLD PEOPLE: *Their wisdom*

63 Eyes

The eye and the mind

1 The eyes are the window of the soul.
   Variants of this proverb substitute "heart" or "mind" for "soul".

2 In the forehead and the eye, the lecture of the mind doth lie.
   "Lecture" here means "explanatory text".
3 The heart's letter is read in the eyes.

The importance of seeing

4 Seeing is believing.
5 One eyewitness is better than two hear-so's.

The need for watchfulness

6 Keep your weather-eye open.
   In nautical usage, a person's "weather-eye" was the eye on that side of the face turned towards the wind, which might (facetiously) be expected to notice any changes in the weather before the other.
7 Keep your mouth shut and your eyes open.
8 Let the cat wink, and let the mouse run.

See also DISCIPLINE: *The watchful master*

64 Fame

Its sources

1 He that sows virtue, reaps fame.
2 Fame is the perfume of heroic deeds.
3 There are many ways to fame.
4 Reputation is often got without merit, and lost without crime.
A near-quotation from Shakespeare's *Othello* (1604), where "deserving" appears instead of "crime".

Its effects

5 Fame is a magnifying glass.
Because it exaggerates the good or bad qualities of the famous.
6 He who leaves the fame of good works after him does not die.
7 From fame to infamy is a beaten road.
8 All fame is dangerous: good, bringeth envy; bad, shame.
9 Any publicity is good publicity.
This adman's adage was first recorded in the USA in the 1930s.

Attitudes to fame

10 Fame is but the breath of the people.
Some variants add "...and that not wholesome."
11 Fame is a thin shadow of eternity.
12 Fame, like a river, is narrowest at its source and broadest afar off.
13 Brave men lived before Agamemnon.
A quotation from Horace's *Odes* (1st century BC); Agamemnon was the leader of the Greeks at the siege of Troy. The implication is that the famous may be neither the first nor the most outstanding in their field.

The value of a good reputation

14 Good fame is better than a good face.
15 A good name is better than riches.
Adapted from Proverbs 22:1.
16 A good name is a rich heritage.
17 A good name keeps its lustre in the dark.
18 Win a good reputation, and sleep at your ease.
19 Reputation serves to virtue, as light does to a picture.

20 The name of an honest woman is mickle worth.
   "Mickle" means "much".
21 He that has lost his credit, is dead to the world.
22 Credit lost is like a Venice-glass broken.
   The fine glass produced in Venice was supposed to be irreparable once cracked.
23 A wounded reputation is seldom cured.
24 A good name is sooner lost than won.

65 Familiarity

Its effects

1 Familiarity breeds contempt.
   Cited by St Augustine of Hippo as "a common proverb" (early 5th century AD).
2 Respect is greater from a distance.
3 Those near the temple deride the gods.
   Chinese proverb.
4 Intimacy lessens fame.
5 No man is a hero to his valet.
   Attributed to the French aristocrat Mme Cornvel (17th century). Variations appear in works by Johnson, Byron, and Carlyle.
6 A prophet is not without honour, save in his own country.
   A biblical quotation: Matthew 13:57. The context is Christ's rejection by the people of Nazareth ("Is not this the carpenter's son?")
7 The reed-player of your own street does not charm.
   Egyptian proverb.
8 No man fears what he has seen grow.
   African proverb.
9 A maid oft seen, and a gown oft worn, are disesteemed and held in scorn.
10 Goods that are much on show lose their colour.
   Brazilian proverb.
11 Custom takes the taste from the most savoury dishes.

Against over-familiarity

12 You should know a man seven years before you stir his fire.

66 Fear

Its sources

1 When we have gold, we are in fear; when we have none, we are in danger.
2 Riches bring care and fears.
3 Love is full of fear.
   A quotation from Ovid's *Heroides* (1st century BC).

Its effects

4 Fear gives wings.
5 Fear has a quick ear.

6 Fear has magnifying eyes.

7 Fear is a great inventor.

8 'Twas fear that first put on arms.

9 Who fears to suffer, suffers from fear.

Its undesirability

10 All fear is bondage.

11 Fear is the prison of the heart.

12 Better pass a danger once, than be always in fear.

13 Better a fearful end than fear without end.

Its value

14 Fear is one part of prudence.
    Variants substitute "distrust" or "suspicion" for "fear".

15 Wise fear begets care.

Its power

16 Fear is stronger than love.

17 All the weapons of war will not arm fear.
    Variants substitute "all the arms of England" (or some other place).

18 There is no medicine for fear.

19 There is no remedy for fear but cut off the head.

Trivial fears

20 He that is afraid of the wagging of feathers, must keep from among wild
    fowl.

21 He that is afraid of wounds, must not come nigh a battle.

22 He that fears every bush must never go a-birding.

23 He that fears every grass must not piss in a meadow.
    A politer version substitutes "walk" for "piss".

24 He that fears leaves, let him not go into the wood.

See also CRUELTY: *Cruelty and fear*; DEATH: *Fear of death*

67 Fine arts

Painting

1 Art improves Nature.

2 Pictures are the books of the unlearned.

3 On painting and fighting look aloof.
   Because a picture may lose some of its effect when viewed at close quarters, and it is dangerous to be close to the scene of fighting.

4 A good painter can draw a devil as well as an angel.

5 Painters and poets have leave to lie.
   Adapted from Horace's *Ars Poetica* (1st century BC).

Poetry

6 There are pictures in poems and poems in pictures.
Chinese proverb.

7 The poet, of all sorts of artificers, is the fondest of his works.

8 A poet is born not made.

9 He's a blockhead that can't make two verses, and he's a fool that makes four.

Music

10 Music is the food of love.
Adapted from Shakespeare's *Twelfth Night* (1602): "If music be the food of love, play on".

11 Music has charms to soothe a savage breast.
A quotation from Congreve's tragedy *The Mourning Bride* (1697). This is frequently misquoted, "beast" being substituted for "breast".

12 Music is the eye of the ear.

13 Music helps not the toothache.

14 Women and music should never be dated.

68 Flattery

Its value

1 Flattery sits in the parlour, when plain-dealing is kicked out of doors.

2 Better fleech the devil than fight him.
"Fleech" means "flatter".

3 Whoso will dwell in court must needs curry favour.

Its sources and effects

4 Imitation is the sincerest form of flattery.
A quotation from Charles Caleb Colton's otherwise forgotten poem *Lacon* (1820).

5 Praise the child, and you make love to the mother.

6 Tell a woman she is fair, and she will soon turn fool.

7 Make yourself all honey, and the flies will devour you.
The warning here is that excessive flattery and obsequious behaviour may arouse contempt.

Its insincerity

8 Dogs wag their tails not so much in love to you as to your bread.

9 Every man bows to the bush he gets bield of.
"Bield" means "shelter".

10 Call the bear 'uncle' till you are safe across the bridge.
Turkish proverb.

Mutual flattery

11 One complimentary letter asks another.

12 Scratch my back and I'll scratch yours.
The allusion is to the mutual grooming of animals.

13 Scratch my breech and I'll claw your elbow.
"Claw" here and in proverb 14 below means to rub or stroke.

14 Claw me, and I'll claw thee.

Flatterers

15 The most deadly of wild beasts is a backbiter, of tame ones a flatterer.
16 Beware of one who flatters unduly; he will also censure unjustly.
  Arabic proverb.
17 As a wolf is like a dog, so is a flatterer like a friend.
18 No foe to a flatterer.
19 A flatterer's throat is an open sepulchre.
20 When the flatterer pipes, then the devil dances.
21 When a lackey comes to hell's door, the devils lock the gates.
  A "lackey" is an obsequious or servile person.

69 Foolishness

Its advantages

1 Children and fools have merry lives.
2 The folly of one man is the fortune of another.
3 Fortune favours fools.
  According to a widespread superstition, fools were both lucky themselves and bringers of luck to those they encountered.
4 God sends fortune to fools.
5 Better be a fool than a knave.

Its dangers

6 Fools and madmen ought not to be left in their own company.
7 Children and fools must not play with edged tools.
8 Fools should not have chopping sticks.
9 Take heed of mad fools in a narrow place.

Its causes

10 The first service a child does his father is to make him foolish.
11 No folly to being in love.
12 Too much money makes one mad.
13 Much learning makes men mad.
  Adapted from Acts 26:24 (where the Romans say this of St Paul).
14 When the moon's in the full, then wit's in the wane.
  The association of the full moon with madness or folly is ancient and widespread.

Its incurability

15 He that is born a fool is never cured.
16 Send a fool to the market and a fool he will return again.
  See TRAVEL: 8–13 for variants of this saying.
17 Fools will be fools still.
18 Once wood, never wise.
  "Wood" here means "mad".

19 Whom Heaven at his birth has endowed as a fool, 'tis a waste of instruction to teach.
Chinese proverb.

20 Fools grow without watering.

Its universality

21 The world is full of fools.
The saying can be traced back to Cicero (1st century BC).

22 Folly is the product of all countries and ages.

23 We have all been fools once in our lives.

24 Every man a little beyond himself is a fool.
"Beyond himself" means "out of his sphere".

25 If folly were grief, every house would weep.

26 Every man is a fool sometimes, and none at all times.

27 If all fools wore feathers we should seem a flock of geese.
Professional fools often wore feathers in their caps.

28 If all fools had baubles, we should want fuel.
Implies that if all fools carried the jester's "bauble" or stick firewood would be in short supply.

29 Who has neither fools nor beggars nor whores among his kindred, was born of a stroke of thunder.
A riposte to someone who attempts to blacken your name by alluding to your foolish or discreditable relatives. For other sayings on this theme see RELATIONS: *Undesirable relations*.

Foolish acts

30 The fool asks much, but he is more fool that grants it.

31 He has great need of a fool, that plays the fool himself.

32 Make not a fool of thyself, to make others merry.

33 He is a fool that forgets himself.

34 He is a fool that kisses the maid when he may kiss the mistress.

35 He is a fool that makes a hammer of his fist.

36 He is not the fool that the fool is, but he that with the fool deals.

37 He is a fool that thinks not that another thinks.
Implies that we consider anyone who holds a different opinion from our own a fool.

38 He is a fool who makes his physician his heir.

39 It is a foolish sheep that makes the wolf his confessor.

40 It is a blind goose that comes to the fox's sermon.

41 A barber learns to shave by shaving fools.
Implies that only a fool allows himself to be practised on by a learner.

42 One cannot do a foolish thing once in one's life, but one must hear of it a hundred times.

43 Wise men make proverbs and fools repeat them.
A handy riposte to anyone who quotes a proverb against you.

44 He is an ass that brays against another ass.

45 A white wall is a fool's paper.
Implies that graffiti is the work of fools.

46 Fools live poor to die rich.

47 He that talks to himself, speaks to a fool.

Characteristics of fools

48 The first degree of folly is to hold one's self wise, the second to profess it, the third to despise counsel.

49 What the fool does in the end, the wise man does at the beginning.
There are two possible implications: that the fool only learns through his errors, or that fools procrastinate.

50 Little things please little minds.
First cited in approximately this form in Disraeli's *Sybil* (1845), although the thought can be traced back to Ovid (1st century BC).

51 Riches serve a wise man but command a fool.
A quotation from the French theologian Pierre Charron (1541–1603).

52 A wise man changes his mind, a fool never.
Some variants have "...but a fool perseveres."

53 Children and fools cannot lie.
Some versions add "drunkards" to the list of truth-tellers.

54 Experience is the mistress of fools.
Like proverbs 55 and 56 below, this implies that fools only learn by making mistakes.

55 Experience keeps a dear school, but fools learn in no other.

56 Wise men learn by other men's harms; fools, by their own.

57 A fool's bolt is soon shot.
To have "shot one's bolt" is to have exhausted one's efforts.

58 Fat paunches have lean pates.
The earliest known citation is in Shakespeare's *Love's Labour's Lost* (c. 1594).

59 Mickle head, little wit.
"Mickle" here means "large".

60 Seldom is a long man wise, or a low man lowly.
Implies that tall people are seldom wise (and small people are rarely meek and humble).

The recklessness of fools

61 Fools rush in where angels fear to tread.
A quotation from Pope's *An Essay on Criticism* (1711); the original context is an attack on those who talk inappropriately in church.

62 While the discreet advise, the fool does his business.
"Advise" here means "seek advice".

63 Wise men propose, and fools determine.

64 A fool always rushes to the fore.

65 A knave and a fool never take thought.

66 From a foolish judge, a quick sentence.

67 Haste and wisdom are things far odd.
"Far odd" means "far apart".

The gullibility of fools

68 A fool and his money are soon parted.

69 A fool believes everything.

70 An easy fool is a knave's tool.

71 Fair words make fools fain.
Implies that fools easily succumb to flattery and false promises. "Fain" means "willing".

72 Fools rejoice at promises.

73 If fools went not to market, bad wares would not be sold.

74 A nod from a lord is a breakfast for a fool.

The talkativeness of fools

75 Empty vessels make the greatest sound.

76 Toom bags rattle.
   "Toom" means "empty".

77 Shallow streams make the most din.

78 A fool's bell is soon rung.

79 A fool's tongue is long enough to cut his own throat.

80 Foolish tongues talk by the dozen.

81 Every ass likes to hear himself bray.

82 The wise hand does not all that the foolish mouth speaks.

83 Wise men silent, fools talk.

84 Wise men have their mouth in their heart, fools their heart in their mouth.

85 If the fool knew how to be silent he could sit amongst the wise.
   Both this and proverb 86 below are based on Proverbs 17:28.

86 Fools are wise as long as silent.

87 For mad words deaf ears.

88 Change of weather is the discourse of fools.

The wisdom of fools

89 A fool may give a wise man counsel.

90 A fool may sometimes speak to the purpose.

91 A fool's bolt may sometimes hit the mark.

92 A fool knows more in his own house than a wise man in another's.

93 A fool may ask more questions in an hour than a wise man can answer in seven years.

94 A fool may throw a stone into a well, which a hundred wise men cannot pull out.

95 Fools set stools for wise folks to stumble at.

96 None is so wise, but the fool overtakes him.

97 Folly and learning often dwell together.

98 Fools are wise men in the affairs of women.

Old fools

99 There's no fool like an old fool.

100 A fool at forty is a fool indeed.
   In this form a quotation from Edward Young's Satires (1725), although the thought is older.

70 Foresight

Its value

1 One good forewit, is worth two afterwits.

2 He is wise who looks ahead.

3 He that looks not before, finds himself behind.

4 A word before is worth two behind.

5 Prevention is better than cure.

The importance of being prepared

6 Providing is preventing.
7 Force without forecast is of little avail.
Like proverbs 8–10 below, this implies that foreseeing problems and being prepared for them is of more use than great strength or skill.
8 Forewarned is forearmed.
9 Forecast is better than work-hard.
10 He is wise that is ware in time.
11 Forethought is easy, repentance hard.
Chinese proverb.
12 Provide for the worst; the best will save itself.
13 In fair weather prepare for foul.
14 Thatch your roof before the rain begins.
15 Have not thy cloak to make when it begins to rain.
16 Although it rain, throw not away your watering-pot.
17 Although the sun shine, leave not your cloak at home.
18 Never rued the man that laid in his fuel before St John.
St John's Day is December 27th; however, the allusion may well be to St John the Baptist, whose feasts are June 24th (Midsummer Day) and August 29th.
19 If you go into a labyrinth, take a clew with you.
A "clew" is a ball of thread, such as that used by the Greek hero Theseus to find his way out of the labyrinth of King Minos in Crete.

Providing for the future

20 First thrive and then wive.
21 Before you marry, be sure of a house wherein to tarry.
22 Honour a physician before thou hast need of him.
Adapted from a passage in the apocryphal book Ecclesiasticus (38:1–2).
23 It is good to work wisely lest a man be prevented.
"Prevented" here means outstripped by events or circumstances.
24 This world is unstable, so saith sage: therefore gather in time, ere thou fall into age.

71 Forgiveness

Its value

1 Pardons and pleasantness are great revenges of slanders.
2 The noblest vengeance is to forgive.
3 Pardon is the choicest flower of victory.
Arabic proverb.
4 He that forgives gains the victory.
African proverb.
5 There is no austerity like forgiveness.
Indian proverb.
6 Mercy surpasses justice.

7 To err is human; to forgive, divine.

A quotation from Pope's *An Essay on Criticism* (1711), although the first part of the saying is much older. A 20th-century workplace variant runs "...; but against company policy."

8 He who forgives others, God forgives him.

Arabic proverb.

9 Forgiveness from the heart is better than a box of gold.

Moorish proverb.

Its dangers

10 Pardon one offence and you encourage many.

11 Pardon makes offenders.

12 Pardoning the bad is injuring the good.

13 Mercy to the criminal may be cruelty to the people.

Its conditions

14 The lion spares the suppliant.

According to a once widespread belief, the lion would refuse to prey on any beast that submitted without a fight.

15 Forgiving the unrepentant is like making pictures on water.

Japanese proverb.

16 Past shame, past grace.

A common variant substitutes "amendment" for "grace".

The need to forgive

17 Let bygones be bygones.

18 Forgive and forget.

19 Forgiveness is perfect when the sin is not remembered.

Arabic proverb.

20 Forgive all but thyself.

21 Wink at small faults.

The unforgiving

22 He that does you an ill turn will never forgive you.

Both this and proverb 23 below are based on the well-known observation of Tacitus in his *Agricola* (c. 98 AD): "It is human nature to hate those you have hurt."

23 The offender never pardons.

The forgiving

24 He that sharply chides, is the most ready to pardon.

25 God gives his wrath by weight, and without weight his mercy.

26 The first faults are theirs that commit them, the second theirs that permit them.

Implies that those who forgive a person a second time for committing the same fault are themselves in the wrong. Compare EXPERIENCE: 31.

72 Friends

Their value

1 Better lose a jest than a friend.
Adapted from the Roman rhetorician Quintilian (1st century AD): the saying warns against losing a friend for the sake of a clever cutting remark.

2 A friend at court is better than a penny in purse.

3 A friend in the market is better than money in the chest.

4 It is good to have some friends both in heaven and hell.

5 He quits his place well that leaves his friend there.

6 Life without a friend, is death without a witness.

7 It's merry when friends meet.
Variants substitute "gossips" or "knaves" for "friends".

8 When friends meet, hearts warm.

9 One enemy is too many; and a hundred friends too few.

10 One God, no more, but friends good store.

11 Friends tie their purse with a cobweb thread.
Implies that friends are ready to open their purses for each other.

12 If friends have faith in each other, life and death are of no consequence.
Chinese proverb.

Their danger

13 Hatred with friends is succour to foes.

14 Better an open enemy than a false friend.

15 It is better to be stung by a nettle than pricked by a rose.
Implies is that it is better to be wronged by an enemy than by a friend.

16 God defend me from my friends; from my enemies I can defend myself.
Now often used in the shorter form "Save us from our friends!"

17 Friends are thieves of time.

18 A reconciled friend is a double enemy.

Their disloyalty

19 Dead men have no friends.

20 Remember man and keep in mind, a faithful friend is hard to find.

21 When good cheer is lacking, our friends will be packing.

22 Misfortune makes foes of friends.

23 Penny in purse will bid me drink, when all the friends I have will not.
Implies that it is better to trust in one's own resources than in the generosity of friends.

24 Poor folks' friends soon misken them.
"Misken" means "desert, disown".

25 Fresh fish and poor friends become soon ill savoured.
Compare HOSPITALITY: 13.

26 Poverty parts fellowship.

27 In time of prosperity, friends will be plenty; in time of adversity, not one amongst twenty.

28 He that ceases to be a friend, never was a good one.

29 Tell nothing to thy friend that thine enemy may not know.

30 Love your friend, but look to yourself.

This and proverb 31 below advise caution in putting one's complete trust in a friend.

31 Whensoever you see your friend, trust to yourself.

Their falseness

32 A false friend and a shadow attend only while the sun shines.

33 There is falsehood in fellowship.

Implies that friendship involves an element of flattery and often proves insubstantial. Variants substitute "flattery" or "fraud" for "falsehood".

34 All are not friends that speak us fair.

35 He that has a full purse never wanted a friend.

36 Rich folk have many friends.

37 The rich knows not who is his friend.

38 When two friends have a common purse, one sings and the other weeps.

True friendship

39 A friend in need is a friend indeed.

That is, a friend who helps out when one is in need must be a true friend. The sentiment can be traced back to Euripides (5th century BC).

40 A friend is never known till a man have need.

41 Prosperity makes friends, adversity tries them.

42 Friends are made in wine and proved in tears.

43 At marriages and funerals, friends are discerned from kinsfolk.

44 Real friendship does not freeze in winter.

45 A friend is another self.

The thought can be traced back to Aristotle's definition of friendship as one soul inhabiting two bodies (4th century BC).

46 A good friend is my nearest relation.

47 Among friends all things are common.

Both this and proverb 48 below can be traced back to the maxims of the Pythagorean brotherhood (6th century BC).

48 Perfect friendship cannot be without equality.

49 A good friend never offends.

50 A true friend is the best possession.

51 They are rich who have true friends.

52 No physician like a true friend.

53 He is a good friend that speaks well of us behind our backs.

54 Greater love hath no man than this, that a man lay down his life for his friends.

Christ's words to the disciples at the Last Supper: John 15:13.

Worthless friends

55 His own enemy is no one's friend.

56 A friend to everybody is a friend to nobody.

57 Trencher friends are seldom good neighbours.

A "trencher" was a platter for serving food. The implication is that such friends will disappear when one can no longer provide them with food and drink.

Old friends

58 The best mirror is an old friend.

59 Friendship, the older it grows, the stronger it is.

60 Old fish, old oil, and an old friend are the best.

61 Old friends and old wine and old gold are best.

62 Old acquaintance will soon be remembered.

Choosing friends

63 Have but few friends, though many acquaintances.

64 Books and friends should be few but good.

65 Select your friend with a silk-gloved hand and hold him with an iron gauntlet.

66 Before you make a friend eat a bushel of salt with him.
   A "bushel" was a unit of measure equal to eight gallons. As only a small amount of salt is eaten at each meal, the implication is that one should spend a long time with a person before becoming his friend.

67 Sudden friendship, sure repentance.

68 Trust not a new friend nor an old enemy.

69 Prove your friend ere you have need.

70 Try your friend before you trust.

71 Go down the ladder when you marry a wife; go up when you choose a friend.
   That is, choose friends from those above you in rank but marry below you.

Maintaining friendship

72 Make not thy friend thy foe.

73 Have patience with a friend rather than lose him forever.

74 Love your friend with his fault.
   Based on a line in the *Satires* of Horace (1st century BC).

75 Friendship cannot stand always on one side.
   Implies that true friendship is based on mutual help and kindness.

76 Friendship increases in visiting friends, but in visiting them seldom.

77 A hedge between keeps friendship green.

78 Little intermeddling makes good friends.

79 When a friend asks, there is no tomorrow.
   Implies that one should not put off a friend's requests with vain promises.

80 Speak well of your friend, of your enemy say nothing.

81 Treat a friend as if he might become a foe.

82 Friendship is a plant which must be often watered.

Losing friends

83 A broken friendship may be soldered, but will never be sound.

84 One may mend a torn friendship but it soon falls in tatters.

85 Fall not out with a friend for a trifle.

86 A friend is not so soon gotten as lost.

87 Lend your money and lose your friend.
Implies that you will lose your friend by demanding repayment of the loan. Shakespeare's version is well known: "Neither a borrower nor a lender be/ For loan oft loses both itself and friend" (*Hamlet, c.* 1600). See also LENDING: 9–15.

88 When love puts in, friendship is gone.

See also ABSENCE: *Its effect on friendship*

73 Gain

Its value

1 Great gain makes work easy.
2 Great pain and little gain will make a man soon weary.
3 No gaining, cold gaming.
    That is, any game (or other enterprise) in which the stakes are low will arouse little enthusiasm.
4 The gains will quit the pains.
5 Pain is forgotten where gain follows.
6 A blow that is profitable does not hurt the neck.
    Arabic proverb.
7 Profit gives no headache.
8 Praise without profit puts little in the pot.

Its sources

9 Gain savours sweetly from anything.
    Implies that the pleasure of gain is not affected by its source, however unsavoury.
10 No pains, no gains.
    Now best known (with both nouns in the singular) as a slogan of the aerobics craze of the 1980s. However, it has been recorded as early as the 17th century.
11 Honour and profit lie not in one sack.
    Because honour may be profitless and some profits are dishonourable.
12 The greatest burdens are not the gainfullest.

Loss and gain

13 There's no great loss without some gain.
14 Where profit is, loss is hidden nearby.
    Japanese proverb.
15 He that loses anything and gets wisdom by it is a gainer by the loss.
16 Sometimes the best gain is to lose.
17 A man may lose more in an hour than he can get in seven.
18 What you lose on the swings you gain on the roundabouts.
    First recorded in the early 20th century. The "swings" suggest unpredictable business or economic trends (or other swings of fortune), while the "roundabouts" are the larger cycles in which everything comes around again.

19 What is lost in the hundred will be found in the shire.
   A "hundred" is a former division of a county or "shire". The implication is that what you lose on a small scale will be recouped as part of the bigger picture.

20 One man's loss is another man's gain.

Losing

21 Loss embraces shame.

22 He loses indeed that loses at last.

23 He that is not sensible of his loss has lost nothing.

24 You cannot lose what you never had.

25 It signifies nothing to play well if you lose.

26 Win at first and lose at last.
   Because early success in e.g. gambling or a business venture will tempt a person to proceed without due care.

27 Losers are always in the wrong.

28 Give losers leave to speak.
   Implies that winners should be patient when losers express their feelings of anger or disappointment.

74 Gambling

Its dangers

1 The devil goes shares in gaming.

2 Keep flax from fire and youth from gaming.

3 Gaming, women, and wine, while they laugh, they make men pine.

4 Play, women, and wine undo men laughing.

5 Women and wine, game and deceit, make the wealth small, and the wants great.

6 He that plays his money ought not to value it.

Cards

7 Cards are the devil's books.
   Variants appear in works by Swift, Burns, and Southey.

8 Lucky at cards, unlucky in love.

Dice

9 The devil is in the dice.
   Dice were sometimes described as "the devil's bones" (being formerly made chiefly of bone).

10 Dicing, drabbing and drinking bring men to destruction.
   A "drab" is a prostitute.

11 The best throw of the dice, is to throw them away.

Betting

12 A wager is a fool's argument.

13 In a bet there is a fool and a thief.

14 On the turf all men are equal – and under it.
A 19th-century saying from the world of horse racing ("the turf"). It implies that in betting on something as unpredictable as a horse race men are as equal as they will be in death.

Gamblers

15 The better gamester, the worser man.
16 Gamesters and race-horses never last long.
17 If the gambler can change, then there is medicine for leprosy.
Chinese proverb.

75 Giving

Its value

1 Riches are like muck, which stink in a heap, but spread abroad make the earth fruitful.
2 Better an apple given than eaten.
3 It is more blessed to give than to receive.
A biblical quotation: Acts 20:35. A common variant substitutes "better" for "more blessed".
4 Better give a shilling than lend and lose half a crown.
5 They are welcome that bring.
6 Give and spend, and God will send.
Like proverbs 7–13 below, this implies that one loses nothing by being generous.
7 The charitable give out at the door and God puts in at the window.
8 He who gives discreetly gains directly.
9 The hand that gives, gathers.
10 Giving much to the poor, doth enrich a man's store.
11 Alms never make poor.
12 Great almsgiving lessens no man's living.
13 What we spent we had; what we gave we have; what we left we lost.
This was reputedly the inscription on the tomb of Edward de Courtenay, third earl of Devonshire (d. 1419), in Tiverton, Devon; the tomb does not survive.

The need for caution

14 He who gives to the unworthy loses doubly.
15 Be just before you are generous.
16 He that has a good memory, gives few alms.
Implies that shrewd people remember persistent beggars.
17 He that gives his goods before he be dead, take up a mallet and knock him on the head.
A reference to the ingratitude of children, who will neglect an ageing parent once he has given up all his wealth and possessions.
18 He learned timely to beg that could not say 'Nay'.
"Timely" here means "quickly".

The need for promptness

19 He gives twice who gives quickly.

20 To refuse and to give tardily is all the same.

21 He that is long a giving knows not how to give.

22 A gift much expected is paid, not given.
    "Paid" here has the sense of "sold".

23 Long tarrying takes all the thanks away.

Generous people

24 Friends tie their purse with a cobweb thread.
    Implies that friends are ready to open their purses for each other.

25 It is a good goose that's ay dropping.

26 The higher the hill, the lower the grass.
    Implies that the richest people are not the most generous.

27 He is more noble that deserves, than he that confers benefits.

False generosity

28 He is free of fruit that wants an orchard.
    Like proverbs 29 and 30 below, this implies that people are always ready to give away what they do not have, or what belongs to another.

29 He is free of horse that never had one.

30 Hens are free of horse corn.

31 Give a thing and take a thing, to wear the devil's gold ring.
    A very old children's rhyme used when a person takes back a previously offered gift.

Small gifts

32 Small gifts make friends, great ones make enemies.

33 He that gives me small gifts, would have me live.

34 He that gives thee a bone, would not have thee die.

35 A little given seasonably, excuses a great gift.

Receiving gifts

36 Who receives a gift, sells his liberty.

37 Benefits make a man a slave.
    Arabic proverb.

38 Benefits bind.

39 Nothing costs so much as what is given us.

40 Nothing freer than a gift.
    A direct contradiction of the preceding proverb.

41 She that takes gifts, herself she sells, and she that gives, does not else.
    Implies that a woman who accepts gifts from a man, or makes presents to him, will be easily seduced.

42 Fear the Greeks bearing gifts.
    A quotation from Virgil's *Aeneid* (1st century BC); the allusion is to the wooden horse, a treacherous "gift" that enabled the Greeks to gain access to Troy and destroy it. When the phrase is used proverbially, "the Greeks" refers to any enemy.

76 Gluttony

Its disadvantages

1 A belly full of gluttony will never study willingly.
2 Fat paunches have lean pates.
   First cited in this form in Shakespeare's *Love's Labour's Lost* (c. 1594).
3 A fat belly does not breed a subtle mind.
4 A full belly neither fights nor flies well.
5 If it were not for the belly, the back might wear gold.
   Refers to those who spend more money on food and drink than on clothes. A common variant is "the belly robs the back."
6 The nearer the bone, the sweeter the flesh.
   This is both a jocular excuse for picking a carcase right to the bone and a way of implying that slim people are more attractive than fat people (but see also proverb 18 below).

Its dangers

7 He that eats till he is sick, must fast till he is well.
8 Many dishes make many diseases.
   The warning here is against overelaborate cuisine rather than simple overeating.
9 Much meat, much malady.
10 A swine over fat, is the cause of his own bane.
11 Greedy eaters dig their graves with their teeth.
12 Gluttony kills more than the sword.
   A variant substitutes "surfeit" for "gluttony".
13 By suppers, more have been killed than Galen ever cured.
   The Greek physician Galen (2nd century AD) was regarded as the supreme authority on medical matters during the middle ages.

Characteristics of gluttons

14 Gluttony is the sin of England.
15 A glutton is never generous.
16 He that has a wide therm had never a long arm.
   "Therm" means "belly". This reiterates the sentiments of proverb 15 above.

Excuses for gluttony

17 Better belly burst than good meat lost.
18 The flesh is aye fairest that is farthest from the bone.
   A direct contradiction of proverb 6 above, implying that a certain plumpness can be attractive.

Needless eating

19 There's little difference between a feast and a bellyful.
   Implies that once hunger has been satisfied, there is nothing to be gained from eating more.
20 Hunger makes dinners, pastime suppers.
   Implies that eating supper is a pleasure rather than a necessity ("dinner" here means the day's main meal).

77 God

His omnipotence

1 God is above all.
2 All must be as God will.
3 That God will have see, shall not wink.
4 Where God will help, nothing does harm.
   Some variants substitute "whom" for "where".
5 What God will, no frost can kill.
6 When God will, no wind but brings rain.
7 The tree that God plants, no wind hurts it.
8 All things are possible with God.
   Adapted from Matthew 19:26.
9 When it pleases not God, the saint can do little.
10 He sits above that deals acres.
   That is, our worldly fortune is in the hands of God.

His wisdom

11 Do the likeliest, and God will do the best.
12 God complains not, but does what is fitting.
13 God is no botcher.
   "Nature" is sometimes substituted for "God".
14 God knows well which are the best pilgrims.
15 They are well guided that God guides.
16 To whom God gives the task, he gives the wit.
17 If God does not give us what we want He gives us what we need.

His goodness

18 That never ends ill which begins in God's name.
19 God, and parents, and our master, can never be requited.
20 God is a good man.
21 He who serves God, serves a good master.

His compassion

22 God tempers the wind to the shorn lamb.
23 God makes the back for the burden.
   That is, God gives us the strength we need to cope with our tasks or troubles. First
   recorded in the early 19th century.
24 God sends cold after clothes.
25 Since God has not bent the top of the palm-tree, He has given a long neck to
   the giraffe.
   Arabic proverb.
26 God strikes not with both hands, for to the sea he made havens, and to
   rivers fords.
27 Heaven takes care of children, sailors, and drunken men.
28 God strikes with his finger, and not with all his arm.

His reliability

29   God comes at last when we think he is farthest off.

30   God provides for him that trusts.

31   He that sows, trusts in God.

32   God never sends mouth but He sends meat.
     Implies that when a new child is born God will always provide sufficient food for it.

33   The constancy of the benefit of the year in their seasons argues a Deity.

His help

34   God helps them that help themselves.
     First cited in this form by Benjamin Franklin (1736) but the thought is much older.

35   God reaches us good things by our own hands.

36   We must not lie down and cry, 'God help us.'

37   God is a good worker, but he loves to be helped.

38   God gives the grain, but we must make the furrow.
     Bohemian proverb. Compare DILIGENCE: 29.

39   For a web begun God sends the thread.

40   God gives, but he does not lock the gate of the fold.
     Bulgarian proverb.

41   Get thy spindle and thy distaff ready and God will send thee flax.

42   God himself is the help of the helpless.
     Indian proverb.

43   Man's extremity is God's opportunity.
     Implies that God is best able to help when man most needs Him.

44   God's help is better than early rising.

45   God's help is nearer than the fair even.
     Implies that God's grace is closer to hand than worldly help or pleasures; compare proverb 53 below.

His grace

46   Divine grace was never slow.
     Variants substitute "late" for "slow".

47   God's grace and Pilling Moss are boundless.
     "Pilling Moss" is a large stretch of marshland near Fleetwood in Lancashire: it was formerly considered bottomless and an inexhaustible source of turf for fuel.

48   Well thrives he whom God loves.

49   Who has God for his friend has the saints in his pocket.

50   Whom God loves, his bitch brings forth pigs.

51   When God loathes aught, men presently loathe it too.
     A reference to the dangers of losing God's grace.

52   The grace of God is enough.

53   The grace of God is worth a fair.

His mysterious ways

54   God moves in a mysterious way.
     The first line of one of Cowper's *Olney Hymns* (1799).

55   Afflictions are sent to us by God for our good.

56 God heals, and the physician has the thanks.
    A variant has "...physician takes the fee."

His forgiveness

57 God gives his wrath by weight, and without weight his mercy.

58 The most high God, sees, and bears: my neighbour knows nothing, and yet
    is always finding fault.

59 God forgives sins, otherwise heaven would be empty.

60 He who forgives others, God forgives him.
    Arabic proverb.

61 Who errs and mends, to God himself commends.
    That is, God forgives the repentant.

Divine retribution

62 God comes with leaden feet, but strikes with iron hands.
    Implies that God is not quick to punish, allowing time for repentance, but when he
    strikes it is with force.

63 The feet of the avenging deities are shod with wool.
    A warning of the silent approach of divine retribution. The saying can be traced back to
    the Roman writer Macrobius (5th century AD).

64 God stays long, but strikes at last.

65 The mills of God grind slowly, yet they grind exceeding small.
    In this form a quotation from Longfellow's translation of "Retribution", a German poem
    by Friedrich von Logau (1604–55). However, there are older variants.

66 God is a sure paymaster.

God and the devil

67 The devil is God's ape.
    Implies that the devil strives to counterfeit or parody the works of God.

68 Where God has his church, the devil will have his chapel.
    Implies that the devil is able to counterfeit religion and virtue. In his satire *The True Born
    Englishman* (1701) Defoe quotes this saying and continues "And 'twill be found upon
    examination/ The latter has the largest congregation."

69 Where God dwells, the devil also has his nest.

70 God sends corn and the devil mars the sack.

71 That which God will give, the devil cannot reave.
    "Reave" means "take away".

God and man

72 God makes and man shapes.

73 God made the country, and man made the town.
    A quotation from Cowper's *The Task* (1785).

74 Man does what he can, and God what he will.

75 Man proposes, God disposes.
    A quotation from Thomas à Kempis's *The Imitation of Christ* (15th century).

78 Goodness

Its value

1 Virtue joins man to God.
2 Virtue and happiness are mother and daughter.
3 Riches adorn the dwelling; virtue adorns the person.
   Chinese proverb.
4 Virtue is a jewel of great price.
5 Virtue is the beauty of the mind.
6 Goodness is better than beauty.
7 There is no poverty where there is virtue, no riches where virtue is not.
   Chinese proverb.
8 Virtue and a trade are the best portion for children.
9 A good heart conquers ill fortune.
10 A good life makes a good death.
11 He dies like a beast who has done no good while he lived.
12 They die well that live well.
13 Virtue has all things in itself.
14 Virtue is its own reward.
   The saying can be traced back to Ovid (early 2nd century AD) and is cited by Spenser,
   Jonson, and Dryden among many others. Note also Quentin Crisp's witty reversal "Vice
   is its own reward" (late 20th century).
15 Virtue is more important than blood.
16 Virtue is the only true nobility.
17 Virtue never grows old.
18 He that sows virtue, reaps fame.
19 Honour is the reward of virtue.
20 Praise is the reflection of virtue.
21 A handful of good life, is better than a bushel of learning.
   A "bushel" was a unit of measurement equal to eight gallons.
22 He that lives well is learned enough.
23 It is not how long, but how well we live.
24 It is good to be good in your time, for you know not how long it will last.
25 A house is a fine house when good folks are within.

Its limitations

26 There is no virtue that poverty destroys not.
27 None so good that it's good to all.
28 That which is good for the back, is bad for the head.
29 That which is good for the head, is evil for the neck and the shoulders.
30 Good for the liver may be bad for the spleen.

Its disadvantages

31 Good things are hard.
   Attributed to the Athenian sages Solon and Pittacus (both 6th century BC).
32 The good is the enemy of the best.
   Implies that being content with good prevents one from striving for better. The saying
   is sometimes reversed to give the opposite meaning: see AMBITION: 18.

33 Good is good, but better carries it.

Its scarcity

34 Good folks are scarce.
Some variants add the advice "..., make much of one."

35 There are two good men: one dead, the other unborn.
Chinese proverb.

36 Virtue is praised by all, but practised by few.

Characteristics of the good

37 A good heart cannot lie.

38 A good man can no more harm than a sheep.

39 He lives long that lives well.

40 Good men must die, but death cannot kill them quite.

41 The sun is never the worse for shining on a dunghill.
Implies that the virtuous are not easily corrupted by contact with impure things or people. The saying can be traced back to the theologian Tertullian (2nd century AD).

42 Good men suffer much.
Chinese proverb.

43 Good people walk on, whatever befall.
Japanese proverb.

44 Show a good man his error, and he turns it to a virtue; but an ill, it doubles his fault.

Good and evil

45 Good and evil are chiefly in the imagination.

46 There is not the thickness of a sixpence between good and evil.

47 Set good against evil.

48 Good is to be sought out and evil attended.
"Attended" here means "prepared for".

49 Better good afar off than evil at hand.

50 It costs more to do ill than to do well.

51 Vice makes virtue shine.

52 Virtue and vice divide the world, but vice has got the greater share.

53 Vice is often clothed in virtue's habit.

See also DEEDS: *Good deeds*

79 Gossip

Its accuracy or inaccuracy

1 Common fame is seldom to blame.
Like proverbs 2–4 below, this implies that gossip generally has an element of truth in it.

2 There's no smoke without fire.

3 Where there are reeds, there is water.

4 There was aye some water where the stirk drowned.
A "stirk" is a young bullock.

5 One learns to know oneself best behind one's back.

6 Gossiping and lying go together.

7 Where there is whispering there is lying.

8 Common fame is a liar.
Some versions have "...a common liar".

9 'They say so' is half a lie.

10 The tale runs as it pleases the teller.

11 A tale never loses in the telling.
Refers to the embellishments added to an item of gossip as it passes from person to person.

Its dangers

12 The gossip of two women will destroy two houses.
Arabic proverb.

13 An ill tongue may do much.

14 He who speaks much of others burns his tongue.

15 He that speaks the thing he should not, hears the thing he would not.
Like proverb 16 below, this implies that those who speak maliciously of others will soon hear bad things said of themselves. The saying can be traced back to the playwright Terence (2nd century BC).

16 He that speaks lavishly shall hear as knavishly.

Its dissemination

17 Go abroad and you'll hear news of home.

18 What is told in the ear of a man is often heard a hundred miles away.
Chinese proverb.

19 Whispered words are heard afar.
Chinese proverb.

20 The noise of the kettledrum goes far.
Arabic proverb.

21 Confide in an aunt and the world will know.

22 If the Nile knows your secret it will soon be known in the desert.
African proverb.

23 Fields have eyes, and woods have ears.

24 Walls have ears.

25 Give a lie twenty-four hours' start, and you can never overtake it.
Variants include the saying popularized (1976) by James Callaghan: "A lie can be half way round the world before the truth has got its boots on."

Gossips and talebearers

26 A gossip speaks ill of all, and all of her.

27 Gossips are frogs, they drink and talk.

28 'Tis merry when gossips meet.

29 A rouk-town's seldom a good housewife at home.
A "rouk-town" is a Yorkshire dialect word for a gossip.

30 Put no faith in tale-bearers.

31 A tale-bearer is worse than a thief.

32 He that is a blab is a scab.

33 Don't tell tales out of school.

34 No names, no pack-drill.
"Pack-drill" is a military punishment in which the offender is made to march up and down with a full pack. The saying, which dates from the World War I era, implies that if no one is named no one can be punished.

35 Avoid a questioner, for he is also a tattler.

36 Who chatters *to* you, will chatter *of* you.

37 The dog that fetches, will carry.
A person who brings you gossip will carry gossip about you to others. A reiteration of proverb 36 above.

38 Were there no hearers, there would be no backbiters.
Both this and proverb 39 below imply that those who listen to gossip are as much at fault as those who speak it.

39 There is nothing to choose between bad tongues and wicked ears.

Telling secrets

40 Thy secret is thy prisoner; if thou let it go, thou art a prisoner to it.
That is, you should guard your secrets as carefully as a gaoler does his charges.

41 He that tells a secret, is another's servant.

42 Three may keep a secret, if two of them are dead.

80 Gratitude

Its value

1 Gratitude preserves old friendships, and procures new.

2 To a grateful man, give money when he asks.
Implies that the requests of the grateful are more likely to be granted than those of the ungrateful.

Its necessity

3 Do not forget little kindnesses and do not remember small faults.
Chinese proverb.

4 When you drink from the stream, remember the spring.
Chinese proverb.

5 Never look a gift horse in the mouth.
Examining a horse's teeth is a way of telling its age. The proverb warns against questioning the value of a gift or a lucky opportunity.

6 Throw no gift again at the giver's head.

7 Beggars can't be choosers.

8 Half a loaf is better than no bread.
Like proverbs 9–26 below, this suggests that one must be thankful for what one has, however little.

9 A crust is better than no bread.

10 Better a louse in the pot than no flesh at all.
Some variants substitute "mouse" for "louse".

11 Better are small fish than an empty dish.

12 Better some of a pudding than none of a pie.

13 A churl's feast is better than none at all.
A "churl" is an archaic term for a miser.

14 Half an egg is better than an empty shell.

15 They that have no other meat, bread and butter are glad to eat.

16 It is better to sup with a cutty than want a spoon.
A "cutty" is a pipe.

17 Better a lean jade than an empty halter.
A "jade" is an old horse.

18 A bad bush is better than the open field.

19 A bad excuse is better than none at all.

20 Better a bare foot than none.

21 One foot is better than two crutches.

22 Better eye sore than all blind.

23 Better to have one eye than be blind altogether.

24 A man were better to be half blind than have both his eyes out.

25 Better my hog dirty home than no hog at all.

26 Something is better than nothing.

Ingratitude

27 Gratitude is the least of virtues, but ingratitude is the worst of vices.

28 Who gives not thanks to men, gives not thanks to God.
Arabic proverb.

29 He is an ill guest that never drinks to his host.

30 The hog never looks up to him that threshes down the acorns.

31 Many a man serves a thankless master.

32 He that keeps another man's dog, shall have nothing left him but the line.
However well you treat such a dog it will show no gratitude, but will run off back to its true master at the first opportunity (leaving you holding the lead).

33 All is lost that is put into a riven dish.
Implies that generosity is wasted on the ungrateful.

81 Greatness

Its dangers

1 A great tree attracts the wind.

2 Great winds blow upon high hills.

3 The bigger they are, the harder they fall.
Usually attributed to the boxer Robert Fitzsimmons, who made the remark before a fight *c.* 1900. The thought is, however, much older.

4 The highest branch is not the safest roost.

5 The highest tree has the greatest fall.

6 He sits not sure that sits too high.

7 Oaks may fall when reeds stand the storm.
The oak here stands for stubbornness as well as greatness, compared to the lowly but pliant reed.

8 High cedars fall when low shrubs remain.

9 Little fishes slip through nets, but great fishes are taken.

10 The bigger the man, the better the mark.
"Mark" here means "target".

11 He who stands high is seen from afar.

12 It is height makes Grantham steeple stand awry.

A reference to the steeple of St Wulfram's church, Grantham, which is 280 feet high and a landmark for many miles around. The implication is that people notice faults in the great that they overlook or ignore in the less exalted.

Its sources

13 Goodness is not tied to greatness, but greatness to goodness.

Implies that while a man's goodness may make him great, his greatness does not necessarily make him good.

14 Some are born great, some achieve greatness, and some have greatness thrust upon them.

A quotation from Shakespeare's *Twelfth Night* (1602).

15 In the country of the blind, the one-eyed man is king.

Implies that even the mediocre may appear great when surrounded by those more incompetent or foolish than themselves.

Its limitations

16 Great trees are good for nothing but shade.

Because they prevent the growth of anything in the vicinity. A variant of this saying was cited by the Romanian sculptor Brancusi, as his reason for refusing Rodin's invitation to work in his studio (1906).

17 The greatest vessel has but its measure.

Characteristics of the great

18 An oak is not felled at one stroke.

19 A truly great man never puts away the simplicity of a child.

Chinese proverb.

20 The boughs that bear most, hang lowest.

A reference to the humility of the truly great.

21 All things that great men do are well done.

22 Great persons seldom see their face in a true glass.

23 Great men have great faults.

24 The greater the man, the greater the crime.

25 Great men's sons seldom do well.

26 A great man and a great river are often ill neighbours.

Some variants add "a great bell" to the list of undesirable neighbours.

27 Great men's favours are uncertain.

28 Hall benches are slippery.

Like proverb 29 below, this reiterates the warning contained in 27 above.

29 There is a sliddery stone before the hall door.

"Sliddery" means "slippery".

30 Serve a great man, and you will know what sorrow is.

31 Eagles don't catch flies.

Implies that the great do not concern themselves with trivial matters.

The great and the small

32 The great and the little have need one of another.

33 If great men would have care of little ones, both would last long.

34 There would be no great ones if there were no little ones.
35 Great oaks from little acorns grow.
36 Every oak has been an acorn.
37 Small is the seed of every greatness.
38 From small beginnings come great things.
39 The little cannot be great unless he devour many.
40 Great businesses turn on a little pin.
41 Great engines turn on small pivots.
42 Great weights hang on small wires.
43 Big fish eat little fish.
44 The great put the little on the hook.
45 Great trees keep down the little ones.

82 Greed

Its sources

1 Riches have made more covetous men, than covetousness hath made rich men.
2 Need makes greed.
   That is, poverty gives rise to covetousness.

Its effects

3 Appetite comes with eating.
   A French saying that can be traced back to Rabelais (1534).
4 Covetousness is always filling a bottomless vessel.
5 The greedy mouth of covetousness is not filled except by the earth of the grave.
   Arabic proverb.
6 The more you get, the more you want.
7 Much would have more.
8 Covetousness is the father of unsatisfied desires.
   African proverb.
9 The pleasure of what we enjoy, is lost by coveting more.
10 Covetousness often starves other vices.
11 Many a one for land takes a fool by the hand.
   A reference to those who marry for money.

Its dangers

12 Covetousness is the root of all evil.
   An adaptation of 1 Timothy 6:10.
13 Covetousness breaks the sack.
   That is, by trying to grasp too much you may lose everything you have; the same moral is presented by proverbs 16 and 17 below.
14 Over covetous was never good.
15 Catch not at the shadow and lose the substance.
   A reference to one of the fables attributed to Aesop (6th century BC), in which a dog carrying a bone in his mouth catches sight of his reflection in a pond and snaps greedily at

the bone reflected there. In doing so, the real bone slips out of his mouth and is lost. Proverbs 16–19 below reiterate the moral of this story.

16 Grasp all, lose all.

17 All covet, all lose.

18 Kill not the goose that lays the golden egg.
    This refers to an ancient Greek fable, concerning a goose that laid a golden egg every day. The greedy owner of the bird killed it, in the vain hope of finding a store of gold inside it, and thus lost his regular source of income.

19 Covetousness brings nothing home.

Characteristics of the greedy

20 It is hard for a greedy eye to have a leal heart.
    "Leal" means "honest".

21 The greedy man and the gileynour are soon agreed.
    Implies that a greedy man will eagerly accept the generous price offered him by a cheat ("gileynour"), who has no intention of paying.

22 Greedy folks have long arms.
    A reference to the ability of the greedy to obtain what they desire, by fair means or foul.

23 Where the carcase is, there shall be the eagles gathered together.
    An adaptation of Matthew 24:28. "Eagles" here refers to any large carrion-eating birds, such as ravens or vultures.

24 The covetous spends more than the liberal.

25 Lechery and covetousness go together.

26 There is little for the rake after the besom.
    Implies that there is little left after the greedy have had their fill (a "besom" is a broom).

27 Three things are insatiable, priests, monks, and the sea.
    Some versions substitute "women" for "monks".

28 Beggars' bags are bottomless.

29 He is not poor that has little, but he that desires much.

See also MISERLINESS

83 Habit

Its power

1 Habit is a second nature.
   With "custom" appearing instead of "habit", this was originally a quotation from Cicero's *De finibus* (1st century BC). The phrase "second nature" is now used to mean any practice, characteristic, etc., that has become so habitual as to seem innate.

2 Men do more things through habit than through reason.

3 Old habits die hard.
   Not recorded in this form until the mid-20th century, although the thought is much older.

4 It is hard to break a hog of an ill custom.

5 It is hard to make an old mare leave flinging.
   "Flinging" here means "kicking".

6 Custom reconciles us to everything.

Its development

7 Habits are at first cobwebs, at last cables.

8 Pursuits become habits.

9 Once a use and ever a custom.
   See also LAW: *Customs*

84 Happiness

Its sources

1 Content is happiness.

2 Children and fools have merry lives.

3 Laughter is the hiccup of a fool.

4 It is comparison that makes men happy or miserable.

5 Let him that would be happy for a day, go to the barber; for a week, marry a wife; for a month, buy him a new horse; for a year, build him a new house; for all his life time, be an honest man.
   There are a number of variations, including the suggestions that the best way to be happy for a day is to "get drunk" and the best recipe for lifelong happiness is to "take up gardening". No version predicts marital happiness for more than a few weeks.

6 Happy is he that chastens himself.

7 Happy is he that is happy in his children.

8 Happy is he whose friends were born before him.
Like proverb 9 below, this is a reference to those who inherit rich estates. Ironic variants substitute "father" or "parents" for "friends".

9 Happy is that child whose father goes to the devil.
Refers to the ill-gotten gains inherited by the child of an avaricious or dishonest man.

10 Happy is she who marries the son of a dead mother.
That is, who has no mother-in-law to contend with.

11 Happy is the country which has no history.
Sometimes attributed to the French political thinker Montesquieu (1681–1755); English variants are cited by Carlyle and George Eliot in the 19th century.

12 Peace in a thatched hut – that is happiness.
Chinese proverb.

13 Sadness and gladness succeed each other.

14 Seill comes not till sorrow be gone.
"Seill" means "happiness".

15 True happiness consists in making happy.
Hindi proverb.

16 All happiness is in the mind.

17 He is happy, that knoweth not himself to be otherwise.

18 He who leaves his house in search of happiness pursues a shadow.
Chinese proverb. The implication is that happiness is to be found at home.

19 Who will in time present pleasure refrain, shall in time to come the more pleasure obtain.

20 Who can sing so merry a note, as he that cannot change a groat?
A "groat" was a coin worth four pennies.

Its effects

21 Pleasant hours fly past.

22 A blithe heart makes a blooming visage.

23 The joy of the heart makes the face fair.

24 A man of gladness seldom falls into madness.

25 Laughter makes good blood.

26 Laugh and grow fat.

27 As long lives a merry man as a sad.

28 With happiness comes intelligence to the heart.
Chinese proverb.

29 When a man is happy he does not hear the clock strike.

30 Merry meet, merry part.
Directly contradicted by proverb 53 below.

Its value

31 Laugh, and the world laughs with you; weep, and you weep alone.
A quotation from Ella Wheeler Wilcox's once popular poem "Solitude" (1872). There are many facetious variants.

32 Better be happy than wise.

33 To weep for joy is a kind of manna.
Manna was the mysterious food that fell with the dew to sustain the Israelites in the wilderness (Exodus 16:13–26).

34 One joy scatters a hundred griefs.
   Chinese proverb.
35 Laughter is the best medicine.
36 One day of pleasure is worth two of sorrow.
37 An ounce of mirth is worth a pound of sorrow.
38 Aye be as merry as be can, for love ne'er delights in a sorrowful man.
   The first clause means "Always be as cheerful as you can..."
39 When good cheer is lacking, our friends will be packing.
40 A merry heart goes all the way.
41 Mirth is the sugar of life.
42 Mustard is a good sauce, but mirth is better.

Its disadvantages

43 Pleasure has a sting in its tail.
44 No joy without annoy.
45 No pleasure without pain.
   Many variants substitute "repentance" for "pain".
46 Short pleasure, long pain.
47 Pleasure is not pleasant unless it cost dear.
48 Take a pain for a pleasure all wise men can.
   That is, sensible people will endure present hardships for the sake of future pleasure.
49 Great happiness, great danger.
50 Sudden joy kills sooner than excessive grief.
51 It is misery enough to have once been happy.
   A commonplace of 16th- and 17th-century English literature, with variants appearing in works by Shakespeare, Thomas Nashe, and Robert Burton, amongst others.
52 Merry is the feast-making till we come to the reckoning.
53 Sorrow is at parting if at meeting there be laughter.

Its ephemerality

54 The mirth of the world dureth but a while.
55 Over jolly dow not.
   "Dow not" means "does not last".
56 Joy and sorrow are next door neighbours.
57 God send you joy, for sorrow will come fast enough.
58 Laugh at leisure, you may greet ere night.
   "Greet" means "weep".
59 Laugh before breakfast, you'll cry before supper.
60 If you sing before breakfast, you'll cry before night.
61 He that sings on Friday, will weep on Sunday.

Handling happiness

62 Happiness is not a horse, you cannot harness it.
   Chinese proverb.
63 Possessed of happiness, don't exhaust it.
64 We should publish our joys, and conceal our griefs.
65 Mirth without measure is madness.
   Like proverbs 66 and 67 below, this recommends moderation in one's joy.

66 It is good to be merry and wise.

67 He laughs ill that laughs himself to death.

68 Of thy sorrow be not too sad, of thy joy be not too glad.

69 He that talks much of his happiness, summons grief.

Jollity

70 There is no jollity but has a smack of folly.

71 It is a poor heart that never rejoices.
First recorded in the mid-19th century.

72 It is good to be merry at meat.

73 It is merry in hall when beards wag all.

74 It's merry when maltmen meet.
Variants substitute "friends", "gossips", or "knaves" for "maltmen".

75 The more the merrier; the fewer the better fare.
The second part of the proverb (which is now largely forgotten) implies that while mirth may increase with the number of guests or merrymakers, shares of food and drink will diminish.

76 A cheerful look makes a dish a feast.

85 Haste

Its dangers

1 Haste is from the devil.
A variant substitutes "hell" for "the devil".

2 It is the pace that kills.

3 Untimeous spurring spills the steed.
"Untimeous" means "untimely"; "spills" here means "spoils". The implication is that an attempt to speed up the natural course of events may be more destructive than constructive.

4 Haste is the sister of repentance.
African proverb.

5 Oft rape rueth.
"Rape" here means "haste".

6 He that soon deemeth, soon repenteth.
"Deemeth" means judges or decides; like proverb 7 below, the saying implies that hasty decisions are often regretted.

7 He that passes judgment as he runs, overtakes repentance.

8 Marry in haste, and repent at leisure.
"Act" is now often substituted for "marry" to make the proverb applicable to other forms of rashness. See also the note at MARRIAGE: 41.

9 A hasty man never wants woe.
Variants substitute "angry" or "wilful" for "hasty".

10 Hurry bequeaths disappointment.
African proverb.

11 Anger and haste hinder good counsel.

12 He begins to build too soon that has not money to finish it.

13 He that rides ere he be ready, wants some of his gear.
"Gear" here means "tools, equipment".

14 The hasty bitch brings forth blind whelps.

15 Haste comes not alone.
Implies that haste is always accompanied by trouble of one kind or another.

16 Haste makes waste.
For a more elaborate version see MARRIAGE: 51.

17 The hasty leaps over his opportunities.

18 Haste trips up its own heels.

19 That tongue does lie that speaks in haste.

20 In haste is error.

21 Haste is the mother of imperfection.
Brazilian proverb.

22 Hasty work, double work.

23 Good and quickly seldom meet.
Implies that what is done in a hurry is seldom done well.

Its inadvisability

24 Make haste slowly.
First cited by the Roman historian Suetonius (1st–2nd century AD), who records it as a favourite saying of the emperor Augustus.

25 There is luck in leisure.

26 Nothing should be done in haste but gripping a flea.

27 Soon enough, if well enough.
That is, a task is performed soon enough if it is done properly.

28 Be not too hasty to outbid another.

29 Hate not at the first harm.

30 Love not at the first look.

31 Affairs, like salt fish, ought to be a good while a-soaking.
The reference is to fish treated with salt as a preservative.

Against recklessness

32 First think, and then speak.

33 Look before you leap.

34 Think on the end before you begin.

35 Score twice before you cut once.
A reference to the need for careful preparation before taking an irreversible action. "Score" refers to the marking of leather by shoemakers.

36 Don't stitch your seam before you've tacked it.
To "tack" a seam is to sew it with loose temporary stitches as a way of marking the pattern.

37 He thinks not well, that thinks not again.

38 Second thoughts are best.
The saying can be traced back to the *Hippolytus* of Euripides (5th century BC).

39 Don't throw out your dirty water until you get in fresh.

40 Don't cut the bough you are standing on.

41 Don't throw the baby out with the bathwater.
In reforming the abuses of an institution, etc., be careful to preserve what is precious and essential.

Haste and speed

42 More haste, less speed.
   Here, as in proverb 43 below, "speed" originally had the sense of "successful performance" rather than "rapidity".

43 Fool's haste is no speed.

44 A hasty man drinks his tea with a fork.
   Chinese proverb.

45 The nearest way is commonly the foulest.
   Like proverbs 46 and 47 below, this implies that short cuts do not always save time.

46 The longest way round is the shortest way home.

47 Better to go about than to fall into the ditch.

48 Slow but sure wins the race.
   The allusion is to the well-known fable of the hare and the tortoise attributed to Aesop (6th century BC). "Steady" is often substituted for "sure".

49 Soft pace goes far.

50 Fair and softly goes far.
   An ironic variant is "Fair and softly, as lawyers go to heaven."

51 Ride softly, that we may come sooner home.

52 He that goes softly goes safely.

See also CHILDREN: *The recklessness of youth*; FOOLISHNESS: *The recklessness of fools*

86 Hatred

Its dangers

1 Hatred is worse than murder.

2 Hatred blasts the crop on the land; envy the fish in the sea.

3 Hatred with friends is succour to foes.

Its relationship to love

4 Love and hate are blood relations.

5 He that cannot hate cannot love.

6 They that too deeply loved too deeply hate.

7 The greatest hate springs from the greatest love.

8 Hatred is blind, as well as love.

9 Better a dinner of herbs where love is than a stalled ox where hate is.
   Adapted from Proverbs 15:17. The words "where love is" are frequently omitted.

Its persistence

10 Old hate never wearies.

11 Rancour sticks long by the ribs.
   That is, it persists long in the heart.

87 Health

Its value

1 Health and gaiety foster beauty.
2 Health and wealth create beauty.
3 Health and money go far.
4 Health is great riches.
5 Health is better than wealth.
   Adapted from a passage in the apocryphal book of Ecclesiasticus (30:15).
6 A good wife and health is a man's best wealth.
7 He who has good health, is young; and he is rich who owes nothing.
8 He that wants health wants all.
9 Health is not valued till sickness comes.

Its sources

10 There's nothing so good for the inside of a man as the outside of a horse.
   A reference to the value of horse-riding as a healthy pastime. The saying is sometimes attributed to the British statesman Lord Palmerston (1784–1865).
11 A cool mouth, and warm feet, live long.
   A "cool mouth" implies moderation in eating and drinking.
12 Dry feet, warm head, bring safe to bed.
13 The head and feet keep warm, the rest will take no harm.
   A variant runs "…, and for the rest live like a beast."
14 Wash your hands often, your feet seldom, and your head never.
15 Early to bed and early to rise, makes a man healthy, wealthy, and wise.
   James Thurber's humorous reversal is well known: "Early to rise and early to bed, makes a man healthy and wealthy and dead" (mid-20th century).
16 A little labour, much health.
17 Poverty is the mother of health.
18 Temperance is the best physic.
19 Where the sun enters, the doctor does not.
20 An apple a day keeps the doctor away.
   Variants are recorded from the mid-19th century onwards. Apples are rich in amino acids, vitamins, and mineral salts.

Sources of ill health

21 Diseases are the price of ill pleasures.
22 Ill air slays sooner than the sword.
23 The air of a window is as the stroke of a cross-bow.
   Like proverbs 24–26 below, this refers to the dangers of sitting in a draught.
24 If cold wind reach you through a hole, say your prayers, and mind your soul.
25 Back to the draught is face to the grave.
   Chinese proverb.
26 Take heed of wind that comes in at a hole, and a reconciled enemy.

Effects of ill health

27 The sickness of the body may prove the health of the soul.
28 Sickness shows us what we are.

29 Sickness soaks the purse.

30 The chamber of sickness is the chapel of devotion.

31 A creaking gate hangs longest.
Implies that the chronically (and querulously) sick often outlive the robust and healthy. "Door" is sometimes substituted for "gate".

32 A dry cough is the trumpeter of death.

33 A priest sees people at their best, a lawyer at their worst, but a doctor sees them as they really are.

Remedies

34 A disease known is half cured.
Often applied metaphorically to nonmedical problems.

35 The best doctors are Dr Diet, Dr Quiet, and Dr Merryman.
Implies that sensible eating, quiet, and a cheerful spirit are the surest remedies for ill health.

36 Kitchen physic is the best physic.
A further reference to the value of good wholesome food as a substitute for drugs and medicaments.

37 Feed a cold and starve a fever.
A variant substitutes "stuff" for "feed". Although now generally interpreted as an encouragement to eat well when suffering from a cold, the proverb was originally a warning that feeding a cold will bring on a fever, which will then have to be cured by fasting.

38 When the sun rises, the disease will abate.
According to Jewish folklore the patriarch Abraham wore a precious stone with healing properties around his neck; it is said that God placed this stone in the sun after Abraham's death.

39 Who pays the physician does the cure.

40 Ready money is a ready medicine.

41 No pain, no cure.
Implies that painful remedies, such as iodine applied to a wound, are the most effective.

The limitations of medicine

42 When a disease returns, no medicine can cure it.
Chinese proverb.

43 Death defies the doctor.

44 A deadly disease neither physician nor physic can ease.

45 If physic do not work, prepare for the kirk.

46 St Luke was a saint and a physician, and yet he died.

47 To the gout, all physicians are blind.
A reference to the incurability of gout.

48 Medicines are not meat to live by.
Like proverb 49 below, this warns against relying too heavily on drugs and medicines; it can also be used in more general contexts, to imply that certain kinds of remedy should not be used habitually.

49 Make not thy stomach an apothecary's shop.

Doctors

50 If the doctor cures, the sun sees it; but if he kills, the earth hides it.
A very old saying that has been attributed to both the Greek philosopher Anarcharsis (7th century BC) and his contemporary the poet Nicocles.

51 One doctor makes work for another.

52 The doctor is often more to be feared than the disease.

53 Physicians kill more than they cure.

Before the medical advances of the later 19th century (notably the widespread use of antiseptics) this may well have been strictly true.

54 Leeches kill with licence.

"Leech" is a former term for a doctor.

55 A young physician fattens the churchyard.

Implies that an inexperienced doctor will make fatal mistakes.

56 If you have a physician for your friend, tip your hat and send him to your enemy.

57 Few lawyers die well, few physicians live well.

58 God heals, and the physician has the thanks.

59 A physician is an angel when employed, but a devil when one must pay him.

60 Hide nothing from thy minister, physician, and lawyer.

61 Every man is a fool or a physician.

Implies that any man who does not know enough about healthy living to be his own doctor must be a fool; some variants specify "after the age of 30 (*or* 40)", suggesting that by this age a person should have learned from his or her experience. In his *Annals* (early 2nd century AD) Tacitus ascribes the saying to the emperor Tiberius, who allegedly refused to consult physicians.

62 A good surgeon must have an eagle's eye, a lion's heart, and a lady's hand.

63 Surgeons cut, that they may cure.

See also DRINKING: *Healthy drinking habits, Unhealthy drinking habits*; EATING: *Undesirable foods, Healthy eating habits, Unhealthy eating habits*; REMEDIES

88 Helping

Its sources

1 One can't help many, but many can help one.

2 All is not at hand that helps.

Implies that help may come from unexpected sources.

3 He that is fallen cannot help him that is down.

Its value

4 Many hands make light work.

As has often been pointed out, this is a direct contradiction of proverb 9 below.

5 Three helping one another, bear the burthen of six.

6 Two heads are better than one.

7 Four eyes see more than two.

8 He must needs swim, that is held up by the chin.

Implies that those who receive assistance and support cannot fail to thrive.

Its dangers

9 Too many cooks spoil the broth.

As has often been pointed out, this is a direct contradiction of proverb 4 above.

10 Two boys are half a boy, and three boys are no boy at all.
This reiterates the sentiments of proverb 9 above; "boy" here has the sense of "menial, underling".

11 He that helps the evil hurts the good.

12 Never catch at a falling knife or a falling friend.

13 Save a stranger from the sea, and he'll turn your enemy.
An old nautical superstition.

14 Save a thief from the gallows and he'll cut your throat.

15 A beggar pays a benefit with a louse.

Its timing

16 When need is highest, help is nighest.

17 When the child is christened, you may have godfathers enough.
Implies that people are always most ready to offer assistance after the job is done.

18 Slow help is no help.

Mutual help

19 One good turn deserves another.

20 One hand washes the other.
A hand cannot wash its partner without receiving the same benefit itself; said in situations where a person provides help, etc., with the clear understanding that this will be repaid.

21 One kindness is the price of another.

22 Kindness lies not aye in one side of the house.
A Scottish saying, spoken by one returning a favour.

23 He that pities another remembers himself.

24 Scratch my back and I'll scratch yours.
The allusion is to the mutual grooming of animals.

25 Scratch my breech and I'll claw your elbow.
"Claw" here and in proverb 26 below means to rub or stroke.

26 Claw me, and I'll claw thee.

27 Give me fire and I'll give you a light.
Arabic proverb.

28 Help, for help in harvest.
Implies that the person one helps now will return the favour in time of greatest need.

See also GOD: *His help*

89 Honesty

Its value

1 Honesty is the best policy.
The British churchman Richard Whately added the observation "...but he who is governed by that policy is not an honest man" (1854).

2 Honesty may be dear bought, but can never be an ill pennyworth.

3 No honest man ever repented of his honesty.

4 Knavery may serve for a turn, but honesty is best at the long run.

5 Plain dealing is a jewel.
   For a cynical variant see proverb 13 below.
6 Plain dealing is best.
7 Open confession is good for the soul.
   The word "open" is now usually omitted.
8 A man never surfeits of too much honesty.
9 Better beg than steal.
10 An honest look covers many faults.

Its disadvantages

11 Honesty is ill to thrive by.
12 Honesty is praised and starves.
13 Plain dealing is a jewel, but they that use it die beggars.
   A cynical variant of proverb 5 above.
14 Confess and be hanged.

Its rarity

15 Plain dealing is praised more than practised.
16 Honesty is a fine jewel; but much out of fashion.
17 Plain dealing is dead, and died without issue.
18 He that resolves to deal with none but honest men, must leave off dealing.

Characteristics of the honest

19 An honest man's word is as good as his bond.
20 Leal heart lied never.
   "Leal" means "honest".
21 Leal folks never wanted gear.
   "Gear" means "possessions".
22 A thread will tie an honest man better than a rope will do a rogue.
23 A true man and a thief think not the same.
24 Honesty keeps the crown of the causeway.
   That is, the honest person may keep to the centre of the pavement rather than slinking
   by the walls; the implication is that the honest have nothing to be ashamed or afraid of.
25 Honest men marry soon, wise men not at all.
26 He is wise that is honest.

90 Honour

Its effects

1 Honours change manners.
2 Honour shows the man.
   Variants substitute "authority", "office", or "place" for "honour".

Its inadequacy

3 Honour buys no beef in the market.
4 Honour without profit is a ring on the finger.

5 Honour and profit lie not in one sack.
Because honour is often profitless and profit sometimes dishonourable.

Its drawbacks

6 Honour and ease are seldom bedfellows.
7 Where there is no honour, there is no grief.
8 Great honours are great burdens.
"Honours" here has the sense of "positions, offices".
9 The post of honour is the post of danger.

Being worthy of honour

10 He that desires honour, is not worthy of honour.
11 It is a worthier thing to deserve honour than to possess it.
12 Honour is the reward of virtue.
13 Who that in youth, no virtue uses, in age all honour him refuses.

91 Hope

Its value

1 Hope is the poor man's bread.
2 If it were not for hope, the heart would break.
3 Hope keeps man alive.
4 Never was cat or dog drowned, that could but see the shore.
5 Hope is grief's best music.
6 A good hope is better than a bad possession.
7 Great hopes make great men.
8 There is more delight in hope than in enjoyment.
Japanese proverb.
9 Tine heart, tine all.
"Tine" means "lose".
10 If fortune torments me, hope contents me.
Often cited in its Italian form *Si fortuna me tormenta, il speranza me contenta*; this is a favourite saying of the braggart Pistol in Shakespeare's 2 Henry IV (c. 1598).
11 In the land of hope there is never any winter.

Its constancy

12 Hope springs eternal in the human breast.
A quotation from Pope's *An Essay on Man* (1733); the poem continues "Man never is, but always to be blest."
13 Hope is the last thing to abandon the unhappy.
14 A drowning man will clutch at a straw.
Now often alluded to in the phrase "to clutch at straws".
15 Death alone can kill hope.

Its disadvantages

16 Too much hope deceives.
17 Hope often deludes the foolish man.

18 Hope is but the dream of those that wake.
   In this form a quotation from Matthew Prior's poem *Solomon* (1718); the thought is much older and has been attributed to Aristotle.

19 Hope is a good breakfast but a bad supper.

20 Who lives by hope will die by hunger.
   A variant runs "…hath a slender diet."

21 He that lives in hope dances to an ill tune.
   A variant has "…dances without music."

22 Hopers go to hell.

23 Hope deferred maketh the heart sick.
   A biblical quotation: Proverbs 13:12.

Hopeful attitudes

24 Hope for the best.
   A common variant adds "…and prepare for the worst."

25 Hope well and have well.

26 While there's life there's hope.
   The thought can be traced back to Cicero (1st century BC) and more distantly to Theocritus (3rd century BC). In English the saying sometimes appears as part of a cynical couplet: "'While there is life, there's hope' he cried/ 'Then why such haste?' – so groaned and died."

27 Bear with evil and expect good.

28 Tomorrow is another day.
   Probably now best known as the closing words of Margaret Mitchell's novel *Gone With the Wind* (1936); however, variants appear as early as the 16th century.

29 He has not lost all who has one cast left.
   "Cast" here refers to a throw of the dice.

See also OPTIMISM

92 Hospitality

Its value

1 If a man receives no guests at home, when abroad he'll have no hosts.
   Chinese proverb.

2 The guest of the hospitable learns hospitality.
   Arabic proverb.

3 Good will and welcome is your best cheer.

4 He that is welcome fares well.

5 Welcome is the best dish.

6 Such welcome, such farewell.

7 It is a sin against hospitality, to open your doors and shut up your countenance.

The guest's behaviour

8 To the man submit at whose board you sit.
   Chinese proverb.

9 He is an ill guest that never drinks to his host.

Outstaying one's welcome

10 Do not wear out your welcome.

11 A constant guest is never welcome.

12 Long visits bring short compliments.
Chinese proverb.

13 Fish and guests smell in three days.

14 The first day a guest, the second day a guest, the third day a calamity.
Indian proverb.

15 The guest who outstays his fellow-guests loses his overcoat.
Chinese proverb.

The uninvited guest

16 An unbidden guest knows not where to sit.

17 An unbidden guest must bring his stool with him.

18 Who comes uncalled, sits unserved.

93 Hunger

Its causes

1 After a famine in the stall, comes a famine in the hall.
Implies that a bad harvest leads to a lack of animal feed, and that both contribute to the hunger of the people. See also COUNTRY LORE: 9.

2 Where coin is not common, commons must be scant.
"Commons" is an archaic word meaning "provisions".

3 They must hunger in frost that will not work in heat.

Its effects

4 Who goes to bed supperless, all night tumbles and tosses.

5 An empty belly bears no body.

6 A sharp stomach makes short devotion.
That is, a hungry person will not spend long saying grace.

7 The belly wants ears.
A reference to the futility of reasoning with a hungry person: the saying is often attributed to Cato the Elder (3rd–2nd centuries BC).

Its advantages

8 Hunger finds no fault with the cookery.

9 Hunger is good kitchen meat.
"Kitchen meat" is anything served as a relish with bread.

10 Hunger is the best sauce.
The thought can be traced back to Cicero (1st century BC).

11 Hunger makes hard beans sweet.

12 A hungry horse makes a clean manger.

13 All's good in a famine.

14 Hunger increases the understanding.
Lithuanian proverb.

Its dangers

15 Hunger and cold deliver a man up to his enemy.

16 A hungry man is an angry man.

Its intensity

17 Hunger is sharper than the sword.

18 Hunger is stronger than love.

19 A hungry man smells meat afar off.

The desperation of the hungry

20 Hunger breaks stone walls.

21 Hunger drives the wolf out of the wood.

22 Hungry dogs will eat dirty puddings.
Sometimes used to imply that the needy will accept money from any source, however tainted.

23 A hungry man is glad to get boiled wheat.
Chinese proverb.

Fasting

24 Who fasts and does no other good, spares his bread and goes to hell.

25 He fasts enough that has had a bad meal.

26 He fasts enough whose wife scolds all dinner-time.

27 Two hungry meals make the third a glutton.
Implies that fasting improves the appetite.

28 He whose belly is full believes not him who is fasting.
"Fasting" here simply means "hungry".

See also EATING: *Appetite*

94 Hypocrisy

Its value

1 Who knows not how to dissemble, knows not how to live.
"Reign" is sometimes substituted for "live"; in this form the saying is sometimes attributed to the Roman emperor Vespasian (9–79 AD) or to Louis XI of France (1422–83).

2 Speak fair and think what you will.

3 Lip-honour costs little, yet may bring in much.

Hypocritical acts

4 The cat and dog may kiss, yet are none the better friends.

5 Many kiss the hand they wish cut off.

6 Many kiss the child for the nurse's sake.

7 He that gives to be seen, will relieve none in the dark.

8 Carrion crows bewail the dead sheep, and then eat them.

9 The cat shuts its eyes while it steals cream.
That is, people blind themselves to any wrong they commit in the course of pleasant or profitable activities.

Hypocritical words

10 Fine words dress ill deeds.

11 Many a one says well that thinks ill.

12 A honey tongue, a heart of gall.

13 He that speaks me fair and loves me not, I'll speak him fair and trust him not.

14 All are not friends that speak us fair.

Religious hypocrisy

15 Pretended holiness is double iniquity.

16 All are not saints that go to church.

17 Bells call others, but themselves enter not into the church.

18 When the fox preaches, then beware your geese.

19 The friar preached against stealing, and had a goose in his sleeve.
   Some variants have the more plausible "pudding" instead of "goose".

20 Some make a conscience of spitting in the church, yet rob the altar.
   A "conscience" here means a "matter of conscience".

21 No rogue like to the godly rogue.

22 If you want to see black-hearted people, look among those who never miss their prayers.
   Chinese proverb.

Against hypocrisy

23 Be what you would seem to be.
   A common variant is "Be what you seem and seem what you are."

24 Kythe in your own colours, that folk may ken you.
   "Kythe" is a Scots word meaning "appear".

95 Idleness

Its causes

1 A light-heeled mother makes a heavy-heeled daughter.
   "Light-heeled" means "nimble"; "heavy-heeled" means "lazy". The implication is that by doing all the work herself an over-busy mother encourages sloth in her daughter.
2 Work for nought makes folks dead sweir.
   "Sweir" means "lazy".
3 Lacking breeds laziness, praise breeds pith.
   "Lacking" here means "criticism"; "pith" means "effort".

Its effects

4 Idleness is the shipwreck of chastity.
5 Love is the fruit of idleness.
6 Pride and laziness would have mickle upholding.
   "Mickle" means "much". A reference to the expense of providing ornaments for the vain and servants for the lazy.
7 Sweet in the bed, and sweir up in the morning, was never a good housewife.
   "Sweir" here means "late".
8 Standing pools gather filth.
9 A sluggard takes an hundred steps because he would not take one in due time.
10 Idle folks have the least leisure.
    Compare DILIGENCE: 45.
11 Who is more busy, than he that has least to do?
    Like proverb 10 above, this implies either that lazy people avoid work by claiming to have no spare time, or that they use up all their time in procrastination and avoidance activities.
12 It is more pain to do nothing than something.
13 The dog that is idle barks at his fleas, but he that is hunting feels them not.

Its dangers

14 The devil finds work for idle hands to do.
    Both this and proverb 15 below are based on a phrase in St Jerome's *Letters* (5th century AD).
15 If the devil find a man idle, he'll set him to work.
16 An idle brain is the devil's workshop.

17 An idle person is the devil's cushion.
Some variants begin "Idleness is…"

18 The devil tempts all, but the idle man tempts the devil.

19 He that is busy, is tempted by but one devil; he that is idle, by a legion.

20 By doing nothing we learn to do ill.
Sometimes attributed to Cato the Elder (3rd–2nd centuries BC).

21 Of idleness comes no goodness.

22 Idleness is the root of all evil.
Sometimes attributed to St Bernard of Clairvaux (1090–1153).

23 Idleness turns the edge of wit.

24 Sloth, like rust, consumes faster than labour wears.

25 Sloth breeds a scab.

26 They must hunger in frost that will not work in heat.

27 An idle youth, a needy age.

28 Idleness is the key of beggary.

29 Laziness goes so slowly that poverty overtakes it.

30 Idleness must thank itself if it goes barefoot.

31 He that lies long abed, his estate feels it.

32 He who sleeps all the morning, may go a begging all the day after.

33 The slothful man is the beggar's brother.

34 The sluggard must be clad in rags.

35 He that gapes until he be fed, well may he gape until he be dead.
A picturesque variant is "You may gape long enough until larks fall into your mouth ready roasted."

Dealing with idleness

36 A lazy ox is little better for the goad.

37 He that is sick of a fever lurden, must be cured by the hazel gelding.
"Fever lurden" means "lazy fever"; a "gelding" here means a young tree (whose branches will serve well for a whip).

38 A horse that will not carry a saddle must have no oats.

39 A lean fee is a fit reward for a lazy clerk.

Lazy people

40 He that does nothing, does ever amiss.

41 Every day is holiday with sluggards.

42 The sluggard's convenient season never comes.

43 For the diligent the week has seven todays, for the slothful seven tomorrows.

44 Idle folks lack no excuses.

45 The slothful is the servant of the counters.
"Counters" here means "prisons".

46 Sluggards are never great scholars.

47 A lazy sheep thinks its wool heavy.

48 As good be an addled egg as an idle bird.
"Addled" means "broken"; the proverb implies that an idle person may as well not have been born.

96 Ignorance

Its advantages

1 Ignorance is the peace of life.
2 Ignorance and incuriosity are two very soft pillows.
3 Wonder is the daughter of ignorance.
4 He that knows nothing, doubts nothing.
5 Where ignorance is bliss, 'tis folly to be wise.
  The closing line of Gray's "Ode on a Distant Prospect of Eton College" (1747).
6 What the eye doesn't see, the heart doesn't grieve over.
7 What you don't know can't hurt you.
8 He that never ate flesh, thinks a pudding a dainty.
9 Acorns were good till bread was found.
  Like proverb 8 above, this implies that ignorance of the finer things of life is better than the discontented knowledge that one cannot have them.

Its disadvantages

10 Ignorance is the night of the mind.
  Chinese proverb.
11 There is no blindness like ignorance.
12 The devil never assails a man except he find him either void of knowledge, or of the fear of God.
13 Science has no enemy but the ignorant.
  "Science" here has the older and wider sense of "learning".
14 Art has no enemy but ignorance.
  "Art" here means "skill, learning".
15 If the blind lead the blind, both shall fall into the ditch.
  A quotation from the Sermon on the Mount: Matthew 15:14.

Its effects

16 Ignorance is the mother of impudence.
  "Presumption" is sometimes substituted for "ignorance".
17 Ignorance is the mother of devotion.
  "Devotion" here means "religious zeal, piety".
18 He that knows little, often repeats it.
19 It is profound ignorance that inspires the dogmatic tone.

97 Imperfection

Nobody is perfect

1 Every man has his faults.
2 He is lifeless that is faultless.
3 No man is infallible.
4 To err is human.
  The proverb predates Pope's well-known line "To err is human: to forgive, divine." (*An Essay on Criticism*, 1711). See also FORGIVENESS: 7.

5 If you don't make mistakes you don't make anything.
   First recorded in the early 20th century. See also proverb 12 below.

6 The best may amend.

7 Every man has his weak side.

8 He is good that failed never.

9 It is a sound head that has not a soft piece in it.

10 Every man is mad on some point.

11 No living man all things can.

12 He who makes no mistakes, makes nothing.
   See also proverb 5 above.

13 He rides sure that never fell.

14 He stands not surely that never slips.

15 Accidents will happen in the best regulated families.
   Although the saying is often associated with Mr Micawber in Dickens's *David Copperfield* (1850), there are several earlier citations.

16 Homer sometimes nods.
   A quotation from Horace's *Ars poetica* (1st century BC) making the point that the greatest poet will err sometimes from a momentary failure of attention. Like proverbs 17 and 18 below, the saying implies that even the great have their limitations.

17 Bernard did not see everything.
   A reference to the great theologian St Bernard of Clairvaux (1090–1153).

18 Arthur could not tame woman's tongue.
   A reference to King Arthur.

Nothing is perfect

19 The best things may be abused.

20 Nothing so good but it might have been better.
   See also OPTIMISM: 6.

21 The best-laid schemes of mice and men gang aft agley.
   A quotation from Burns's poem "To a Mouse" (1786). "Gang aft agley" means "often go awry".

22 There are spots even in the sun.

23 The best cloth may have a moth in it.

24 The best cart may overthrow.

25 No garden without its weeds.

26 No land without stones, or meat without bones.

27 No silver without its dross.

28 There is no pack of cards without a knave.

29 No rose without a thorn.
   A commonplace of Elizabethan and 17th-century verse.

30 Every light has its shadow.

31 No sun without a shadow.

32 No day so clear but has dark clouds.

33 No summer, but has its winter.

34 There was never a good town but had a mire at one end of it.

35 Wherever a man dwell, he shall be sure to have a thorn-bush near his door.

36 No larder but has its mice.

37 Every bean has its black.

38 Every path has a puddle.

39 It is a good tree that has neither knap nor gaw.
   A "knap" is a knob; a "gaw" is a blemish.
40 He is a gentle horse that never cast his rider.
41 It is a good horse that never stumbles.
   Sometimes completed with the rhyming line "And a good wife that never grumbles."
42 He who wants a mule without fault, must walk on foot.
43 He that seeks a horse or a wife without fault, has neither steed in his stable
   nor angel in his bed.

See also WISDOM: *The fallibility of the wise*

98 Inconvenience

Its necessity

1 No convenience without its inconvenience.
2 Every commodity has its discommodity.
3 Suffer the ill and look for the good.
   "Suffer" here has the sense of "endure".
4 The cat would eat fish and would not wet her feet.
5 He that would have eggs must endure the cackling of hens.
   Hens cackle (rather than cluck) when they are about to lay.
6 Better a mischief than an inconvenience.
   Implies that it is better to have a small inconvenience now than to endure greater
   inconvenience at a later date.
7 A stumble may prevent a fall.
8 It is better to kiss a knave than to be troubled with him.

99 Inquisitiveness

Its dangers

1 Curiosity killed the cat.
   First recorded in the USA in the earlier 20th century.
2 Curiosity is endless, restless, and useless.
3 Listeners never hear good of themselves.
   "Eavesdroppers" is often substituted for "listeners".
4 He who peeps through a hole, may see what will vex him.
5 He that gazes upon the sun, shall at last be blind.
6 He that pries into every cloud, may be stricken with a thunderbolt.
7 That fish will soon be caught that nibbles at every bait.
8 Spur a jade a question, and she'll kick you an answer.
   A "jade" is a horse. The saying implies that a nosy or impertinent question will provoke
   a cutting answer.
9 Ask no questions and hear no lies.
   Variants of this common saying appear in works by Goldsmith, Scott, and Kipling.

Against meddling

10 Mind your own business.

11 Meddle not with another man's matter.

12 Skeer your own fire.
    "Skeer" means "rake out".

13 The stone that lies not in your gate breaks not your toes.

14 Enquire not what boils in another's pot.

15 Put not thy hand between the bark and the tree.
    A warning against meddling in family quarrels.

16 Little intermeddling makes good friends.

17 Little meddling makes much rest.

18 Come not to counsel uncalled.
    That is, don't give advice until it's asked for.

19 Every man knows his own business best.

100 Justice

Its value

1 In justice is all virtue found in sum.
2 Justice will not condemn even the devil himself wrongfully.
3 Though the sword of justice is sharp, it will not slay the innocent.
  Chinese proverb.
4 Right wrongs no man.
5 A just war is better than an unjust peace.
  A quotation from *Annals* of Tacitus (early 2nd century AD). The reverse had been stated by Cicero (1st century BC).

Injustice

6 Extreme justice is extreme injustice.
  Implies that to apply a law to the letter, without taking any extenuating circumstances into account, is a form of injustice.
7 Much law, but little justice.
8 There's one law for the rich, and another for the poor.
  First recorded in the early 19th century.
9 One man may steal a horse, while another may not look over a hedge.
  Implies that through personal favour or prejudice, the misdeeds of one person may be overlooked while a trivial action by another is condemned. To "look over a hedge" was formerly a euphemism for urinating in the open air (of men).

Fair judgment

10 Hear all parties.
11 There are two sides to every question.
  Sometimes attributed to the Greek philosopher Protagoras (5th century BC).
12 Every medal has its reverse.
13 Give the devil his due.
14 Give credit where credit is due.
15 Comparisons are odious.
  Implies that it is unfair to pass judgment on one person by comparing him or her with another.
16 Circumstances alter cases.

Fair play

17 Fair play's a jewel.
18 Fair exchange is no robbery.
19 What's sauce for the goose is sauce for the gander.
   Implies that what is appropriate for a man is equally appropriate for a woman.
20 One dog, one bull.
   A reference to the former sport of bull-baiting.
21 Two to one is odds.
   Like proverb 22 below, this refers to the unfairness of an uneven match.
22 Many dogs may easily worry one hare.

Sharing fairly

23 Share and share alike.
24 It is no play where one greets and another laughs.
   "Play" here means "fair play" and "greets" means "cries".
25 Turn about is fair play.

See also LAW

101 Kindness

Its value

1 A kind heart loseth nought at last.
2 It is cheap enough to say, 'God help you.'
3 Pity is akin to love.
4 Charity construes all doubtful things in good part.
   Adapted from St Paul's teaching on charity in 1 Corinthians 13:7.
5 Charity covers a multitude of sins.
   A biblical quotation: 1 Peter 4:8. Whereas the meaning of the biblical text is that love overcomes sin, the saying is now often used to imply that charity may conceal or disguise wrongdoing.
6 Kindness is the noblest weapon to conquer with.
7 An iron anvil should have a hammer of feathers.
   Implies that a kind gentle approach may be the best way to win over a stubborn person.
8 The rough net is not the best catcher of birds.
9 To fright a bird is not the way to catch her.
10 Honey catches more flies than vinegar.
11 Where men are well used, they'll frequent there.

Its dangers

12 Tender-handed stroke a nettle, and it stings you for your pains; grasp it like a man of mettle, and it soft as silk remains.
   A quotation from "Verses Written on a Window in Scotland", a short poem by Aaron Hill (1685–1750).
13 Kind hearts are soonest wronged.
14 Let an ill man lie in thy straw, and he looks to be thy heir.
   Like proverbs 15 and 16 below, this warns against letting unscrupulous people take advantage of one's kindness.
15 Give a clown your finger, and he will take your hand.
16 Give him an inch and he'll take a yard.
   Variants substitute "mile" or "ell" for "yard".
17 Sometimes clemency is cruelty, and cruelty clemency.

Its sources

18 Kindness cannot be bought for gear.
   That is, it cannot be bought with gifts.

19 Kindness comes of will.
   That is, it cannot be forced.
20 We can poind for debt but not for kindness.
   "Poind" means "distrain". The proverb implies that no one has a legal obligation to be kind.

Kind words

21 Fair words break no bones.
22 Fair words hurt not the mouth.
23 Good words are good cheap.
   "Good cheap" means "a good bargain" (because they cost nothing).
24 A good word costs no more than a bad one.
25 Good words cost nought.
26 There is great force hidden in a sweet command.
   Implies that gentle firmness may be more effective than loud threats.

102 Knowledge

Its sources

1 Doubt is the key of knowledge.
   Persian proverb.
2 He that nothing questions, nothing learns.
3 He that travels far, knows much.
4 Knowledge is a wild thing and must be hunted before it can be tamed.
   Persian proverb.

Its effects

5 Learning makes a good man better and an ill man worse.
6 A man's studies pass into his character.
7 Pursuits become habits.

Its value

8 Knowledge is the mother of all virtue; all vice proceeds from ignorance.
9 Knowledge is power.
   A maxim associated with Francis Bacon (1561–1626), who used Latin variants of this phrase in several of his works.
10 Knowledge is no burthen.
   Implies that knowledge can be carried about everywhere.
11 Learning is a treasure which accompanies its owner everywhere.
   Chinese proverb.
12 Learning makes a man fit company for himself.
13 Learning is the eye of the mind.
14 Wit without learning is like a tree without fruit.
15 A man of great memory without learning, has a rock and a spindle, and no stuff to spin.
   "Rock" here means "distaff".
16 When house and land are gone and spent, then learning is most excellent.
   Implies that learning enables one to survive without material wealth.

17 No knave to the learned knave.

18 With Latin, a horse, and money, you may travel the world.
"Latin" here symbolizes learning.

19 A dwarf on a giant's shoulders sees further of the two.
A reference to the value of knowledge acquired from one's predecessors. The saying is often attributed to Sir Isaac Newton, who modestly applied a variant of these words to himself (1675), but there are earlier citations. In tribute to Newton the words "Standing on the shoulders of giants" appear around the rim of £2 coins in the UK.

Its inadequacy

20 Knowledge makes one laugh, but wealth makes one dance.

21 Knowledge without practice makes but half an artist.

22 Learning without wisdom is a load of books on an ass's back.
Japanese proverb.

23 Experience without learning is better than learning without experience.

24 The greatest scholars are not the best preachers.

25 The greatest clerks are not the wisest men.
"Clerks" means "scholars".

Its unimportance

26 He that lives well is learned enough.

27 A handful of good life is better than a bushel of learning.

Its dangers

28 Knowledge is folly, except grace guide it.

29 Learning in the breast of a bad man is as a sword in the hand of a madman.
Some variants substitute "prince" for "bad man".

30 Much learning makes men mad.
Adapted from Acts 26:24 (where the Romans say this of St Paul).

31 Much science, much sorrow.
"Science" here means "learning".

32 A little learning is a dangerous thing.
A quotation from Pope's *An Essay on Criticism* (1711). The poem continues: "Drink deep, or taste not the Pierian spring:/ There shallow draughts intoxicate the brain,/ And drinking largely sobers us again."

Characteristics of scholars

33 The love of money and the love of learning rarely meet.

34 Poverty is the common fate of scholars.
Chinese proverb.

35 He that robs a scholar, robs twenty men.
Implies that many of the things stolen from a scholar will have been previously borrowed from other people.

See also EDUCATION; EXPERIENCE.

L

103 Lateness

Its disadvantages

1 Who comes late, lodges ill.
2 He that comes last to the pot, is soonest wroth.
   "Wroth" means "angry".
3 Far behind must follow the faster.
4 Late-comers are shent.
   "Shent" means "ruined".
5 He that rises not early, never does a good day's work.
6 He that rises late, must trot all day.
7 The gods send nuts to those who have no teeth.
   A reference to opportunities that come too late to be of any use.

Its compensations

8 Better late than never.
   A maxim that can be traced back to Livy (1st century BC) and other classical authors.
9 Better late ripe and bear, than early blossom and blast.
10 Late was often lucky.
11 They are far behind that may not follow.
12 Never too late to learn.
   Variants substitute "old" for "late" and "mend", "repent", or "do well" for "learn".
13 The last suitor wins the maid.

See also EARLINESS; REGRET: *Its futility, The futility of hindsight*

104 Law

Its sources

1 Good laws often proceed from bad manners.
   See also OPTIMISM: 26.
2 The law grows of sin, and chastises it.
3 Many lords, many laws.
4 New lords, new laws.
5 Law governs man, reason the law.

Its inconsistency

6 There's one law for the rich, and another for the poor.
First recorded in the early 19th century.

7 The law is not the same at morning and at night.

8 The law is an ass.
A saying familiarized by Dickens's *Oliver Twist* (1838), in which it is said by Mr Bumble; there are, however, several earlier citations.

9 Laws catch flies but let hornets go free.
Sometimes attributed to the Athenian sage Solon (7th century BC) or his contemporary Anacharsis.

Its inadequacy

10 You cannot make people honest by Act of Parliament.
"Sober" is sometimes substituted for "honest".

11 A coach and four may be driven through any Act of Parliament.
Because of the many inevitable loopholes. Often attributed (with particular reference to the 1652 Act of Settlement punishing Irish rebels) to the English judge Sir Stephen Rice (1637–1715).

12 Every law has a loophole.

13 Where drums beat, laws are silent.
Implies that the law has little weight in a state of war. Adapted from a maxim of the Roman orator Cicero (1st century BC).

14 Much law, but little justice.

15 A penny-weight of love is worth a pound of law.

16 In a thousand pounds of law, there's not an ounce of love.

17 We can poind for debt but not for kindness.
"Poind" means "distrain". The proverb implies that no one has a legal obligation to be kind.

18 Law cannot persuade, where it cannot punish.

19 Many things lawful are not expedient.
A biblical quotation: 1 Corinthians 6:12.

Its dangers

20 Law is a bottomless pit.

21 The more laws, the more offenders.
Adapted from an aphorism in Tacitus's *Annals* (early 2nd century AD). The saying can be used to make two different points: that the existence of many laws in a country points to the badness of the national character; or that an over-regulated society tends to encourage, rather than deter, law-breaking.

22 One suit of law breeds twenty.

23 Wrong laws make short governance.
Implies that those who make unjust laws will not enjoy their authority for long.

Its expense

24 Agree, for the law is costly.

25 A lean agreement is better than a fat judgment.

26 Law is a lickpenny.
A "lickpenny" is a person or thing that eats up money.

27 Lawsuits consume time, and money, and rest, and friends.

28 Win your lawsuit and lose your money.
Chinese proverb.

29 Go to law for a sheep and lose your cow.

30 A lawyer's opinion is worth nothing unless paid for.

31 Lawyers' gowns are lined with the wilfulness of their clients.

Keeping the law

32 Abundance of law breaks no law.
Implies that it is better to do more than is required by law than to break the law.

33 Law makers should not be law breakers.

34 We live by laws not by examples.

Lawyers

35 A good lawyer, an evil neighbour.

36 The better lawyer is the worse Christian.

37 A client twixt his attorney and counsellor is like a goose twixt two foxes.

38 A good lawyer must be a great liar.

39 Few lawyers die well, few physicians live well.

40 A lawyer never goes to law himself.

41 He that is his own lawyer has a fool for a client.

42 Hide nothing from thy minister, physician, and lawyer.

43 Kick an attorney downstairs and he'll stick to you for life.

44 Two attorneys can live in a town, when one cannot.
Implies that one attorney makes work for the other.

Judges

45 A good judge conceives quickly, judges slowly.

46 From a foolish judge, a quick sentence.

47 A judge knows nothing unless it has been explained to him three times.
Adapted from a saying (1961) of Hubert Lister Parker, a former Lord Chief Justice. It alludes (ironically) to the doctrine that a judge's summing up should take account only of admissible evidence presented in court.

Legal maxims

48 No wrong without a remedy.

49 The law does not concern itself about trifles.

50 Ignorance of the law excuses no man.
Most legal systems have refused to admit ignorance of the law as a defence because such a claim is almost impossible to confute. The observation that "Lawyers are the only persons in whom ignorance of the law is not punished" has been attributed to Jeremy Bentham (1748–1832).

51 No man is bound to criminate himself.
Under English law witnesses can refuse to answer a question if (in the judge's opinion) the answer might lead to criminal proceedings.

52 Every one is held to be innocent until he is proved guilty.
It is a well-known principle of English law that a defendant must be acquitted unless the prosecution proves its case "beyond reasonable doubt"; although the principle is long-established, this form of words is no older than the early 20th century.

53 Possession is nine points of the law.
Implies that actual control or possession of something is a strong presumption that one is the rightful owner of it. Although the saying is common, no such principle has ever been recognized in English law. The proverb refers to the medieval practice of settling questions of ownership according to a points system, in which full legal entitlement depended on satisfying ten (or sometimes twelve) points. It is now sometimes used in an ironic sense implying "the law favours the rich" or "might is right".

54 The act of God does wrong to none.
In English law an "act of God" is a sudden unavoidable catastrophe (such as a flood, earthquake, etc.) resulting from natural causes; the proverb means that no one can be held legally responsible for such occurrences.

55 Every dog is allowed one bite.
A reference to the leniency of the law with regard to a person's first offence.

56 Once a way and aye a way.
Implies that nobody has the authority to close or divert a public right of way.

57 The father to the bough, the son to the plough.
This refers to the law that allowed the offspring of a hanged criminal to inherit his lands.

Customs

58 With customs we live well, but laws undo us.

59 The command of custom is great.

60 Custom rules the law.

61 Custom has the force of law.

62 Custom is the plague of wise men, and the idol of fools.

63 Custom without reason is but ancient error.
Sometimes attributed to St Cyprian (3rd century AD).

64 A bad custom is like a good cake, better broken than kept.

65 So many countries, so many customs.

66 Every land has its own law.

See also CORRUPTION: *Corruption at law*; JUSTICE

105 Lending

Against lending

1 Better give a shilling than lend and lose half a crown.

2 Lend only that which you can afford to lose.

3 Lend never that thing thou needest most.

4 He who has but one coat cannot lend it.

5 Lend sitting and you will run to collect.

6 Neither a borrower nor a lender be.
A quotation from Polonius's speech of advice in Shakespeare's *Hamlet* (c. 1600); the speech continues "For loan oft loses both itself and friend."

7 The world still he keeps at his staff's end, that needs not to borrow and never will lend.

8 A horse, a wife, and a sword may be shewed, but not lent.
Some variants add "a faithful servant" to the list of things that should not be lent.

Its dangers

9   If you would make an enemy, lend a man money, and ask it of him again.

10 Lend your money and lose your friend.
See also note to proverb 6 above.

11 Lending nurses enmity.
Arabic proverb.

12 When I lent, I was a friend; and when I asked, I was unkind.

13 Lend, and lose the loan, or gain an enemy.

14 Give a loan and buy a quarrel.
Indian proverb.

15 Lend money to a bad debtor and he will hate you.
Chinese proverb.

16 He that lends, gives.

17 Lending is like throwing away; being paid is like finding something.
Chinese proverb.

18 The leeful man is the beggar's brother.
"Leeful" means "ready to lend".

19 Lend and lose; so play fools.

20 He that lends his pot may seethe his kail in his loof.
"Kail" is broth; "loof" means "palm of the hand".

21 Lend your horse for a long journey, you may have him return with his skin.

Usurers

22 God keep me from four houses, a usurer's, a tavern, a spital, and a prison.
A "spital" was a hospital for the sick and needy.

23 Usury is murder.
Hebrew proverb.

24 Usurers are always good husbands.

25 Usurers live by the fall of heirs, as swine by the dropping of acorns.

26 To speak of a usurer at the table mars the wine.

106 Liberty

Its value

1   Liberty is more worth than gold.

2   Liberty is a jewel.

3   Freedom is a fair thing.

4   Lean liberty is better than fat slavery.

5   A bean in liberty is better than a comfit in prison.
A "comfit" was a type of sweet.

6   Better hand loose than in an ill tethering.
Implies that the freedom of celibacy is preferable to a bad marriage.

7   An ox, when he is loose, licks himself at pleasure.
A further reference to the freedom of the single state.

8   No love is foul, nor prison fair.

Its effects

 9 Too much liberty spoils all.
10 Liberty is not licence.
   A warning of the possible abuse of liberty.

Losing one's liberty

11 Who loses his liberty loses all.
12 Who receives a gift, sells his liberty.
13 He that marries for wealth, sells his liberty.

107 Life

Its brevity

 1 Life is but a span.
   Adapted from Psalms 39:5.
 2 Life is half spent before we know what it is.
 3 Man's life is like a candle in the wind, or hoar-frost on the tiles.
   Chinese proverb.
 4 Art is long, life is short.
   Also familiar in its Latin form, *Ars longa, vita brevis*. The saying is attributed to Hippocrates
   (5th–4th centuries BC), the founder of the medical profession, and originally meant that
   life is too short to acquire skills or learning in any depth. However, it is now frequently
   used to imply that painting, sculpture, etc., last for longer than the brief span of human
   life.
 5 Life is short and time is swift.

Its unpleasant aspects

 6 Long life has long misery.
 7 Life is not all beer and skittles.
   First recorded in the mid-19th century: sometimes attributed to Thomas Hughes in his
   Tom Brown's Schooldays (1857) but there are earlier citations.
 8 Life would be too smooth, if it had no rubs in it.
   A "rub" is any roughness or inequality.

Attitudes to life

 9 Life is sweet.
10 The life of man is a winter's day and a winter's way.
11 Our whole life is but a greater and longer childhood.
12 Life begins at forty.
   This well-established catchphrase originated as the title of a book (1932) by the US author
   William B. Pitkin, in which he attempted to address the issues raised by longer
   life and greater leisure. It was further popularized by a song of the same title, recorded
   by Sophie Tucker in 1937.
13 Life means strife.
14 Life is a pilgrimage.
15 Life is a shadow.
16 Every day of thy life is a leaf in thy history.

17 Life is just a bowl of cherries.
   The title of a popular song (1931) by Lew Brown.

The value of long life

18 They who live longest, will see most.
19 The longer we live, the more farlies we see.
   "Farlies" means "wonders".

See also DEATH: *The manner of death*

108 Likelihood

Probability

1 A thousand probabilities do not make one truth.
2 Likely lies in the mire, and unlikely gets over.
   "Likely" here denotes a person thought to have good possibilities of success and "unlikely" the opposite. The wider implication is that the probable often gives way to the
   improbable.

Possibility

3 Possibilities are infinite.
4 All things are possible with God.
   Adapted from Matthew 19:26.
5 Whatever man has done, man may do.
6 Every may be has a may not be.
7 May-bee was ne'er a gude honey bee.
8 If ifs and ans were pots and pans, there'd be no trade for tinkers.
   Some variants have "… there'd be no work for tinkers' hands." Used as a riposte to any
   overconfident statement that is built on a conditional clause (i.e. one beginning "If…").
9 'If' and 'An' spoils many a good charter.
   Here, as in poverb 7 above, "an" is a dialect word meaning "if"; a "charter" here means
   a contract.
10 Like to die fills not the churchyard.

Improbability

11 Pigs might fly, if they had wings.
   A variant is "Pigs may fly, but they are very unlikely birds." The abbreviated form "And
   pigs might fly" is now commonly used to express scepticism about any predicted event.
12 If the sky falls we shall catch larks.
13 If my aunt had been a man, she'd have been my uncle.
   Used to ridicule those who raise absurd points of the "what if?" kind.
14 The age of miracles is past.
   A phrase now mainly used to express scepticism about a predicted or promised out-
   come. It originated in the widely held Protestant belief that miracles ceased with those
   recorded in the New Testament (contrary to the Catholic view that they continue to
   occur within the pale of the Church).

Impossibility

15 Nothing is impossible to a willing heart.

16 Nought's impossible, as t'auld woman said when they told her calf had swallowed grindlestone.

"Grindlestone" means "grindstone".

17 The difficult is done at once; the impossible takes a little longer.

Now the official motto of the US armed forces, the saying was formerly associated with the French politician Charles Alexandre de Calonne, who was charged with reforming France's desperate financial position in the 1780s; the failure of his measures led directly to the Revolution of 1789.

18 No one is bound to do impossibilities.

A general principle of English contract law.

19 No man can do two things at once.

20 No man can sup and blow together.

21 A man cannot be in two places at once.

22 No man can flay a stone.

23 It is hard to sail over the sea in an egg-shell.

There was formerly a widespread folk belief that witches did precisely this.

24 Solomon was a wise man, and Samson was a strong man, yet neither of them could pay money before they had it.

25 You can't get blood out of a stone.

Often applied to those who have no money with which to pay their debts.

26 You can't get a quart into a pint pot.

27 You can't make bricks without straw.

That is, you cannot make (or do) something without the essential materials. The allusion is to Pharaoh's oppression of the Hebrews in Exodus 5:6; in fact, Pharaoh did not demand that the Hebrews make bricks without straw but that they gather their own straw (previously supplied) while keeping to the existing production quotas.

28 Nothing comes of nothing.

A maxim of Greek philosophy that can be traced back to the 7th century BC. Variants appear in works by Chaucer, Marlowe, and Shakespeare.

109 Love

Its blindness

1 Love is blind.

Cupid, the Roman god of love, is represented as a blindfolded child. The phrase appears in a number of Shakespeare's plays.

2 If Jack's in love, he's no judge of Jill's beauty.

3 Love sees no faults.

4 In the eyes of the lover, pock-marks are dimples.

5 No love is foul, nor prison fair.

Its irrationality

6 Love is without reason.

7 Love is lawless.

The saying can be traced back through Chaucer to the Roman philosopher Boethius (6th century).

   8 Affection blinds reason.

   9 No folly to being in love.

  10 One cannot love and be wise.
> A more elaborate variant has "To love and be wise is scarce granted to God above."

  11 Lovers are madmen.

Its value

  12 To be beloved is above all bargains.

  13 A penny-weight of love is worth a pound of law.

  14 Love covers many infirmities.
> A secularized version of 1 Peter 14:8; see KINDNESS: 5.

  15 Where love fails, we espy all faults.

  16 Faults are thick where love is thin.

  17 Labour is light where love doth pay.

  18 Love makes one fit for any work.

  19 He that has love in his breast, has spurs in his sides.

  20 Love is free.

  21 In love is no lack.

  22 Love locks no cupboards.

  23 True love kythes in time of need.
> "Kythes" means "shows itself".

  24 All the world loves a lover.
> A near quotation from Emerson's essay "Love" (1840s), where "mankind" appears rather than "the world".

  25 Love is the touchstone of virtue.

  26 'Tis better to have loved and lost than never to have loved at all.
> A quotation from Tennyson's *In Memoriam* (1850), where the context is bereavement rather than romantic disappointment.

Its power

  27 Love conquers all.
> Also familiar in the Latin form *Amor vincit omnia*.

  28 Love rules his kingdom without a sword.

  29 Love makes the world go round.
> The title of a French popular song of the 1850s.

  30 Love makes all men equal.

  31 Love and business teach eloquence.

  32 Love makes a wit of the fool.

  33 Love makes all hard hearts gentle.

  34 Love laughs at locksmiths.
> The title of an operetta (1803) by George Colman the Younger; the same idea is expressed in Shakespeare's *Venus and Adonis* (1593).

  35 Love will find a way.

  36 Love will go through stone walls.

  37 Love cannot be compelled.
> Variants can be found in Chaucer, Spenser, and Shakespeare.

  38 A man has choice to begin love, but not to end it.

  39 Perfect love casteth out fear.
> A biblical quotation: 1 John 4:18.

40 Love is as strong as death.
    A biblical quotation: Song of Solomon 8:6. The verse continues "...; jealousy is as cruel as the grave".

41 Love and a cough cannot be hid.
    Variations substitute or add "light", "fire", "smoke", "gout", and "an itch" as things that can no more be concealed than love.

Its universality

42 He that does not love a woman, sucked a sow.

43 Love and leprosy few escape.
    Chinese proverb.

Its steadfastness

44 Old love will not be forgotten.

45 Old love does not rust.

46 Sound love is not soon forgotten.

47 True love never grows old.

48 Love will creep where it may not go.
    "Creep" here means "crawl"; "go" means "walk upright".

49 Love without end has no end.
    Implies that true selfless love will last forever, whereas false love, which has a particular aim ("end") in view, will fade as soon as its goal is attained.

Its ups and downs

50 The course of true love never did run smooth.
    A quotation from Shakespeare's *A Midsummer Night's Dream* (c. 1595).

51 Never rely on love or the weather.

52 Of honey and gall in love there is store.
    Some versions add "The honey is much, but the gall is more."

53 Love is sweet in the beginning but sour in the ending.

54 Love is a sweet torment.

55 War, hunting, and love are as full of trouble as pleasure.

Its disadvantages

56 Love is full of fear.

57 When love puts in, friendship is gone.

Its dangers

58 Love and pease-pottage are two dangerous things.
    The implication is that one attacks the heart and the other the stomach; "pease-pottage" is a dish of boiled peas notorious for causing flatulence. A variant states that "... both will make their way".

59 The love of the wicked is more dangerous than their hatred.

60 They love too much that die for love.

Its inadequacy

61 Fear is stronger than love.

62 Of soup and love, the first is the best.

63 'Sweet-heart' and 'Honey-bird' keeps no house.
That is, loving endearments will not provide for and manage a household.

Its silence

64 Love speaks, even when the lips are closed.
65 When love is greatest, words are fewest.
66 Whom we love best, to them we can say least.
67 Next to love, quietness.

Its sources

68 Congruity is the mother of love.
69 Likeness causes liking.
70 Looks breed love.
"Looks" here means "glances" rather than "appearance".
71 Love begets love.
72 Love is the loadstone of love.
That is, love is attracted to love.
73 Love is the true reward of love.
74 Love needs no teaching.
75 Love is not found in the market.
76 Love is the fruit of idleness.

Its remedies

77 Cold pudding will settle your love.
Implies that love, like pudding, cools and becomes less appetising after a short time.
Compare proverb 90 below.
78 Time, not the mind, puts an end to love.
79 In love's wars, he who flies is conqueror.
Implies that the only remedy for love is to run away.
80 No herb will cure love.
The saying can be traced back to Ovid's *Metamorphoses* (late 1st century BC).

Its rules and conditions

81 All is fair in love and war.
Sometimes attributed to Nathan Bedford Forrest (1821–77), a Confederate general in the
US Civil War (and subsequently first leader of the Ku Klux Klan); a brilliant commander,
he was noted for his brutal and unscrupulous tactics. However, there are several citations
from earlier in the 19th century and the sentiment is older still.
82 Love is a game in which both players always cheat.
83 Love me, love my dog.
Implies that in loving a person one must also love those who are close to him or her. The
earliest recorded use is in a sermon by St Bernard of Clairvaux (12th century).

Its tactics

84 Love delights in praise.
85 Scorn at first makes after-love the more.
A quotation from Shakespeare's *The Two Gentlemen of Verona* (c. 1592).
86 He that would the daughter win, must with the mother first begin.

87 Follow love and it will flee thee: flee love and it will follow thee.
"Glory" or "pleasure" is sometimes substituted for "love".

88 The last suitor wins the maid.

89 He that woos a maid, must seldom come in her sight; but he that woos a widow must woo her day and night.

90 Puddings and paramours should be hotly handled.
Implies that neither puddings nor love should be allowed to grow cold. Compare proverb 77 above.

Courtship

91 To woo is a pleasure in a young man, a fault in an old.

92 A man may woo where he will, but he will wed where his hap is.
"Hap" here means "fate, destiny".

93 Happy is the wooing that is not long a-doing.

94 Sunday's wooing draws to ruin.

95 When petticoats woo, breeks may come speed.
That is, when women ("petticoats") do the courting it is well for the men ("breeks" or britches).

Lover's quarrels

96 Lovers' quarrels are soon mended.

97 The quarrel of lovers is the renewal of love.
A near quotation from Terence's comedy *Andria* (2nd century BC).

98 Jove laughs at lovers' perjuries.
A quotation from Ovid's *Ars amatoria* (1st century BC); variants appear in works by Shakespeare, Dryden, and others.

99 Biting and scratching is Scots folk's wooing.

Young love

100 Calf love, half love; old love, cold love.

101 Love of lads and fire of chats is soon in and soon out.
"Chats" are wood-chips.

102 Lad's love's a busk of broom, hot awhile and soon done.
"Busk" is a dialect word for "bush"; broom burns quickly and is then consumed.

103 No love like the first love.

New love

104 The new love drives out the old love.

105 One love expels another.

106 It is best to be off with the old love before you are on with the new.

107 As good love comes as goes.

108 Many a heart is caught in the rebound.
First recorded in the late 19th century.

Unrequited love

109 Love without return is like a question without an answer.

110 There is more pleasure in loving than in being beloved.

Parental love

111 It is a dear collop that is cut out of thine own flesh.
   A "collop" is a slice or morsel, here referring to one's offspring.

112 A mother's love never ages.

113 A mother's love is best of all.

114 No love to a father's.

115 Love the babe for her that bare it.
   Like proverbs 116 and 117 below, this implies that if a man loves a woman he must also love her children.

116 If you love the boll, you cannot hate the branches.
   "Boll" means "bole, trunk".

117 He that loves the tree, loves the branch.

Love and faith

118 Love asks faith, and faith asks firmness.
   "Asks" here means "requires".

119 Where love is, there is faith.

120 Where there is no trust there is no love.

Love and jealousy

121 Love being jealous, makes a good eye look asquint.

122 Love is never without jealousy.

123 Love and lordship like no fellowship.
   This may be interpreted in two ways: that neither love nor lordship will tolerate a rival; or that love and lordship (i.e. authority or majesty) are not compatible. When used in this second sense, the saying adapts a line in Ovid's *Metamorphoses* (late 1st century BC); writers to use the proverb in the first sense include Chaucer and Spenser.

Love and money

124 Love does much, money does everything.

125 Love lasts as long as money endures.

126 Money is the sinews of love as well as of war.
   The saying "Money is the sinews of war" derives from the *Philippics* of Cicero (44 BC).

127 When poverty comes in at the door, love flies out of the window.

128 Love lives in cottages as well as in courts.

See also ABSENCE: *Its effect on love*; HATRED: *Its relationship to love*; MARRIAGE: *Marriage and love*

110 Loyalty

Its value

1 Loyalty is worth more than money.

2 Faithfulness is a sister of love.

3 The subject's love is the king's lifeguard.
   Sometimes attributed to Cicero (1st century BC).

Loyalty between companions

4 There is honour among thieves.
In this form, the earliest known citation is from Jeremy Bentham (early 19th century); however the thought is much older.

5 One thief will not rob another.
Compare CRIME: 37.

6 Dog does not eat dog.
The sense of this proverb is now more often reversed in variants of the phrase "dog eat dog", used to indicate a state of ruthless competition.

7 Hawks will not pick out hawks' eyes.

8 One mule scrubs another.
"Scrub" here means "scratch" or "rub".

9 One barber shaves another gratis.

10 Tarry breeks pays no fraught.
"Tarry breeks" refers to seamen; "fraught" means "freight" (i.e. charges for transporting cargo).

Divided loyalties

11 No man can serve two masters.
A biblical quotation: Matthew 6:24.

12 You cannot run with the hare and hunt with the hounds.

13 If you can't ride two horses at once, you shouldn't be in the circus.
A contradiction of proverb 12 above. The saying was coined by the British socialist MP James Maxton, when arguing against a proposed rule change disallowing dual membership of the Independent Labour Party and the Labour Party (c. 1935).

Disloyalty

14 Rats desert a sinking ship.
The earliest recorded use of this idea occurs in Shakespeare's *The Tempest* (1611); however, the notion that rats and mice forsake a house that is close to collapse is older.

15 No tie can oblige the perfidious.

111 Luck

Its unpredictability

1 God sends good luck and God sends bad.

2 A blind man may sometimes hit the mark.

3 It chances in an hour, that happens not in seven years.

4 Fortune is blind.
The goddess Fortune was conventionally depicted as a blindfolded woman turning a large wheel.

5 Fortune is fickle.

6 Fortune to one is mother, to another is stepmother.

7 You never know your luck.

Its uncertainty

8 The footsteps of fortune are slippery.

9 The highest spoke in fortune's wheel, may soon turn lowest.

10 Fortune is weary to carry one and the same man always.

11 Fortune is made of glass.
Implies that fortune is shiny and attractive but brittle.

12 When a fool finds a horseshoe, he thinks aye the like to do.
Implies that it is foolish to rely on perpetual good fortune after just one lucky occurrence. The horseshoe is an emblem of good luck.

13 He that quits certainty and leans to chance, when fools pipe he may dance.

Its value

14 It is better to be born lucky than rich.

15 Good luck reaches further than long arms.

16 An ounce of luck is worth a pound of wisdom.

17 Better be born lucky than wise.

18 Hap and halfpenny goods enough.
"Hap" means "luck". The implication is that as long as one has luck, great wealth is unnecessary.

Its drawbacks

19 Great fortune brings with it great misfortune.

20 When the wagon of fortune goes well, spite and envy hang on to the wheels.
Chinese proverb.

21 Every flow has its ebb.

Ill luck

22 If anything can go wrong, it will.
This modern proverb is known as Murphy's Law. Both the proverb and the name have been attributed to George Nichols, a leading engineer at the US aircraft firm of Northrop in the 1940s; he is said to have based the idea on a remark by a colleague named Murphy, who was involved in conducting safety trials for the company. Alternatively, the name has been linked to a poster campaign by the US navy (mid-20th century), featuring a blundering character named Murphy who continually made mistakes. Murphy's Law is also known as Sod's Law or Spode's Law.

23 The bread never falls but on its buttered side.
Perhaps the most frequently cited example of Murphy's Law (see proverb 22 above); however, it predates the formulation of that law, dating from the mid-19th century.

24 There's no fence against ill fortune.

25 Bad luck often brings good luck.

26 The worse luck now, the better another time.

The power of fortune

27 Fortune is the mistress of the field.

28 Fortune, not prudence, rules the life of men.

29 No man can make his own hap.
"Hap" means "luck".

30 Fortune can take from us nothing but what she gave us.

The lucky

31 Lucky men need no counsel.

32 He dances well to whom fortune pipes.

33 A cat has nine lives.
A reference to the cat's apparent ability to escape death, either through agility or sheer good luck.

34 Fortune favours those who use their judgment.

35 Fortune favours fools.

36 A little wit will serve a fortunate man.
That is, a lucky man will not be handicapped by a lack of intelligence.

37 The more knave, the better luck.

38 The more wicked, the more lucky.

39 Thieves and rogues have the best luck, if they do but scape hanging.

40 Fortune knocks once at least at every man's gate.

41 Every dog has his day.

42 Some have the hap, some stick in the gap.
"Hap" here means "good luck".

43 The devil looks after his own.
Like proverb 44 below, this is quoted when other people have a stroke of good fortune.

44 The devil's children have the devil's luck.

See also SUPERSTITIONS

112 Lust

Its causes

1 When the belly is full, the mind is among the maids.

2 Without Ceres and Bacchus, Venus grows cold.
A quotation from the Roman playwright Terence (2nd century BC). Ceres is the goddess of agriculture, Bacchus the god of wine, and Venus the goddess of love; the implication is that without food and wine a man loses his desire to make love.

3 If it wasn't for meat and good drink, the women might gnaw the sheets.
The implication here is the same as that of proverb 2 above.

4 Wine and youth increase love.

5 Beauty's sister is vanity, and its daughter lust.

6 The postern door makes thief and whore.
Implies that the back door of a house provides the necessary concealment for dishonest servants and unfaithful wives.

Its effects

7 When the heart is full of lust, the mouth's full of leasings.
A reference to the lies told by a lustful person in order to win over the object of his or her desires.

8 Lechery and covetousness go together.

9 A lewd bachelor makes a jealous husband.

10 Grass grows not upon the highway.
A reference to the supposed barrenness of prostitutes.

Its dangers

11 A libertine life is not a life of liberty.

12 Of the myriad vices lust is the worst.
Chinese proverb.

13 Hunting, hawking, and paramours, for one joy a hundred displeasures.

14 Dicing, drabbing and drinking bring men to destruction.
A "drab" is a prostitute.

15 Gaming, women, and wine, while they laugh, they make men pine.

16 Play, women, and wine undo men laughing.
"Play" here means "gambling".

17 Thieves and whores meet at the gallows.

Its expense

18 Three things cost dear: the caresses of a dog, the love of a whore, and the invitation of a host.
"Host" here means the keeper of a tavern.

19 Whores affect not you but your money.
"Affect" here means "love".

20 Wine and wenches empty men's purses.

21 Whoring and bawdry do often end in beggary.

22 Women and wine, game and deceit, make the wealth small, and the wants great.

23 What is got over the devil's back is spent under his belly.
Implies that ill-gotten gains are often squandered in dissolute living.

Its universality

24 A man is known to be mortal by two things, sleep and lust.

25 Who has neither fools nor beggars nor whores among his kindred, was born of a stroke of thunder.
Like proverb 26 below, this is a riposte to someone who attempts to blacken your name by alluding to family scandals.

26 It is a poor kin that has neither whore nor thief in it.

Whores

27 Once a whore and ever a whore.

28 A whore repents as often as water turns to sour milk.
Arabic proverb.

29 Never was strumpet fair.

30 A whore in a fine dress is like a clean entry to a dirty house.

31 Whoredom and grace dwelt ne'er in one place.

32 Whores and rogues always speak of their honour.

113 Marriage

Its advantages

1 He that is needy when he is married, shall be rich when he is buried.
   Implies that those who know straitened circumstances early in their adult life will learn prudence and thereby become wealthy.

2 Age and wedlock tames man and beast.
   Some variants have "...brings a man to his nightcap"; others substitute "winter" for "age".

3 Single long, shame at length.

4 He who marries might be sorry; he who does not will be sorry.

5 The married man has many cares, the unmarried one many more.

6 A man without a wife is but half a man.

7 A good wife and health is a man's best wealth.

8 A cheerful wife is the joy of life.

9 A good wife's a goodly prize, saith Solomon the wise.
   The allusion is probably to the description of the perfect wife in Proverbs 31:10–31; authorship of this Old Testament book was formerly ascribed to King Solomon.

10 Two things do prolong thy life: a quiet heart and a loving wife.

11 As your wedding ring wears, your cares will wear away.

Its disadvantages

12 Wedlock is a padlock.

13 A married man turns his staff into a stake.
   Implies that the walking stick carried (symbolically) by the roving bachelor becomes, on marriage, a stake to which he is tethered.

14 A married woman has nothing of her own but her wedding-ring and her hair-lace.
   Until 1870 married women in England and Wales had no legal rights over their own property.

15 Maids want nothing but husbands, and when they have them they want everything.

16 Wife and children are bills of charges.

17 Mills and wives are ever wanting.

18 It is hard to wive and thrive both in a year.

19 A young man married is a man that's marr'd.
   A quotation from Shakespeare's *All's Well that Ends Well* (1602).

20 He that has a wife, has strife.

21 Matrimony is a school in which one learns too late.

Its undesirability

22 Advise none to marry or go to war.

23 Better hand loose than in an ill tethering.
Implies that the freedom of celibacy is preferable to a bad marriage.

24 An ox, when he is loose, licks himself at pleasure.
A further reference to the freedom of the single state.

25 Why buy a cow when milk is so cheap?

26 Honest men marry soon, wise men not at all.

27 Next to no wife, a good wife is best.

28 An ill marriage is a spring of ill fortune.

29 Better be half hanged, than ill wed.

30 Needles and pins, needles and pins: when a man marries his trouble begins.

31 Many a man sings that wife home brings; wist he what he brought, weep he might.
"Wist" means "knew".

32 We bachelors laugh and show our teeth, but you married men laugh till your hearts ache.

Its risks

33 Marriage is a lottery.

34 Marriage makes or mars a man.

35 Marriage halves our griefs, doubles our joys, and quadruples our expenses.

Its inevitability

36 Marriages are made in heaven.
Some variants add "...but consummated on earth".

37 Marriage is destiny.

38 Hanging and wiving go by destiny.

39 A man may woo where he will, but he will wed where his hap is.
"Hap" here has the sense of "fate, destiny".

40 Wives must be had, be they good or bad.

The need for caution

41 Marry in haste, and repent at leisure.
Modern corruptions of this proverb include "Marry in haste, and repent in the suburbs" and "Marry in haste, and repent at Reno" (the US city of Reno was formerly notorious for the ease with which divorces could be obtained there).

42 Marriage rides upon the saddle and repentance upon the crupper.
The "crupper" is the rump of a horse.

43 In wiving and thriving a man should take counsel of all the world.
That is, you cannot take too much advice in matters of marriage or commerce.

44 Keep your eyes wide open before marriage, and half shut afterwards.

The importance of material well-being

45 First thrive and then wive.

46 Before you marry, be sure of a house wherein to tarry.

47 More belongs to marriage than four bare legs in a bed.

48 Bare walls make giddy housewives.

49 A house well-furnished makes a woman wise.

50 Toom pokes will strive.
"Toom" means "empty"; a "poke" is a bag or sack. The implication is that lack of food and money causes quarrels in a household.

51 Haste makes waste, and waste makes want, and want makes strife between the goodman and his wife.

The dowry

52 Better a portion in a wife than with a wife.
"Portion" means "dowry".

53 A great dowry is a bed full of brambles.

54 He that marries for wealth, sells his liberty.

55 Never marry for money, ye'll borrow it cheaper.
A variant has "Never marry for money, but marry where money is."

56 Marry not an old crony, or a fool, for money.

57 Many a one for land takes a fool by the hand.

58 Money makes marriage.

59 A tocherless dame sits long at home.
"Tocherless" means "without a dowry".

60 A poor beauty finds more lovers than husbands.

61 A poor man gets a poor marriage.

Choosing a partner

62 The good or ill hap of a good or ill life, is the good or ill choice of a good or ill wife.

63 In choosing a wife, and buying a sword, we ought not to trust another.

64 Refuse a wife with one fault, and take one with two.
The advice here is not to be too particular when choosing a wife.

65 A maid marries to please her parents; a widow to please herself.

66 He has fault of a wife, that marries mam's pet.
That is, a spoiled daughter will prove a bad wife.

67 Take a vine of a good soil, and the daughter of a good mother.

68 It is good grafting on a good stock.

69 It is better to marry a shrew than a sheep.
Implies that a bad-tempered wife is preferable to a spiritless one.

70 One sheaf of a stook is enough.
The advice here is against marrying twice into the same family.

71 Better be an old man's darling than a young man's slave.

72 A young maid married to an old man is like a new house thatched with old straw.

73 Old men, when they marry young women, make much of death.
Implies that when an old man embraces his young wife he embraces death, for she will bring him to an early grave.

74 An old man who weds a buxom young maiden, bids fair to become a freeman of Buckingham.
"Freeman of Buckingham" is here a jocular expression meaning "cuckold" (probably by
the association of "buck" with "horns").

75 Better wed over the mixen than over the moor.
Implies that it is better to marry someone from one's own neighbourhood. The "mixen"
or "midden" was a compost heap in the back yard.

76 Like blood, like good, and like age, make the happiest marriage.
"Good" here means "wealth".

77 Marry your like.
The saying can be traced back to Ovid's *Heroides* (1st century BC).

78 Better one house spoiled than two.
Implies that two ill-tempered people should marry each other, so that only one household is marred by their presence. It was the novelist Samuel Butler who remarked (1884)
of Thomas Carlyle and his wife Jane, that it was very good of God to let them marry "and
so make only two people miserable instead of four."

79 Go down the ladder when you marry a wife; go up when you choose a friend.
That is, choose friends from those above you in rank but marry below you.

80 A wife is sought for her virtue, a concubine for her beauty.
Chinese proverb.

81 Choose not a wife by the eye only.

82 Choose a wife by your ear rather than by your eye.
That is, avoid marrying a scold however beautiful.

83 Choose a wife on a Saturday rather than a Sunday.
Implies that on a Sunday women are dressed in their best clothes and are therefore not
seen in their true light.

84 An ugly wife and a lean piece of ground protect the house.
Chinese proverb.

85 A fair wife and a frontier castle breed quarrels.

86 Who has a fair wife needs more than two eyes.

87 He that has a white horse and a fair wife, never wants trouble.

The ideal time

88 He that marries ere he be wise, will die ere he thrive.

89 A young man should not marry yet, an old man not at all.
Sometimes attributed to the Cynic philosopher Diogenes (4th century BC).

90 Early wed, early dead.
Variants include "Early bridals make early burials."

91 It is good to marry late or never.

92 He that marries late, marries ill.

93 It is time to set in, when the oven comes to the dough.
Both this and proverb 94 below imply that the right time to marry is when the woman
courts the man.

94 It is time to yoke, when the cart comes to the caples.
"Caples" means "horses".

95 He is a fool that marries his wife at Yule, for when the corn's to shear the
bairn's to bear.
Implies that the first child of such a union will be born at harvest time, the busiest season of the year.

The husband's importance

96 A good husband makes a good wife.
    A variant substitutes "bad" for "good" in each case. See also proverb 100 below.

97 When the goodman is from home, the good wife's table is soon spread.
    Implies that money for food will be short when the husband is away.

98 He is an ill husband who is not missed.

99 If the husband be not at home, there is nobody.

The wife's importance

100 A good wife makes a good husband.
     See also proverb 96 above.

101 He that will thrive must ask leave of his wife.
     A reference to the wife's responsibility for the household finances.

102 The wife is the key of the house.

103 The grey mare is the better horse.
     Said in cases where the wife ("grey mare") is thought to rule the husband.

104 The foot on the cradle and hand on the distaff is the sign of a good house-
     wife.

The dominant wife

105 He that has a wife has a master.

106 The most master wears no breech.
     Implies that the wife is the dominant member of a household.

107 Where the mistress is the master, the parsley grows the faster.
     This curious saying probably implies that families grow more rapidly when the wife is the
     dominant partner. A number of folk remedies and superstitions associate parsley with the
     female reproductive role; note also the former saying that newborn babies are "found
     under a parsley bush".

108 An obedient wife commands her husband.

109 It is a sorry flock where the ewe bears the bell.
     Implies that it is a sorry household where the wife is in command (the sheep chosen to
     lead a herd is often given a bell).

110 As the goodman says, so say we; but as the good wife says, so must it be.

The scolding wife

111 Scolds and infants never lin bawling.
     "Lin" means "cease".

112 A groaning horse and a groaning wife never fail their master.
     Like proverb 113 below, this implies that a scolding wife is a good housewife.

113 If a hen does not prate, she will not lay.
     Hens cackle when they are laying.

114 A deaf husband and a blind wife are always a happy couple.

115 Husbands are in heaven whose wives scold not.

116 Wae's the wife that wants the tongue, but weel's the man that gets her.
     "Wae's" means "woe is"; "weel's" means "well is".

117 It is a good horse that never stumbles, and a good wife that never grumbles.

118 It is a sad house where the hen crows louder than the cock.

119 Three things drive a man out of his house – smoke, rain, and a scolding wife.
   The earliest known citation is in a work by Pope Innocent III (1160–1216); the saying is based loosely on Proverbs 19:13 and 27:15.

120 Who has a scold, has sorrow to his sops.

Handling one's wife

121 You may ding the devil into a wife, but you'll never ding him out of her.
   "Ding" means "beat".

122 If you make your wife an ass, she will make you an ox.
   That is, if you treat your wife badly she will make a fool of you.

123 He that lets his horse drink at every lake, and his wife go to every wake, shall never be without a whore and a jade.

124 He that tells his wife news, is but newly married.
   Implies that it is unwise to confide in one's wife.

125 If you sell your purse to your wife, give your breeks into the bargain.
   The warning here is that a wife who has control over her husband's money has total control in the household. "Breeks" are trousers.

Losing one's wife

126 He that loses his wife and sixpence, has lost a tester.
   "Tester" is a former slang word for a sixpenny piece.

127 'Tis a sweet sorrow to bury an outrageous wife.

128 A dead wife's the best goods in a man's house.

The in-laws

129 Happy is she who marries the son of a dead mother.

130 She is well married, who has neither mother-in-law nor sister-in-law by her husband.

131 Mother-in-law and daughter-in-law are a tempest and hail storm.

132 The mother-in-law remembers not that she was a daughter-in-law.

Marriage and love

133 Marriage is the tomb of love.

134 Love is a fair garden and marriage a field of nettles.

135 It is unlucky to marry for love.

136 Who marries for love without money, has good nights and sorry days.

137 Love is a flower which turns into fruit at marriage.

138 Marry first, and love will follow.

139 Where there's marriage without love, there will be love without marriage.

Superstitions concerning marriage

140 A growing moon and a flowing tide are lucky times to marry in.
   According to a widespread body of superstitions, a waxing moon and an incoming tide were the most propitious times for any important enterprise.

141 Marry in Lent, and you'll live to repent.

142 Marry in May, rue for aye.
   The belief that May is an unlucky month for weddings can be traced back to Roman times and is mentioned by Ovid in his *Fasti* (1st century BC). The superstition may have arisen from the major festivals of virginity and the dead held in that month. By contrast,

June was considered the most propitious month for weddings – perhaps because of its association with Juno, the protectress of women and marriage. The tradition of the "June bride" continues to this day in Western countries.

143 They that marry in green, their sorrow is soon seen.

The colour green was associated with sexual jealousy (the "green-eyed monster"). More generally, it was considered an unlucky colour because of its association with the "little folk" or fairies.

144 Happy is the bride the sun shines on, and the corpse the rain rains on.

145 Change your name but not the letter, change for worse, and not for better.

Implies that it is unlucky for the initial letter of one's married name to be the same as that of one's maiden name.

146 If you carry a nutmeg in your pocket, you'll be married to an old man.

147 Two bachelors drinking to you at once; you'll soon be married.

148 One wedding brings another.

Remarriage

149 The first wife is matrimony, the second company, the third heresy.

150 Frequent remarriage gives room for scandal.

151 The woman who marries many is disliked by many.

Marrying widows

152 He that marries a widow and two children marries three thieves.

Implies that a widow will appropriate her husband's property to provide for her fatherless children. Some variants conclude the proverb "…has three back doors to his house."

153 He that marries a widow, will often have a dead man's head thrown in his dish.

Like proverb 154 below, this refers to the unfavourable comparisons a widow may make between her old and new husbands.

154 Never marry a widow unless her first husband was hanged.

155 Marry a widow before she leaves mourning.

156 Take heed of a person marked and a widow thrice married.

Fear and suspicion of those with birthmarks was once widespread.

Marrying off one's children

157 Building and marrying of children are great wasters.

A reference to the expense of wedding festivities.

158 Marry your daughter and eat fresh fish betimes.

Implies that the marriage of one's daughter, like the eating of fresh fish, should be carried out as soon as possible.

159 Marry your daughters betimes, lest they marry themselves.

160 Marry your son when you will, your daughter when you can.

114 Mind

Its importance

1 The mind is the man.

The thought can be traced back to Cicero (1st century BC).

2 What is a man but his mind?

3 A man is well or woe as he thinks himself so.

4 There is nothing either good or bad but thinking makes it so.
A quotation from Shakespeare's *Hamlet* (c. 1600).

5 A mind enlightened is like heaven; a mind in darkness is like hell.
Chinese proverb.

6 It is the riches of the mind only that make a man rich and happy.

7 If the brain sows not corn, it plants thistles.

Changing one's mind

8 A man will never change his mind if he has no mind to change.

9 A wise man changes his mind, a fool never.

10 A woman's mind and winter wind change oft.

Freedom of thought

11 Thought is free.

12 One may think that dares not speak.

13 The rope has never been made that binds thoughts.

Misunderstanding

14 Misunderstanding brings lies to town.

15 Who understands ill, answers ill.

16 Who wrong hears, wrong answer gives.

17 Ill hearing makes ill rehearsing.
"Rehearsing" here means "repeating".

The power of reason

18 Reason rules all things.

19 Reason binds the man.
A variant adds "…but the devil could never bind the wife."

20 Reason governs the wise man and cudgels the fool.

21 Hearken to reason, or she will be heard.

22 A man without reason is a beast in season.

See also EYES: *The eye and the mind*

115 Miserliness

Its effects

1 Avarice hoards itself poor; charity gives itself rich.

2 Little good comes of gathering.

3 If a man is a miser, he will certainly have a prodigal son.

4 Narrow gathered, widely spent.
Implies that wealth accumulated by penny-pinching often ends up being squandered.

5 He that measures oil shall anoint his fingers.
Implies that miserliness will become evident and taint a person's reputation.

6 Sow thin and mow thin.

7 Nothing enters into a close hand.

8 Covetous men's chests are rich, not they.
9 Gold does not belong to the miser, but the miser to gold.
   Arabic proverb.
10 Don't spoil the ship for a ha'porth of tar.
   The warning here is that refusing to make a small expense may result in a great loss. The proverb originally referred to sheep (pronounced "ship" in certain parts of the country) and the use of tar to treat their wounds.
11 Many tine half-mark whinger for the halfpenny thong.
   "Tine" means "lose"; a "half-mark whinger" is a dagger worth half a mark (i.e. about seven shillings).

Characteristics of the miserly

12 Poverty wants many things, and avarice all.
13 A poor man wants some things, a covetous man all things.
14 Fools live poor to die rich.
15 Covetous men live drudges, to die wretches.
16 He that hoards up money, takes pains for other men.
17 A rich miser is poorer than a poor man.
   Arabic proverb.
18 The covetous man is good to none and worst to himself.
19 The ass loaded with gold still eats thistles.
   A reference to the refusal of the miser to spend money on personal luxuries.
20 The brother had rather see the sister rich than make her so.
21 The devil's mouth is a miser's purse.

Avarice and age

22 Avarice is the only passion that never ages.
23 When all sins grow old, covetousness is young.
24 The older the bird the more unwillingly it parts with its feathers.

See also THRIFT

116 Moderation

Its value

1 Moderation in all things.
   The saying can be traced back to Hesiod (8th century BC).
2 Measure is treasure.
   The saying probably derives from the "golden mean" recommended by Horace (*Odes*, 1st century BC).
3 Measure is medicine.
4 The half is better than the whole.
5 Measure is a merry mean.
6 The mean is the best.
7 Virtue is found in the middle.
8 Safety lies in the middle course.
9 It is good to be neither too high nor too low.
   Chinese proverb.

10 Reason lies between the spur and the bridle.
11 Too much spoils, too little does not satisfy.
12 Soft fire makes sweet malt.
   Malt (for brewing or distilling) is prepared by allowing barley or other grain to germinate and then drying it over a gentle heat.
13 Love me little, love me long.
   Implies that a calm and durable affection is better than a sudden passion.

Against excess

14 Better go away longing than loathing.
15 Leave off with an appetite.
16 Make not your sail too big for the ballast.
   A sailing vessel that does so is in danger of overturning. The warning is against over-enthusiasm.
17 Sow with the hand, and not with the whole sack.
   The saying can be traced back to Plutarch (1st–2nd centuries AD).
18 Take no more on than you're able to bear.
19 Do not all you can; spend not all you have; believe not all you hear; and tell not all you know.
20 Never take a stone to break an egg, when you can do it with the back of your knife.
21 Never draw your dirk when a dunt will do.
   A "dirk" is a dagger; "dunt" means "blow".
22 Take not a musket to kill a butterfly.
23 Burn not your house to fright the mouse away.
24 There is measure in all things.
   The saying can be traced back to Horace's *Satires* (1st century BC).
25 You can have too much of a good thing.
   A saying denounced by G. K. Chesterton (1906) as "a blasphemous belief, which at one blow wrecks all the heavens that men have hoped for."

The dangers of excess

26 Too much of ought is good for nought.
27 Too much pudding will choke a dog.
28 Too much honey cloys the stomach.
29 If in excess even nectar is poison.
30 Mirth without measure is madness.
31 A little wind kindles, much puts out the fire.
32 He that forsakes measure, measure forsakes him.
33 He that measures not himself is measured.
   That is, judged.

Extremes

34 Every extremity is a fault.
35 Extreme law is extreme wrong.
   Implies that to apply a law to the letter, without taking any extenuating circumstances into account, is a form of injustice.
36 No extreme will hold long.

37 Extremes meet.

Like proverb 38 below, this implies that any virtue, belief, emotion, etc., indulged in to excess may approach the opposite extreme. Thus a person may verge on extreme arrogance by being excessively humble. The earliest known citation is by Pascal (1662).

38 Too far east is west.

39 From the sublime to the ridiculous is only a step.

Adapted from a passage in Paine's *The Age of Reason* (1795). The saying is frequently attributed to Napoleon, who used it when describing his disastrous retreat from Moscow (1812) to the diplomat D. G. De Pradt.

40 Extremes are dangerous.

See also CONTENTMENT: *Having enough*

117 Months

January

1 Who in Janiveer sows oats, gets gold and groats; who sows in May, gets little that way.

"Janiveer" is January; a "groat" was a coin worth four pennies.

2 If grass look green in Janiveer, 'twill look the worser all the year.

It was a widespread belief among farmers that a mild January presaged a late spring and poor summer.

3 If one knew how good it were to eat a hen in Janivere; had he twenty in the flock, he'd leave but one to go with the cock.

This refers to the former lack of fresh meat in January.

4 At Twelfth Day the days are lengthened a cock-stride.

Twelfth Day is January 6th.

5 On St Distaff's Day neither work nor play.

St Distaff's Day (January 7th) was so called because it was the day on which household tasks were resumed after the Christmas festivities.

6 Yule is come and Yule is gone, and we have feasted well; so Jack must to his flail again, and Jenny to her wheel.

February

7 Februeer doth cut and shear.

8 On Candlemas Day, you must have half your straw and half your hay.

That is, you should make sure that half your winter supply of animal fodder is still remaining on Candlemas Day (February 2nd).

9 On Candlemas Day, throw candle and candlestick away.

A reference to the lengthening days at this time of year. There may also be a reference to the Anglican Church's former custom of not using candles at vespers and litanies between Candlemas Day and All Saints' Day (November 1st).

10 Sow or set beans in Candlemas waddle.

"Waddle" here means the waning of the moon. See also COUNTRY LORE: 17.

11 On St Valentine, all the birds of the air in couples do join.

St Valentine's Day is February 14th. This folk belief is referred to by both Chaucer and Shakespeare.

12 St Valentine, set thy hopper by mine.
   Implies that this is a good time to begin sowing (a "hopper" is a seed-basket).
13 On St Valentine's Day cast beans in clay, but on St Chad sow good or bad.
   St Chad's Day is March 2nd. "Good or bad" refers to the weather.
14 On Valentine's Day, will a good goose lay; if she be a good goose, her dame
   well to pay, she will lay two eggs before Valentine's Day.
15 St Matthee shut up the bee.
   A reference to St Matthias's Day (February 24th).
16 St Matthi lay candlesticks by.
   See proverb 9 above and note.
17 St Matthie sends sap into the tree.
18 St Mattho, take thy hopper, and sow.

March

19 March borrowed from April three days, and they were ill.
   A reference to unseasonal weather at the end of March; the last three days of the month
   were often known as the "borrowing" or "borrowed" days. In Scotland February was
   similarly said to borrow three days from January.
20 March comes in like a lion and goes out like a lamb.
21 March comes in with adder heads and goes out with peacock tails.
   In Britain, March is generally the month in which adders emerge from hibernation and
   peacocks begin to display their tails.
22 In March, kill crow, pie, and cadow, rook, buzzard, and raven; or else go desire them to seek a new haven.
   "Pie" means "magpie"; "cadow" means "jackdaw". These birds, which were all generally regarded as nuisances or birds of ill-omen, begin to pair and build their nests in
   March.
23 In March, the birds begin to search; in April the corn begins to fill; in May,
   the birds begin to lay.
   "Search" here means "pair".
24 If you kill one flea in March, you kill a hundred.
25 On the first of March, the crows begin to search.
   See the note to proverb 23 above.
26 St David's Day, put oats and barley in the clay.
   St David's Day is March 1st.
27 David and Chad: sow peas good or bad.
   St Chad's Day is March 2nd. Here (as in proverb 28 below) "good or bad" refers to the
   weather.
28 Before St Chad every goose lays, both good and bad.
29 First comes David, next comes Chad, and then comes Winneral as though he
   were mad.
   "Winneral" refers to St Winwaloe's Day (March 3rd); "mad" refers to the windy weather
   common at this time of year.
30 St Benedick, sow thy pease, or keep them in thy rick.
   St Benedict's Day is March 21st.
31 Salmon and sermon have their season in Lent.
   Because eating meat was forbidden during this season of abstinence.
32 Marry in Lent, and you'll live to repent.

33 On Mothering Sunday, above all other, every child should dine with its mother.

34 At Easter, let your clothes be new, or else be sure you will it rue.
It was once a widespread custom for people to don their new clothes for the spring on Easter Sunday.

35 When Easter Day lies in Our Lady's lap, then, O England, beware of a clap.
"Lady" refers to the Feast of the Annunciation, or Lady Day (March 25th); while "clap" here means "blow, misfortune".

April

36 On the first of April, you may send a fool whither you will.
The reasons why April 1st ("All Fools Day") became associated with folly and practical jokes are now obscure; there is no record of such customs in Britain before the late 17th century. There may be some link with the return of the cuckoo, a bird traditionally associated with folly and madness, at around this time (see proverb 37 below).

37 On the first of April, hunt the gowk another mile.
"Gowk" means "cuckoo" or "simpleton"; to "hunt the gowk" meant to send someone on a fool's errand or play a trick on them.

38 The cuckoo comes in April, and stays the month of May; sings a song at midsummer, and then goes away.

39 On the third of April comes in the cuckoo and nightingale.

40 The cuckoo goes to Beaulieu Fair to buy him a greatcoat.
The fair at Beaulieu in Hampshire was held on April 15th, the day when the cuckoo was often said to arrive in England (contrary to proverb 39 above).

41 Mackerel's in season when Balaam's ass speaks in church.
A reference to the former lesson for the second Sunday after Easter (Numbers 22), which concerns Balaam and his talking ass.

42 If they blow in April, you'll have your fill; but if in May, they'll all go away.
A reference to the blossoming of fruit trees.

May

43 A swarm in May is worth a load of hay; a swarm in June is worth a silver spoon; but a swarm in July is not worth a fly.
By July there is little time for the bees to store up honey before the flowers begin to fade.

44 May makes or mars the wheat.

45 Set sage in May, and it will grow alway.

46 Shear your sheep in May, and shear them all away.
Implies that this is too soon to shear sheep, as cold weather may still be in store.

47 He that is in a town in May, loses his spring.

48 May-day, pay-day, pack rags and go away.
A reference to the former custom of hiring workers on May 1st.

49 A May cold is a thirty-day cold.
Implies that colds caught in May are hard to shake off.

50 He that is hanged in May, will eat no flannes in midsummer.
"Flannes" are custards or pancakes.

51 Marry in May, rue for aye.
The belief that May is an unlucky month for weddings can be traced back to Roman times and is mentioned by Ovid in his *Fasti* (1st century BC). The superstition may have arisen from the major festivals of virginity and the dead held in that month. By contrast,

June was considered the most propitious month for weddings – probably because of its association with Juno, the protectress of women and marriage. The tradition of the "June bride" continues to this day in Western countries.

52 May birds come cheeping.
The implication is that children born in May are sickly and unhealthy.

53 May never goes out without a wheat-ear.

54 Be it weal or be it woe, beans blow before May does go.
"Weal or...woe" here refers to good or bad weather; "blow" means "blossom".

55 Ne'er cast a clout till May be out.
The advice here is not to discard winter clothing until the end of May or, following an erroneous alternative interpretation, until the may (hawthorn) blossom appears.

June

56 If you look at your corn in May, you'll come weeping away; if you look at the same in June, you'll come home in another tune.

57 He who bathes in May, will soon be laid in clay; he who bathes in June, will sing a merry tune.

58 Barnaby bright, Barnaby bright, the longest day and the shortest night.
Before the calendar reform of 1752, St Barnabas's Day (June 11th) was the longest day of the year. Compare proverb 76 below.

July

59 Till St James's Day be come and gone, you may have hops or you may have none.
St James's Day is July 25th.

August

60 After Lammas corn ripens as much by night as by day.
Lammas Day (August 1st) traditionally marked the beginning of the corn harvest.

61 St Bartholomew brings the cold dew.
St Bartholomew's Day is August 24th.

September

62 September blow soft, till the fruit's in the loft.

63 On Holyrood Day the devil goes a-nutting.
Holyrood or Holy Cross Day is September 14th.

64 St Matthew get candlesticks new.
St Matthew's Day is September 21st; the reference is to the shortening days at this time of year.

65 Michaelmas chickens and parsons' daughters never come to good.
Michaelmas is September 29th.

66 The Michaelmas moon rises aye alike soon.
The "harvest moon" (the full moon nearest the autumnal equinox) rises soon after sunset for several evenings in a row; these long moonlit evenings were traditionally used for completing the cereal harvest.

67 Michaelmas rot comes never in the pot.
A reference to sheep afflicted with the liver disease known as "rot". This was often contracted in the early autumn, meaning that the sheep needed to be slaughtered in Lent, when eating their meat was forbidden.

68 The devil sets his foot on the blackberries on Michaelmas Day.
According to an old folk belief, the devil landed in a blackberry bush when he was cast out of heaven on Michaelmas Day (the feast of his nemesis, St Michael the archangel). He is therefore said to spoil the blackberry crop by cursing, stamping, or spitting on it at this time of year.

October

69 On St Luke's Day the oxen have leave to play.
The first ploughing after harvest was generally completed by St Luke's Day (October 18th). Fittingly, the ox is the traditional symbol of St Luke.

70 Simon and Jude all the ships on the sea home they do crowd.
The feast day of SS Simon and Jude is October 28th. It was considered inadvisable for ships to put out to sea after this time (see also proverb 71 below).

November

71 November take flail; let ship no more sail.
The advice is that in November the thresher should take up his flail and sailors should not venture out to sea.

72 On the first of November, if the weather holds clear, an end of wheat-sowing do make for this year.

73 Set trees at Allhallontide and command them to prosper; set them after Candlemas and entreat them to grow.
Allhallontide (All Hallows) is the first week in November; Candlemas is February 2nd.

74 St Andrew the King, three weeks and three days before Christmas comes in.
St Andrew's Day is November 30th.

December

75 On Lady Day the latter, the cold comes on the water.
A reference to the Festival of the Conception of the Virgin Mary (December 8th).

76 St Thomas gray! St Thomas gray! the longest night and the shortest day.
St Thomas's Day is December 21st. Compare proverb 58 above.

77 On St Thomas the Divine kill all turkeys, geese, and swine.

78 Blessed be St Stephen, there is no fast upon his even.
Most of the Church's festivals were preceded by a fast day; St Stephen (December 26th) was an obvious exception, it being the day after Christmas.

79 If you bleed your nag on St Stephen's Day, he'll work your work for ever and aye.

See also SEASONS; WEATHER

N

118 Names

Their importance

1 A man lives a generation; a name to the end of all generations.
Japanese proverb.

2 Names and natures do often agree.

3 Names are debts.
Implies that a person is obliged to live up to the meaning of his or her name.

Their unimportance

4 What's in a name?
Both this saying and proverb 5 below are quotations from Shakespeare's *Romeo and Juliet* (c. 1595).

5 A rose by any other name would smell as sweet.

6 Man dies and leave a name; the tiger dies and leaves a skin.
Chinese proverb.

See also ENGLAND: *English names*; FAME: *The value of a good reputation*

119 Nature

Her power

1 Nature draws more than ten teams.
A reference to ploughing with animals.

2 Nature will have her course.
Now more often heard in the form "Let Nature take its course."

3 Fix thy pale in Severn, Severn will be as before.
A reference to the river Severn, implying the futility of any attempt to alter the course of Nature. A "pale" is a fence or boundary.

4 Let Uther-Pendragon do what he can, the river Eden will run as it ran.
Uther-Pendragon was a legendary British prince (the father of Arthur) who is said to have attempted to change the course of this Cumbrian river in order to fortify his castle.

Her wisdom

5 Nature is the true law.

6 Nature does nothing in vain.
The maxim can be traced back to Aristotle's *Politics* (4th century BC).

7 Nature is no botcher.
8 Nature, time, and patience are the three great physicians.
9 He that follows Nature, is never out of his way.

Other characteristics

10 Nature abhors a vacuum.
  The saying can be traced back to Plutarch (1st–2nd centuries AD) although the idea is older, being a commonplace of Aristotelian physics.
11 Nature hates all sudden changes.
12 Nature is content with a little.
13 Nature is conquered by obeying her.
  Often attributed to Francis Bacon (1561–1626).

Nature and art

14 Art improves Nature.
  Here, as in proverb 15 below, "art" means "skill, craft".
15 Nature passes art.
  "Passes" here means "surpasses".
16 That which Nature paints never fades.

120 Necessity

Its power

1 Necessity knows no law.
  A legal maxim that dates from the middle ages if not earlier.
2 Necessity is a powerful weapon.
3 There is no such conquering weapon as the necessity of conquering.
4 Necessity breaks iron.
5 Necessity has no holiday.
6 Needs must when the devil drives.

Its effects

7 Necessity is the mother of invention.
  Compare POVERTY: 38.
8 Necessity and opportunity may make a coward valiant.

121 Neighbours

Their importance

1 No one is rich enough to do without his neighbour.
2 We can live without our friends, but not without our neighbours.
3 Choose your neighbour before your house and your companion before the road.
  Arabic proverb.
4 You must ask your neighbour if you shall live in peace.
5 A good neighbour, a good morrow.

6 To have a good neighbour is to find something precious.
Chinese proverb.

7 A near neighbour is better than a far-dwelling kinsman.

8 All is well with him who is beloved of his neighbours.

9 It is not as thy mother says, but as thy neighbours say.
That is, don't heed the praises of those who are too close to you to form an objective view but listen to the more disinterested opinions of your neighbours.

10 He who wants to know himself should offend two or three of his neighbours.

Bad neighbours

11 An ill neighbour is an ill thing.

12 A great man and a great river are often ill neighbours.
Some variants add "a great bell" to the list of undesirable neighbours.

13 A good lawyer, an evil neighbour.

14 He's an ill neighbour that is not missed.

Privacy

15 Love your neighbour, yet pull not down your hedge.
A prudent amendment of the injunction given at Matthew 22:39.

16 A hedge between keeps friendship green.

17 Good fences make good neighbours.
Cited by Robert Frost in his well-known poem "Mending Wall" (1914).

18 An Englishman's home is his castle.
The saying, which is sometimes attributed to the jurist Sir Edward Coke (1552–1634), reflects the common-law principle that a person has the right to be unmolested in his or her own home. It is now mainly used to emphasize the Englishman's love of privacy and independence. Variants substitute "man" for "Englishman" or "house" for "home".

122 News

Good news

1 No news is good news.

2 He that brings good news, knocks hard.
Because he is confident of a good reception.

Bad news

3 Bad news travels fast.
Because people take a perverse pleasure in passing it on.

4 Ill news comes apace.

5 Ill news comes unsent for.

6 Ill news never comes too late.

7 Ill news comes often on the back of worse.

8 Ill news is too often true.

Hearing news

9 If you will learn news, you must go to the oven or the mill.

10 Go abroad and you'll hear news of home.
11 Stay a little, and news will find you.

Telling news

12 Good news may be told at any time, but ill in the morning.
13 He that tells his wife news, is but newly married.
   Implies that it is unwise to confide in one's wife.

O

123 Obedience

Its value

1 Obedience is the mother of success.
2 He that cannot obey, cannot command.
   The saying has been traced back to Seneca (1st century AD).
3 Do as you're bidden and you'll never bear blame.

Its effects

4 An obedient wife commands her husband.
5 Obedience is much more seen in little things than in great.
6 Nature is conquered by obeying her.
   Sometimes attributed to Francis Bacon (1561–1626).

Its necessity

7 Obedience is the first duty of a soldier.
   First recorded in the mid-19th century.
8 They that are bound must obey.
9 Do as I say, not as I do.
   Based ultimately on Matthew 23:3. Now most familiar as the retort of exasperated parents to their disobedient (but observant) children.
10 Do as the friar says, not as he does.

Disobedience

11 Forbid a thing, and that women will do.
   Adapted from a line in Ovid's *Amores* (1st century BC).
12 Forbidden fruit is sweet.
   An allusion to Genesis 3:6.
13 That which one most foreheets, soonest comes to pass.
   "Foreheets" means "forbids".

124 Occupations

The value of a trade

1 Who hath a good trade, through all waters may wade.
2 Who has a trade, has a share everywhere.
   Like proverb 3 below, this implies that those with a useful trade can thrive anywhere.

3 He who has an art, has everywhere a part.
4 They that can cobble and clout, shall have work when others go without.
"Clout" here means to make or mend clothes.
5 Trade is the mother of money.
6 A handful of trade is a handful of gold.
7 A useful trade is a mine of gold.
8 An occupation is as good as land.
9 He that learns a trade, has a purchase made.
10 Virtue and a trade are the best portion for children.
11 He that has no good trade, it is to his loss.
12 A trade is better than service.
13 A man of many trades, begs his bread on Sunday.
Like proverbs 14 and 15 below, this implies that to specialize in one trade is far more profitable than to dabble in many.
14 A dozen trades, thirteen miseries.
15 Jack of all trades, master of none.

The need for tradesmen

16 If things did not break, or wear out, how would tradesmen live?
17 Let all trades live.
A remark made when something is accidentally broken, alluding to the thought expressed in proverb 16 above.
18 Tradesmen live upon lack.

Rivalry within trades

19 Two of a trade never agree.
20 One potter envies another.
Implies that every man envies potential rivals within his own field. The saying can be traced back to Hesiod (8th century BC).
21 A vinegar seller does not like another vinegar seller.
Arabic proverb.

Sticking to one's trade

22 Let the cobbler stick to his last.
A "last" is the wooden or metal form used to fashion boots or shoes. The saying refers to a story told about the Greek painter Appelles (4th century BC). When a cobbler found fault with the detail of a shoe fastening in one of Appelles's paintings, the artist gratefully accepted the criticism and altered the work. When the same cobbler then went on to criticize the leg of one of the figures, Appelles indignantly told him to keep to his trade.
23 The gunner to his linstock, and the steersman to the helm.
A "linstock" was a forked stick used by gunners to hold a lighted match.
24 Every man to his trade.

Millers and bakers

25 Millers are the last to die of famine.
Implies that the miller always steals a little from the grain brought to him to be ground. Proverbs 26–30 below all refer to the alleged dishonesty of millers and bakers.
26 Millers and bakers do not steal: people bring it to them.
27 Three dear years will raise a baker's daughter to a portion.

28 The miller is honest who has hair on his teeth.

29 What is bolder than a miller's neck-cloth, which takes a thief by the neck every morning?

30 Put a miller, a weaver, and a tailor in a bag, and shake them; the first that comes out will be a thief.

Tailors

31 Tailors and writers must mind the fashion.

32 The tailor must cut three sleeves to every woman's gown.
Like proverbs 33–35 below, this refers to the alleged dishonesty of tailors.

33 A hundred tailors, a hundred millers, and a hundred weavers are three hundred thieves.

34 Never trust a tailor that does not sing at his work.

35 There is knavery in all trades, but most in tailors.

Nurses

36 Nurses put one bit in the child's mouth and two in their own.

37 One year a nurse, and seven years the worse.

38 The nurse is valued till the child has done sucking.

39 The nurse's tongue is privileged to talk.

Sailors

40 Sailors' fingers must all be fish-hooks.
Because of their need to hold on to the rigging or ropes, etc., in rough seas.

41 Sailors have a port in every storm.

42 Sailors go round the world without going into it.

43 Sailors get money like horses, and spend it like asses.

44 Seamen are the nearest to death, the furthest from God.

45 A seaman, if he carries a millstone, will have a quart out of it.
A reference to the drinking habits of sailors.

Soldiers

46 Nails are not made from good iron, nor soldiers from good men.
Chinese proverb.

47 To take from a soldier ambition, is to take off his spurs.

48 Old soldiers never die, they simply fade away.
This derives from a popular marching song of the British army during World War I (sung to the tune of the hymn "Kind Words Can Never Die"). The phrase is now associated with General Douglas MacArthur, who quoted it during his valedictory speech to Congress in 1941.

49 Soldiers in peace are like chimneys in summer.

50 The blood of the soldier makes the glory of the general.

51 Soldiers fight, and kings are heroes.
Hebrew proverb.

52 It is better to have no son than one who is a soldier.
Chinese proverb.

See also HEALTH: *Doctors*; LAW: *Lawyers, Judges*; SERVANTS

125 Old people

Their wisdom

1 An old man's sayings are seldom untrue.
2 If you wish good advice, consult an old man.
3 If the old dog bark, he gives counsel.
4 An old dog barks not in vain.
5 The devil knows many things because he is old.
6 Years know more than books.
7 It is good to follow the old fox.
8 The ox when weariest treads surest.
   The earliest known citation is in a letter from the old St Jerome to the younger St Augustine of Hippo (early 5th century AD).
9 Let aye the belled wether break the snow.
   A "belled wether" is a ram with a bell tied round its neck so that the rest of the flock will hear and follow. The implication is that it is best to follow the lead of the old and experienced.
10 Old foxes want no tutors.
11 An old fox is not easily snared.
12 You cannot catch old birds with chaff.
13 No playing with a straw before an old cat.
14 An old knave is no babe.
15 No knave to the old knave.
16 Put an old cat to an old rat.
   Implies that only the experience of the old will prove a match for the wiliness of their contemporaries.

Their value

17 There is beild aneath an auld man's beard.
   "Beild" means "shelter".
18 An old wise man's shadow is better than a young buzzard's sword.
   "Buzzard" here means "fool".
19 It is good sheltering under an old hedge.
20 The best wine comes out of an old vessel.
21 There's many a good tune played on an old fiddle.
   First recorded in the early 20th century.
22 Good broth may be made in an old pot.
23 An old cart well used may outlast a new one abused.
24 An old man in a house is a good sign.
25 An old ox makes a straight furrow.
   A reference to the value of an old person's experience.

Their uselessness

26 When bees are old, they yield no honey.
27 Old cattle breed not.
28 An old man is a bed full of bones.
29 Old vessels must leak.

Their folly

30 There's no fool like an old fool.

31 The brains don't lie in the beard.

32 Old age doesn't protect from folly.

33 Both folly and wisdom come upon us with years.

34 Though old and wise, yet still advise.
    "Advise" here means "seek advice".

35 Never too old to learn.
    Variants substitute "late" for "old" and "mend", "repent", or "do well" for "learn".

36 Old men are twice children.
    The saying can be traced back to Aristotle (4th century BC).

Their infirmities

37 Old age is sickness of itself.
    The saying can be traced back to Terence (2nd century BC).

38 Old age is a hospital that takes in all diseases.

39 A hundred disorders has old age.

40 Old age is a malady of which one dies.

41 Old churches have dim windows.
    A reference to the failing eyesight of the old.

Their influence

42 As the old cock crows, so crows the young.

43 The young pig grunts like the old sow.

44 Where old age is evil, youth can learn no good.

Their tales

45 When the teeth fall out, the tongue wags loose.
    Chinese proverb.

46 An old man never wants a tale to tell.

47 Old men and travellers may lie by authority.
    Variants add "soldiers", "physicians", and "poets" to the list of confirmed liars.

48 Old wives were aye good maidens.
    A reference to old people's claims that they were virtuous and sober when young.

Handling the old

49 An old ox will find a shelter for himself.

50 He wrongs not an old man that steals his supper from him.
    Implies that the old should not be overfed.

51 Remove an old tree and it will wither to death.
    A warning against forcing old people to move house.

52 You can't teach an old dog new tricks.
    Implies that old people, who are set in their ways, cannot cope with new ideas.

53 An old dog bites sore.
    The advice here is not to provoke an old person.

The generation gap

54 Youth and age will never agree.

55 Young men think old men fools, and old men know young men to be so.

56 The old cow thinks she was never a calf.

The inevitability of old age

57 Old age comes stealing on.

58 You cannot have two forenoons in the same day.

59 Old be, or young die.

60 If you would not live to be old, you must be hanged when you are young.

Old age and death

61 They that live longest, must die at last.

62 The cure for old age is the grave.

63 The more thy years, the nearer thy grave.

64 An old man's staff is the rapper of death's door.

65 Death sends his challenge in a grey hair.
   Arabic proverb.

66 Grey hairs are death's blossoms.

67 Of young men die many, of old men scape not any.

68 Young men may die, but old must die.

69 Old men go to death, death comes to young men.

70 The old man has his death before his eyes; the young man behind his back.

71 When age is jocund, it makes sport for death.

72 None so old that he hopes not for a year of life.

73 When an old man will not drink, go to see him in another world.
   Implies that death is at hand when an old person refuses a drink.

See also CHILDREN: *The recklessness of youth*

126 Opportunity

Making the most of opportunities

1 Opportunity seldom knocks twice.
   The talent-spotting show *Opportunity Knocks*, a long-running fixture on British TV (1956–77, subsequently revived), took its name from this proverb.

2 Christmas comes but once a year.

3 Make hay while the sun shines.

4 Strike while the iron is hot.
   The allusion is to work in a blacksmith's forge. Some variants add "...and polish it at leisure."

5 Hoist your sail when the wind is fair.

6 Gather ye rosebuds while ye may.
   A quotation from Herrick's poem "To the Virgins, to Make Much of Time" (1648).

7 Put out your tubs when it is raining.

8 If heaven drops a date, open your mouth.
   Chinese proverb.

9 Take the goods the gods provide.
   The saying can be traced back to Plautus (3rd century BC).

10 When the shoulder of mutton is going, 'tis good to take a slice.
11 Make not a balk of good ground.
    A "balk" is a ridge of land left unploughed.
12 The tide must be taken when it comes.
13 Time and tide wait for no man.
14 Take time by the forelock.
    The Greek god Kairos, who represented Occasion or Opportunity, was depicted with a full lock of hair on the forehead but bald behind – signifying that the critical moment must be seized as it comes because once past it is irretrievable.
15 Take time when time comes.
    See also TIME: 36.
16 Life is short and time is swift.
17 An occasion lost cannot be redeemed.
18 The mill cannot grind with the water that is past.
19 He that will not when he may, when he will he shall have nay.
20 When fortune smiles, embrace her.

127 Optimism

Optimistic attitudes

1 Look on the bright side.
2 When one door shuts, another opens.
3 There are as good fish in the sea as ever came out of it.
   The variant "plenty more fish in the sea" is now more common; the context is usually one of consolation for a romantic disappointment.
4 When the sun sets, the moon rises; when the moon sets, the sun rises.
   Chinese proverb.
5 Bode good, and get it.
   "Bode" means "expect".
6 Nothing so bad but it might have been worse.
   See also IMPERFECTION: 20.
7 Nothing is to be presumed on, or despaired of.
   The proverb adapts a saying of St Augustine of Hippo (4th–5th centuries AD), who wrote of the two thieves crucified with Christ: "Do not despair; one of the thieves was saved. Do not presume; one of the thieves was damned."
8 God's in his heaven; all's right with the world.
   A quotation from Browning's *Pippa Passes* (1841).
9 All is for the best in the best of all possible worlds.
   A saying associated with the optimistic philosopher Dr Pangloss in Voltaire's *Candide* (1759), who continues to talk in this vein despite a series of grotesque misfortunes; the novel satirizes the optimistic doctrine of Leibnitz.

Things will improve

10 He that falls today may rise tomorrow.
11 It will all come right in the wash.
12 When things are at the worst they begin to mend.
13 There is a good time coming.
14 All is not lost that is in danger.

15 The darkest hour is that before the dawn.
16 A foul morning may turn to a fair day.
17 Cloudy mornings turn to clear afternoons.
18 After black clouds, clear weather.
19 After a storm comes a calm.
   Another well-known phrase states the converse: "the calm before the storm".

Nothing is all bad

20 Every cloud has a silver lining.
   The proverb derives from a line in Milton's *Comus* (1634).
21 It's an ill wind that blows nobody any good.
   Originally a sailing reference.
22 It's a hard-fought field, where no man escapes unkilled.
23 It is an ill bargain where no man wins.
24 There is good land where there is foul way.
25 Ill for the rider, good for the abider.
   Like proverb 24 above, this implies that the most fertile land is usually muddy and thus inconvenient for the rider.
26 Of evil manners, spring good laws.
   A variant of LAW: 1.
27 After a typhoon there are pears to gather up.
28 No great loss but some small profit.
   "But" here means "without".
29 Ill luck is good for something.
30 Nothing but is good for something.
31 Nothing so bad in which there is not something of good.
32 The bee sucks honey out of the bitterest flowers.

Nothing is permanent

33 All wrong will end.
34 Nothing that is violent is permanent.
35 All that is sharp is short.
36 The sharper the storm, the sooner it's over.
37 Be the day never so long, at length comes evensong.
38 The longest day has an end.
39 The longest night will have an end.
40 Even the weariest river winds somewhere safe to sea.
41 It is a long lane that has no turning.
42 The tide never goes out so far but it always comes in again.

See also HOPE

P

128 Parents

Their importance

1 God, and parents, and our master, can never be requited.
2 A father's goodness is higher than the mountains; a mother's goodness is deeper than the sea.
   Japanese proverb.
3 One father is enough to govern one hundred sons, but not a hundred sons one father.
4 One father is more than a hundred schoolmasters.
5 An ounce of mother is worth a ton of priest.
6 A man's mother is his other God.
   African proverb.

Their influence

7 Parents are patterns.
8 Like father, like son.
9 Like mother, like daughter.
10 The birth follows the belly.
   Like proverb 11 below, this implies that the mother is likely to have a greater influence than the father over the child.
11 The mother's side is the surest.
12 The hand that rocks the cradle rules the world.
   A quotation (slightly abridged) from William Ross Wallace's poem "What Rules the World" (1865).

Their subjectivity

13 He whose father is judge, goes safe to his trial.
14 The owl thinks her own young fairest.
15 There's only one pretty child in the world, and every mother has it.
16 It is not as thy mother says, but as thy neighbours say.
   That is, don't heed the praises of those who are too close to you to form an objective view, but listen to the more disinterested opinions of your neighbours.

The mother's kindness

17 The good mother says not, 'Will you?' but gives.
18 The mother's breath is aye sweet.

Old parents

19 The old pearl-oyster produces a pearl.
    Chinese proverb.

20 Late children, early orphans.

21 The offspring of those that are very old, or very young, lasts not.

Step-parents

22 With the arrival of the stepmother the father becomes a stepfather.
    Afghan proverb.

23 Take heed of a stepmother: the very name of her suffices.

24 Put another man's child in your bosom, and he'll creep out at your elbow.
    Implies that a child will never have any natural affection for an adoptive or step-parent.

See also CHARACTER: *Hereditary influences*; LOVE: *Parental love*

129 Passion

Its sources

1 There is no heat of affection, but is joined with some idleness of brain.

2 A man is a lion in his own cause.

Its effects

3 Glowing coals sparkle oft.
    The meaning is explained by proverb 4 below.

4 When the heart is a fire, some sparks will fly out of the mouth.

5 He that burns most, shines most.

6 Hot love, hasty vengeance.

7 The end of passion is the beginning of repentance.

8 Hot love is soon cold.

9 Soon hot, soon cold.

10 Nothing that is violent is permanent.

11 After a storm comes a calm.
    Another well-known phrase states the converse: "the calm before the storm".

12 No man can guess in cold blood what he may do in a passion.

13 To a boiling pot, flies come not.
    "Flies" here stand for any minor nuisances.

14 The stream stopped swells the higher.
    Like proverb 15 below, this refers to the effect of suppressing passion.

15 Fire that's closest kept burns most of all.

Its value

16 He freezes who does not burn.

17 Never do things by halves.

Its dangers

18 Zeal without knowledge is a runaway horse.
    The phrase "zeal without knowledge" is adapted from Romans 10:2.

19 Zeal is fit only for wise men, but is found mostly in fools.

20 Zeal without prudence is frenzy.

21 Mettle is dangerous in a blind horse.

22 Zeal, when it is a virtue, is a dangerous one.

23 Serving one's own passions is the greatest slavery.

130 Patience

Its importance

1 Patience is a virtue.

2 Let patience grow in your garden alway.
   "Patience" was a popular name for a species of dock, *Rumex patientia* (hence also the allusions in proverbs 3 and 29 below).

3 Patience is a flower that grows not in every one's garden.

4 Patience is the best buckler against affronts.
   "Buckler" means "shield".

5 Patience surpasses learning.

6 Patience is the knot which secures the seam of victory.
   Chinese proverb.

7 Patience is the key of joy, but haste is the key of sorrow.
   Arabic proverb.

8 Though God take the sun out of heaven, yet we must have patience.

9 He that will be served, must be patient.

10 They also serve who only stand and wait.
   A quotation from Milton's sonnet "On His Blindness" (1650s).

Its rewards

11 Patient men win the day.

12 The world is for him who has patience.

13 Everything comes to him who waits.
   "All things" is often substituted for "everything".

14 Long looked for comes at last.

15 Be still, and have thy will.

16 He that can stay, obtains.

17 Patience, time, and money accommodate all things.

18 He that has patience, has fat thrushes for a farthing.

19 Who has no haste in his business, mountains to him seem valleys.

20 The hindmost dog may catch the hare.

21 With patience the mulberry leaf becomes a silk gown.
   Chinese proverb.

22 With the trowel of patience we dig out the roots of truth.

23 It is in the garden of patience that strength grows best.

Its dangers

24 Patience provoked turns to fury.
   Variants include the well-known line from Dryden's *Absalom and Achitophel* (1681) "Beware the fury of a patient man".

25 The string of a man's sack of patience is generally tied with a slip knot.

26 Patience under old injuries invites new ones.
Implies that to tolerate injuries or insults with patience may provoke further attack.

Patience as a remedy

27 Patience is the remedy of the world.
28 Patience is a remedy for every grief.
29 Patience is a plaster for all sores.
Alludes to the widespread use of *Rumex patientia* in poultices for sores, wounds, etc. (see note to proverb 2 above).
30 No remedy but patience.
31 Patience with poverty is all a poor man's remedy.
32 Nature, time, and patience are the three great physicians.

Against impatience

33 A little impatience will spoil great plans.
Chinese proverb.
34 A watched pot never boils.
Implies that time appears to pass more slowly when one is impatiently waiting for something to happen. First recorded in the mid-19th century.
35 Rome was not built in a day.
Like proverbs 36–45 below, this is aimed at those who are impatient to see the results of their own or someone else's labours.
36 A strong town is not won in an hour.
37 An oak is not felled at one stroke.
38 No man is his craft's master the first day.
39 All things are difficult before they are easy.
40 Children learn to creep ere they can go.
Here, as in proverb 41 below, "creep" means "crawl" and "go" means "walk".
41 First creep, and then go.
42 We must learn to walk before we can run.
43 Learn to say before you sing.
44 First things first.
First recorded in the late 19th century.
45 He who would climb the ladder must begin at the bottom.

131 Paying

Its necessity

1 Mills will not grind if you give them not water.
2 As good play for nought as work for nought.
3 Work for nought makes folks dead sweir.
"Sweir" means "lazy".
4 Service without reward is punishment.

Its effects

5 Corn him well, he'll work the better.
The reference is to the feeding of horses. Applied to any person whose industriousness is directly related to the size of his fee.

6 The purse of the patient protracts the disease.
  Contrary to the preceding proverb, this implies that those who are being well paid for their work may draw it out longer than is necessary.

7 Wage will get a page.

8 Merry is the feast-making till we come to the reckoning.

9 Sweet appears sour when we pay.

10 The reckoning spoils the relish.

The dangers of not paying

11 He that cannot pay, let him pray.

12 He must pay with his body that cannot pay with money.

13 He that cannot pay in purse must pay in person.

14 If you pay not a servant his wages, he will pay himself.
   That is, you will encourage pilfering or other dishonesty.

Methods of payment

15 Pay beforehand was never well served.

16 Pay beforehand and your work will be behindhand.

17 Payment in advance is evil payment.

18 He who wants the work badly done has only to pay in advance.

19 He that pays last never pays twice.
   Advice to defer payment until the job is completely finished. However, the saying has sometimes been used as an ironic rebuke to late payers.

20 The best payment is on the peck bottom.
   A "peck" was a vessel used for measuring grain. The proverb implies that it is best to receive immediate payment for one's wares.

21 It is best to take half in hand and the rest by and by.

Good and bad payers

22 A good payer is master of another's purse.

23 A good paymaster needs no surety.

24 A good paymaster never wants workmen.

25 A good paymaster may build Paul's.
   A reference to St Paul's Cathedral in London.

26 If you pay peanuts, you get monkeys.
   A phrase used to justify high wages or salaries; first recorded in the 1960s.

27 An ill paymaster never wants excuse.

28 Sore cravers are aye ill payers.
   Implies that those who are most eager to obtain something are least prompt in paying for it.

29 Trust is dead, ill payment killed it.

Privileges of the one who pays

30 He who pays the piper calls the tune.
   First recorded in the late 19th century.

31 Let him that pays the lawing choose the lodging.
   "Lawing" means "reckoning".

The mercenary

32 He that serves God for money, will serve the devil for better wages.
33 Virtue flies from the heart of a mercenary man.

See also BORROWING: *Repayment of debts*

132 Peace

Its value

1 Where there is peace, God is.
2 To live peaceably with all breeds good blood.
3 Peace makes plenty.
   Some variants extend this to make a complete cycle: "…, plenty makes pride, pride makes envy (*or* ambition), envy makes war, war makes poverty, poverty makes peace."
4 By wisdom peace, by peace plenty.
   Some variants add "…, by plenty war."
5 The secret wall of a town is peace.

War and peace

6 He that will not have peace, God gives him war.
7 If you want peace, you must prepare for war.
   A quotation from Vegetius, a Latin writer on warfare (5th century AD).
8 Clothe thee in war: arm thee in peace.
9 A just war is better than an unjust peace.
   A quotation from the *Annals* of Tacitus (early 2nd century AD).
10 He that makes a good war, makes a good peace.
11 Better a lean peace than a fat victory.
12 Better an egg in peace than an ox in war.
13 War makes thieves, and peace hangs them.
14 Of all wars, peace is the end.
15 It is a great victory that comes without blood.

Making peace

16 The stick is the surest peacemaker.
   Like proverbs 17–19 below, this implies that peace can best be achieved by violence or by the threat of violence.
17 'Tis safest making peace with sword in hand.
18 Weapons breed peace.
19 One sword keeps another in the sheath.

133 People and places

Africa

1 Africa always brings something new.
   A quotation from Pliny the Elder's *Historia naturalis* (1st century AD). In the form "Out of

Africa, always something new" this saying provided the title for Karen Blixen's book *Out of Africa* (1937) and the subsequent film (1985).

2 The African race is an indiarubber ball; the harder you dash it to the ground, the higher it will rise.
African proverb.

3 The riches of Egypt are for the foreigners therein.
Arabic proverb. A reference to the fact that most of Egypt's rulers have been foreigners.

4 Truly at weaving wiles the Egyptians are clever.

Asia

5 In China we have only three religions, but we have a hundred dishes we can make from rice.
Chinese proverb. Compare ENGLAND: 11.

6 In China are more tutors than scholars, and more physicians than patients.
Chinese proverb.

7 A Chinaman is ill only once in his life, and that is when he is dying.
Russian proverb.

8 If a Bengali is a man, what is a devil?
Indian proverb.

9 The more you plunder a Turk the richer he is.

10 Where the Turk's horse once treads, the grass never grows.
A reference to the destructive power of the former Turkish empire.

11 The tyranny of the Turk is better than the justice of the Arab.
Arabic proverb. The Ottoman Turks ruled the Arab world for some 300 years (until 1918).

12 The understanding of an Arab is in his eyes.
Arabic proverb.

Europe

13 The emperor of Germany is the king of kings; the king of Spain, king of men; the king of France, king of asses; the king of England, the king of devils.
In the middle ages the Holy Roman Empire, ruled from 962 by German kings, was the greatest secular power in Europe.

14 The Italians are wise before the deed, the Germans in the deed, the French after the deed.

15 In settling an island, the first building erected by a Spaniard will be a church; by a Frenchman, a fort; by a Dutchman, a warehouse; and by an Englishman, an alehouse.

16 Learn in Italy; clothe yourself in Germany; flirt in France; banquet in Poland.

17 In Spain, the lawyer; in Italy, the doctor; in France, the flirt; in Germany, the artisan; in England, the merchant; in the Balkans, the thief; in Turkey, the soldier; in Poland, a Treasury official; in Moscow, the liar – can all make a living.

18 Malta would be a delightful place if every priest were a tree.

19 Every Czech is a musician.

20 Finland is the devil's country.
A reference to the physical geography of the country (mainly forests, lakes, and marshes) rather than to its inhabitants.

France

21 France is a meadow that cuts thrice a year.
   A reference to the richness of the farming land in much of France.

22 He that will France win, must with Scotland first begin.
   The reference is to the various English attempts to conquer France in the middle ages; a wise monarch would make sure that he had subdued the Scots in the north before embarking on a campaign across the Channel.

23 The day of France's ruin, is the eve of the ruin of England.
   A saying first recorded at the time of the Thirty Years' War (1618–48); it implies that the collapse of French power would leave England at the mercy of Spain.

24 Every French soldier carries a marshal's baton in his knapsack.
   This saying has been attributed both to Louis XVIII and to Napoleon.

25 The French would be the best cooks in Europe if they had got any butcher's meat.

26 Have the Frenchman for thy friend, not for thy neighbour.

27 The Frenchman is a scoundrel.

28 The English love; the French make love.

29 When the Ethiopian is white, the French will love the English.

30 The friendship of the French is like their wine, exquisite but of short duration.

31 Only a dog and a Frenchman walks after he has eaten.

32 Good Americans, when they die, go to Paris.
   A saying attributed to the US wit Thomas Gold Appleton (1812–84).

33 The Bourbons learn nothing and forget nothing.
   The Bourbons were the ruling family of France at the time of the Revolution of 1789. As originally coined, by the general Charles François du Périer Dumouriez in 1795, the phrase was directed at the courtiers who surrounded Louis XVIII in his exile. On the restoration of the monarchy in 1814 it was given a new currency by Talleyrand, who applied it to the returning royalist emigrés, and by Napoleon, who first applied it to the Bourbons themselves. The Bourbons' inability to learn the lessons of the Revolution or to forget their own injuries led to their overthrow in a second revolution in 1830.

Italy

34 The Englishman Italianate is a devil incarnate.
   An Elizabethan saying.

35 All things are to be bought at Rome.
   Sometimes given in the form "All things are sold for money at Rome", which has a slightly different implication.

36 Genoa has mountains without wood, sea without fish, women without shame, and men without conscience.

37 See Naples and die.
   A reference to the beauty of Naples and its environs, presuming that earth has nothing more beautiful to show. The saying is recorded in Goethe's *Italian Journey* (1787).

38 The Neapolitan is wide-mouthed and narrow-handed.
   "Narrow-handed" here means "tight-fisted, mean".

39 A man would live in Italy, but he would choose to die in Spain.
   This implies that while Italy is the more pleasant place to live, the Catholic faith is more strictly practised in Spain.

Spain and Portugal

40 Nothing ill in Spain but that which speaks.

41 The Spaniard is a bad servant, but a worse master.

42 The Basque is faithful.

43 He who has not seen Seville, has not seen a wonder.

44 A bad Spaniard makes a good Portuguese.
    Implies that the best of the Portuguese are no better than the worst Spaniards.

45 A blue eye in a Portuguese woman is a mistake of nature.

Germany

46 When a snake gets warm on ice, then a German will wish well to a Czech.

47 The German's wit is in his fingers.
    Implies that a German's practical skills are superior to his intellectual ability.

Holland

48 The Netherlands are the cockpit of Christendom.
    "Cockpit" here means an area of civil strife and war. "The Netherlands", used here in the
    historical sense of "the Low Countries" (Holland, Belgium, and Luxembourg), were the
    scene of repeated struggles between the European powers in the 16th and 17th centuries.

49 God made the earth but the Dutch made Holland.
    A reference to the large areas of Holland that have been reclaimed from the sea by drain-
    ing and damming.

Hungary

50 Outside Hungary there is no life; if there is any it is not the same.

51 Where there is a Hungarian there is anger; where there is a Slovak there is a
    song.

52 Do not trust a Hungarian unless he has a third eye on his forehead.

Poland

53 Poland is the peasant's hell, the Jew's paradise, the citizen's purgatory, the
    noble's heaven, and the grave of the stranger's gold.

54 What an Englishman cares to invent, a Frenchman to design, or a German to
    patch together, the stupid Pole will buy.

55 When God made the world He sent to the Poles some reason and the feet of
    a gnat, but even this little was taken away by a woman.

56 God save us from a Polish bridge!

Russia

57 In Russia as one must; in Poland as one wishes.
    This Polish proverb was coined in the days of Russian serfdom (abolished in 1861).

58 Russian friendship does not get sour.

59 The cold is Russia's cholera.

60 Scratch a Russian and you'll find a Tartar.

61 If you can deal with an Armenian, you can deal with the devil.
    Persian proverb.

62 Trust a snake before a Jew, a Jew before a Greek, but never trust an Armenian.

Greece

63 After shaking hands with a Greek, count your fingers.

64 The Greeks only tell the truth once a year.

Britain

65 All countries stand in need of Britain, and Britain of none.

66 An Englishman is never happy but when he is miserable, a Scotchman never at home but when he is abroad, and an Irishman never at peace but when he is fighting.
For further references to the migratory Scots and belligerent Irish see proverbs 67, 69, and 77 below.

67 The Englishman weeps, the Irishman sleeps, but the Scottishman gangs while he gets it.
"Gangs while" means "gets going until". The proverb refers to the supposed behaviour of the English, Irish, and Scottish when in need.

68 The Irishman for a hand, the Welshman for a leg, the Englishman for a face, and the Dutchman for a beard.
Implies that the Irish have the best hands, the Welsh the best legs, and so on.

Scotland

69 A Scot, a rat, and a Newcastle grindstone travel all the world over.
Newcastle grindstones were formerly considered the best in the world and widely exported.

70 The Scot will not fight till he sees his own blood.

71 Biting and scratching is Scots folk's wooing.

72 A Scotsman is always wise behind the hand.
"Behind the hand" means "after the event, with hindsight".

73 Forth bridles the wild Highlandman.
A reference to the river Forth as a barrier against Highland raids; the saying is referred to by both Scott and Stevenson.

74 A Scottish mist will wet an Englishman to the skin.
"Scotch mist" is a facetious English expression for steady rain; the proverb implies that the Scots are inured to weather conditions that the more delicate English find intolerable.

75 Had Judas betrayed Christ in Scotland he might have repented before he could have found a tree to hang himself on.
Refers to the barrenness of large parts of the Highlands.

Ireland

76 An Irishman before answering a question always asks another.
The other question referred to is "Why do you ask?"

77 Put an Irishman on the spit, and you can always get another Irishman to baste him.
A reference to Ireland's long history of civil strife; cited by Shaw in his Preface to *John Bull's Other Island* (1912).

78 Will any, but an Irishman, hang a wooden kettle over the fire?

79 The citizens of Cork are all akin.
Several Tudor chroniclers noted that the people of Cork, a largely English settlement, mistrusted outsiders so much that they only married among themselves.

80 Limerick was, Dublin is, and Cork shall be, the finest city of the three.
Recorded as an "old prophecy" in 1859.

Wales

81 Anglesey is the mother of Wales.
Probably a reference to the fertility of the farming land on the island; possibly to its status as one of the earliest centres of Celtic civilization in Wales.

82 Powys is the paradise of Wales.
Attributed to the 6th-century bard Taliesin.

83 Snowdon will yield sufficient pasture for all the cattle of Wales put together.

84 The older the Welshman, the more madman.

85 The Welshman keeps nothing until he has lost it.
The Welsh are only roused to protect their lands or heritage after these have been lost and regained. Originally a comment on the medieval resistance to English rule, but also applicable to e.g. the 20th-century revival of the Welsh language.

See also ENGLAND

134 Perseverance

Its value

1 Perseverance kills the game.

2 It's dogged as does it.

3 Have at it, and have it.
To "have at" something is to attack it (an idiom originating from fencing).

4 Slow but sure wins the race.
One may achieve more by steady perseverance than by rash haste; the allusion here is to the same fable as proverb 5 below. "Steady" is often substituted for "sure".

5 The tortoise wins the race while the hare is sleeping.
A reference to the well-known fable attributed to Aesop (6th century BC).

6 The race is not to the swift, nor the battle to the strong.
A biblical quotation: Ecclesiastes 9:11.

7 The snail slides up the tower at last, though the swallow mounteth it sooner.

8 Better never to begin than never to make an end.

9 Good to begin well, better to end well.
Implies that a good beginning is of no value unless one perseveres to the end. Contrast BEGINNINGS: 11 and 12.

10 Things that are hard to come by are much set by.
"Set by" means "valued".

11 The best things are hard to come by.

12 The best fish swim near the bottom.

Its effects

13 Feather by feather, the goose is plucked.
One of many proverbs to point out that small repeated actions may have a large cumulative effect: for further examples see proverbs 14–20 below and SMALL THINGS: 7–16.

14 Grain by grain, and the hen fills her belly.

15 Step after step the ladder is ascended.

16 By one and one the spindles are made.
    The reference is to the laborious process of hand-spinning yarn from natural fibre; for commercial purposes, a single fully wound spindle was held to consist of some 15 120 yards of cotton or 14 400 yards of linen yarn (in both cases, over 13 km).

17 Spit on a stone, and it will be wet at the last.

18 Constant dripping wears away the stone.

19 Little strokes fell great oaks.
    Variants appear in works by Chaucer, Erasmus, and Shakespeare.

20 A mouse in time may bite in two a cable.

Against giving up

21 Never say die.
    Never give up hope. The phrase was popularized (and may even have been invented) by Dickens, who used it in several novels. It is the catchphrase of Grip the Raven in *Barnaby Rudge* (1841).

22 Seek till you find, and you'll not lose your labour.

23 If at first you don't succeed, try, try, try again.
    From a brief didactic poem often quoted in 19th-century writings for children (author unknown; the earliest recorded citation is from 1850).

24 He that shoots oft at last shall hit the mark.

25 Oft ettle, whiles hit.
    A Scots version of proverb 24 above. "Ettle" means "aim"; "whiles" means "sometimes".

26 Forsaken by the wind, you must use your oars.

27 That which will not be butter, must be made into cheese.
    After an initial failure, one should try a different approach.

Seeing things through

28 In for a penny, in for a pound.
    Once committed to an enterprise, one should see it through whatever the cost.

29 He who rides a tiger is afraid to dismount.
    Once embarked on a risky or alarming enterprise it may be more dangerous to give up than to go on. Originally a Chinese proverb. Churchill's pre-war warning is well known: "Dictators ride to and fro upon tigers which they dare not dismount. And the tigers are getting hungry."

135 Possession

Its value

1 A bird in the hand is worth two in the bush.
   A very old proverb with variants in most languages and cultures, some of which are listed below.

2 Better a sparrow in the hand than a pigeon on the roof.

3 A thousand cranes in the air are not worth one sparrow in the fist.
   Arabic proverb.

4 A pullet in the pen is worth a hundred in the fen.
   A pullet is a young hen.

5 A bird in the soup is better than an eagle's nest in the desert.
   Chinese proverb.

6 A feather in hand is better than a bird in the air.

7 Better an egg today than a hen tomorrow.

8 Better to have than wish.

9 Better is one *Accipe*, than twice to say *Dabo tibi*.
   That is, it is better to be given something once than to be promised it twice. *Accipe* is Latin for "take it"; *dabo tibi* is Latin for "I shall give it to you."

10 Have is have.

11 Own is own.

Having and keeping

12 Better keep now than seek anon.
    "Anon" means "soon" or "shortly".

13 Better say "here it is", than "here it was".

14 He who gets does much, but he who keeps does more.

15 What you have, hold.
    Of medieval origin. In later times often heard in the form "What we have we hold", implying defiance or refusal to compromise rather than simple carefulness.

Laws of possession

16 Possession is nine points of the law.
    Implies that actual control or possession of something is a strong presumption that one is the rightful legal owner of it. Although the saying is common, no such principle has ever been recognized in English law. The proverb refers to the medieval practice of settling questions of ownership according to a points system, in which full legal entitlement depended on satisfying ten (or sometimes twelve) points. It is now sometimes used in an ironic sense implying "the law favours the rich" or "might is right".

17 Finders keepers, losers weepers.
    Although this may often be the case in practice, the law recognizes no such principle. Unless it has been deliberately abandoned, lost property remains the property of the owner and anyone who appropriates it without consent is guilty of theft. A variant substitutes "seekers" for "weepers".

18 Finding's keeping.

19 *Meum, tuum, suum*, set all the world together by the ears.
    That is, disputes about ownership cause trouble all over the world. *Meum, tuum, suum* is Latin for "mine, yours, his".

20 Every man should take his own.

21 What's yours is mine and what's mine is my own.
    Usually an ironic comment on someone else's selfish attempt to have things both ways.

True possession

22 The gown is his that wears it, and the world his that enjoys it.

23 Goods are theirs that enjoy them.

24 A man has no more goods than he gets good of.

136 Poverty

Its causes

1 Who dainties love, shall beggars prove.

2 There are God's poor and the devil's poor.
"God's poor" are those whose poverty results from misfortune; "the devil's poor" are those who have brought poverty upon themselves by greed or extravagance.

3 Who spends before he thrives, will beg before he thinks.

4 He that has it and will not keep it; he that wants it and will not seek it; he that drinks and is not dry, shall want money as well as I.

5 Nothing is to be got without pains except poverty.

6 An idle youth, a needy age.

7 Idleness is the key of beggary.

8 Idleness must thank itself if it go barefoot.

9 Plenty makes poor.
Having more than enough encourages carelessness, which leads to poverty. The saying can be traced back to Ovid's *Metamorphoses* (1st century BC).

10 He who of plenty will take no heed, shall find default in time of need.
"Default" here means a failure to meet one's financial obligations.

Its effects

11 Poverty is an enemy to good manners.

12 A moneyless man goes fast through the market.

13 Need makes the naked man run.
Poverty spurs on the desperate. Often cited together with SORROW: 22.

14 Need makes the old wife trot.

15 The worth of a thing is best known by the want of it.

16 Wealth is best known by want.

17 When poverty comes in at the door, love flies out of the window.
A very old proverb with variants in most European languages.

Its advantages

18 A beggar can never be bankrupt.

19 It is a good thing to eat your brown bread first.
Implies that poverty in early life is good preparation for future wealth. Brown (i.e. rye) bread was formerly the staple food of the poor.

20 Poor folk are fain of little.
Poor people are easily pleased ("fain" means "glad"). The same thought is expressed in proverbs 21 and 22 below.

21 Where nothing is, a little does ease.

22 Poor folks are glad of porridge.

23 A horn spoon holds no poison.
Those who can afford nothing better than a horn spoon (formerly the cheapest kind of utensil and a byword for poverty) are not worth poisoning; therefore they need have no fear of murderers or thieves. This sentiment is echoed in several of the proverbs below.

24 He that has nothing need fear to lose nothing.

25 He that has no money needs no purse.

26 No naked man is sought after to be rifled.

27 The beggar may sing before the thief.

28 If we have not the world's wealth, we have the world's ease.

29 Who can sing so merry a note, as he that cannot change a groat?
A "groat" was a former coin worth four pennies.

30 Little gear, less care.
"Gear" means "goods, possessions".

31 Little wealth, little care.

32 Lowly sit, richly warm.

33 Small riches hath most rest.

34 The poor sit on the front benches in Paradise.

35 He that has little is the less dirty.

36 Nothing have, nothing crave.

37 Poor folk fare the best.

38 Poverty is the mother of all arts.
Compare NECESSITY: 7.

39 Poverty is the mother of health.

Its disadvantages

40 A poor man's table is soon spread.

41 Where coin is not common, commons must be scant.
"Commons" is an archaic term for "provisions".

42 Want of money, want of comfort.

43 An empty purse causes a full heart.

44 A light purse makes a heavy heart.

45 An empty purse fills the face with wrinkles.

46 It is easier to commend poverty than to endure it.

47 Poverty is no disgrace, but it is a great inconvenience.
Noted as "a common saying" among the villagers in Flora Thompson's *Lark Rise to Candleford* (1945).

48 Health without money is half an ague.

49 He that has little shall have less.

50 He that has nought shall have nought.

51 He that has nothing is not contented.

52 A man without money is no man at all.

53 The poor man pays for all.

54 The poor suffer all the wrong.

55 The poor man's shilling is but a penny.
An old proverb making the still-relevant point that it is always more expensive to be poor than to be rich: the poor have little ready money and no bargaining power and must therefore pay for everything on the most disadvantageous terms.

56 He that is in poverty, is still in suspicion.
Sometimes attributed to Cato the Elder (3rd–2nd centuries BC).

57 No woe to want.
That is, there is no greater woe than poverty.

58 Poor men have no souls.
Like proverb 59 below, this refers to the medieval church's practice of saying requiem masses only for those rich enough to pay for them – an abuse widely condemned by 16th-century reformers.

59 Penniless souls must pine in purgatory.

Its dangers

60 Poverty is the mother of crime.

61 He that brings up his son to nothing, breeds a thief.

62 The devil dances in an empty pocket.
Apart from the obvious meaning, this alludes to the fact that for many centuries English coins were marked on the back with a cross – a sign that could be expected to drive the devil away from a well-stocked pocket.

63 The poorer one is, the more devils one meets.
Chinese proverb.

64 An empty sack cannot stand upright.
Originally a reference to the moral or physical weakness of the poor. However, the phrase is now more often used as a jocular excuse for taking food or drink.

65 It is a hard task to be poor and leal.
"Leal" means "honest".

66 There is no virtue that poverty destroys not.

67 Poverty obstructs the road to virtue.

68 Poverty is the worst guard for chastity.

69 Need makes greed.

70 Poverty breeds strife.

71 When we have gold, we are in fear; when we have none we are in danger.

Its relative unimportance

72 He who is content in his poverty, is wonderfully rich.

73 He is not poor that has little, but he that desires much.

74 Poverty does not hurt him who has not been rich before.

75 Poor men go to heaven as soon as rich.

76 Put the poor man's penny and the rich man's penny in ae purse, and they'll come out alike.
"Ae" means "one".

77 He is poor that God hates.
Implies that to lack God's grace is far more serious than to lack money.

78 Poverty is not a shame; but the being ashamed of it is.

79 Poverty is not a crime.

80 Want of wit is worse than want of gear.
"Gear" here means "possessions".

81 It is better to be a beggar than a fool.

82 Better beg than steal.

Poverty and wealth

83 Poverty and wealth are twin sisters.

84 From clogs to clogs is only three generations.
Clogs were wooden-soled shoes worn by mill and factory workers in the north of England. The implication is that if a poor man works hard to ensure a comfortable life for his children, they will squander all his accumulated wealth and their own children will once again be obliged to work for their living. A modern variant of this proverb substitutes "shirtsleeves" for "clogs".

85 Bear wealth, poverty will bear itself.

86 Better go to heaven in rags than to hell in embroidery.

87 Better a wee fire to warm us than a mickle fire to burn us.
Implies that it is better to have the comforts of a small amount of money than the dangers of a large fortune. "Mickle" means "great".

88 Content lodges oftener in cottages than palaces.

89 Better be envied than pitied.
The saying can be traced back to Herodotus (5th century BC).

90 Better leave than lack.
Implies that it is better to have too much than not enough.

91 The dainties of the great are the tears of the poor.

92 The pleasures of the mighty are the tears of the poor.

93 The pride of the rich makes the labour of the poor.

94 The rich man spends his money, the poor man his strength.
Chinese proverb.

95 A poor man's cow dies, a rich man's child.

96 The rich man has his ice in the summer and the poor man gets his in the winter.
First recorded in the early 20th century.

97 The sorrows of the rich are not real sorrows; the comforts of the poor are not real comforts.
Chinese proverb.

98 Poor men seek meat for their stomach; rich men stomach for their meat.

99 The rich man may dine when he will, the poor man when he may.

100 The rich man thinks of the future, the poor man thinks of today.
Chinese proverb.

101 Rich men are stewards for the poor.
Implies that the rich are caretakers rather than owners of their wealth, and as such should always be ready to give to the poor.

102 Beggars breed, and rich men feed.
Sometimes used to explain the constant supply of, and demand for, domestic servants.

Contempt for the poor

103 The devil wipes his tail with the poor man's pride.
Less polite versions substitute "arse" for "tail".

104 God help the rich, the poor can beg.
An ironic description of the attitude of the wealthy in times of economic crisis.

105 There's one law for the rich, and another for the poor.
First recorded in the early 19th century.

106 Little Jock gets the little dish, and it holds him aye long little.
The implication is that poverty is prolonged by bad treatment of the poor.

107 The poor man is aye put to the worst.

108 A poor man's tale cannot be heard.

109 The reasons of the poor weigh not.

110 Wood in a wilderness, moss in a mountain, and wit in a poor man's breast, are little thought of.

111 The skilfullest wanting money is scorned.

Qualities of the poor

112 Under a ragged coat lies wisdom.

113 Poor and liberal, rich and covetous.

114 Patience with poverty is all a poor man's remedy.

115 Be patient in poverty and you may become rich.
Chinese proverb.

116 Poverty and anger do not agree.
Arabic proverb.

117 Bashfulness is an enemy to poverty.
That is, bashfulness is a great disadvantage to a poor man.
118 He that has no honey in his pot, let him have it in his mouth.
Like proverb 119 below, this implies that the poor man must be a glib speaker.
119 He that has not silver in his purse, should have silk on his tongue.

See also MARRIAGE: *The importance of material well-being*; PRIDE: *Pride and poverty*

137 Praise

Its value

1 True praise roots and spreads.
2 Praise is always pleasant.
3 Praise is the reflection of virtue.
4 They that value not praise, will never do anything worthy of praise.
5 Praise youth and it will prosper.
6 Lacking breeds laziness, praise breeds pith.
"Lacking" here means "censure"; "pith" means "effort".

Its dangers

7 Too much praise is a burden.
8 Praise none too much, for all are fickle.
9 Praise by evil men is dispraise.

Its effects

10 Praise is a spur to the good, a thorn to the evil.
11 Praise makes good men better, and bad men worse.
12 Praise the child, and you make love to the mother.
13 Who praises St Peter does not blame St Paul.
The common saying "to rob Peter to pay Paul" is probably related to this proverb.
14 Good words anoint us, and ill do unjoint us.
"Anoint" here means "heal", while "unjoint" means "disable".

Its inadequacy

15 Praise is not pudding.
The most familiar variant is Pope's line from *The Dunciad* (1728) about impoverished writers weighing "solid pudding against empty praise".
16 Praises fill not the belly.
17 Praise without profit puts little in the pot.

Self-praise

18 Self-praise is no recommendation.
19 A man's praise in his own mouth stinks.
20 He that praises himself, spatters himself.
21 He has ill neighbours, that is fain to praise himself.
22 Neither praise nor dispraise thyself; thy actions serve the turn.

138 Pride

Its dangers

1 Pride goes before a fall.
   A misquotation from Proverbs 16:18. The full quotation is "Pride goeth before destruction, and an haughty spirit before a fall."
2 Pride goes before, and shame follows after.
3 When pride rides, shame lacqueys.
   To "lacquey" is to follow or attend. The saying has been attributed to King Louis XI of France (1423–83).
4 Pride is the sworn enemy to content.
5 Pride is a flower that grows in the devil's garden.
6 Pride increases our enemies, but puts our friends to flight.
7 Pride, joined with many virtues, chokes them all.

Its sources

8 Heresy is the school of pride.
9 Plenty breeds pride.
   See PEACE: 3 and note.

Its effects

10 Pride and grace dwelt never in one place.
11 Pride and laziness would have mickle upholding.
    "Mickle" means "much". A reference to the expense of providing ornaments for the vain and servants for the lazy.
12 I proud and thou proud, who shall bear the ashes out?

Pride and poverty

13 Pride and poverty are ill met, yet often seen together.
14 Charity and pride do both feed the poor.
    Implies that the wealthy often give alms for motives of pride or status.
15 Pride may lurk under a threadbare coat.
16 A proud mind and a beggar's purse agree not together.

Characteristics of the proud

17 It is good beating proud folks, for they'll not complain.
18 Bastard brood is always proud.
19 Pride had rather go out of the way than go behind.
    Implies that proud people will not accept advice or guidance.
20 Likeness begets love, yet proud men hate one another.
21 Pride with pride will not abide.
22 Pride will spit in pride's face.
23 Pride often wears the cloak of humility.
    Like proverbs 24 and 25 below, this implies that to proclaim one's humility is in itself a form of pride.
24 There are those who despise pride with a greater pride.
    The saying arises from a story about the philosophers Diogenes and Plato (5th–4th centuries BC). Diogenes, who was known for his somewhat theatrical poverty, once visited Plato's house, where he was disgusted to see a rich carpet on the floor. "Thus I tread the

pride of Plato under my feet!" he cried. "So you do" replied Plato, "but it is with another kind of pride just as great as mine."

25 It is not a sign of humility to declaim against pride.

The need for humility

26 No man so good, but another may be as good as he.

27 No man is indispensable.

28 The best of men are but men at best.
   A saying associated with the English parliamentary general John Lambert (1619–83).

29 Remember you are but a man.
   According to legend Philip of Macedon (4th century BC), the founder of the Macedonian empire, had a servant whose job it was to repeat these words to him every morning.

30 He that will not stoop for a pin, shall never be worth a pound.

31 It is a proud horse that will not bear his own provender.

32 He is a proud tod that will not scrape his own hole.
   "Tod" means "fox".

139 Promises

Their unreliability

1 Promises are like pie-crust, made to be broken.

2 Eggs and oaths are easily broken.

3 Promises are either broken or kept.

4 A man apt to promise, is apt to forget.

5 The day obliterates the promise of the night.
   Arabic proverb.

6 Vows made in storms are forgotten in calms.

7 Men may promise more in a day than they will fulfil in a year.

8 Many fair promises in marriage making, but few in tocher paying.
   "Tocher" means "dowry". The proverb implies that people are very ready to make
   promises until these threaten to involve them in some expense.

9 Words and feathers the wind carries away.

10 Words are but wind.

Their obligation

11 Promise is debt.

12 An ox is taken by the horns, and a man by his word.

Breaking one's word

13 A man that breaks his word, bids others be false to him.

14 To him that breaks his trust, let trust be broken.

15 He loses his thanks who promises and delays.

Promising too much

16 He that promises too much, means nothing.
   Like proverbs 17 and 18 below, this implies that those who make lavish promises are unlikely to keep them.

17 To offer much, is a kind of denial.
18 Who gives to all, denies all.

Promise and performance

19 Promises may make friends, but 'tis performances keep them.
20 One acre of performance, is worth twenty of the land of promise.
21 Between promising and performing, a man may marry his daughter.
22 A long tongue is a sign of a short hand.
   Implies that those who are most eager to make promises are the least likely to keep them.

140 Proverbs

Their value

1 A good maxim is never out of season.
2 The genius, wit, and spirit of a nation are discovered in its proverbs.
   A maxim attributed to Francis Bacon, who compiled (1594) one of the earliest collections of proverbs in English.
3 Great consolation may grow out of the smallest saying.
4 A proverb is an ornament to language.
5 The proverb cannot be bettered.
6 Hold fast to the words of your ancestors.

Their truth

7 Common proverb seldom lies.
8 Old saws speak truth.
9 There is no disputing a proverb, a fool, and the truth.
10 Proverbs cannot be contradicted.
11 Though the proverb is abandoned, it is not falsified.

Their sources

12 Proverbs are the children of experience.
13 Maxims are the condensed good sense of nations.
14 Proverbs are the wisdom of the streets.
15 Wise men make proverbs and fools repeat them.
   A handy riposte to anyone who quotes a proverb against you.
16 A proverb is the wit of one and the wisdom of many.
   Attributed to the British statesman Lord John Russell (1792–1878).
17 A proverb comes not from nothing.

Their brevity

18 Death and proverbs love brevity.
19 A proverb is shorter than a bird's beak.

Their permanence

20 Time passes away, but sayings remain.
21 Proverbs are like butterflies, some are caught, others fly away.

Q

141 Quarrelling

Its sources

1 Contention's roots are three: women, land, and gold.
Indian proverb.

2 Women and dogs set men together by the ears.
Some variants add "wine" to the list of troublemakers.

3 Poverty breeds strife.

4 It takes two to make a quarrel.

5 The second word makes the quarrel.
Japanese proverb. The "second word" here means the angry reply to an insult, criticism, etc.

6 Two cats and a mouse, two wives in one house, two dogs and a bone, never agree in one.

7 Two sparrows on one ear of corn make an ill agreement.

8 Two suns cannot shine in one sphere.
According to tradition, this was Alexander the Great's answer to Darius III, king of Persia, when the latter attempted to make terms (c. 333 BC). The phrase is mainly used in a political context, with some variants adding "...and two kings cannot reign in one kingdom."

9 Youth and age will never agree.

10 The mother of mischief is no bigger than a midge's wing.
A reference to the trivial causes of many quarrels.

Its effects

11 Quarrelling dogs come halting home.
"Halting" here means "limping".

12 Quarrelsome dogs get dirty coats.

13 Brabbling curs never want sore ears.
"Brabbling" means "brawling".

14 Brawling booteth not.
"Booteth" means "profits".

15 Two dogs strive for a bone, and a third runs away with it.

16 Yelping curs will raise mastiffs.
Implies that a trivial quarrel among subordinates may lead to more serious disputes between the powerful.

17 By scratching and biting, cats and dogs come together.

18 In too much dispute truth is lost.
19 Strife never begets a gentle child.
African proverb.
20 Broken bones well set become stronger.
Implies that a quarrel between two parties, once settled, may help to strengthen their relationship.
21 Woe to the house where there is no chiding.
22 When thieves fall out, honest men come by their own.
23 It is good fishing in troubled waters.
Implies that situations of unrest or dispute may be successfully exploited by a third party.
24 Divide and rule.
An old political maxim, implying that a shrewd ruler will encourage disputes amongst those who might otherwise unite against his or her authority.

The need to agree

25 Fools bite one another, but wise men agree together.
26 Agree, for the law is costly.
27 One bad general is better than two good ones.
Because two generals may not agree as to the best course of action. Sometimes attributed to Abraham Lincoln (1860s).
28 United we stand, divided we fall.
The original context for this slogan was the uniting of the American colonies against British rule in the 1770s.
29 A house divided against itself cannot stand.
Adapted from Mark 3:25.
30 Kingdoms divided soon fall.
31 Birds in their little nests agree.
A quotation from Isaac Watts's moralizing poems for young children "Love Between Brothers and Sisters" (1715).

The quarrelsome

32 Of two disputants, the warmer is generally in the wrong.
33 Wranglers never want words.
34 Cavil will enter at any hole, and if it find none it will make one.
Implies that those who are determined to quarrel will always find some excuse to do so.

Settling a quarrel

35 Spread the table, and contention will cease.
36 The difference is wide that the sheets will not decide.
Implies that most quarrels between a couple may be settled in bed.
37 Dogs will redd swine.
"Redd" means "settle, put in order". The proverb refers to the use of a third party to settle disputes.
38 He that can make a fire well, can end a quarrel.

142 Regret

Its futility

1 What's done cannot be undone.
   A well-known variant is "What's done is done", a quotation from Shakespeare's *Macbeth* (c. 1606).
2 It is too late to call back yesterday.
3 Things past cannot be recalled.
4 It is too late to grieve when the chance is past.
5 It is no use crying over spilt milk.
6 Never grieve for what you cannot help.
7 Past cure, past care.
8 A word spoken is past recalling.
9 For a lost thing, care not.
10 A hundred pounds of sorrow pays not one ounce of debt.
11 Sorrow will pay no debt.
12 Win or lose, never regret.
   Chinese proverb.
13 Repentance comes too late.
14 Repentance is the virtue of fools.

Its undesirability

15 Fly that pleasure which pains afterward.
16 Repentance is a bitter physic.
17 Repentance is a pill unwillingly swallowed.

Its sources

18 Remorse is lust's dessert.
19 No pleasure without repentance.
20 Short pleasure, long repentance.
21 The end of passion is the beginning of repentance.
22 Short acquaintance brings repentance.
23 Sudden friendship, sure repentance.
24 From hearing, comes wisdom; from speaking, repentance.

The futility of hindsight

25 It is easy to be wise after the event.

26 If things were to be done twice, all would be wise.
27 Beware of 'Had I wist'.
"Wist" means "known".
28 After wit comes ower late.
Here, as in proverb 29 below, "after wit" means "the wisdom of hindsight". "Ower" means "ever".
29 After wit is dear bought.
30 A word before is worth two behind.
31 It's too late to shut the stable door after the horse has bolted.
Until the 20th century the most common form was "…after the horse has been stolen."
32 When the daughter is stolen, shut Pepper Gate.
A reference to a former gate of the city of Chester, through which (it is said) the mayor's daughter was once stolen away by her lover. The mayor is alleged to have had the gate shut up after the incident.
33 It is no time to stoop when the head is off.
34 We never know the worth of water till the well is dry.

The value of repentance

35 Repentance is the loveliest of the virtues.
Chinese proverb.
36 Repentance is not to be measured by inches and hours.
37 Repentance is good, but innocence is better.
38 Who errs and mends, to God himself commends.
39 A fault confessed is half redressed.
40 Never too late to repent.

143 Relations

Their value

1 Blood is thicker than water.
That is, family relationships will prove stronger than any other kind. Not recorded in this form before the early 19th century.
2 Kinsman helps kinsman, but woe to him that has nothing.
3 It is good to be near of kin to land.

Their unreliability

4 Many kinsfolk, few friends.
Mainly said by those who feel neglected by their more prosperous relatives.
5 At marriages and funerals, friends are discerned from kinsfolk.
Because such occasions reveal a person's true well-wishers.
6 A near neighbour is better than a far-dwelling kinsman.
7 Wheresoever you see your kindred, make much of your friends.
8 Do no business with a kinsman.
Indian proverb.

Undesirable relations

9 There's a black sheep in every flock.
First recorded in the early 19th century.

10 Every family has a skeleton in the cupboard.
First recorded in the mid-19th century.

11 Even the Son of Heaven has his poor relations.
Chinese proverb. "Son of Heaven" was a title given to the emperor.

12 It is a poor kin that has neither whore nor thief in it.
Like proverbs 13–18 below, this is a retort to someone who attempts to discredit you by alluding to your discreditable relatives.

13 It is a sairy wood that has never a withered bough in it.
"Sairy" means "poor".

14 In good pedigrees there are governors and chandlers.
That is, men of both high and low degree (a "chandler" was a shopkeeper or trader).

15 Who has neither fools nor beggars nor whores among his kindred, was born of a stroke of thunder.

16 Every family cooking-pot has one black spot.
Chinese proverb.

17 Shame in a kindred cannot be avoided.

18 A man cannot bear all his kin on his back.
Implies that nobody can be held responsible for the faults of his relations.

Looking after one's relations

19 Charity begins at home.

20 A man should keep from the blind and give to his kin.

21 Keep your ain fish-guts to your ain sea-maws.
"Ain" means "own"; "sea-maws" are gulls.

Family affairs

22 It is an ill bird that fouls its own nest.
Implies that one should not publicly criticize or denigrate one's own family.

23 Don't wash your dirty linen in public.
Implies that one should not discuss family scandals or quarrels in public. The saying is sometimes attributed to Napoleon.

144 Religion

Its value

1 Religion is the rule of life.

2 A man without religion is like a horse without a bridle.

3 One may live without father or mother, but one cannot live without God.

4 The devil never assails a man except he find him either void of knowledge, or of the fear of God.

5 Have God and have all.

6 He loses nothing who keeps God for his friend.

7 The best way to travel is towards heaven.

8 Meat and mass never hindered any man.
Implies that one's business is never harmed by making the time to eat or pray. See also proverb 97 below.

9 When God is made the master of a family, he orders the disorderly.

Its limitations

10 Put your trust in God, but keep your powder dry.

Advice allegedly given by Oliver Cromwell to his troops while crossing a river during his Irish campaign (1649). Like proverb 11 below, it implies that one should not allow faith in God to prevent one from being severely practical.

11 Praise the Lord and pass the ammunition.

A remark allegedly made by a US naval chaplain during the Japanese attack on Pearl Harbor (1941). The phrase later supplied the title of a popular song by Frank Loesser (1943).

12 The man of God is better for having his bows and arrows about him.

13 It matters not what religion an ill man is of.

Implies that religion can do little to improve an evil person.

14 St Luke was a saint and a physician, and yet he died.

The need for respect

15 Religion, credit, and the eye are not to be touched.

Because these are all sensitive matters.

16 Jest not with the eye, or with religion.

17 King Harry robbed the church, and died a beggar.

A reference to Henry VIII's dissolution of the monasteries (1536–40).

18 Never dog barked against the crucifix but he ran mad.

Heaven and hell

19 Better go to heaven in rags than to hell in embroidery.

20 Hell is wherever heaven is not.

21 Heaven and hell are within the heart.

Chinese proverb.

22 All of heaven and hell is not known till hereafter.

23 This world is nothing, except it tend to another.

The way to heaven

24 No coming to heaven with dry eyes.

25 Crosses are ladders that lead to heaven.

"Crosses" here refers to the cross of Christ, a symbol of suffering.

26 In rain and sunshine cuckolds go to heaven.

27 He that will enter into Paradise must have a good key.

28 A man must go old to the court, and young to a cloister, that would go from thence to heaven.

Implies that many years spent at court will corrupt the soul, and that turning to God in one's old age may not be enough.

29 There is no going to heaven in a sedan.

An earlier variant, "We cannot go to heaven in a featherbed", is recorded as a favourite saying of Sir Thomas More.

30 Gold goes in at any gate except heaven's.

31 Poor men go to heaven as soon as rich.

32 The way to heaven is alike in every place.

Sometimes attributed to the philosopher Diogenes (5th century BC), who is said to have used these words to rebuke someone who complained that he would not die in his own country.

33 The way to heaven is as ready by water as by land.
Sometimes attributed to the English sailor Sir Humphrey Gilbert (d. 1583), who is said to have used these words to encourage his crew during a tempest. However, the saying has also been attributed to other famous seafarers.

The way to hell

34 The descent to hell is easy.
A quotation from Virgil's *Aeneid* (1st century BC), describing Aeneas's descent to the underworld; the poem continues "but the return is very difficult."

35 The road to hell is paved with good intentions.
In earlier forms of the proverb (pre-19th century) it is hell itself that is so paved. The saying has been attributed to St Bernard of Clairvaux (1090–1153).

36 Who fasts and does no other good, spares his bread and goes to hell.

37 Hell is always open.

38 Hopers go to hell.

39 Long in court, deep in hell.

False devotion

40 The devil was sick, the devil a saint would be; the devil was well, the devil a saint was he.
Like proverbs 41–43 below, this implies that people tend to turn to religion in time of need, only to discard it again when things take a turn for the better.

41 Danger makes men devout.

42 Some are atheists only in fair weather.

43 The porter calls upon God only when he is under the load.
Arabic proverb.

Heresy

44 Heresy is the school of pride.

45 Heresy may be easier kept out than shook off.

46 Turkey, heresy, hops, and beer came into England all in one year.
Turkeys were introduced to England from the New World at about the same time (the 1520s) that Protestant doctrines began to arrive from Germany; the same period saw beer, which is flavoured with hops, replace ale as the favoured drink of the English. Some variants add "carp" to the list of novelties.

47 For the same man to be a heretic and a good subject, is impossible.

48 With the gospel, one becomes a heretic.

Religious differences

49 An atheist is one point beyond the devil.
Because at least the devil believes in God.

50 A complete Christian must have the works of a Papist, the words of a Puritan, and the faith of a Protestant.
Traditionally, Catholic teaching has stressed the value of good works while Protestantism has insisted that salvation comes through faith alone; the proverb implies that Puritans are noted for neither faith nor works but only "words".

51 The Jews spend at Easter, the Moors at marriages, the Christians in suits.
"Easter" here refers to the Passover feast and "suits" to lawsuits.

52 Henry the Eighth pulled down monks and their cells, Henry the Ninth should pull down bishops and their bells.

A reference to Henry VIII's dissolution of the monasteries (1536–40); many Puritans took the view that the Reformation had not gone far enough and that a similar approach should be taken to the structures of the Church of England.

53 '*Pater noster*' built churches, and 'Our Father' pulls them down.

A further reference to the dissolution of the monasteries; the Latin form "*Pater noster*" represents the Catholic Church and "Our Father" the Church of England.

54 There is no rain – the Christians are the cause.

A popular proverb in ancient Rome, where natural calamities were frequently blamed on the Christians. It is noted in St Augustine of Hippo's *The City of God* (413 AD).

55 He that is of all religions is of no religion.

Religious martyrs

56 No religion but can boast of its martyrs.

57 The blood of the martyrs is the seed of the church.

A quotation from the Christian writer Tertullian (2nd–3rd centuries AD).

58 It is not the suffering, but the cause which makes a martyr.

59 It is better to be a martyr than a confessor.

In Roman Catholic teaching the martyrs ranked above all other saints, including the "confessors", who had shown great courage in proclaiming their faith. The proverb implies that it is better to show your faith through action and suffering rather than through words.

The church

60 The church is an anvil which has worn out many hammers.

61 The nearer the church, the farther from God.

Now mainly used to imply that those who are most involved with religious institutions are often the least Christian in their lives. Formerly, however, the proverb reflected a belief that people who live near church buildings have a tendency to be irreligious or immoral.

62 The kirk is aye greedy.

Like proverb 63 below, a reference to the much resented practice of tithing.

63 What the church takes not, the exchequer carries away.

Sunday

64 The better the day, the better the deed.

An excuse for doing something that should not be done on the Sabbath day.

65 A man had better ne'er been born as have his nails on a Sunday shorn.

However, according to another old superstition Saturday was the unlucky day for cutting one's nails: see DAYS: 7.

66 He that hangs himself on Sunday, shall hang still uncut down on Monday.

67 If you go nutting on Sundays, the devil will come to help and hold the bough for you.

68 Sunday's wooing draws to ruin.

69 When Sunday comes it will be holy day.

70 If you have done no ill the six days, you may play the seventh.

Men of the church

71 A house-going parson makes a church-going people.

72 Like people, like priest.
    A biblical quotation: Hosea 4:9. There are two possible implications: that the godliness (or otherwise) of the people depends on that of the priest; or that the people get the priests they deserve.

73 Such priest, such offering.
    Implies that the size of gifts made to the church reflects the quality of the priest.

74 Clergymen's sons always turn out badly.

75 Once a parson always a parson.
    Variants substitute "bishop" or "priest" for "parson". The proverb alludes to the doctrine that holy orders are indelible.

76 Parsons are souls' waggoners.

77 He that preaches, gives alms.

78 Saturday is the working day and Monday the holiday of preachers.

79 The greatest scholars are not the best preachers.

80 A pope by voice, a king by birth, an emperor by force.
    The saying refers to the means by which these high offices may be attained ("voice" here means "choice, election").

81 If you would be pope, you must think of nothing else.

82 A monk out of his cloister is like a fish out of water.
    A maxim from the *Decretum*, the principal compilation of medieval canon law (12th century).

83 He that cannot do better, must be a monk.

84 Take heed of an ox before, of a horse behind, of a monk on all sides.

85 The devil and the dean begin with a letter; when the devil gets the dean, the kirk will be the better.

86 Weel's him and wae's him that has a bishop in his kin.
    Implies that there are both advantages and disadvantages of having relatives in the church.

87 Pigeons and priests make foul houses.
    A warning not to bring a priest into one's household, because his meddling will cause trouble. A variant substitutes "doves and dominies (*i.e.* schoolmasters)".

88 No mischief but a woman or a priest is at the bottom of it.

89 Women, priests, and poultry, have never enough.

90 Three things are insatiable, priests, monks, and the sea.

Prayer

91 A short prayer penetrates heaven.
    The earliest known citation is in Langland's *Piers Plowman* (late 14th century).

92 The fewer the words, the better the prayer.

93 If your heart is in your prayer, God will know it.

94 Even the prayers of an ant reach to heaven.
    Japanese proverb.

95 Labour as long lived, pray as ever dying.

96 Prayer should be the key of the day and the lock of the night.

97 Prayers and provender hinder no man's journey.
    The implication is the same as that of proverb 8 above.

98 The prayers of the wicked won't prevail.

99 The family that prays together stays together.
    This was the slogan of the Family Rosary Crusade, a US Roman Catholic movement of
    the 1940s led by a Father Patrick Peyton; it was apparently devised by an advertising
    copywriter named Al Scalpone. The slogan is now mainly associated with the so-called
    Moral Majority, a conservative movement among evangelical Christians in the USA.

The Bible

100 The Bible is the religion of Protestants.
     A quotation from William Chillingworth's tract *The Religion of Protestants* (1637); the
     words "...and the Bible only..." are often added.
101 There is nothing patent in the New Testament that is not latent in the Old.
102 Prosperity is the blessing of the Old Testament, adversity the blessing of the
     New.
     A quotation from Francis Bacon's *Essays* (1625).

See also CORRUPTION: *Religious corruption*; DEVIL; GOD; HYPOCRISY: *Religious hypocrisy*

145 Remedies

Their reliability

1 No wrong without a remedy.
   An old legal maxim.
2 There is a salve for every sore.
3 There is a remedy for all things but death.
4 There is a remedy for everything, could men find it.
5 For every evil under the sun, there is a remedy or there is none: if there be
   one, try and find it; if there be none, never mind it.

The nature of the remedy

6 Adapt the remedy to the disease.
   Chinese proverb.
7 Seek your salve where you get your sore.
   It was a common axiom of folk medicine, later adopted as the basis of homeopathy, that
   the cause of any malady would also yield a cure for it.
8 The hand that gave the wound must give the cure.
   This is usually quoted to refer to the "wound" of love.
9 Take a hair of the dog that bit you.
   The advice here is that the unpleasant after-effects of drunkenness may be relieved by
   consuming more alcohol. The saying originates from an old superstititon that the bite of
   a dog could be healed by burning and consuming one of its hairs.
10 One poison drives out another.
    Variants substitute "nail", "love", "fire", or "heat" for "poison".
11 The smell of garlic takes away the smell of onions.
    One ironic variant suggests "To take away the smell of onion eat a leek, to take away the
    smell of the leek eat garlic, and to take away the smell of the garlic eat a turd."
12 Desperate cuts must have desperate cures.
    "Diseases" is often substituted for "cuts".

13 Take away the cause, and the effect must cease.
14 Destroy the nests and the birds will fly away.
   That is, destroy the places where undesirable people gather and they will disperse.
15 If you don't like the heat, get out of the kitchen.
   If you can't stand the pressure that is inseparable from positions of authority, make way for someone who can. The saying is usually associated with President Harry S. Truman, who used it when explaining his decision to step down in 1952. Truman himself attributed it to one of his military advisers, Major General Harry Vaughan.
16 The remedy may be worse than the disease.
   Implies that measures taken to solve a problem may themselves cause a worse problem.

See also ANGER: *Its remedies*; DEATH: *Its consolations*; HEALTH: *Remedies*; LOVE: *Its remedies*; PATIENCE: *Patience as a remedy*; SORROW: *Remedies for sorrow*

146 Resolution

Its value

1 Bold resolution is the favourite of providence.
2 Every task is easy to a resolute man.
   Chinese proverb.
3 The resolved mind has no cares.
4 In things that must be, it is good to be resolute.
.5 A cat in gloves catches no mice.
   A warning against over-cautiousness.

Indecision

6 He who hesitates is lost.
7 The woman that deliberates is lost.
   A quotation, referring to matters of love, from Addison's play *Cato* (1713).
8 The longer you look at it the less you will like it.
9 Between two stools one falls to the ground.
10 When in doubt, do nowt.
   "Nowt" means "nothing".

147 Responsibility

Personal responsibility

1 Every man is the architect of his own fortune.
   The saying can be traced back to the historian Sallust (1st century BC).
2 Every man is the son of his own works.
3 Let every sheep hang by his own shank.
   Like proverbs 4–6 below, this implies that everybody should rely on their own initiative and hard work.
4 Every herring must hang by its own gill.
5 Every tub must stand on its own bottom.
6 Let every pedlar carry his own burden.
7 A burthen of one's own choice is not felt.

8 That sick man is not to be pitied who has his cure in his sleeve.

9 The evils we bring on ourselves are the hardest to bear.

10 As you make your bed, so you must lie on it.
Like proverbs 11–19 below, this implies that one must accept responsibility for one's own actions, however unpleasant the consequences may be. Owing to the reference to "bed", this proverb is often applied to cases involving sexual activity.

11 As you sow, so you reap.
Adapted from Galatians 6:7.

12 As you bake so shall you eat.
A variant substitutes "brew...drink" for "bake...eat".

13 He that takes the devil into his boat, must carry him over the sound.

14 He that has shipped the devil, must make the best of him.

15 He that has his hand in the lion's mouth, must take it out as well as he can.

16 If you leap into a well, Providence is not bound to fetch you out.

17 Wite yourself if your wife be with bairn.
"Wite" means "blame".

18 That which a man causes to be done, he does himself.

19 They that dance must pay the fiddler.

Joint responsibility

20 It takes two to tango.
This modern proverb derives from the title of a popular song (1952) by Hofmann and Manning. It is often used in sexual contexts, to imply that in any consensual act the parties must be regarded as equally responsible. When used in cases of political negotiation, etc., the implication is somewhat different – that agreement cannot be reached without give-and-take on both sides.

21 Everybody's business is nobody's business.
Like proverb 22 below, this implies that where responsibility is shared, it is likely to be neglected.

22 A pot that belongs to many is ill stirred and worse boiled.

23 Corporations have neither bodies to be punished nor souls to be damned.
A saying of the English judge Lord Thurlow (1731–1806).

Shifting the blame

24 A bad workman always blames his tools.

25 A bad shearer never had a good sickle.

26 The absent party is always to blame.

27 Deaf men go away with the blame.

28 Many a one blames his wife for his own unthrift.

29 Every one puts his fault on the times.

30 One does the scathe, and another has the scorn.
"Scathe" means "harm".

31 When one falls, it is not one's foot that is to blame.
Chinese proverb.

32 He that cannot beat the ass, beats the saddle.

33 How can the cat help it, if the maid be a fool?
Implies that if the cat steals food or causes some other damage, it is the maid's fault for not putting things out of the animal's reach.

34 The dog bites the stone, not him that throws it.

35 Put the saddle on the right horse.
That is, put the blame on those who deserve to bear it.

Making excuses

36 He who excuses himself, accuses himself.

37 Bad excuses are worse than none.

38 A bad excuse is better than none at all.

39 It is good to have a cloak for the rain.
That is, it is good to have an excuse ready in case you need it.

40 A good shift may serve long, but it will not serve for ever.
"Shift" here means "excuse".

41 He that would hang his dog, gives out first that he is mad.
Implies that when we intend to act harshly towards somebody we will usually seek justification by accusing him or her of some fault.

42 It is easy to find a stick to beat a dog.
That is, if you wish to attack somebody or something an excuse can usually be found for doing so.

43 Idle folks lack no excuses.

44 An ill paymaster never wants excuse.
"Wants" here means "lacks".

45 A woman need but look on her apron-string to find an excuse.

46 Find a woman without an excuse, and find a hare without a meuse.
A "meuse" is a gap in a hedge.

148 Revenge

Its inevitability

1 Blood will have blood.
Adapted from Genesis 9:6.

2 Where blood has been spilt the tree of forgetfulness cannot flourish.
Brazilian proverb.

3 Where vice is, vengeance follows.

Its sources

4 The noblest vengeance is to forgive.

5 Pardons and pleasantness are great revenges of slanders.

6 Neglect will kill an injury sooner than revenge.
The meaning is made clearer by proverb 7 below.

7 The remedy for injuries is not to remember them.

8 Living well is the best revenge.

Its effects

9 To lament the dead avails not and revenge vents hatred.

10 Revenge never repairs an injury.

11 To take revenge is often to sacrifice oneself.
African proverb.

12 Don't cut off your nose to spite your face.

Attitudes to revenge

13 Revenge is sweet.

Used (with variants) by Jonson, Milton, and Sheridan.

14 Revenge is a morsel for God.

This Italian proverb alludes to the biblical doctrine that revenge belongs to God alone (Romans 12:19) – but hints that He has reserved it to Himself because of its extreme sweetness.

15 He who cannot revenge himself is weak, he who will not is vile.

16 An eye for an eye, and a tooth for a tooth.

This concept of retribution is expressed on a number of occasions in the Old Testament (e.g. Exodus 21:23–25). It is specifically condemned by Christ in Matthew 5:38.

17 Turn the other cheek.

Adapted from the same passage of the Sermon on the Mount (Matthew 5:38–39) referred to in the note above.

Delayed revenge

18 Revenge, the longer it is delayed, the crueller it grows.

19 Revenge is a dish that can be eaten cold.

A common variant has "…best eaten cold."

20 Revenge of a hundred years still has its sucking teeth.

That is, it is still in its infancy. Another Italian proverb reflecting the culture of *vendetta*.

149 Royalty

Its power

1 The king can do no wrong.

An English common-law maxim that states the so-called "prerogative of perfection", under which the sovereign is immune from all civil and criminal proceedings. Although the sovereign's personal immunity remains, since 1947 it has been possible to take civil action against the Crown (i.e. government departments and other public bodies).

2 Kings have long arms.

The saying can be traced back to Ovid's *Heroides* (1st century BC).

3 Kings have many ears and many eyes.

4 What the king wills, that the law wills.

The proverb arose from the high-handed action of King Alfonso VI of Castile (d. 1109), who ended a protracted dispute about whether the Mozarabic or the Roman liturgy should be used in his kingdom by throwing the former into the fire.

5 He whom a prince hates, is as good as dead.

Sometimes attributed to Thomas Howard, 3rd duke of Norfolk (1473–1554), who held high office under Henry VIII. Norfolk went in and out of favour as the king successively married and executed two of his nieces (Anne Boleyn and Catherine Howard). He was finally condemned to death for treason in 1546 but Henry died before the sentence could be carried out.

6 The king never dies.

Like proverb 7 below, this makes the point that although individual monarchs may die, the office of sovereign is never vacant.

7 The king is dead; long live the king!

Its drawbacks

  8 Crowns have cares.
  9 Uneasy lies the head that wears a crown.
     A quotation from Shakespeare's *2 Henry IV* (*c.* 1598).
 10 Content lodges oftener in cottages than palaces.
 11 Many eyes are upon the king.
 12 It is the lot of a king to do well but to be ill spoken of.

Its inadequacy

 13 A crown is no cure for the headache.
 14 Content is more than a kingdom.

Characteristics of the monarch

 15 The king's word is worth more than another man's oath.
     Sometimes attributed to the philosopher Isocrates (4th century BC), in his correspondence with Nicocles, king of Cyprus.
 16 A king's face should give grace.
 17 Princes are venison in heaven.
     Implies that princes go to heaven as rarely as venison is eaten in England.
 18 Kings are out of play.
     Another reference to the immunity of monarchs and their affairs (see proverb 1 above).

The monarch and his subjects

 19 Like king, like people.
     This may be used to emphasize the moral influence of the monarch over the people; or to imply that the people get the ruler they deserve.
 20 He that is hated of his subjects, cannot be counted a king.
 21 The subject's love is the king's lifeguard.
     The saying can be traced back to Seneca's *De clementia* (1st century AD).
 22 When the prince fiddles, the subject must dance.
 23 When the king makes a mistake, all the people suffer.
     Chinese proverb.
 24 When the head aches, all the body is the worse.
     The "head" here refers to the king, and the "body" to his people.

Serving the monarch

 25 No service to the king's.
     A common variant adds "...and no fishing to the sea", thereby implying that royal service is dangerous as well as profitable.
 26 King's chaff is worth other men's corn.
     Implies that although the monarch's service may not carry the best wages, it has other advantages and benefits.

Courtiers

 27 At court, every one for himself.
 28 Whoso will dwell in court must needs curry favour.
 29 The king's cheese goes half away in parings.
     A reference to the dishonesty of courtiers.

The insecurity of court life

30 A king's favour is no inheritance.
31 Favour will as surely perish as life.
32 Courtiers are shod with watermelon rind.
    Which is very slippery.
33 He that lives in court dies upon straw.

The dangers of court life

34 Nearest the king, nearest the widdie.
    "Widdie" means "gallows".
35 Far from Jupiter, far from thunder.
36 Far from court, far from care.
37 Long in court, deep in hell.

150 Sacrifice

Its necessity

1 You can't make an omelette without breaking eggs.
   Originally a French proverb; first recorded in English in the mid-19th century. The context is often one of political or revolutionary violence.
2 You must lose a fly to catch a trout.
3 He who does not kill hogs, will not get black puddings.

Its value

4 A hook's well lost to catch a salmon.
5 Venture a small fish to catch a great one.
6 Throw out a sprat to catch a mackerel.
7 Better a little loss than a long sorrow.
8 Better cut the shoe than pinch the foot.
9 If thine eye offend thee, pluck it out.
   A biblical quotation: Matthew 18:9.
10 Better eye out than always ache.
   Adapted from the same biblical text as proverb 9 above. Another proverb states the opposite view: "Better eye sore than always blind."
11 Lose a leg rather than a life.

151 Safety

Its sources

1 There is safety in numbers.
   The earliest known citation is from Jane Austen's *Emma* (1816). The saying is loosely based on Proverbs 11:14.
2 It is safe riding in a good haven.
   "Riding" here means "lying at anchor".
3 The death of the wolves is the safety of the sheep.
4 Out of debt, out of danger.
5 Out of office, out of danger.
6 Nought is never in danger.
   "Nought" here refers to a worthless person or thing.

7 He that never climbed never fell.
A variant substitutes "rode" for "climbed".

8 A hole in the ice is dangerous only to those who go skating.
Chinese proverb.

9 The way to be safe is never to be secure.
Like proverb 10 below, this implies that a sense of security may make one careless and unaware of potential danger. Compare DANGER: 30–32.

10 He that is secure is not safe.

11 Safety lies in solitude.
Persian proverb.

12 Safe bind, safe find.

The value of security

13 Better be safe than sorry.
A variant substitutes "sure" for "safe".

14 It is best to be on the safe side.

15 It is good walking with a horse in one's hand.
Like proverbs 16–19 below, this refers to the importance of having contingency plans.

16 Good riding at two anchors, men have told, for if one break the other may hold.

17 Venture not all in one bottom.
"Bottom" here means "vessel".

18 Don't put all your eggs in one basket.

19 The mouse that has but one hole is quickly taken.

Compare DANGER: *Against taking risks*

152 Seasons

Spring

1 When you can tread on nine daisies at once, spring has come.

2 A late spring is a great blessing.

3 The spring is not always green.

4 Plan the whole year in the spring.
Chinese proverb.

5 In the spring a young man's fancy lightly turns to thoughts of love.
A quotation from Tennyson's poem *Locksley Hall* (1842).

6 When the cuckoo comes, he eats up all the dirt.
Implies that the arrival of the cuckoo announces the end of the unpleasant weather of winter and heralds the beginning of spring.

Summer

7 Summer is a seemly time.

8 Look for summer on the top of an oak tree.
A reference to the sprouting of the oak tree, which is supposed to herald the beginning of summer.

9 An English summer, two fine days and a thunderstorm.
First recorded in the mid-19th century.

Autumn

10 Of fair things the autumn is fair.

11 When fern grows red, then milk is good with bread.
Based on the belief that milk is thicker in the autumn than in the summer.

12 A grassy autumn presages a spring of many deaths.

Winter

13 A good winter brings a good summer.

14 Winter eats what summer lays up.

15 Winter is summer's heir.

16 He that passes a winter's day, escapes an enemy.

17 Every mile is two in winter.
A reference to the difficulty of travelling in the winter.

18 If Candlemas Day be fair and bright, winter will have another flight; if on Candlemas Day it be shower and rain, winter is gone, and will not come again.
Candlemas Day is February 2nd. In the USA this is known as Groundhog Day, owing to a belief that the groundhog emerges from hibernation on this date. If the weather is bright enough for the animal to see its shadow (so the belief runs), then it will return to its hole for another six weeks; if, however, the weather is gloomy then winter is over and the groundhog will remain outside to forage and play.

See also MONTHS; WEATHER

153 Self

Protecting one's own interests

1 When everyone takes care of himself, care is taken of all.

2 Look after number one.
"Number one" refers to oneself. Variants are first recorded in the late 18th century.

3 Number one is the first house in the row.

4 Yourself first, others afterward.
Chinese proverb.

5 Every man for himself, and the devil take the hindmost.

6 Every man for himself, and God for us all.

7 He that is ill to himself will be good to nobody.

8 He helps little that helps not himself.

9 God helps them that help themselves.
The earliest known citation in this form is by Benjamin Franklin (1735), but the thought is much older.

10 Mind other men, but most yourself.

11 Near is my coat, but nearer is my shirt.
Like proverb 12 below, this implies that one's own interests and those of close relations must take precedence over anything else.

12 Near is my shirt, but nearer is my skin.

13 The shoemaker's son always goes barefoot.
A reference to those who neglect their own interests or those of their families.

14 Self-preservation is the first law of nature.
   The thought can be traced back to Cicero's *De finibus* (1st century BC). English variants appear in works by Donne, Dryden, and Scott.

15 Everything would fain live.

16 Look to thyself when thy neighbour's house is on fire.

17 No man fouls his hands in his own business.
   That is, there is nothing dishonest in furthering one's own interests.

18 If tha does owt for nowt, do it for thysen.
   "Owt" means "anything"; "nowt" means "nothing". A longer version runs "Hear all, see all, say nowt, tak' all, keep all, gie nowt, and if ..."

Selfishness

19 He is a slave of the greatest slave, who serves nothing but himself.

20 We are not born for ourselves.

21 Sel, sel, has half-filled hell.
   "Sel" means "self".

22 He is unworthy to live who lives only for himself.

23 Who eats his cock alone, must saddle his horse alone.
   Implies that those who live for themselves alone must not expect any help from others.

24 Every man will have his own turn served.

25 Every man is nearest himself.

26 The parson always christens his own child first.
   Sometimes used as a jocular excuse for serving oneself first at table.

27 The tod never sped better than when he went his own errand.
   "Tod" means "fox".

28 He that is warm thinks all so.

Against relying on others

29 If you would be well served, serve yourself.

30 If thou thyself canst do it, attend no other's help or hand.

31 If you want a thing well done, do it yourself.

32 If you want a thing done, go; if not send.

33 Command your man, and do it yourself.

34 He that by the plough would thrive, himself must either hold or drive.

35 Self do, self have.

36 He who depends on another dines ill and sups worse.

The dangers of oneself

37 Every man is his own worst enemy.

38 No man has a worse friend than he brings from home.

39 Beware of no man more than thyself.

Subjectivity

40 Every man likes his own thing best.

41 Our own opinion is never wrong.

42 Men are blind in their own cause.

43 No one ought to be judge in his own cause.
   An old legal maxim.
44 A fox should not be of the jury at a goose's trial.
45 Lookers-on see most of the game.
   A reference to the objectivity of the neutral observer.
46 Each priest praises his own relics.
47 Ask mine host whether he have good wine.

Self-knowledge

48 Know thyself.
   The words inscribed on the oracle of Apollo at Delphi (6th century BC). This motto, which
   has often been taken to encapsulate the ancient Greek philosophy of life, has been vari-
   ously attributed to Thales, Pythagoras, and Solon.
49 Every man is best known to himself.
50 Who knows himself knows others.
   Chinese proverb.
51 No man is the worse for knowing the worst of himself.
52 No man has ever yet thoroughly mastered the knowledge of himself.

Self-pity

53 Every horse thinks its own pack heaviest.
54 Every one thinks his sack heaviest.
55 He that bewails himself has the cure in his hands.

See also DISCIPLINE: *Self-discipline*; PRAISE: *Self-praise*; RESPONSIBILITY: *Personal
responsibility*

154 Servants

Hiring servants

1 Choose none for thy servant who has served thy betters.
2 If you would have a good servant, take neither a kinsman nor a friend.
3 Choose a horse made, and a man to make.
   Implies that while an unschooled horse is difficult to handle, the best servants are those
   who may be moulded to one's own needs.
4 He that is manned with boys, and horsed with colts, shall have his meat
   eaten, and his work undone.
   A warning against hiring servants who are too young.
5 Who wishes to be ill-served, let him keep plenty of servants.
6 He that would be well served, must know when to change his servants.
7 A servant and a cock must be kept but a year.

The good servant

8 A good servant should never be in the way and never out of the way.
   Originally said by Charles II of his page of honour Sidney Godolphin (1645–1712), a future
   Lord Treasurer under James II and Anne.

9 A good servant should have the back of an ass, the tongue of a sheep, and the snout of a swine.
The first to bear burdens patiently, the second to speak meekly, and the third to eat whatever he or she is given.

10 A servant is known by his master's absence.
That is, by his behaviour when he is not being supervised.

11 A good servant must come when you call him, go when you bid him, and shut the door after him.

12 A servant that is diligent, honest, and good, must sing at his work like a bird in the wood.

13 He that serves well needs not ask his wages.
"Ask" here means "ask for".

Handling one's servants

14 A good servant must have good wages.

15 If you would wish the dog to follow you, feed him.

16 If you pay not a servant his wages, he will pay himself.
That is, you will encourage pilfering or other dishonesty.

17 Servants will not be diligent, where the master's negligent.

18 Master easy, servant slack.
Chinese proverb.

19 Like master, like man.
The saying can be traced back to Cicero (1st century BC).

Making use of one's servants

20 Why keep a dog and bark yourself?

Their potential danger

21 So many servants, so many enemies.
The saying can be traced back to Cato the Elder (3rd–2nd centuries BC).

22 Give a slave a rod, and he'll beat his master.

23 Hounds and horses devour their masters.

24 A mastiff grows the fiercer for being tied up.

Servants as masters

25 Servants make the worst masters.

26 Neither beg of him who has been a beggar, nor serve him who has been a servant.

27 An ill servant will never be a good master.

28 One must be a servant before one can be a master.

Good and bad masters

29 He that serves a good master shall have good wages.

30 Serve a noble disposition, though poor, the time comes that he will repay thee.

31 Serve a great man, and you will know what sorrow is.

32 Many a man serves a thankless master.

The undesirability of servitude

33 He who serves is not free.

34 Lean liberty is better than fat slavery.

35 No man loves his fetters, be they made of gold.

36 Service is no inheritance.
Like proverb 37 below, this refers to the financial insecurity of working as a servant.

37 A young serving-man, an old beggar.

The need for subservience

38 If the master say the crow is white, the servant must not say 'tis black.

39 Servants should put on patience, when they put on a livery.

40 As long as you serve the tod, you must bear up his tail.
"Tod" means "fox". The implication is that the servant should not consider any task too menial.

41 An ass pricked must needs trot.

42 An ass must be tied where the master will have him.

43 They that are bound must obey.

155 Shame

Its sources

1 Loss embraces shame.

2 Poverty is not a shame; but the being ashamed of it is.

3 Single long, shame at length.
Like proverb 4 below, this implies that those who remain long single will eventually make unworthy marriages.

4 Long a widow weds with shame.

Its effects

5 Better die with honour than live with shame.
A modern variant, sometimes attributed to the Spanish Republican heroine La Pasionaria (1895–1989), is "Better die on your feet than live on your knees."

6 So long as there is shame, there is hope for virtue.

The shameless

7 Past shame, past grace.
A common variant substitutes "amendment" for "grace".

8 He that has no shame, has no conscience.

9 He who has no shame before the world, has no fear before God.

10 He who is without shame, all the world is his.

Hiding one's shame

11 When an ass kicks you, never tell it.
Implies that there is shame in allowing oneself to be injured by a fool.

12 Who is a cuckold and conceals it, carries coals in his bosom.

13 He that has horns in his bosom, let him not put them on his head.

Like proverb 14 below, this implies that the man who suspects his wife of infidelity does best to keep his fears to himself. Both sayings allude to the symbolic horns of the cuckold.

14 Wise men wear their horns on their breasts, fools on their foreheads.

156 Silence

Its value

1 Silence is golden.
An abbreviated version of proverb 23 below.

2 Silence is of the gods.
Chinese proverb.

3 Silence is the sweet medicine of the heart.
Chinese proverb.

4 A good bestill is worth a groat.
"Bestill" ("be still") is a command to be silent; a groat was a coin worth four pennies.

5 A close mouth catches no flies.

6 It is good to have a hatch before the door.
Like proverb 7 below, this implies that one should be able to keep silent when necessary. A "hatch" here means a wicket or gate.

7 Good that the teeth guard the tongue.

8 A still tongue makes a wise head.

9 No wisdom to silence.

10 A wise head makes a close mouth.

11 Silence never makes mistakes.
Hindi proverb.

12 If you keep your tongue prisoner, your body may go free.

13 He knows enough that knows nothing if he knows how to hold his peace.

14 Neglect will kill an injury sooner than revenge.
Like proverb 15 below, this implies that it is more effective to remain silent than to retaliate when insulted.

15 No reply is best.

16 Silence is a woman's best garment.
The thought can be traced back to Sophocles (5th century BC).

17 Quietness is a great treasure.

18 Silence catches a mouse.

19 Sorrow makes silence her best orator.

Its effects

20 Silence means consent.
A variant substitutes "gives" for "means". Although the maxim is familiar in legal contexts, no such principle is accepted in English law.

21 Silence and thinking can no man offend.

22 Silence does seldom harm.

Silence and speech

23 Speech is silver, silence is golden.
A German proverb, not recorded in English until the mid-19th century; now often abbreviated to the last three words.

24 Talking comes by nature, silence by understanding.

25 Wise men silent, fools talk.

26 He that speaks sows, and he that holds his peace gathers.

27 There is a time to speak and a time to be silent.
Adapted from Ecclesiastes 3:7.

28 More have repented speech than silence.
Sometimes attributed to the Greek orator Isocrates (5th–4th centuries BC).

29 Better say nothing, than not to the purpose.

30 Speak fitly, or be silent wisely.

Characteristics of the silent

31 He that is silent, gathers stones.

32 Still waters run deep.
An example of a proverb that has completely changed its meaning. Before the 19th century it was used to point out that a fair appearance can be dangerously deceptive; since then, it has been used in a mainly favourable sense, to suggest that a person with a placid manner may have hidden depths.

33 Beware of a silent man and still water.

34 From a choleric man withdraw a little; from him that says nothing for ever.
Implies that silent anger is more lasting and dangerous than noisy ill-temper.

35 Dumb dogs are dangerous.

See also TALKING: *Hearing and speaking, Saying little*

157 Similarity

Its sources

1 Like breeds like.

2 Like father, like son.
Variants of this proverb are too numerous to list; for a few examples see e.g. PARENTS: 9; ROYALTY: 19; SERVANTS: 19.

Its effects

3 Like cures like.
Attributed to Samuel Hahnemann (1755–1843), the founder of homeopathic medicine.

4 Like blood, like good, and like age, make the happiest marriage.

5 Likeness causes liking.
The saying has been attributed to both Aristotle and the philosopher Boethius (5th–6th centuries AD).

6 No like is the same.
Implies that similar things are never identical.

7 Great minds think alike.
Not recorded in this form until the early 20th century, although the thought is older; the saying is now mainly used facetiously, to point out any coincidence of thought.

8 Like will to like.

9 Birds of a feather flock together.
Adapted from Ecclesiastes 27:9; "of a feather" means "of the same species".

10 Jackdaw always perches by jackdaw.

11 Scabby donkeys scent each other over nine hills.
   Implies that rogues will seek each other's company.
12 Hedgehogs lodge among thorns, because themselves are prickly.
   Implies that difficult people will surround themselves with difficulties.

158 Skill

Its value

1 Skill and confidence are an unconquered army.
2 Skill will accomplish what is denied to force.
3 'Tis skill, not strength, that governs a ship.
4 Sticking goes not by strength, but by guiding of the gully.
   "Sticking" means "stabbing"; "gully" means "knife".
5 Great strokes make not sweet music.
   Implies that skilful handling of an instrument will produce better results than force.
6 Skill is no burden.

Its necessity

7 Well to work and make a fire, it does care and skill require.
8 There is an art even in roasting apples.
9 Will is no skill.
10 If thy hand be bad, mend it with good play.
   That is, with practice.

Its inadequacy

11 The skilfullest wanting money is scorned.
12 Often a full dexterous smith forges a very weak knife.
13 Nature passes art.
   "Art" here means "skill, craft": "passes" means "surpasses".

Its evidence

14 A good archer is not known by his arrows, but his aim.
15 The best carpenter makes the fewest chips.
   Implies that a skilful worker avoids untidiness and waste.

159 Sleep

Its value

1 Sleep is better than medicine.
2 The beginning of health is sleep.
3 Sleep is a priceless treasure; the more one has of it the better it is.
   Chinese proverb.
4 Sleep is the poor man's treasure.
5 In sleep all passes away.

Its effects

6 In sleep, what difference is there between Solomon and a fool?
   The biblical king Solomon was reputed the wisest of men.

7 One slumber invites another.

8 A man is known to be mortal by two things, sleep and lust.

9 Sleep is the greatest thief, for it steals half one's life.

The right amount

10 One hour's sleep before midnight, is worth two after.

11 Five hours sleeps a traveller, seven a scholar, eight a merchant, and eleven
    every knave.

12 Nature requires five, custom takes seven, idleness takes nine, and wickedness
    eleven.

13 Six hours' sleep for a man, seven for a woman, and eight for a fool.
    This saying was a favourite of George III but is doubtless older.

14 Seven hours' sleep will make a clown forget his design.
    "Clown" here means "countryman, rustic".

Against sleeping too long

15 There will be sleeping enough in the grave.

16 He who sleeps all the morning, may go a begging all the day after.

17 The sleepy fox has seldom feathered breakfasts.

Sleep and death

18 Sleep is the brother of death.
    Hypnos (sleep) and Thanatos (death) were twin brothers in Greek mythology.

19 Sleep is the image of death.

Dreams

20 Dream of a funeral and you hear of a marriage.

21 After a dream of a wedding comes a corpse.

22 Friday night's dream on the Saturday told, is sure to come true be it never so
    old.

23 Morning dreams come true.
    A very old belief, alluded to in Horace's *Satires* (1st century BC).

24 Dreams go by contraries.
    For two of the best-known examples of this common folk belief see proverbs 20 and 21
    above.

25 Dreams are lies.

26 To believe in one's dreams is to spend all one's life asleep.
    Chinese proverb.

27 Golden dreams make men awake hungry.

28 A dream grants what one covets when awake.

29 In dreams and in love nothing is impossible.

30 God creates dreams.
    African proverb.

31 When troubles are few, dreams are few.
    Chinese proverb.

160 Small things

Their value

1 The best things come in small packages.
   Variants substitute "good" for "the best" or "parcels" for "packages". The saying is often used by short people as a response to insults or teasing; in this case a common retort is "And poison comes in small bottles."

2 A little body often harbours a great soul.

3 Small is beautiful.
   The title of a book (1973) by the German-born economist E. F. Schumacher, in which he decried the expansionism then prevalent in business and management thinking. The phrase, which is now used in almost any context, was devised not by Schumacher himself but by his English publishers.

4 Little fish are sweet.
   Often used to imply that small gifts or favours will always be popular.

5 Little sticks kindle the fire; great ones put it out.
   Like proverb 6 below, this is used to urge a moderate approach.

6 A little wind kindles, much puts out the fire.

7 Every little helps.
   For some of the many variants on this theme see proverbs 8–16 below and PERSEVERANCE: *Its effects*.

8 Everything helps, quoth the wren, when she pissed into the sea.
   A variant substitutes "ant" for "wren".

9 One grain fills not a sack, but helps his fellow.

10 Many a little makes a mickle.
   "A mickle" means "a lot".

11 Many a mickle makes a muckle.
   A nonsensical variant of proverb 10 above; "mickle" and "muckle" are synonymous.

12 Many small make a great.

13 Many drops make a shower.

14 Many sands will sink a ship.
   "Sands" here means "grains of sand".

15 Penny and penny laid up will be many.

16 Little and often fills the purse.

17 Small rain lays great dust.

18 Small rain allays great winds.

19 One may see day at a little hole.
   Implies that a small detail may reveal the whole truth about something.

20 The little wimble will let in the great auger.
   A "wimble" is a gimlet; this tool is often used to bore a small hole in wood, etc., to prepare for the auger, a larger boring tool.

21 No hair so small but has his shadow.
   Implies that even the smallest things have an effect beyond themselves.

22 For want of a nail the shoe was lost; for want of a shoe the horse was lost; for want of a horse the rider was lost.
   The proverb illustrates the importance of such small details as the nail in a horse's shoe.

23 Straws show which way the wind blows.
   Implies that trivial incidents may reveal an underlying trend and thereby herald momentous events. The proverb is often alluded to in the phrase "straws in the wind".

Their potential danger

24 A little fire burns up a great deal of corn.

25 Of a small spark, a great fire.

26 A small leak will sink a great ship.
   Mainly used to suggest that constant expenditure, however small, will eventually bring ruin.

27 A little stone in the way overturns a great wain.

28 There is no man, though never so little, but sometimes he can hurt.

29 No viper so little, but has its venom.

30 The fly has her spleen, and the ant her gall.

31 Hair and hair makes the carl's head bare.
   "Carl" means "man". The implication is that many small expenditures may eventually cause financial ruin.

The unimportance of size

32 God oft has a great share in a little house.

33 A short prayer penetrates heaven.

34 The greatest calf, is not the sweetest veal.

35 The greatest crabs be not all the best meat.

36 An inch is as good as an ell.
   An "ell" was a former measure of length, used mainly to measure cloth; originally calculated from the length of a man's forearm, it was later standardized at 45 inches in England and 37 inches in Scotland.

37 They think a calf a muckle beast that never saw a cow.
   "Muckle" means "large". The implication is that the perception of size is relative.

38 A little and good fills the trencher.
   Implies that it is the quality rather than the quantity of food that is important.

Small people

39 Men are not to be measured by inches.

40 Seldom is a long man wise, or a low man lowly.
   Implies that tall people are rarely wise, and small people are rarely meek and humble.

41 Short folk are soon angry.

42 Short folk's heart is soon at their mouth.

43 A little pot is soon hot.

44 As sore fight wrens as cranes.
   Implies that a small person, when provoked, will fight as ardently as anyone else.

See also GREATNESS: *The great and the small*

161 Solitude

Its effects

1 Solitude dulls the thought, too much company dissipates it.

2 Solitude is the nest of thought.

3 A wise man is never less alone than when he is alone.
Adapted from Cicero's *De officiis* (1st century BC), in which the saying is attributed to the great general Scipio Africanus.

4 A soul alone neither sings nor weeps.

Its advantages

5 Solitude is often the best society.

6 Better be alone than in bad company.

7 Safety lies in solitude.
Persian proverb.

8 A man is safe when alone.
Arabic proverb.

9 He travels fastest who travels alone.
A near quotation from the "L'Envoi" to Kipling's tale "The Story of the Gadsbys" (1890).

Its disadvantages

10 It is better to want meat than guests or company.

11 Better strife than solitude.

12 No joy emanates from a lonely person.

13 Misery loves company.
Implies not just that the miserable seek companionship, but that they find satisfaction in seeing others as unhappy as themselves.

14 Woe to him that is alone.
A partial quotation from Ecclesiastes 4:10; the full text continues "...when he falleth; for he hath not another to help him up."

15 The lone sheep is in danger of the wolf.

Characteristics of the solitary

16 Man if he lives alone is either a god or a devil.
Like proverb 17 below, this is adapted from Aristotle's *Politics* (4th century BC), where "beast" appears instead of "devil".

17 A solitary man is either a beast or an angel.

Loneliness in a crowd

18 A great city, a great solitude.

19 A crowd is not company.
A quotation from Francis Bacon's essay "Of Friendship" (1625).

162 Sorrow

Its sources

1 It is comparison that makes men happy or miserable.

2 It is misery enough to have once been happy.
A commonplace of 16th- and 17th-century English literature, with variants appearing in works by Shakespeare, Thomas Nashe, and Robert Burton amongst others.

3 Much science, much sorrow.
"Science" here means "learning".

4 It is a sad burden to carry a dead man's child.

5 Sadness and gladness succeed each other.

6 Sorrow is born of excessive joy.
Chinese proverb.

7 When it thunders in March, it brings sorrow.
Thundery weather in winter or early spring was thought to herald scarcity in summer.

8 Sorrow is at parting if at meeting there be laughter.

9 He that talks much of his happiness, summons grief.

10 Will is the cause of woe.

11 Will will have will, though will woe win.
Implies that although wilfulness invariably causes sorrow, the wilful person still insists on having his or her own way.

Its effects

12 When good cheer is lacking, our friends will be packing.

13 Grief pent up will break the heart.

14 The wound that bleeds inwardly is most dangerous.

15 The greater grief drives out the less.

16 New grief awakens the old.

17 Sorrow kills not, but it blights.

18 Aye be as merry as be can, for love ne'er delights in a sorrowful man.
The first clause means "Always be as cheerful as you can..."

19 Sorrow and an evil life makes soon an old wife.

20 Small sorrows speak; great ones are silent.
A quotation from the Roman play *Hippolytus* (1st century AD), which was formerly attributed to Seneca. The implication is that true grief cannot be put into words. Compare SUFFERING: 4 and 6.

21 Sorrow makes silence her best orator.

22 Sorrow makes websters spin.
"Webster" means "weaver". Often cited together with POVERTY: 13.

Its compensations

23 The remembrance of past sorrows is joyful.
A quotation from Seneca's play *Hercules Furens* (1st century AD).

24 No weal without woe.

25 No coming to heaven with dry eyes.

26 Nothing dries sooner than tears.
A quotation from Cicero's *De oratore* (1st century BC).

27 A bellowing cow soon forgets her calf.
Implies that sorrow, once expressed, is transitory. The allusion is to the noisy but short-lived grieving of cows when first separated from their calves.

Its inevitability

28 You cannot prevent the birds of sadness from flying over your head, but you can prevent them from nesting in your hair.
Chinese proverb.

29 Life and misery began together.

30 We weeping come into the world, and weeping hence we go.

31 No day passes without some grief.

32 He is a fool that is not melancholy once a day.

33 Long life has long misery.

34 Sorrow comes unsent for.

A variant begins "Sorrow and bad weather..."

Its undesirability

35 Better a little loss than a long sorrow.

36 Better two skaiths than one sorrow.

"Skaith" means "harm". Like proverb 35 above, this implies that losses can be made up, whereas sorrow has a lasting effect on the soul.

Handling sorrow

37 Hang sorrow, cast away care.

38 Never lay sorrow to your heart when others lay it to their heels.

Implies that one should not allow oneself to be upset by the desertion or ingratitude of others.

39 He bears misery best, that hides it most.

40 He is worth no weal that can bide no woe.

41 When sorrow is asleep, wake it not.

42 Make not two sorrows of one.

The advice here is that while lamenting a loss, one should not increase one's sadness by lamenting one's sorrow at the loss.

43 Of thy sorrow be not too sad, of thy joy be not too glad.

44 It is ill to put a blithe face on a black heart.

A reference to the difficulty of disguising one's sorrow.

Remedies for sorrow

45 A cure for all sorrows is conversation.

46 Misery loves company.

Implies not just that the miserable seek companionship, but that they find satisfaction in seeing others as unhappy as themselves.

47 He grieves sore who grieves alone.

48 Two in distress make sorrow less.

49 Grief is lessened when imparted to others.

50 Time tames the strongest grief.

The thought can be traced back to Terence (2nd century BC); some variants begin "Time and thought (or thinking)..."

51 Patience is a remedy for every grief.

52 A sorrow is an itching place which is made worse by scratching.

Japanese proverb.

53 There's no cure for sorrow but to put it underfoot.

54 All griefs with bread are less.

Implies that a sufficient diet is a partial remedy for sorrow.

See also HAPPINESS: *Its ephemerality*

163 Spending

Its dangers

1 Who spends before he thrives, will beg before he thinks.
2 Young prodigal in a coach, will be an old beggar barefoot.
3 Who spends more than he should, shall not have to spend when he would.
4 Who will not keep a penny, never shall have many.
5 Who more than he is worth does spend, he makes a rope his life to end.
6 Always taking out of the meal-tub, and never putting in, soon comes to the bottom.
7 A small leak will sink a great ship.
  Implies that constant expenditure, however small, will eventually bring ruin.
8 He who flings gold away with his hands seeks it with his feet.

Its causes

9 Easy come, easy go.
  Implies that money gained with little effort is spent as easily. Variants substitute "lightly" or "quickly" for "easy". The phrase is now used to suggest any kind of relaxed insouciant attitude.
10 Soon gotten, soon spent.
11 So got, so gone.
12 Early master, long knave.
  Implies that a youth who receives his inheritance too soon will squander it and end up working as a servant ("knave").
13 Narrow gathered, widely spent.
  Implies that wealth accumulated by penny-pinching often ends up being squandered.

Its effects

14 Fat housekeepers make lean executors.
  Implies that those whose household expenses are too lavish will have little to leave in their wills.
15 Silks and satins put out the fire in the chimney.
  A reference to the hardship caused by spending money on luxuries.
16 Who dainties love, shall beggars prove.
17 Lavishness is not generosity.
18 The prodigal robs his heir; the miser himself.

Living within one's income

19 Cut your coat according to your cloth.
20 Let your purse be your master.
21 Spend as you get.
22 Stretch your arm no further than your sleeve will reach.
  Don't extend yourself beyond your means.
23 Everyone stretches his legs according to the length of his coverlet.
  A "coverlet" is a blanket or bedspread; some variants add that those who extend themselves further will "stretch in the straw".
24 Lay your wame to your winning.
  That is, suit your household expenditure to your income. "Wame" means "stomach, appetite".

Wise spending

25 If you can spend much, put the more to the fire.
That is, if you can afford to live well, don't stint on basic expenditures. A variant substitutes "fore" for "fire".

26 Spend not where you may save; spare not where you must spend.

27 To a good spender, God is the treasurer.

28 Spend and be free, but make no waste.

29 Know when to spend and when to spare, and you need not be busy; you'll ne'er be bare.

30 That penny is well spent that saves a groat.
A "groat" was a former coin worth four pennies.

31 Sow with the hand, and not with the whole sack.
The saying can be traced back to Plutarch (1st–2nd centuries AD).

32 Scatter with one hand, gather with two.

Characteristics of the prodigal

33 Great spenders are bad lenders.

34 He that has but four and spends five, has no need of a purse.

35 Sailors get money like horses, and spend it like asses.

See also THRIFT: *Its drawbacks*

164 Strength

Its sources

1 Strength grows stronger by being tried.

2 He may bear a bull that has borne a calf.
A reference to a Greek parable in which a wrestler built up his strength by carrying a calf around on his shoulders.

3 Union is strength.
"Unity" or "concord" are often substituted for "union". A common slogan for trade unions or federalist movements.

4 Weak things united become strong.
The saying can be traced back to Homer's *Iliad* (8th century BC).

5 Men, not walls make a city safe.
Adapted from Thucydides's *History of the Peloponnesian War* (4th century BC). The saying implies that the courage and loyalty of its inhabitants may prove a stronger means of defence for a city than walls of stone.

6 Better a castle of bones than of stones.
This has the same implication as proverb 5 above.

Its power

7 Might is right.
The saying can be traced back to Lucan's *Pharsalia* (1st century AD).

8 The strong man and the waterfall channel their own path.

9 God is always on the side of the big battalions.
A quotation from the *Letters* (1696) of Mme de Sévigné, where the saying is attributed to the military leader Henri, Vicomte de Turenne (1611–75). The proverb implies that

although both sides in a battle may claim to have God's support, it is the stronger side that wins. Variants substitute "Providence" or "Fortune" for "God".

Its limitations

10 Not even Hercules could contend against two.

11 A man can do no more than he can.

12 You may break a horse's back, be he never so strong.

13 The race is not to the swift, nor the battle to the strong.
A biblical quotation: Ecclesiastes 9:11.

14 Sticking goes not by strength, but by guiding of the gully.
"Sticking" here means "stabbing"; "gully" means "knife".

15 If the lion's skin cannot, the fox's shall.
Implies that what cannot be gained by strength must be gained by cunning. The saying has been attributed to Lysander, the Spartan naval commander in the Peloponnesian War (5th century BC).

16 Wisdom is better than strength.

17 Policy goes beyond strength.

18 Subtlety is better than force.

19 A chain is no stronger than its weakest link.
First recorded in the mid-19th century.

165 Success

Its value

1 Nothing succeeds like success.
Because everyone wants to be on the winning side; a saying first recorded in English in the mid-19th century. Variants include Wilde's "Nothing succeeds like excess" (1893).

2 He plays best that wins.

3 In all games, it is good to leave off a winner.

Its effects

4 Success makes a fool seem wise.

5 He seems wise with whom all things thrive.

6 On the day of victory no fatigue is felt.
Arabic proverb.

7 Success has many friends.
A well-known modern variant is "Success has many fathers, while failure is an orphan" (often attributed to the Italian Fascist leader Galeazzo Ciano, 1940s).

Failure

8 You can't win them all.
Like proverb 9 below, an expression of resigned acceptance after some failure. The first recorded citation is from Raymond Chandler's *The Long Goodbye* (1954).

9 You win some, you lose some.

10 Failure teaches success.
Modern variants include the now almost proverbial "There's no success like failure" (from Bob Dylan's song "Love Minus Zero/No Limit", 1965).

11 Man learns little from success, but much from failure.
Arabic proverb.

12 The vulgar will keep no account of your hits, but of your misses.

13 A miss is as good as a mile.
Implies that when an objective is missed, the margin of failure is irrelevant.

166 Suffering

Its sources

1 Afflictions are sent to us by God for our good.

2 Who knows much will suffer much.

3 To have a stomach and lack meat; to have meat and lack a stomach; to lie in bed and cannot rest; are great miseries.
"Stomach" here means "appetite".

Its effects

4 Who suffers much is silent.
Compare SORROW: 20–21.

5 Suffering does not manifest itself.

6 Small pain is eloquent.
Implies that true suffering cannot be put into words, and people only complain about minor ills.

Its compensations

7 Crosses are ladders that lead to heaven.
As in proverbs 8 and 20 below, "crosses" here refers to the cross of Christ, a symbol of suffering.

8 No cross, no crown.
The title of a tract written by the Quaker leader William Penn during his imprisonment (1668–69) in the Tower of London. In the text, now regarded as one of the classics of Quakerism, Penn wrote: "No pain, no palm; no thorns, no throne; no gall, no glory; no cross, no crown." "Crown" here refers to the reward of the blessed in heaven.

9 Pain is forgotten where gain follows.

10 Pain is gain.
See also DILIGENCE: 35 and note.

11 No pleasure without pain.

12 Take a pain for a pleasure all wise men can.
That is, sensible people will endure present hardships for the sake of future pleasure.

13 Of sufferance, comes ease.
"Sufferance" here means "patience, forbearance".

14 Suffering is better than care.
"Suffering" here means "patient endurance".

15 Suffering is bitter, but its fruits are sweet.

16 Bitter pills may have blessed effects.

Its inevitability

17 We must suffer much or die young.
Implies that old age is mainly suffering.

18 He that lives long suffers much.

19 Mickle must a good heart thole.
"Mickle" means "much"; "thole" means "suffer".

20 Each cross has its inscription.
Implies that suffering does not come by chance, specific afflictions being destined for particular people.

21 Pain is the price that God puts upon all things.
Adapted from Hesiod's *Works and Days* (8th century BC).

Physical pain

22 There is no pain like the gout and toothache.

23 Pride feels no pain.

24 Pride must be pinched.
Like proverb 23 above, this refers to the suffering inflicted by tight shoes, low-cut dresses, etc., worn for the sake of vanity.

167 Superstitions

Good luck

1 He that would have good luck in horses, must kiss the parson's wife.
This curious saying probably relates to the former belief that horses were preyed upon by witches and evil spirits.

2 There is luck in odd numbers.
A very old belief that can be traced back to the numerological doctrines of Pythagoras and his followers. It is alluded to by Virgil, Spenser, and Shakespeare.

3 Third time lucky.
Like proverbs 4–6 below, this is an encouragement to attempt something a third time having failed twice. It reflects the ancient and widespread belief that three is a propitious number.

4 The third is a charm.

5 The third time pays for all.

6 All things thrive at thrice.

7 Shitten luck is good luck.
Said by someone who treads in animal dung or is otherwise befouled.

8 Turn the money in your pocket when you hear the cuckoo.
This action is supposed to ensure that one will not be short of money throughout the following year.

9 The robin and the wren are God's cock and hen; the martin and the swallow are God's mate and marrow.
This refers to the belief that it is lucky to have swallows and martins nesting around one's house, and that it is unlucky to kill a robin or wren. "Marrow" is a dialect word meaning "companion".

Bad luck

10 Lucky at cards, unlucky in love.

11 Lucky at life, unlucky in love.

12 A whistling woman and a crowing hen are neither fit for God nor men.
Some variants add "a crooning cow" to the list of bad omens.

13 A whistling girl does rouse the devil.

Many superstitions attach ill-luck to whistling (e.g. those prevalent in theatres, mines, and on shipboard). The idea that it is particularly abhorrent among females may have its origin in an old story that a woman whistled while the nails for the crucifixion were being forged.

Averting misfortune

14 He who would wish to thrive, must let spiders run alive.

The good luck attached to spiders and their webs may reflect their role in killing flies, which carry disease. There is also a fanciful legend that a spider hid the infant Jesus from the agents of Herod by spinning a web to conceal him.

15 Touch wood; it's sure to come good.

Many people still routinely "touch wood" to ward off the ill-fortune that may be brought on by boasting or complacency. Although the practice has been linked to pagan beliefs in the sacred significance of certain trees, there is no evidence for it before the early 20th century.

16 Rowan tree and red thread make witches tine their speed.

"Tine" means "lose". A reference to the former belief that a rowan cross tied to the door with a red thread would keep witches away. It was commonly believed that red objects (such as rowan berries) had the power to ward off evil.

Omens of death

17 The croaking raven bodes death.

This belief dates back to Roman times (Cicero was supposedly amongst those warned of his death in this manner) and is alluded to frequently by Shakespeare and the Eliza-bethans. It has been suggested that the raven, an eater of carrion, may have an acute sense of smell that enables it to recognize the odour of decay from some distance.

18 Soon tod, soon with God.

"Tod" here means "having teeth". The implication is that babies who cut their teeth early will die young.

19 No moon no man.

This refers to the belief that children born between the old and new moons will not survive to adulthood.

Physical characteristics

20 Cold hands, warm heart.

First recorded in the early 20th century.

21 A moist hand argues an amorous nature.

A moist palm was also held to be a sign of fertility in women.

22 A dimple in the chin, your living comes in; a dimple in the cheek, your living to seek.

23 A dimple in the chin, a devil within.

24 Blue eyes, true eyes.

The colour blue was generally associated with truth and loyalty.

25 To a red man read thy rede; with a brown man break thy bread; at a pale man draw thy knife; from a black man keep thy wife.

A reference to the colour of a man's hair as an indicator of his personality ("read one's rede" means "discuss one's plans"). The same notion is expressed in the rhyme "The red is wise, the brown trusty, the pale envious, and the black lusty."

Miscellaneous omens and charms

26 When a picture leaves the wall, someone then receives a call.
   A portrait falling from the wall was also thought to herald the death of that person.

27 If you rock the cradle empty then you shall have babies plenty.

28 Meet on the stairs and you won't meet in heaven.

29 See a pin and pick it up, all the day you'll have good luck; see a pin and let it
   lie, you'll want a pin before you die.
   There are numerous variations. The superstition probably arose from a fear of witches,
   who were thought to use pins and other bits of metal in their spells.

30 Yellow's forsaken, and green's forsworn, but blue and red ought to be worn.
   In traditional colour symbolism, yellow stood for cowardice and treachery and green for
   jealousy; blue generally stood for truth and red for love.

31 One for sorrow, two for mirth; three for a wedding, four for a birth; five for
   silver, six for gold; seven for a secret, not to be told; eight for heaven, nine
   for hell; and ten for the devil's own sel.
   The proverb refers to the number of magpies or crows seen during a walk; numerous
   variants are recorded from the mid-19th century onwards. "Sel" means "self".

The superstitious

32 Nothing but what is ominous, to the superstitious.

33 He that follows freits, freits will follow him.
   "Freits" means "omens". The saying implies that to meddle with omens and superstitions is itself unlucky.

See also DAYS; EATING: *Table manners and superstitions*; MARRIAGE: *Superstitions
concerning marriage*; SLEEP: *Dreams*

T

168 Talking

Its dangers

1 Birds are entangled by their feet, and men by their tongues.
2 He that strikes with his tongue, must ward with his head.
   "Ward" here means "ward off blows".
3 The tongue talks at the head's cost.
4 The ass that brays most eats least.
5 A bleating sheep loses her bit.
6 Many words, many buffets.
7 Much babbling is not without offence.
8 He who says what he likes shall hear what he does not like.
   Compare GOSSIP: 15–16.
9 A man may say too much, even upon the best subjects.
10 When all men speak, no man hears.
11 Let not thy tongue run away with thy brains.
12 Let not your tongue run at rover.
   "At rover" means "unrestrained".
13 Little can a long tongue lein.
   "Lein" means "conceal".
14 Talk much, and err much.
15 Better the foot slip than the tongue.
16 Words have wings, and cannot be recalled.
17 A word and a stone let go cannot be called back.
   A quotation from Horace's *Ars poetica* (1st century BC).
18 While the word is in your mouth, it is your own; when 'tis once spoken 'tis another's.
19 Words bind men.

Its value

20 The lame tongue gets nothing.
21 Dumb men get no lands.
22 Spare to speak and spare to speed.
   Implies that those who are reluctant to speak out will not make much progress in life.
23 Speak and speed, ask and have.
24 The squeaking wheel gets the grease.
   First recorded in the mid-20th century.

25 He that speaks well, fights well.

26 The tongue is the rudder of our ship.
   Adapted from James 3:4.

27 The voice is the best music.

28 Good words cool more than cold water.

29 The bird is known by his note, the man by his words.

Its inadequacy

30 Fine words butter no parsnips.
   Variants substitute "soft" or "fair" for "fine". Parsnips are usually served with a garnish of butter.

31 Fair words fill not the belly.

32 Fair words will not make the pot play.
   "Play" here means "boil".

33 He who gives fair words, feeds you with an empty spoon.

34 Good words fill not a sack.

Its futility

35 Talk is but talk; but 'tis money buys land.
   A rhyming variant begins "Words are but sand; but..."

36 Talking pays no toll.

37 Save your breath to cool your porridge.

Idle threats

38 Barking dogs seldom bite.

39 Great barkers are no biters.

40 Dogs that bark at a distance bite not at hand.

41 Threatened folk live long.
   Like proverbs 42–44 below, this implies that threats need not be feared as they are rarely carried out.

42 There are more men threatened than stricken.

43 Warned folks may live.

44 Long mint, little dint.
   "Mint" means "intended"; "dint" means "struck".

45 If you cannot bite, never show your teeth.

The tongue as a weapon

46 A good tongue is a good weapon.

47 Under the tongue men are crushed to death.

48 The tongue breaks bone, and herself has none.
   Adapted from Proverbs 25:15.

49 The tongue stings.

50 The tongue is more venomous than a serpent's sting.

51 There is no venom to that of the tongue.

52 The tongue is not steel yet it cuts.

53 Words cut more than swords.

54 Words are but wind, but blows unkind.

55 Words may pass, but blows fall heavy.

56 Sticks and stones may break my bones, but words will never hurt me.
   Usually the response of one child to another who has been calling names. First recorded in the late 19th century.

Speaking ill

57 Never speak ill of the dead.
   A maxim attributed to the Spartan philosopher Chilo (6th century BC).

58 It is a good tongue that says no ill, and a better heart that thinks none.
   Often used ironically to imply that one could say something unpleasant if one chose.

59 To speak ill of others is the fifth element.
   According to ancient and medieval philosophy, all things in creation were made from the four basic elements of earth, air, fire, and water. The saying has two possible implications: that malicious talk is essential and ubiquitous; or that it is something completely superfluous, like a fifth element.

60 Say well or be still.

61 Of him that speaks ill, consider the life more than the word.

62 Ill will never said well.

63 Ill words are bellows to a slackening fire.

64 Good words anoint us, and ill do unjoint us.

The truth of the spoken word

65 What the heart thinks, the tongue speaks.

66 Speech is the picture of the mind.
   "Image" or "index" is often substituted for "picture".

67 In many words, a lie or two may escape.

68 In many words, the truth goes by.

Hearing and speaking

69 From hearing, comes wisdom; from speaking, repentance.

70 Hear much, speak little.

71 Hear and see and say nothing.

72 He that hears much and speaks not at all, shall be welcome both in bower and hall.

73 Keep your mouth shut and your ears open.
   "Eyes" is sometimes substituted for "ears".

74 Nature has given us two ears, two eyes, and but one tongue; to the end we should hear and see more than we speak.
   Attributed to the stoic philosopher Zeno of Citium in Diogenes Laertius's *Lives of the Philosophers* (3rd century AD); other writers have attributed the saying to the historian Xenophon and the orator Demosthenes.

75 It is better to play with the ears than the tongue.

76 Hear twice before you speak once.

Saying little

77 Brevity is the soul of wit.
   A quotation from Shakespeare's *Hamlet* (c. 1600). In this original context "wit" meant "wisdom" rather than "clever humour".

78 Few words are best.

79 Deliver your words not by number but by weight.

80 Least said soonest mended.
81 Who knows most, speaks least.
82 Tell not all you know, all you have, or all you can do.
83 Whom we love best, to them we can say least.
84 Half a word is enough for a wise man.
   Like proverbs 85–87 below, this implies that a small hint or indirect suggestion is sufficient for those who will understand.
85 A word to the wise is enough.
   This proverb is also known as *Verb. sap.*, an abbreviation of its Latin form *Verbum sapienti sat est.*
86 Send a wise man on an errand and say nothing to him.
87 A nod is as good as a wink to a blind horse.
   The last four words are now often omitted.

The need for tact

88 All truths are not to be told.
89 Ale sellers should not be tale-tellers.
90 Masters should be sometimes blind, and sometimes deaf.
91 Discreet women have neither eyes nor ears.
92 Name not a rope, in his house that hanged himself.
93 Although there exist many thousand subjects for elegant conversation, there are persons who cannot meet a cripple without talking about feet.
   Chinese proverb.

Language

94 That is not good language which all understand not.
95 Think with the wise, but talk with the vulgar.
   Implies that one's thoughts should be those of the discerning, but one's language should be that of the common people.

Conversation

96 Conversation makes one what he is.
97 Conversation teaches more than meditation.
98 Education begins a gentleman, conversation completes him.
99 He that converses not, knows nothing.
100 Sweet discourse makes short days and nights.
101 Talk of the devil, and he is bound to appear.
   A remark made when a person mentioned in conversation unexpectedly arrives on the scene (now often abbreviated to the first four words). It originally reflected a superstitious belief that it was dangerous to mention the devil by name.

Characteristics of the talkative

102 Many speak much who cannot speak well.
103 He cannot speak well, that cannot hold his tongue.
104 Flow of words is not always flow of wisdom.
105 Empty vessels make the most sound.
106 Great talkers fire too fast to take aim.

107 The mill that is always going grinds coarse and fine.
Implies that those who talk constantly will often say what is better left unsaid.

108 Great talkers are like leaky pitchers, everything runs out of them.

109 He must have leave to speak who cannot hold his tongue.
A reference to the often impolite insistence of the talkative to voice their opinions.

110 The eternal talker neither hears nor learns.

111 The tongue of idle persons is never still.

See also DEEDS: *Words and deeds*; FOOLISHNESS: *The talkativeness of fools*; SILENCE: *Silence and speech*; WOMEN: *Their tongue*

169 Temptation

Its sources

1 All temptations are found either in hope or fear.

2 The righteous man sins before an open chest.
Like proverb 3 below, this implies that even the most virtuous will be seduced when wrongdoing is made too easy.

3 An open door may tempt a saint.

4 At open doors dogs come in.

5 The hole calls the thief.

6 Opportunity makes the thief.

7 A bad padlock invites a picklock.

8 He that shows his purse, longs to be rid of it.
A variant ends "…, bribes the thief."

9 He that is busy, is tempted by but one devil; he that is idle, by a legion.

10 The devil tempts all, but the idle man tempts the devil.

11 How can a crow sleep soundly when the figs are ripe?
Indian proverb.

Handling temptation

12 Everything tempts the man who fears temptation.

13 Greater is he who is above temptation than he who, being tempted, overcomes.

14 Better keep the devil at the door than turn him out of the house.
Implies that it is easier to abstain completely from vice than to master a weakness that has become habitual.

15 Away goes the devil when he finds the door shut against him.

16 It is easy to keep a castle that was never assaulted.
Implies that one cannot claim to have resisted temptation when one has never been tempted.

17 Say to pleasure, 'Gentle Eve, I will none of your apple.'
An allusion to Genesis 3:1–7.

18 If you can't be good, be careful.
First recorded in the early 20th century. The phrase is generally used as a valediction, with an obvious sexual innuendo. Some variants add "…and if you can't be careful, have fun" or "…, name it after me."

170 Thrift

Its value

1 Thrift is a great revenue.
   The saying can be traced back to Cicero (1st century BC). Variants substitute "sparing" or "parsimony" for "thrift".

2 Thrift is the philosopher's stone.
   According to alchemical belief, the philosopher's stone was capable of turning base metals into gold.

3 No alchemy to saving.

4 Better spare to have of thine own, than ask of other men.

5 A good saver is a good server.

6 Industry is fortune's right hand, and frugality her left.

7 A penny saved is a penny earned.

8 Of saving, comes having.

9 Spare well and have well.

10 Sparing is the first gaining.

11 Frugality is the mother of virtue.

12 A little saving is no sin.

13 He who works begins well; he who economizes ends better.

14 Better spared than ill spent.

15 Better spare at brim than at bottom.
   Like proverb 16 below, this implies that it is prudent to make economies while one still has plenty. The saying can be traced back to Hesiod (8th century BC).

16 It is too late to spare when the bottom is bare.

17 Penny and penny laid up will be many.

18 Little and often fills the purse.

19 A pin a day is a groat a year.
   A "groat" was a coin worth four pennies.

20 Placks and bawbees grow pounds.
   "Placks" and "bawbees" were small Scottish coins.

21 Take care of the pence, and the pounds will take care of themselves.
   Sometimes attributed to William Lowndes (1652–1724), secretary to the Treasury under Queen Anne and George I. (Lowndes is also said to have originated the phrase "ways and means").

22 Spare when you're young, and spend when you're old.

23 He that saves his dinner will have the more for his supper.
   "Dinner" and "supper" here refer to youth and old age.

24 If youth knew what age would crave, it would both get and save.

25 For age and want save while you may: no morning sun lasts a whole day.

26 Save something for the man that rides on the white horse.
   A reference to the white hair of old age.

27 Keep something for the sore foot.
   The "sore foot" refers to gout and thus more generally to the needs and afflictions of old age.

28 Keep some till furthermore come.

29 Keep something for a rainy day.

Its drawbacks

30 You can't take it with you when you die.
An excuse for spending one's money, as savings will be of no use after one's death. Proverbs 31–33 below reiterate this idea.

31 Shrouds have no pockets.

32 What we spent we had; what we gave, we have; what we left, we lost.

33 There was a wife that kept her supper for her breakfast, and she died ere day.

34 Better to die a beggar than live a beggar.

35 He who saves for tomorrow saves for the cat.

36 Cats eat what hussies spare.
"Hussies" means "housewives".

37 Spend, and God will send; spare, and ever bare.

38 The groat is ill saved that shames the master.
A "groat" was a coin worth four pennies; the "shame" referred to is that of being thought a miser or pauper.

39 There is no economy in going to bed early to save candles if the result be twins.
Chinese proverb.

40 Penny wise, pound foolish.
A reference to those whose stinginess leads them to make false economies.

Against waste

41 Waste not, want not.
"Want" here means "lack".

42 Waste makes want.

43 Spend and be free, but make no waste.

44 Better shake out the sack than start a full bag.

45 Shameful leaving is worse than shameful eating.

46 Make not orts of good hay.
"Orts" are scraps or leavings.

Good housekeeping

47 Everything is of use to a housekeeper.

48 Mending and doing without keep the house.

49 Mend your clothes, and you may hold out this year.

50 Patch by patch is good housewifery, but patch upon patch is plain beggary.

51 Think no labour slavery that brings in penny saverly.
"Saverly" means "by saving". The implication is that any task that avoids future expense, such as mending or repairing, is worthwhile.

52 Provision in season makes a rich house.
A reference to the value of buying each food when it is in season and therefore at its cheapest.

53 Some savers in a house do well.

See also MISERLINESS; SPENDING: *Wise spending*

171 Time

Its value

1 Time cures all things.

2 Time is a great healer.

3 Nature, time, and patience are the three great physicians.

4 Time tames the strongest grief.

5 Time works wonders.

6 Patience, time, and money accommodate all things.

7 Time is money.
The earliest known citation in this form is by Benjamin Franklin (1748), although the thought is older.

8 An inch of gold will not buy an inch of time.
Chinese proverb.

9 He that has time, has life.

10 Gain time, gain life.

11 The crutch of time does more than the club of Hercules.
Time was traditionally depicted as an old man leaning on a crutch. The proverb implies that slow change over time achieves more than brute force.

12 With time and art, the leaf of the mulberry-tree becomes satin.
Silkworms were traditionally fed on mulberry leaves.

13 Time and straw make medlars ripe.
The fruit of the medlar is not edible until it has fallen from the tree and begun to decay.

Its effects

14 Time devours all things.
A quotation from Ovid's *Metamorphoses* (1st century BC).

15 Time is a file that wears and makes no noise.

16 Time undermines us.

17 Time is the rider that breaks youth.

18 Time tries all things.

19 Time will tell.
Not recorded in this form until the early 20th century, although the thought is ancient.

20 Time tries truth.

21 Time is the father of truth.

22 Truth is time's daughter.

Its passing

23 Time flies.
In its familiar Latin form, *Tempus fugit*, the saying is an abbreviated quotation from Virgil's *Georgics* (1st century BC).

24 Time flees away without delay.

25 Time has wings.

26 Time is, time was, and time is past.
According to legend, these were the portentous words uttered by the miraculous brazen head created by Friar Roger Bacon (13th century). On speaking the last phrase the head fell down and was smashed to pieces.

27 For the busy man time passes quickly.
Chinese proverb.

28 The sun has stood still, but time never did.
An allusion to Joshua 10:12–14, which describes how the sun stood still in the heavens at Joshua's command.

29 Time and tide wait for no man.

30 Time stays not the fool's leisure.

Losing time

31 What greater crime than loss of time?

32 Time spent in vice or folly is doubly lost.

33 Lose an hour in the morning and you'll be all day hunting for it.

34 If you lose your time, you cannot get money or gain.

35 Time lost cannot be recalled.
Variants include "Lost time is not found again."

36 Take time when time comes, lest time steal away.
A variant has "… while time serves…"

The appropriate time

37 There is a time and place for everything.
Like proverb 38 below, this is adapted from Ecclesiastes 3:1 ("To everything there is a season…").

38 Everything is good in its season.

The past

39 Other times, other manners.
A French saying, first recorded in English in the late 19th century.

40 Now is now, and then was then.

41 It is too late to call back yesterday.

42 Things past cannot be recalled.

43 There are no birds in last year's nests.
A quotation from Quixote's valedictory speech in the last chapter of Cervantes's *Don Quixote* (1605–15).

The present

44 Things present are judged by things past.

45 Today is the scholar of yesterday.
"Scholar" here means "pupil"; an ancient Roman saying implying that we must continually learn from the past.

46 The golden age was never the present age.

The future

47 The time to come is no more ours than the time past.

48 None knows what will happen to him before sunset.

49 This morning knows not this evening's happenings.
Chinese proverb.

50 He that would know what shall be, must consider what has been.

51 History repeats itself.
Although not recorded in this form until the mid-19th century the thought is ancient. Marx (1852) attributed the idea to Hegel (1770–1831) while adding the famous qualification: "the first time as tragedy, the second as farce."

52 What has been, may be.
53 Coming events cast their shadows before.
   A quotation from Thomas Campbell's ballad "Lochiel's Warning" (1803).

172 Travel

Its value

1 Travel broadens the mind.
   First recorded in the early 20th century.
2 He that travels far, knows much.
3 Much travel is needed to ripen a man's rawness.
   Persian proverb.
4 Much travelling teaches how to see.
   African proverb.
5 He who does not travel will not know the value of men.
   African proverb.

Its effects

6 Travellers change climates, not conditions.
   "Conditions" here means "character". The observation can be traced back to Horace's *Epistles* (1st century BC).
7 One may change place but not change the mind.
8 If an ass goes a-travelling, he'll not come home a horse.
   Some of the numerous variants of this proverb are given below.
9 Who goes a beast to Rome, a beast returns.
10 Send a fool to France and he'll come back a fool.
   A variant substitutes "the market" for "France".
11 Send a donkey to Paris, he'll return no wiser than he went.
12 Lead a pig to the Rhine, it remains a pig.
13 Travel makes a wise man better, but a fool worse.
14 No man was ever made more healthful by a dangerous sickness, or came home better from a long voyage.
15 Travellers should correct the vice of one country, by the virtue of another.
16 A traveller may lie with authority.
   Variants add "old men", "soldiers", "physicians", etc., to travellers as confirmed liars.
17 Travellers and poets have leave to lie.
18 Don't put tricks upon travellers.
   Implies that travellers know too much to be easily fooled.
19 He that goes far, has many encounters.

The value of staying at home

20 There's no place like home.
   The saying can be traced back to Hesiod (8th century BC).
21 East, west, home's best.
   A German saying, first recorded in English in the mid-19th century.
22 Home is home, though it be never so homely.
23 The hare always returns to her form.
   A "form" is a hare's nest.

24 The bird loves her nest.

25 One's own fire is pleasant.

26 Dry bread at home is better than roast meat abroad.

27 The smoke of a man's own country is better than the fire of another's.
Some variants substitute "house" for "country".

28 Home is where the heart is.
First recorded in English in the late 19th century. An ironic modern variant substitutes "mortgage" for "heart".

29 He that would be well, needs not go from his own house.

30 Better at home than a mile from it.
Chinese proverb.

31 Far from home, near thy harm.

32 Much spends the traveller more than the abider.

33 A gentleman ought to travel abroad, but dwell at home.

34 Being on sea, sail; being on land, settle.

The needs of the traveller

35 To travel through the world, it is necessary to have the mouth of a hog, the legs of a stag, the eyes of a falcon, the ears of an ass, the shoulders of a camel, and the face of an ape, and, overplus, a satchel full of money and patience.
Variants add "a tongue to flatter all" and "a conscience as broad as the king's highway".

36 The heaviest baggage for a traveller is an empty purse.

37 With Latin, a horse, and money, you may travel the world.

38 Nothing so necessary for travellers as languages.

173 Trial

Its necessity

1 First try and then trust.

2 Prove your friend ere you have need.

3 If you trust before you try, you may repent before you die.

4 All things are good unseyit.
"Unseyit" means "untried".

Its methods

5 The proof of the pudding is in the eating.

6 Gold is tried in the fire.
To "try" gold is to separate the metal from its ore by heating. The phrase appears several times in the Bible (Zechariah 13:9, 1 Peter 1:7) to imply that the truly worthy are revealed by trial and suffering.

7 Calamity is the touchstone of a brave mind.
Implies that bravery can only be truly assessed in time of danger.

8 You may know by a handful the whole sack.

Experimenting

9 Make your experiment on a worthless object.

10 Try your skill in galt first, and then in gold.
"Galt" means "clay".

11 A surgeon experiments on the heads of orphans.

Proving

12 The exception proves the rule.
Originally a legal maxim making the point that where certain cases are noted as exceptions to a law, this implicitly confirms the law for all other cases not so excepted. The saying is now used rather loosely to justify any kind of inconsistency.

13 Never try to prove what nobody doubts.

14 That which proves too much, proves nothing.

Evidence

15 One reason is as good as fifty.

16 One swallow does not make a summer.
Implies that a single item of evidence is not sufficient to prove a case.

17 Every picture tells a story.
The saying seems to have begun life as an advertising slogan. Newspaper advertisements for a brand of patent backache pills (1900s) carried the phrase beneath pictures claiming to show a "London woman" before and after taking the remedy.

174 Trouble-making

Its sources

1 He that seeks trouble never misses.

2 Make ado and have ado.
Implies that those who make trouble will have trouble.

3 Take away fuel, take away flame.

Against trouble-making

4 Leave well alone.
"Well" is here a noun, meaning "what is well". "Let" is often substituted for "leave".

5 Let sleeping dogs lie.

6 Wake not a sleeping lion.

7 He who rouses a sleeping tiger exposes himself to danger.
Chinese proverb.

8 It is easier to raise the devil than to lay him.

9 Raise no more devils than you can lay.

10 Kindle not a fire that you cannot extinguish.

11 Rip not up old sores.
"Wounds" is often substituted for "sores".

12 Put not fire to flax.

13 Pouring oil on the fire is not the way to quench it.

175 Trust

Its effects

1 Trust helps many both up and down.
2 Trust makes way for treachery.
3 In trust is treason.
  A direct contradiction of proverb 9 below.
4 Trust is the mother of deceit.
5 Trusting too much to others is the ruin of many.
6 He that trusts much, obliges much.

Its value

7 God provides for him that trusts.
8 Trusting often makes fidelity.
9 In trust is truth.
  A direct contradiction of proverb 3 above.

The need for caution

10 Better known than trusted.
11 In choosing a wife, and buying a sword, we ought not to trust another.
12 Who trusts to rotten boughs, may fall.
13 Trust not a great weight to a slender thread.
14 First try and then trust.
15 If you trust before you try, you may repent before you die.
16 Try your friend before you trust.
17 When you go to dance, take heed whom you take by the hand.
18 Trust not a new friend or an old enemy.
19 Trust not a woman when she weeps.
  One variant adds "… nor a dog when it pisses."
20 Never trust a sleeping dog, a swearing Jew, a praying drunkard, or a weeping woman.
21 Three things are not to be trusted: a cow's horn, a dog's tooth, and a horse's hoof.
22 While you trust to the dog, the wolf slips into the sheepfold.
23 If we are bound to forgive an enemy, we are not bound to trust him.
  "Always forgive your enemies – but never forget their names" was a maxim of the US politician Robert Kennedy (1960s).
24 He that speaks me fair and loves me not, I'll speak him fair and trust him not.
25 Tell money after your own father.
  "Tell" here means "count". The implication is that even one's own parents are not to be trusted.

Distrust

26 Remember to distrust.
  Attributed to the poet and philosopher Epicharmus (6th–5th centuries BC).
27 He who trusts not, is not deceived.
28 Wise distrust is the parent of security.

29 If one does not trust enough, one does not meet with trust.
Chinese proverb.

30 Mistrust is an axe at the tree of love.

31 Where there is no trust there is no love.

32 Trust is dead, ill payment killed it.

176 Truth

Its value

1 Truth is God's daughter.

2 Truth has always a sure bottom.

3 Fair fall truth and daylight.

4 Better speak truth rudely, than lie covertly.

5 Truth never grows old.

6 Truthfulness becomes the gentleman.

Its power

7 Truth is mighty and will prevail.
Adapted from the apocryphal book of 1 Esdras (4:41). Variants include the closing lines of Coventry Patmore's poem "Magna est Veritas" (1895): "When all its work is done the lie shall rot;/ The truth is great and shall prevail,/ When none cares whether it prevail or not."

8 Truth may walk through the world unarmed.
Arabic proverb.

9 Truth will conquer, falsehood will kill.

10 Though a lie be swift, the truth overtakes it.

11 Truth will out.

12 Truth will come to light.

13 Truth and oil are ever above.
Implies that the truth will always rise above any attempts to conceal it.

14 Truth has no answer.
That is, there can be no answer or objection to what is evidently true.

15 Facts are stubborn things.

Its straightforwardness

16 Truth is truth.

17 Truth's best ornament is nakedness.

18 The truth shows best being naked.

19 Craft must have clothes, but truth loves to go naked.

20 Truth needs no colours.
"Colours" here means "specious embellishments" or "figures of rhetoric". A common but obscure variant is "Truth *fears* no colours"; here the last word has the additional sense of "regimental flag, ensign" (symbolizing military force).

21 Truth has no need of rhetoric.

22 The language of truth is simple.

23 Truth needs not the ornament of many words.

24 In many words, the truth goes by.

25 In too much dispute, truth is lost.

26 Truth seeks no corners.

That is, it has no need of secrecy or indirection.

27 Truth may be blamed, but cannot be shamed.

28 Truth fears no trial.

Its sources

29 Face to face, the truth comes out.

30 Children and fools cannot lie.

Some versions add "drunkards" to the list of truth-tellers.

31 A fool may sometimes tell the truth.

32 The devil sometimes speaks the truth.

33 Dying men speak true.

There was formerly a widespread belief that the words of the dying were inspired or prophetic.

34 A good heart cannot lie.

35 There is truth in wine.

Equally familiar in its Latin form, *In vino veritas*, which is sometimes attributed to Pliny the Elder (1st century AD). A Greek version has been attributed to the semilegendary poet Alcaeus (7th century BC).

36 What everybody says must be true.

37 Many a true word is spoken in jest.

38 What is new cannot be true.

39 Tell a lie and find a truth.

Implies that a lie often has the effect of uncovering a more important truth.

40 Time is the father of truth.

41 Truth is time's daughter.

42 In trust is truth.

43 Truth lies at the bottom of a well.

That is, it is remote and inaccessible except to deep research. The saying has been attributed to several of the early Greek philosophers, notably Heraclitus (6th–5th centuries BC) and Democritus (5th–4th centuries BC).

44 Truth often hides in an ugly pool.

Chinese proverb.

Its dangers

45 Truth breeds hatred.

The saying can be traced back to the Roman playwright Terence (2nd century BC).

46 Four good mothers have four bad daughters: truth, hatred; prosperity, pride; security, peril; familiarity, contempt.

47 Truth finds foes, where it makes none.

48 Truth and roses have thorns about them.

49 Truth has a scratched face.

50 Follow not truth too near the heels, lest it dash out thy teeth.

A warning to historians and biographers from the preface to Raleigh's *History of the World* (1614). Some versions substitute "eyes" for "teeth".

51 The greater the truth, the greater the libel.

A legal adage sometimes attributed to William Murray, 1st Earl of Mansfield, who presided at the trial of John Wilkes for seditious libel (1780), and sometimes to Edward

Law, 1st Baron Ellenborough, who acted as chief prosecutor at state trials in the 1790s before becoming a notoriously reactionary Lord Chief Justice (1802–18). The saying, which reflects the former use of the libel laws to suppress sedition, makes the point that a defamatory statement may be all the more damaging for being completely true. As a statement of the law it is at best a half-truth. According to the strict letter of the law, the truth of an alleged libel is not an absolute defence, as it must also be shown that publication served the public good. In practice, however, no modern jury would convict if a "libel" were shown to be true.

52 Speak the truth and run.

53 He who speaks the truth must have one foot in the stirrup.

Its unwelcomeness

54 Truth is a spectre that scares many.

55 The truest jests sound worst in guilty ears.

56 Sooth bourd is no bourd.

That is, a true jest is no jest; said when a satirical remark is considered too close to the bone.

57 Sooth saws be to lords lothe.

True sayings are odious to the rich and powerful.

58 The sting of a reproach is in the truth of it.

Its strangeness

59 Truth is stranger than fiction.

An abbreviated quotation from Byron's *Don Juan* (1823). A variant substitutes "fact" for "truth".

Telling the truth

60 Tell the truth and shame the devil.

61 No one was ever ruined by speaking the truth.

Hindi proverb.

62 Hide nothing from thy minister, physician, and lawyer.

63 All truths are not to be told.

U

177 Use

Its value

1 The used key is always bright.
   Like proverbs 2–5 below, this is a warning against neglect or sloth.
2 Iron with use grows bright.
3 Iron not used soon rusts.
   Sometimes attributed to Cato the Elder (3rd–2nd centuries BC).
4 Use legs and have legs.
   Implies that talents or faculties must be used if they are not to atrophy.
5 Drawn wells are seldom dry.

Usefulness

6 Keep a thing seven years and you will find a use for it.
7 Lay things by, they may come to use.
8 All's fish that comes to the net.
   Like proverb 9 below, this implies that everything is of some use.
9 All's grist that comes to the mill.
10 Water is a boon in the desert, but the drowning man curses it.

See also EXPERIENCE: *Its value*

W

178 War

Its dangers

1 Famine, pestilence, and war are the destruction of a people.
2 War is death's feast.
3 When war begins, then hell opens.
4 Wars bring scars.
5 In war all suffer defeat, even the victors.
6 He that strikes with the sword, shall be beaten with the scabbard.
7 He who lives by the sword dies by the sword.
   Adapted from Matthew 26:52.
8 All may begin a war, few can end it.
   Adapted from a maxim in Machiavelli's *History of Florence* (1521–24).
9 Who preaches war, is the devil's chaplain.
10 Advise none to marry or to go to war.
11 War, hunting, and love, are as full of trouble as pleasure.
12 On painting and fighting look aloof.
   Because a picture may lose some of its effect when viewed at close quarters, and it is
   dangerous to be close to the scene of fighting.

Its rules and tactics

13 All is fair in love and war.
   Sometimes attributed to Nathan Bedford Forrest (1821–77), a Confederate general in the
   US Civil War (and subsequently first leader of the Ku Klux Klan); a brilliant commander,
   he was noted for his brutal and unscrupulous tactics. However, there are several citations
   from earlier in the 19th century and the sentiment is older still.
14 In war, it is not permitted twice to err.
   First said of the Athenian general Lamachus (5th century BC), leader of an ill-fated expedition against Sicily.
15 He is the best general who makes the fewest mistakes.
   A saying of Sir Ian Hamilton (1853–1947), commander in chief of the ill-fated Gallipoli
   campaign (1915).
16 Cities are taken by the ears.
   A reference to the use of propaganda.
17 He that fights and runs away, may live to fight another day.
   This is sometimes completed with the addition "But he that is in battle slain, will never
   rise to fight again." The thought is sometimes attributed to Demosthenes (4th century
   BC), who used his oratory to urge continuing Athenian resistance to Macedonian power.

18 Attack is the best form of defence.
In its usual US form, "The best defense is a good offense", this is an abbreviated quotation from George Washington (1799). Like proverb 19 below, the saying may be applied to any aggressive situation.

19 Fight fire with fire.

Attitudes to war

20 War is sweet to them that know it not.

21 War is the sport of kings.
A misquotation from Dryden's *King Arthur* (1691), substituting "sport" for "trade".

Weapons

22 All the weapons of war will not arm fear.
Variants substitute "all the arms of England" (or some other place).

23 England were but a fling, save for the crooked stick and the greygoose wing.
That is, the conquest of England would be easy but for the bow and arrow; a reference to the fabled skill of English archers in battle.

The futility of violence

24 The crutch of time does more than the club of Hercules.
Time was traditionally depicted as an old man leaning on a crutch. The proverb implies that slow change over time achieves more than brute force.

25 Though the left hand conquer the right, no advantage is gained.
Chinese proverb.

26 When all is gone, and nothing left, what avails the dagger with the dudgeon-heft?
Most common daggers had a hilt ("heft") made of boxwood ("dudgeon").

See also OCCUPATIONS: *Soldiers*; PEACE: *War and peace*; TALKING: *The tongue as a weapon*

179 Weakness

Its dangers

1 The weaker goes to the pot.

2 The weakest goes to the wall.

3 The weaker has the worst.

4 The thread breaks where it is weakest.

5 Whether the pitcher strikes the stone, or the stone the pitcher, it is bad for the pitcher.
Like proverb 6 below, this implies that the weak always come off worst in disputes with the strong.

6 The earthen pot must keep clear of the brass kettle.

Its redeeming features

7 Weak things united become strong.
The saying can be traced back to Homer's *Iliad* (8th century BC).

8 Willows are weak, yet they bind other wood.

9 A mouse may help a lion.
   A reference to one of the fables attributed to Aesop (6th century BC). The implication is that there are occasions when the weak may help the strong out of difficulties.

Characteristics of the weak

10 Weak men had need be witty.
11 Wiles help weak folk.

Exploitation of the weak

12 Every one leaps over the dyke where it is lowest.
   Like proverbs 13–15 below, this implies that people tend to take advantage of the weak and lowly, who put up the least resistance.
13 Where the hedge is lowest, men may soonest over.
14 A low hedge is easily leaped over.
15 The least boy always carries the greatest fiddle.
   That is, the greatest loads are placed on those least able to bear them (because the weak are also the least able to resist).

The weakness of mankind

16 Flesh is frail.
   A near-quotation from Matthew 26:41; see WILL: 6 and note.
17 Men are not angels.
18 Every man has the defects of his qualities.
   First recorded in the late 19th century.
19 Whatever is made by the hand of man, by the hand of man may be overturned.

180 Wealth

Its advantages

1 Rich men may have what they will.
   A variant substitutes "do" for "have".
2 He that has money has what he wants.
   A variant concludes "…has all."
3 A heavy purse makes a light heart.
4 Ready money is a ready medicine.
5 A rich man can do nothing wrong.
6 Rich men's spots are covered with money.
7 There is no companion like the penny.
8 They that have got good store of butter, may lay it thick on their bread.
   Like proverbs 9 and 10 below, this refers to the freedom of the rich to live and spend as they please.
9 Where there is store of oatmeal, you may put enough in the crock.
10 He that hath the spice, may season as he list.
11 He that has a good harvest may be content with some thistles.
   Implies that the rich can put up with small inconveniences.
12 Fat sorrow is better than lean sorrow.
   Implies that it is better to be rich and unhappy than poor and unhappy. The saying was

often used in a marital context, to imply (cynically) that since one is almost certain to be unhappy in marriage one might as well marry for money.

13 Knowledge makes one laugh, but wealth makes one dance.

Its disadvantages

14 The rich knows not who is his friend.

15 Riches are but the baggage of virtue.
Implies that riches are an impediment to active virtue; the saying paraphrases a remark in Francis Bacon's essay "Of Riches" (1607–12).

16 Much coin, much care.

17 Riches bring care and fears.

18 He that has lands, has quarrels.
A common variant substitutes "war" for "quarrels".

19 The longest at the fire soonest finds cold.
Implies that those who are most accustomed to wealth and comfort will suffer most in time of hardship.

20 Much money makes a country poor, for it sets a dearer price on everything.
An early (17th century) statement of the so-called quantity theory of money, later to become the central doctrine of monetarism.

21 Plenty is no dainty.
Implies that one ceases to appreciate a thing when one has a surfeit of it.

22 Abundance of things engenders disdainfulness.

23 Plenty makes poor.
Having more than enough encourages carelessness, which leads to poverty. The saying can be traced back to Ovid's *Metamorphoses* (1st century BC).

24 Riches have wings.
An abbreviated version of Proverbs 13:5. This warning that wealth may be short-lived is echoed in proverbs 25 and 26 below.

25 Ready money will away.

26 Money is round, and rolls away.

27 Riches take away more pleasures than they give.
Chinese proverb.

28 Where wealth is established it is difficult for friendship to find a place.

Its dangers

29 Money is the root of all evil.
A misquotation from 1 Timothy 6:10. The correct version is "the love of money is the root of all evil." Variants substitute "riches", "covetousness", or "idleness" for "money".

30 The abundance of money ruins youth.

31 Abundance, like want, ruins many.

32 As the carl riches he wretches.
"Carl" means "man, fellow"; "wretches" means "declines morally".

33 A rich man's money hangs him oftentimes.

34 Riches serve a wise man but command a fool.
A quotation from the French theologian Pierre Charron (1541–1603).

35 When we have gold, we are in fear; when we have none we are in danger.

36 It is easier for a camel to go through the eye of a needle, than for a rich man to enter into the kingdom of God.
A biblical quotation: Matthew 19:24.

37 A man's wealth is his enemy.

38 Too much money makes one mad.

39 Wealth infatuates as well as beauty.
    Chinese proverb.

40 Riches rather enlarge than satisfy appetites.

41 Set a beggar on horseback, and he'll ride to the devil.
    A reference to the effects of sudden wealth. Variants include "…and he will never alight" and "…and he will ride his horse to death."

Its importance

42 A gentleman without an estate is like a pudding without suet.
    Alludes to the making of black pudding from pigs' blood and suet, etc.

43 Good blood makes bad puddings without groats or suet.
    "Groats" were both fragments of crushed grain and coins worth four pennies; for the implied meaning see proverb 42 above.

44 Money makes the man.

45 Money makes the pot boil.
    Some variants add "…though the devil pisses on the fire."

46 Put money in thy purse.
    In Shakespeare's *Othello* (1604) this is the cynical advice of Iago to the would-be lover Rodrigo.

47 Money is often lost for want of money.

48 Wealth is the test of a man's character.

49 Talk is but talk; but 'tis money buys land.
    A rhyming variant begins "words are but sand; but…"

50 It is not what is he, but what has he.
    Implies that a person's wealth is more important than his or her character. When the female pronoun is used, the context is generally that of a man choosing a prospective wife.

Its relative unimportance

51 The best things in life are free.
    First recorded in the early 20th century. The phrase formed the title of one popular song (1927) but was later rejected in another, Bradford and Gordy's "Money" (1950s): "They say the best things in life are free/ But you can give them to the birds and bees/ I want money!"

52 Money isn't everything.
    First recorded in the early 20th century.

53 Riches alone make no man happy.

54 The greatest wealth is contentment with a little.

55 He is not rich that possesses much, but he that is content with what he has.

56 He is rich enough that wants nothing.

57 He is rich enough who lacks not bread.
    The saying can be traced back to the writings of St Jerome (early 5th century AD).

58 Health is better than wealth.

59 Better wit than wealth.

60 Without wisdom, wealth is worthless.
    Based loosely on Psalms 16:16.

61 A good name is better than riches.

Adapted from Proverbs 22:1.

62 Wisest is he who recks not who is rich.
"Reck" means "pay heed to, care about".

63 Gold is but muck.
A reference to gold's humble origins in the earth.

64 Shrouds have no pockets.
A reminder that wealth is of no importance after death.

65 You can't take it with you when you die.
First recorded in the mid-19th century; "go" is often substituted for "die".

66 A thousand pounds, and a bottle of hay, is all one thing at doomsday.
"Bottle" here means "bundle".

Its sources

67 Money makes money.
Like proverbs 68–72 below, this implies that the best source of wealth is wealth itself.

68 Every man bastes the fat hog.

69 He that has plenty of goods shall have more.

70 He that has a goose, will get a goose.
Implies that the wealthy will receive gifts and favours while the poor go empty-handed.

71 Put two pennies in a purse and they will draw together.
That is, they will breed.

72 Money would be gotten if there were money to get it with.

73 Peace makes plenty.
Some variants extend this to make a complete cycle: "..., plenty makes pride, pride makes envy (*or* ambition), envy makes war, war makes poverty, poverty makes peace."

74 By wisdom peace, by peace plenty.
Some variants add "..., by plenty war."

75 Widows are always rich.

76 Where there's muck there's brass.
"Brass" here means "money". Like proverb 77 below, this implies that the most lucrative occupations are not necessarily the cleanest, physically or morally.

77 Muck and money go together.

78 Provision in season makes a rich house.
A reference to the value of buying food when it is in season and therefore at its cheapest.

79 Early to bed and early to rise, makes a man healthy, wealthy and wise.
James Thurber's humorous reversal is well known: "Early to rise and early to bed, makes a man healthy and wealthy and dead" (mid-20th century).

80 He that will be rich before night, may be hanged before noon.
Implies that many sources of rapidly acquired wealth are outside the law.

81 The town for wealth, the country for health.

Its effects

82 Wine and wealth change wise men's manners.

83 Plenty breeds pride.
See also proverb 73 above and note.

84 Manners and money make a gentleman.

85 Jack would be a gentleman if he had money.

86 A thief passes for a gentleman when stealing has made him rich.

87 Gold dust blinds all eyes.

88 Wealth makes worship.
89 Every one is akin to the rich man.
90 Land was never lost for want of an heir.
    Implies that the rich are never short of those claiming kindred or friendship.
91 Rich folk have many friends.
92 He that has a full purse never wanted a friend.
93 Prosperity makes friends, adversity tries them.
94 A rich man's joke is always funny.

The power of money

95 Beauty is potent but money is omnipotent.
96 Moyen does mickle, but money does more.
    "Moyen" means "influence", "mickle" means "much".
97 What will not money do?
98 What cannot gold do?
99 Money will do anything.
100 Money will do more than my lord's letter.
101 Money makes a man free everywhere.
    A variant runs "Money recommends a man everywhere."
102 With Latin, a horse, and money, you may travel the world.
103 Health and money go far.
104 He that has gold may buy land.
105 Gold goes in at any gate except heaven's.
106 An ass laden with gold climbs to the top of the castle.
    That is, gold may secure an entrance to even the most impregnable stronghold. According to tradition, this was a favourite saying of Philip of Macedon (4th century BC), the founder of the Macedonian empire. Whenever Philip's spies reported that a city or fortress was too strongly defended to be taken, he would reply in these words, implying that bribery would always prevail where force could not.
107 A golden key opens every door.
108 A silver key can open an iron lock.
109 All things are obedient to money.
    From a passage in the apocryphal book of Ecclesiasticus (10:19).
110 Be it for better, be it for worse, do you after him that bears the purse.
111 Money answereth all things.
    A biblical quotation: Ecclesiastes 10:19.
112 Patience, time, and money accommodate all things.
113 Money is the only monarch.
114 Money governs the world.
115 Money is the ace of trumps.
116 Money makes the mare to go.
117 Money talks.
    Variants include Aphra Behn's "Money speaks in a language all nations understand" (1681) and Bob Dylan's "Money doesn't talk, it swears" (1965).
118 When money speaks the world is silent.
119 Gold is an orator.
120 You may speak with your gold, and make other tongues dumb.
    The thought can be traced back to Horace (1st century BC).

121 Money is the sinews of war.
A quotation from Cicero's *Philippics* (44 BC). See also LOVE: 126.

Handling wealth

122 Dally not with women or money.
123 Gear is easier gained than guided.
"Gear" here means "wealth". The saying implies that it is easier to become rich than to use one's wealth with discretion.
124 Money is a good servant, but a bad master.

Characteristics of the rich

125 Poor and liberal, rich and covetous.
126 They that hold the greatest farms, pay the least rent.
Implies that the richest people show the least gratitude to God for their good fortune.
127 He is wise that is rich.
128 The love of money and the love of learning rarely meet.

See also LOVE: *Love and money*; MARRIAGE: *The dowry*; POVERTY: *Poverty and wealth*

181 Weather

Forecasting

1 If the cock crows on going to bed, he's sure to rise with a watery head.
A forecast of rain.
2 If the cock moult before the hen, we shall have weather thick and thin; but if the hen moult before the cock, we shall have weather hard as a block.
3 When the peacock loudly bawls, soon we'll have both rain and squalls.
4 When black snails on the road you see, then on the morrow rain will be.
5 When the glow-worm lights her lamp, the air is always damp.
6 The gull comes against the rain.
7 If the robin sings in the bush, then the weather will be coarse; but if the robin sings on the barn, then the weather will be warm.
8 The full moon brings fair weather.
9 So many days old the moon is on Michaelmas Day, so many floods after.
Michaelmas Day is September 29th.
10 Near burr, far rain.
The "burr" is the halo that sometimes appears around the moon. As this proverb makes clear, such a halo was thought to presage fine weather only when it appeared close to the orb of the moon ("near burr"); otherwise the forecast was the opposite (see proverbs 11 and 12 below).
11 When round the moon there is a brugh, the weather will be cold and rough.
"Brugh" means "halo".
12 If the moon shows a silver shield, be not afraid to reap your field; but if she rises haloed round, soon we'll tread on deluged ground.
13 Pale moon does rain, red moon does blow: white moon does neither rain nor snow.
14 The farther the sight, the nearer the rain.

15 Sound travelling far and wide, a stormy day will betide.

16 Many haws, many snaws.

An abundance of hedgerow fruit ("haws") is often considered a bad omen, it being assumed that nature has provided extra food to sustain the birds through a hard winter ("snaws" means "snowstorms").

17 If the oak's before the ash, then you'll only get a splash; if the ash precedes the oak, then you may expect a soak.

This well-known saying refers to the order in which the two trees come into leaf.

18 March in Janiveer, Janiveer in March I fear.

"Janiveer" is January. The implication is that March weather in January presages wintry weather in March.

19 The paleness of the pilot is a sign of a storm.

20 Long foretold, long last; short notice, soon past.

Implies that the duration of a spell of weather depends on the length of time for which it has been predicted by the barometer. The saying is noted in Jerome's *Three Men in a Boat* (1899).

21 Evening red and morning grey help the traveller on his way; evening grey and morning red bring down rain upon his head.

22 Red sky at night, shepherd's delight; red sky in the morning, shepherd's warning.

A variant substitutes "sailor" for "shepherd".

Wind

23 The devil is busy in a high wind.

A reference to the damage caused by gales.

24 No weather is ill if the wind be still.

25 If wind follows sun's course, expect fair weather.

That is, if the wind veers from the east to the west.

26 When the wind veers against the sun, trust it not, for back 'twill run.

27 Where the wind is on Martinmas Eve, there it will be the rest of winter.

Martinmas is November 11th.

28 A windy March and a rainy April make a beautiful May.

29 March winds and April showers bring forth May flowers.

30 March wind kindles the adder and blooms the thorn.

31 March whisker was never a good fisher.

Implies that a windy March is not favourable to the fisherman.

32 When the wind is in the north, the skilful fisher goes not forth.

33 The north wind does blow, and we shall have snow.

34 Northern wind brings weather fair.

35 Northerly wind and blubber, brings home the Greenland lubber.

A sailors' proverb alluding to Greenland whaling voyages. However, there is also a play on words here: "Greenland lubber" implies a "green (i.e. inexperienced) landlubber" and "blubber" can mean a wild boiling sea.

36 If the wind is north-east, three days without rain, eight days will pass before south wind again.

37 When the wind is in the east, it is neither good for man nor beast.

In the British Isles easterly winds are often sharp and severe.

38 Easterly winds and rain bring cockles here from Spain.
"Cockle" is the name of a disease that turns wheat black and also of a weed that grows in cornfields.

39 When the wind is in the east on Candlemas Day, there it will stick till the second of May.
Candlemas Day is February 2nd.

40 When the wind is in the south, it's in the rain's mouth.

41 When the wind is south it blows your bait into a fish's mouth.
According to Walton's *The Compleat Angler* (1653) the south wind was considered particularly favourable for fishing.

42 A southerly wind and a cloudy sky, proclaim a hunting morning.

43 A southerly wind with showers of rain will bring the wind from west again.

44 When the wind is in the west, the weather is at its best.
Since classical times the west wind has been associated with mild weather, the arrival of spring, and good luck generally.

45 When the wind is west, the fish bite best.

46 Do business with men when the wind is in the north-west.

Rain

47 April showers bring forth May flowers.

48 An April flood carries away the frog and her brood.

49 In April Dove's flood is worth a king's good.
A reference to the river Dove, which runs between Staffordshire and Derbyshire.

50 Some rain, some rest.
A reference to the respite granted to outdoor workers during a shower of rain.

51 More rain, more rest; more water will suit the ducks best.

52 Many rains, many rowans; many rowans, many yawns.
An abundance of rowans, the fruit of the mountain ash, was thought to predict a poor harvest. "Yawns" are light grains of corn.

53 A May flood never did good.

54 After a rainy winter, a plentiful summer.

55 A shower in July, when the corn begins to fill, is worth a plow of oxen, and all belongs there till.
The last phrase means "and all that goes with it".

56 A dripping June sets all in tune.

57 When England wrings, Thanet sings.
The Isle of Thanet in Kent has dry chalky soil that needs plenty of rain.

58 If it rains on Easter Day, there shall be good grass but very bad hay.

59 If on the eighth of June it rain, it foretells a wet harvest men sain.

60 If the first of July it be rainy weather, 'twill rain more or less for four weeks together.

61 St Swithin's Day, if thou dost rain, for forty days it will remain; St Swithin's Day, if thou be fair, for forty days 'twill rain na mair.
"Na mair" means "no more". St Swithin's Day is July 15th. Swithin (or Swithun) was an Anglo-Saxon bishop of Winchester who died in 862. According to the story, as he lay dying he asked to be buried outside his cathedral door "so that the sweet rain of heaven might fall upon his body." This request was carried out, but following Swithin's canonization his relics were translated to a new shrine in the cathedral on July 15th 971. Legend has it that attempts to exhume and reinter the saint's body were frustrated for

some time by prolonged heavy rainfall, which many interpreted as a miraculous sign of his displeasure. In France a similar story is told about St Médard's Day (June 8th): see also proverb 62 below.

62 If St Vitus's Day be rainy weather, it will rain for thirty days together.
St Vitus's Day is June 15th.

63 Rain from the east: wet two days at least.

64 Rain before seven: fine before eleven.

65 The rain comes scouth when the wind's in the south.
"Scouth" means "heavily".

66 It rains by planets.
A reference to the former belief that rainfall was governed by the planets.

67 Rain, rain, go away, come again another day.
A popular children's rhyme with many variants.

68 If it rains when the sun is shining, the devil is beating his wife.
Some variants add "…with a shoulder of mutton". The meaning and origin of the saying are obscure.

69 Bright rain makes fools fain.
Foolish people believe that a patch of brightness in the sky after a shower of rain presages fine weather. "Fain" means "happy, eager".

Rainbows

70 If two rainbows appear at one time, they presage rain to come.

71 A rainbow at morn, put your hook in the corn; a rainbow at eve, put your head in the sheave.

72 A rainbow in the morning is the shepherd's warning; a rainbow at night is the shepherd's delight.
A variant substitutes "sailor" for "shepherd".

Thunderstorms

73 Dunder do gally the beans.
"Dunder" is thunder; "gally" means "frighten". The implication is that thunder causes beans to grow quickly.

74 When April blows his horn, it's good both for hay and corn.
A reference to thunder in April.

75 When it thunders in March, it brings sorrow.
Thundery weather in winter or early spring was thought to herald scarcity in summer.

76 Winter thunder bodes summer hunger.

77 Winter's thunder and summer's flood never boded Englishman good.

78 Winter's thunder makes old man's wonder.
A reference to the ominous nature of a winter thunderstorm.

79 No tempest, good July, lest corn look ruely.
A plea for a stormless lead-up to the corn harvest; "ruely" means "poorly".

80 Beware of an oak, it draws the stroke; avoid an ash, it counts the flash; creep under the thorn, it can save you from harm.
A warning against sheltering from lightning under an oak or an ash tree.

Clouds

81 When Bredon Hill puts on his hat, ye men of the vale beware of that.
Bredon Hill is a prominent isolated hill in Worcestershire. The warning is that when there

are clouds around the top of the hill there will soon be rain or storms on the plain below. The regional variants of this proverb are too numerous to list; there are also several versions of the ironic saying "If you can see the top of —Hill it will rain; if you can't, it is raining."

82 If the clouds look as if scratched by a hen, get ready to reef your topsails then.
To "reef" sails is to reduce their area, as in expectation of a high wind.

83 Mackerel sky and mares' tails make lofty ships carry low sails.
A "mackerel sky" is dappled with small white clouds; "mares' tails" are long streaks of cirrus cloud.

84 Red clouds in the east, rain the next day.

85 When it gangs up i' sops, it'll fau down i' drops.
Implies that small clouds ("sops") gathering around the sides of a mountain are a sign of rain.

86 In the old of the moon, a cloudy morning bodes a fair afternoon.

Fog

87 When Tottenham wood is all on fire, then Tottenham street is nought but mire.
"Tottenham Wood" is a former name for the Wood Green area of northeast London, which remained largely rural until the later 19th century. The proverb implies that when fog hangs over the wood like the smoke from a fire, it is a sign of heavy rain to come.

88 So many mists in March, so many frosts in May.

89 When the mist comes from the hill, then good weather it doth spill; when the mist comes from the sea, then good weather it will be.

Cold weather

90 A cold April the barn will fill.

91 A cold May and a windy makes a full barn and a findy.
"Findy" means "substantial".

92 Cold weather and knaves come out of the north.

93 As the day lengthens, the cold strengthens.
Points out that February and early March are often the coldest part of the winter.

94 There is a good steward abroad when there is a windfrost.
Implies that there is no need to supervise workmen in cold weather, as they are obliged to work hard in order to keep warm.

Snow

95 A snow year, a rich year.

96 Snow for a se'nnight is a mother to the earth, for ever after a stepmother.
A "se'nnight" is a week. The saying implies that a brief period of snow may be good for the earth's fertility but a longer one will be harmful.

97 Under water, famine; under snow, bread.

98 Widecombe folks are picking their geese, faster, faster, faster.
A saying used by the people of south Devon during a snowstorm; the village of Widecombe stands high up on Dartmoor.

Frost

99 A white frost never lasts more than three days.

100 Many frosts and many thowes make many rotten yowes.
"Thowes" are thaws; "yowes" are ewes.

101 The first and last frosts are the worst.

102 He that is surprised with the first frost, feels it all the winter after.

103 Hail brings frost in the tail.

Sun

104 On Candlemas Day, if the sun shines clear, the shepherd had rather see his
wife on the bier.
Candlemas Day is February 2nd. It was commonly believed that bright weather on this
date heralded a long period of cold weather. See also SEASONS: 17.

105 Remember on St Vincent's Day, if the sun his beams display, be sure to mark
the transient beam, which through the casement sheds a gleam; for 'tis a
token bright and clear of prosperous weather all the year.
St Vincent's Day is January 22nd.

106 A gaudy morning bodes a wet afternoon.

107 The morning sun never lasts a day.
Often applied warningly to youthful prodigies or those who achieve early success in
some new enterprise.

108 A morning sun, and a wine-bred child, and a Latin-bred woman, seldom end
well.
A "wine-bred child" implies an overindulged young girl and a "Latin-bred woman"
means a female scholar or bluestocking.

109 If red the sun begins his race, expect that rain will flow apace.

110 If the sun goes pale to bed, 'twill rain tomorrow, it is said.

111 If the sun in red should set, the next day surely will be wet; if the sun should
set in grey, the next will be a rainy day.

112 When the sun sets in a bank, a westerly wind we shall not want.
The "bank" refers to a bank of dark cloud.

113 When the sun sets bright and clear, an easterly wind you need not fear.

114 The March sun causes dust, and the winds blow it about.

115 The March sun raises, but dissolves not.
Implies that the March sun is warm enough for the wind to raise a dust but not hot
enough to disperse any lingering frosts or snow.

Mild weather

116 The Welshman had rather see his dam on the bier, than to see a fair
Februeer.
Like proverb 104 above, this warns that a bright February often heralds a period of severe
cold.

117 A green Yule makes a fat churchyard.
It is still a common belief that mild weather in winter is ominous because it preserves
harmful germs, etc.

118 A fair day in winter is the mother of a storm.

119 Summer in winter, and a summer's flood, never boded England good.

120 If Janiveer's calends be summerly gay, 'twill be winterly weather till the calends of May.
"Janiveer" is January. The "calends" of a month are the first day.

Dry weather

121 If in February there be no rain, 'tis neither good for hay nor grain.

122 Dry August and warm does harvest no harm.

123 Drought never bred dearth in England.

124 If the 24th of August be fair and clear, then hope for a prosperous autumn that year.

125 If St Paul's Day be fair and clear, it will betide a happy year.
St Paul's Day is January 25th.

126 A peck of March dust, and a shower in May, makes the corn green and the fields gay.
Like proverbs 127 and 128 below, this emphasizes the value of a dry March. A "peck" was a former measure for grain, etc., equal to eight quarts.

127 A bushel of March dust is worth a king's ransom.
A "bushel" was a unit of measure equal to eight gallons.

128 March dust and May sun, makes corn white and maids dun.

See also MONTHS; SEASONS

182 Will

Its power

1 Where there's a will there's a way.

2 That which two will, takes effect.

3 You can lead a horse to the water, but you can't make him drink.

4 To bow the body is easy, to bow the will is hard.
Chinese proverb.

Its inadequacy

5 Will is no skill.

6 The spirit is willing, but the flesh is weak.
Based on Matthew 26:41, where the disciples excuse themselves for having fallen asleep in Christ's hour of anguish.

Its effects

7 He who wills the end, wills the means.
Implies that anyone who truly resolves to achieve a certain end must be prepared to accept the necessary means, however repugnant.

8 Will buys and money pays.

9 Will is the cause of woe.

10 Will will have will, though will woe win.
Implies that although wilfulness invariably causes sorrow, the wilful person still insists on having his or her own way.

Willingness

11 Where your will is ready, your feet are light.

12 All things are easy, that are done willingly.

13 It is easy to do what one's own self wills.

14 Nothing is impossible to a willing heart.

15 Fate leads the willing, but drives the stubborn.

16 All lay load on the willing horse.

17 Never spur a willing horse.
The thought can be traced back to Ovid's *Ars amatoria* (1st century BC).

18 One volunteer is worth two pressed men.
"Pressed" here means "forced into military service".

Unwillingness

19 Nothing is easy to the unwilling.

20 He that complies against his will, is of his own opinion still.
A quotation from Samuel Butler's *Hudibras* (1678).

21 If the lad go to the well against his will, either the can will break or the water will spill.

22 It is a thrawn faced bairn that is gotten against the father's will.
"Thrawn" means "crooked, twisted". The saying implies that unwilling actions will be carried out poorly or ungraciously.

23 A forced kindness deserves no thanks.

Stubbornness

24 Obstinate oxen waste their strength.
Chinese proverb.

25 Swine, women, and bees cannot be turned.

26 A wilful man will have his way.

27 He that will to Cupar, maun to Cupar.
Cupar is a town in Fife, Scotland. "Maun" means "must".

28 None so blind as those who will not see.

29 None so deaf as those who will not hear.

30 Little birds that can sing and won't sing should be made to sing.

31 He that will not go over the stile, must be thrust through the gate.

Wishes

32 Mere wishes are silly fishes.

33 Wishes can never fill a sack.

34 If wishes were horses, beggars would ride.
One variant adds "…; if turnips were watches, I'd wear one by my side."

35 If wishes were butter-cakes, beggars might bite.

36 If wishes were thrushes, then beggars would eat birds.

37 Wishers and woulders be no good householders.

38 'Had I fish' was never good with garlic.
A further illustration of the inadequacy of idle wishes. Variants substitute "mustard" or "butter" for "garlic".

39 The wish is father to the thought.
Adapted from Shakespeare's *2 Henry IV* (1598).

40 We soon believe what we desire.

See also WOMEN: *Their wilfulness*

183 Wisdom

Its sources

1 The wind in one's face makes one wise.
"The wind in one's face" here implies adversity or difficulty.

2 Trouble brings experience and experience brings wisdom.

3 Experience is the mother of wisdom.
Some variants add "…and memory the father".

4 From hearing, comes wisdom; from speaking, repentance.

5 A still tongue makes a wise head.

6 Early to bed and early to rise, makes a man healthy, wealthy, and wise.
James Thurber's humorous reversal is well known: "Early to rise and early to bed, makes a man healthy and wealthy and dead" (mid-20th century).

7 The brains don't lie in the beard.
Implies that the old are not always wise.

8 Wisdom goes not always by years.

9 No man is born wise or learned.

10 Wisdom is neither inheritance nor legacy.
Implies that wisdom can neither be inherited from one's parents nor passed on to one's children.

11 Under a ragged coat lies wisdom.

12 Wisdom sometimes walks in clouted shoes.
"Clouted (*i.e.* patched) shoes" here symbolize poverty.

Its value

13 Wisdom is a treasure for all time.
Japanese proverb.

14 Wisdom is more to be envied than riches.

15 Without wisdom, wealth is worthless.
Adapted from Proverbs 16:16.

16 Better wit than wealth.

17 Want of wit is worse than want of gear.
"Gear" means "possessions, goods".

18 He that has money in his purse, cannot want a head for his shoulders.
Implies that wisdom is of great importance in the handling of money.

19 Wisdom is the least burdensome travelling pack.
Implies that wisdom can be carried about everywhere.

20 A wise man is never less alone than when he is alone.
Adapted from Cicero's *De officiis* (1st century BC), in which the saying is attributed to the great general Scipio Africanus.

21 Wisdom and virtue are like the two wheels of a cart.
Japanese proverb.

22 Wit and wisdom is good warison.
"Warison" means "provision, store".

23 Well goes the case when wisdom counsels.

24 He commands enough that obeys a wise man.

25 A wise man never wants a weapon.

26 Wisdom is better than strength.

27 What is not wisdom, is danger.

28 By wisdom peace, by peace plenty.
Some variants add "…, by plenty war."

29 A wise man is a great wonder.

30 An ounce of mother wit is worth a pound of learning.

31 It is good to be merry and wise.
Implies that merriment should be tempered with wisdom.

Its unimportance

32 Better be happy than wise.

33 A little wit will serve a fortunate man.
Implies that a man who has good fortune does not need great wisdom.

Evidence of wisdom

34 It is a great point of wisdom to find out one's own folly.

35 It is wit to pick a lock and steal a horse, but wisdom to let them alone.

36 He that is truly wise and great, lives both too early and too late.
A great wise man lives "too early" because he is ahead of his time and "too late" because of the good he could have done if born earlier. Sometimes used as a facetious excuse for arriving too late or too early.

37 He is wise enough that can keep himself warm.

38 He is a wise man who, when he is well, can keep so.
That is, who knows when to leave well alone.

39 He is wise that has wit enough for his own affairs.

40 He is not wise, who is not wise for himself.
The saying can be traced back to Cicero (1st century BC).

41 He has a good judgment that relies not wholly on his own.

42 He is wise that is ware in time.

43 He is wise that knows when he's well enough.

44 Wisest is he who recks not who is rich.
"Reck" means "pay heed to, care about".

45 A wise man cares not for what he cannot have.

46 He has wisdom at will, that with an angry heart can hold him still.

47 He was very wise who first gave a reward.

48 What the fool does in the end, the wise man does at the beginning.
There are two possible implications: that the fool only learns through his errors, or that fools procrastinate.

49 Honest men marry soon, wise men not at all.

50 The fool wanders, the wise man travels.

51 Riches serve a wise man but command a fool.
A quotation from the French theologian Pierre Charron (1541–1603).

52 No wisdom to silence.

53 Wise men silent, fools talk.

54 Wise men have their mouth in their heart, fools their heart in their mouth.

55 A wise head makes a close mouth.

56 He is wise that is honest.

57 Wise is the man who has two loaves, and sells one to buy a lily.
Chinese proverb. The saying implies that once a man's material needs are taken care of, he should seek beauty.

Characteristics of the wise

58 The wise seek wisdom, a fool has found it.

59 He that is a wise man by day is no fool by night.

60 A wise man changes his mind, a fool never.
    Some variants have "…but a fool perseveres."

61 A wise man needs not blush for changing his purpose.

62 A wise man esteems every place to be his own country.
    Implies that the wise are at ease wherever they are. The saying has been attributed to both Plato and Diogenes (5th–4th centuries BC).

63 A wise man may sometimes play the fool.

64 No man can play the fool so well as the wise man.
    Sometimes attributed to Cato the Elder (3rd–2nd centuries BC).

65 Wise men propose, and fools determine.

66 Reason governs the wise man and cudgels the fool.

67 Fools bite one another, but wise men agree together.

The fallibility of the wise

68 No man is wise at all times.

69 The wisest man may fall.

70 Wise men are caught in wiles.

71 A wise man commonly has foolish children.

72 If the wise erred not, it would go hard with fools.

73 Great wits have short memories.

See also FOOLISHNESS: *The wisdom of fools*; OLD PEOPLE: *Their wisdom*

184 Women

Their danger

1 Women are the snares of Satan.
    A commonplace of early and medieval Christian teaching, referring ultimately to the Adam and Eve story (Genesis 3).

2 Women are the devil's nets.

3 A wicked woman and an evil is three halfpence worse than the devil.

4 There is no devil so bad as a she-devil.

5 Women and dogs set men together by the ears.
    Some variants add "wine" to the list of troublemakers.

6 No war without a woman.

7 No mischief but a woman or a priest is at the bottom of it.

8 Weal and women cannot pan, but woe and women can.
    "Pan" means "come together". The implication is that women are more often the source of sorrow than of good fortune.

9 Women's counsel is cold.
    An old Icelandic saying. "Cold" here means "deadly, fatal".

10 Take heed of a young wench, a prophetess, and a Latin woman.
    Both here and in proverb 11 below a "Latin woman" implies a bluestocking or female scholar.

11 A morning sun, and a wine-bred child, and a Latin-bred woman, seldom end well.

A "wine-bred child" implies an overindulged young girl.

12 Women are like wasps in their anger.

13 Hell hath no fury like a woman scorned.

Based on a quotation from Congreve's tragedy *The Mourning Bride* (1697); the thought is much older and can be traced back to the *Medea* of Euripides (5th century BC). In classical mythology the Furies were goddesses of vengeance who lived in hell (Tartarus).

14 Women in state affairs are like monkeys in glass shops.

Their value

15 All women are good.

Often used ironically, or with the addition "either for something or nothing."

16 If a woman were as little as she is good, a pease-cod would make her a gown and a hood.

A "pease-cod" is a pea-pod.

17 Woeful is the household that wants a woman.

18 Women are necessary evils.

Variants add "wind" "fire" and "water" to the list of necessary evils.

Their capriciousness

19 A woman is a weathercock.

20 A woman's mind and a winter wind change oft.

21 Women are as wavering as the wind.

Their impulsiveness

22 A woman's thoughts are afterthoughts.

Indian proverb.

23 A woman either loves or hates in extremes.

Their wilfulness

24 Women must have their wills while they live, because they make none when they die.

Until 1870 married women in England and Wales had no legal rights over their own property.

25 Women will have their wills.

26 Swine, women, and bees cannot be turned.

27 Forbid a thing, and that women will do.

Adapted from a line in Ovid's *Amores* (1st century BC).

Their dissimulation

28 Women naturally deceive, weep and spin.

29 Women may blush to hear what they were not ashamed to do.

30 A maid and a virgin is not all one.

31 Maidens should be meek till they be married.

Some variants add "…and then they may burn kirks."

32 Women are saints in church, angels in the street, and devils at home.

Their tears

33 Women laugh when they can, and weep when they will.

34 Early rain and a woman's tears are soon over.

35 It is no more pity to see a woman weep, than to see a goose go barefoot.

36 Trust not a woman when she weeps.
One variant adds "…nor a dog when it pisses."

Their lack of wisdom

37 When an ass climbs a ladder, we may find wisdom in women.

38 Women have long hair and short brains.

39 A woman cuts her wisdom teeth when she is dead.

40 A woman's advice is no great thing, but he who won't take it is a fool.

Their reasoning

41 'Because' is a woman's reason.

42 Take the first advice of a woman and not the second.
Implies that the first advice, based on intuition, will be more reliable than the second, based on inferior reasoning.

43 A woman need but look on her apron-string to find an excuse.

44 Find a woman without an excuse, and find a hare without a meuse.
A "meuse" is a gap in a hedge.

Their tongue

45 A woman's sword is her tongue, and she does not let it rust.

46 A woman's strength is in her tongue.

47 Arthur could not tame woman's tongue.
A reference to King Arthur.

48 A woman's tongue wags like a lamb's tail.

49 A woman's tongue is the last thing about her that dies.

50 One tongue is enough for a woman.
Sometimes attributed to John Milton, who allegedly gave this as his reason for refusing to let his daughters learn Latin and Greek.

51 Women are great talkers.

52 Women will say anything.

53 A woman's answer is never to seek.
That is, she always has a ready retort.

54 Women will have the last word.

55 Many women, many words; many geese, many turds.

56 Women and sparrows twitter in company.
Japanese proverb.

57 Where there are women and geese, there wants no noise.

58 Three women make a market.
A reference to the noise generated by three women.

59 Three women, three geese, and three frogs make a market.
A German variant of proverb 58 above.

60 Silence is a woman's best garment.
The thought can be traced back to Sophocles (5th century BC).

61 Maidens must be mild and meek, swift to hear and slow to speak.

62 Maidens should be seen, and not heard.
   A saying later applied to children of both sexes; see CHILDREN: 37.

63 The gist of a lady's letter is in the postscript.
   This may imply that a woman's written communications are as rambling as her speech;
   or that she cunningly disguises her real purpose in writing.

64 A sieve will hold water better than a woman's mouth a secret.

65 A woman conceals what she knows not.
   There are two possible implications: that women like to create an air of spurious mystery;
   or that the only secrets women can keep are those of which they have no knowledge.

Their needs

66 Women, priests, and poultry, have never enough.

67 A ship and a woman are ever repairing.
   Implies that women are always demanding new clothes and possessions, etc.

68 Two daughters and a back door are three arrant thieves.
   A reference to the expense of bringing up daughters. The "back door" is the means by
   which dishonest servants dispose of goods stolen from their masters.

Their duties

69 A woman's place is in the home.
   First recorded in the mid-19th century.

70 Women and hens are lost by gadding.

71 House goes mad when women gad.

72 A woman's work is never done.
   First recorded as the title of a 17th-century Scottish ballad, although the thought is much
   older.

Handling women

73 Dally not with women or money.

74 A woman and a glass are ever in danger.
   Implies that women are morally frail and easily ruined.

75 Who has a woman has an eel by the tail.

76 Women and music should never be dated.
   Implies that the age of a woman should neither be asked nor told.

77 Never trust a woman, even if she has borne you seven children.
   Japanese proverb.

78 From the evil woman guard yourself, and the good one never trust.

79 Let no woman's painting breed thy stomach's fainting.
   That is, don't be overcome with lust for a woman's cosmetic beauty.

80 A woman, a dog, and a walnut-tree, the more you beat them the better they
   be.
   It was formerly believed that beating a walnut tree would increase its yield.

81 All women may be won.

82 Tell a woman she is fair, and she will soon turn fool.

83 A maid that laughs is half taken.

84 A woman kissed is half won.

85 Women resist in order to be conquered.

86 Nineteen nay-says of a maiden are half a grant.

87 Maids say 'Nay' and take it.

88 Saying 'No' a woman shakes her head lengthwise.
Japanese proverb. "Lengthwise" here implies up and down, suggesting that a woman nods assent as she says "No".

Man and woman

89 Women's instinct is often truer than men's reasoning.
90 Women in mischief are wiser than men.
91 Man is the head, but woman turns it.
92 Men make houses, women make homes.
93 A woman has an eye more than a man.
94 A woman is flax, man is fire, the devil comes and blows the bellows.
95 Woman is the confusion of man.
A quotation from the medieval encyclopedist Vincent of Beauvais (13th century). A punning variant substitutes "woe" for "confusion".
96 Men get wealth and women keep it.
Implies that men are better at acquiring wealth but women are better at saving it.
97 A clever man will build a city, a clever woman will lay it low.
Chinese proverb.
98 A woman is the weaker vessel.
Adapted from 1 Peter 3:7.
99 A man of straw is worth a woman of gold.
100 Man, woman, and devil, are the three degrees of comparison.
101 A bad woman is worse than a bad man.
102 The female of the species is more deadly than the male.
A quotation from Kipling's poem "The Female of the Species" (1919).
103 Deeds are males, and words are females.
An Italian proverb; in the original language it refers to the fact that the nouns *fatti* and *parole* are male and female respectively.
104 A man is as old as he feels, and a woman as old as she looks.
20th century. The many facetious variants include "A man is only as old as the woman he feels", attributed to Groucho Marx.

See also MARRIAGE: 100–128

185 World

Its size

1 The world is a long journey.
2 The world is a wide place.
3 It's a small world.
Like proverb 4 below, this is mainly said when friends meet by accident in a quite unexpected place; or when new acquaintances find that they already have mutual friends.
4 The world is but a little place, after all.

Its perpetual motion

5 The world turns as a ball.
6 The world goes on wheels.

Attitudes to the world

7 The world is like a dancing girl – it dances for a little while to everyone.
Arabic proverb.

8 The world is a net, the more we stir in it, the more we are entangled.

9 The world is bound to no man.

10 The world is a mirror; show thyself in it, and it will reflect thy image.
Arabic proverb.

11 The world is a stage and every man plays his part.
In English, the classic comparison of human life to a stage play is the long speech "All the world's a stage…" in Shakespeare's *As You Like It* (1599); the thought, however, is much older, occurring in several classical authors.

12 The world is a ladder for some to go up and some down.

13 The world is nought.

14 This world is nothing, except it tend to another.

15 It is a good world, but they are ill that are on it.

186 Worry

Its sources

1 Riches bring care and fears.

2 Much coin, much care.

3 Little gear, less care.
"Gear" means "possessions".

4 Little wealth, little care.

5 He that has no ill fortune, is troubled with good.
Implies that certain people will always find something to worry about.

Its effects

6 Care brings grey hair.

7 It is not work that kills, but worry.
First recorded in the late 19th century.

8 A poet in adversity can hardly make verses.
Implies that worry prevents the mind from functioning as it should.

Its futility

9 Hang care.

10 Care killed the cat.

11 Care is no cure.

12 A pound of care will not pay an ounce of debt.

13 It will be all the same a hundred years hence.
A 20th-century saying implying that few things matter very much in the long run.

Sharing one's problems

14 A trouble shared is a trouble halved.
A variant substitutes "problem" for "trouble"; first recorded in the early 20th century.

15 It is good to have company in trouble.

Against worrying about the future

16 Sufficient unto the day is the evil thereof.
A biblical quotation: Matthew 6:34.

17 Don't cross the bridge till you get to it.
First recorded in the mid-19th century.

18 Take things as they come.

19 Don't cry before you are hurt.

20 Dearths foreseen come not.

21 Our worst misfortunes are those which never befall us.
Variants have been used by Jefferson, Disraeli, and Churchill.

22 Sorrow is soon enough when it comes.

23 Let your trouble tarry till its own day comes.

24 Don't meet troubles half-way.

25 Never trouble trouble till trouble troubles you.

26 Let the morn come, and the meat with it.
That is, don't worry about tomorrow's provisions.

187 Worth

Its assessment

1 A man's worth is the worth of his land.

2 A man is valued as he makes himself valuable.

3 Worth has been underrated, ever since wealth has been overrated.
That is, since time began.

4 The worth of a thing is what it will bring.
Adapted from a couplet in Samuel Butler's *Hudibras* (1664).

5 The worth of a thing is best known by the want of it.

6 Blessings brighten as they take their flight.

7 The cow knows not what her tail is worth till she has lost it.

8 You never miss the water till the well runs dry.

9 If you would know the value of a ducat, try to borrow one.

10 Would you know what money is, go borrow some.

11 What costs little, is less esteemed.

12 The more cost, the more honour.

13 A penny at a pinch is worth a pound.

14 That thing which is rare is dear.
A variant has "The rarest is the fairest."

Everything has some value

15 All things in their being are good for something.

16 It is a poor dog that is not worth the whistling.

17 Willows are weak, yet they bind other wood.

18 There is no tree but bears some fruit.

188 Writing

The written word

1 The pen is mightier than the sword.
  A quotation from Edward Bulwer-Lytton's otherwise forgotten poem *Richelieu* (1839); the thought, however, is much older and can be traced back to Cicero (1st century BC).

2 The calf, the goose, the bee: the world is ruled by these three.
  "The calf" refers to parchment, "the goose" to the quill-pen, and "the bee" to sealing-wax.

3 Pen and ink is wit's plough.

4 The pen is the tongue of the hand.

5 The thought has good legs, and the quill a good tongue.
  A variant ends "...quill has wings."

6 Pens may blot, but they cannot blush.

7 The mouth is wind, the pen is a track.

8 Words fly, writings remain.
  Also used in its Latin form, *Littera scripta manet.*

9 Writing destroys the memory.

Books

10 Literature is a good staff but a bad crutch.
   Attributed to Sir Walter Scott (1771–1832).

11 You cannot open a book without learning something.
   Chinese proverb.

12 A book that is shut, is but a block.

13 Every book must be chewed to get out its juice.
   Chinese proverb.

14 A great book is a great evil.
   A quotation from the poet and scholar Callimachus (3rd century BC).

15 A wicked book is the wickeder because it cannot repent.

Writers

16 Like author, like book.

17 The style is the man.
   Implies that the style of writing reveals the personality of the author. In this form the saying is a quotation from the Comte de Buffon's *Discours sur le style* (1753), an address to the Académie Française that is itself regarded as a model of the French classical style. However, the idea that literary style shows or reveals the author is much older.

18 Tailors and writers must mind the fashion.

See also FINE ARTS: *Poetry*

A.'s well... 55:5
Almost A. and well nigh... 40:31
Alms A. never make poor 75:11
Almsgiving Great a.... 75:12
Alone A soul a.... 161:4
  Better be a.... 161:6
  Man if he lives a.... 161:16
Alton Through the pass of A.... 58:68
Altrincham The Mayor of A.... 58:67
Ambition A. loses many a man 4:14
  A. makes people diligent 4:1
Ambitious Every a. man is a captive...
  4:16
Amend Some do a.... 10:37
  The best may a. 97:6
Americans Good A.... 133:32
Andrew St A. the King... 117:74
Angels Men are not a. 179:17
Anger A. and haste... 5:4
  A. begins with folly... 5:14
  A. dies quickly... 5:20
  A. ends in cruelty 5:8
  A. has no eyes 5:11
  A. is a short madness 5:21
  A. makes a rich man hated... 5:3
  A. punishes itself 5:5
  A. restrained... 5:29
  The a. is not warrantable... 5:22
Anglesey A. is the mother of Wales
  133:81
Angry An a. man never wants woe 5:2
  He that is a. is seldom at ease 5:1
  He that is a. without a cause... 5:34
  He who slowly gets a.... 5:23
  If you be a.... 5:26
  Two things a man should never be a.
    at... 5:33
  When a man grows a.... 5:12
  When a man is a.... 5:15
  When a., count a hundred 5:24
Answer A soft a.... 5:28
  Never a. a question... 8:11
  Such a. as man gives... 44:18
Ant The a. had wings... 4:25
Anvil When you are an a.... 28:47
Ape An a.'s an ape... 7:43
Apparel A. makes the man 50:3
Appearances A. are deceptive 7:1
Appetite A. comes with eating 82:3
Apple An a. a day... 53:59
  Better an a. given... 75:2

No good a.... 18:11
The a. never falls... 18:8
Apple-pie An a. without some cheese...
  53:50
Apples The a. on the other side... 28:41
April An A. flood... 181:48
  A. showers... 181:47
  If they blow in A.... 117:42
  In A. Dove's flood... 181:49
  On the first of A., hunt the gowk...
    117:37
  On the first of A., you may send a
    fool... 117:36
  On the third of A.... 117:39
  When A. blows his horn... 181:74
Archer A good a.... 158:14
Architect Every man is the a.... 147:1
Army An a. marches... 53:2
  An a. of stags... 9:15
Arrival With the a. of the stepmother...
  128:22
Arrow An a. shot upright... 44:12
Art A. has no enemy... 96:14
  A. improves Nature 119:14
  A. is long... 107:4
  He who has an a.... 124:3
  In every a.... 54:19
  There is an a. even in roasting apples
    158:8
Arthur A. could not tame... 184:47
  A. himself had but his time 39:10
Ashamed Never be a. to eat your meat
  53:73
Ask A. and it shall be given you 8:5
  A. a silly question... 8:10
  A. but enough... 22:1
  A. much to have a little 22:2
  A. no questions... 8:12
  Better to a. the way... 8:4
  He that cannot a.... 8:1
  You must a. your neighbour... 121:4
Asks He that a. faintly... 8:15
Ass An a. endures his burden... 56:8
  An a. laden with gold... 180:106
  An a. must be tied... 154:42
  An a. pricked... 154:41
  Every a. likes to hear... 69:81
  Every a. thinks himself worthy... 60:15
  He is an a.... 69:44
  If an a. goes a-travelling... 172:8

If one, two, or three tell you you are an a.... 34:26

The a. loaded with gold... 115:19

The a. that brays most... 168:4

When all men say you are an a.... 34:25

When an a. climbs a ladder... 184:37

When an a. kicks you... 155:11

Wherever an a. falls... 62:23

Atheist An a. is one point... 144:49

Atheists Some are a. only in fair weather 144:42

Attack A. is the best form... 178:18

Attorneys Two a. can live... 104:44

August If the twenty-fourth of A.... 181:124

Aunt If my a. had been a man... 108:13

Austerity There is no a.... 71:5

Author Like a.... 188:16

Authority A. shows the man 9:10

Autumn A grassy a.... 152:12

Avarice A. hoards itself poor... 115:1

A. is the only passion... 115:22

Avoid A. a questioner... 79:35

Away If a person is a.... 1:19

B

Babbling Much b.... 168:7

Baby Don't throw the b. out... 85:41

Bacchus B. has drowned... 51:25

Bachelors B.' wives and maids' children... 3:60

Two b. drinking to you... 113:147

We b. laugh... 113:32

Back The b. door... 33:6

Bacon He loves b. well... 53:71

Bad A b. penny... 10:36

B. luck often brings... 111:25

No man ever became thoroughly b.... 29:21

Nothing so b. but it might have been worse 127:6

Nothing so b. in which there is not something of good 127:31

Where b.'s the best... 20:8

Bairn It is a thrawn faced b.... 182:22

Bait The b. hides the hook 7:14

Bake As you b. so shall you eat 147:12

Balance The b. distinguishes not... 60:26

Balk Make not a b. of good ground 126:11

Ball If the b. does not stick to the wall... 42:2

Barber A b. learns to shave... 69:41

One b. shaves another gratis 110:9

Bare B. walls... 113:48

Better a b. foot... 80:20

Bargain A good b.... 22:40

At a good b.... 22:14

Don't b. for fish... 6:11

It is an ill b.... 127:23

Barkers Great b.... 168:39

Barking B. dogs... 168:38

Barnaby B. bright... 117:58

Barter He is fond of b.... 46:18

Bartholomew St B. brings the cold dew 117:61

Bashfulness B. is an enemy... 8:3

Basket-justice A b.... 29:44

Basque The B. is faithful 133:42

Bastard B. brood... 138:18

Bastes Every man b. the fat hog 180:68

Bathes He who b. in May... 117:57

Battle It is an ill b.... 46:6

Be What must b., must be 45:5

Bean A b. in liberty... 106:5

Every b. has its black 97:37

Beans Sow b. in the mud... 30:15

Bear A man may b.... 56:9

B. and forbear 56:4

Call the b. 'uncle'... 68:10

He may b. a bull... 164:2

Beard A b. well lathered... 12:15

If the b. were all... 7:6

It is not the b.... 7:5

Beast Who goes a b. to Rome... 172:9

Beat He that cannot b. the ass... 147:32

If you can't b. 'em... 25:8

You may b. a horse... 30:32

Beaten Better to be b.... 23:9

Beauty A thing of b.... 11:59

B. and folly... 11:9

B. and honesty... 11:8

B. draws more than oxen 11:11

B. fades... 11:29

B. is but a blossom 11:30

B. is eloquent... 11:13

B. is in the eye... 11:35

B. is no inheritance 11:27

B. is only one layer 11:2

B. is only skin-deep 11:1

B. is potent... 11:28

B. may have fair leaves... 11:3
B. opens locked doors 11:12
B.'s sister... 11:52
B. without bounty... 11:21
B. won't make the pot boil 11:23
Because B. is a woman's reason 184:41
Bed As you make your b.... 147:10
  Better go to b. supperless... 14:3
  Go to b. with the lamb... 52:9
  Who goes to b. supperless... 93:4
Bee The b. sucks honey... 127:32
Beef It is good b.... 53:37
  Such b.... 55:11
Been What has b., may be 171:52
Bees B. that have honey... 7:15
  No b., no honey... 48:17
  When b. are old... 125:26
  Where b. are, there is honey 48:16
Before He that looks not b.... 70:3
Beg Better b. than steal 136:82
  He learned timely to b.... 75:18
  Neither b. of him... 154:26
Beggar A b. can never be bankrupt 136:18
  A b. pays a benefit... 88:15
  Every b. is descended... 60:21
  It is better to be a b.... 136:81
  Set a b. on horseback... 180:41
  The b. may sing... 136:27
Beggars B.' bags... 82:28
  B. breed... 136:102
  B. can't be choosers 80:7
Begin All may b. a war... 178:8
  Better never to b.... 134:8
  Good to b. well... 134:9
Beginning A good b.... 12:11
  An ill b.... 12:12
  Every b. is hard 12:7
  Everything must have a b. 12:1
  If the b. is good... 12:10
  Such b.... 12:13
Begins He b. to build too soon... 85:12
  He who b. many things... 48:54
Begun Well b. is half done 12:14
Behind Far b. must follow the faster
103:3
  They are far b.... 103:11
Beild There is b. aneath... 125:17
Being All things in their b.... 187:15
Belief B. is better than investigation 13:8
Believe B. no tales... 13:12
  B. nothing of what you hear... 13:10

B. well... 13:5
To b. in one's dreams... 159:26
We soon b.... 13:1
Believes He that b. all... 13:9
Belled Let aye the b. wether... 125:9
Bellowing A b. cow... 162:27
Bells B. call others... 94:17
Belly A b. full of gluttony... 76:1
  Better b. burst... 76:17
  He whose b. is full... 93:28
  If it were not for the b.... 76:5
  The b. carries the legs 53:3
  The b. wants ears 93:7
  When the b. is full, the bones... 112:1
  When the b. is full, the mind... 112:1
Beloved To be b.... 109:12
Bend Better b. than break 25:9
Benedick St B., sow thy pease... 117:30
Benefits B. bind 75:38
  B. make a man a slave 75:37
Bengali If a B. is a man... 133:8
Bernard B. did not see everything 97:17
Best All is for the b.... 127:9
  B. is best cheap 22:42
  The b. cart... 97:24
  The b. cloth... 97:23
  The b. go first 39:62
  The b. is the enemy... 4:18
  The b. of friends... 55:8
  The b. of men... 138:28
  The b. things are hard to come by
    134:11
  The b. things in life... 180:51
  The b. things may be abused 97:19
Bestill A good b.... 156:4
Best-laid The b. schemes... 97:21
Bet In a b. there is a fool... 74:13
Better Be it for b., be it for worse...
180:110
  B. sit still... 4:19
  He that cannot do b.... 144:83
  If b. were within... 55:10
Bewails He that b. himself... 153:55
Beware B. of an oak... 181:80
  B. of breed 15:24
  B. of 'Had I wist' 142:27
  B. of no man... 153:39
  It is good to b.... 62:37
Beyond Every man a little b. himself...
69:24

Bible The B. is the religion of Protestants 144:100

Bidden Do as you're b.... 123:3

Bigger The b. the man... 81:10
The b. they are... 81:3

Bind B. the sack... 56:12

Birchen B. twigs break no ribs 49:25

Bird A b. in the hand... 135:1
A b. in the soup... 135:5
Every b. loves to hear... 24:2
It is an ill b.... 143:22
The b. is known by his note... 168:29
The b. loves her nest 172:24

Birds B. are entangled... 168:1
B. in their little nests agree 141:31
B. of a feather... 157:9
B. once snared... 62:25
Little b. that can sing... 182:30
There are no b.... 171:43

Birth B. is much... 15:3
Great b. is a very poor dish... 15:31
Our b. made us mortal... 39:44
The b. follows the belly 128:10

Bite If you cannot b.... 168:45

Biter The b. is sometimes bit 44:11

Biting B. and scratching... 109:99

Bitten He that has been b. by a serpent... 62:26
Once b.... 62:21

Bitter B. pills... 166:16

Blab He that is a b.... 79:32

Black A b. hen... 7:40
A b. plum... 7:39
After b. clouds... 127:18
B. will take no other hue 18:32
There's a b. sheep... 143:9

Black-hearted If you want to see b. people... 94:22

Blacks Two b. do not make a white 10:54

Blames He that b. would buy 22:5
Many a one b. his wife... 147:28

Blate A b. cat... 49:21

Bleating A b. sheep... 168:5

Bleed If you b. your nag... 117:79

Blessed B. be St Stephen... 117:78
B. is the eye... 58:22

Blessings B. brighten... 187:6

Blind A b. man may sometimes... 111:2
A man should keep from the b.... 143:20
A man were better to be half b.... 80:24

If the b. lead the blind... 96:15
It is a b. goose... 69:40
Men are b.... 153:42
None so b.... 182:28
The b. man's peck... 22:33

Blindness There is no b.... 96:11

Blister A b. will rise... 40:12

Blithe A b. heart... 84:22
It is ill to put a b. face... 162:44

Blockhead He's a b. that can't make two verses... 67:9

Blood All b. is alike ancient 60:10
B. is thicker... 143:1
B. will have blood 148:1
B. will tell 18:14
Good b. makes bad puddings... 15:30
Like b.... 113:76
The b. of the martyrs... 144:57
The b. of the soldier... 124:50
Where b. has been spilt... 148:2
You can't get b.... 108:25

Blow A b. that is profitable... 73:6

Blows He that b. best... 44:3

Blue A b. eye in a Portuguese woman... 133:45
B. are the faraway hills 7:27
B. eyes... 167:24
There may be b.... 47:6

Boast Great b.... 24:15
They can do least who b. loudest 24:13

Boastful Never be b.... 24:11

Boil B. not the pap... 6:14
Whether you b. snow... 55:12

Boiling To a b. pot... 129:13

Boisterous A b. horse... 49:6

Bold A b. heart... 31:7
Be not too b. with your biggers or betters 37:47
B. men have generous hearts 31:20
B. resolution... 146:1
He was a b. man... 53:38
It is a b. mouse... 31:30
Nothing so b. as a blind mare 31:31

Bolder What is b. than a miller's neckcloth... 124:29

Bone The nearer the b.... 76:6

Bonny A b. bride is soon buskit... 11:54

Book A b. that is shut... 188:12
A great b.... 188:14
Every b. must be chewed... 188:13
You cannot open a b.... 188:11

You can't tell a b.... 7:32
Books B. and friends... 72:64
Booted They that are b.... 7:12
Born A man had better ne'er been b....
144:65
As soon as man is b.... 39:13
He that is b. a fool... 69:15
He that is b. to be hanged... 45:7
He that is once b.... 39:15
Men know where they were b.... 39:24
We are not b. for ourselves 153:20
Who is b. fair... 11:56
Borrow Not so good to b.... 14:7
Borrowed A b. loan... 14:26
B. garments... 14:10
B. thing... 14:25
Borrower Neither a b. nor a lender be
14:8
The b. is servant to the lender 14:21
Borrowing He that goes a b.... 14:17
Borrows He that b. binds himself... 14:12
He that b. must pay again... 14:20
Who b. to build... 16:7
Both You cannot have it b. ways 20:1
Boughs The b. that bear most... 81:20
Bound No man is b.... 104:51
They that are b.... 154:43
Bourbons The B. learn nothing... 133:33
Bourd B. not with Bawty... 37:49
They that b. wi' cats... 37:22
Bow A b. long bent... 56:15
To b. the body is easy... 182:4
Bows Every man b. to the bush... 68:9
Boys B. will be boys 19:32
B. will be men 19:42
He that is manned with b.... 154:4
Two b. are half a boy... 88:10
Brabbling B. curs... 141:13
Brag B. is a good dog... 24:7
Braggers Great b.... 24:14
Brain If the b. sows not corn... 114:7
Brains The b. don't lie... 125:31
Brave A b. arm... 31:17
A b. man may fall... 31:19
A b. man's wounds... 31:18
B. men lived... 64:13
None but the b.... 31:9
Some have been thought b.... 32:19
To a b. and faithful man... 31:24
Brawling B. booteth not 141:14
Bread B. is the staff of life 53:1

Man cannot live by b. alone 53:15
The b. never falls... 111:23
Break If things did not b.... 124:16
You may b. a horse's back... 164:12
Breaks A man that b. his word... 139:13
To him that b. his trust... 139:14
Breams He that has b. in his pond...
53:35
Breath The first b.... 39:14
Bred The best b.... 15:2
What is b. in the bone... 18:13
Bredon When B. Hill puts on his hat...
181:81
Breeks Tarry b.... 110:10
Brevity B. is the soul of wit 168:77
Brewing It is a sairy b.... 17:38
Bribe A b. will enter... 29:27
Neither b.... 29:26
Bricks You can't make b.... 108:27
Bride Happy is the b. the sun shines on...
113:144
Bridle It is the b. and spur... 49:5
Shake a b. over a Yorkshire tike's grave...
58:29
Bright B. rain... 181:69
Look on the b. side 127:1
Brings He that b. good news... 122:2
He that b. himself... 37:21
He that b. up his son to nothing...
136:61
Broken A b. friendship... 72:83
B. bones well set... 141:20
Broth Good b. may be made... 125:22
Brother The b. had rather see the sister
rich... 115:20
Brown It is a good thing to eat your b.
bread first 136:19
Bucket Put not the b. too often in the
well 56:17
Buckles Every man b. his belt... 47:9
Build Don't b. the sty... 6:13
Building B. and borrowing... 16:3
B. and marrying... 16:4
B. is a sweet impoverishing 16:2
B. is a thief 16:1
No good b.... 12:16
Bullet Every b.... 45:8
Bully A b. is always a coward 32:17
Burden It is not the b.... 56:10
Too long b.... 56:11
Burdens The greatest b.... 73:12

Burn B. not your house... 116:23
Burns He that b. most... 129:5
Burnt The b. child... 62:22
Burthen A b. of one's own choice... 147:7
Bush A bad b.... 80:18
Bushel A b. of March dust... 181:127
Busiest B. men find the most leisure time
  48:45
Business B. before pleasure 22:24
  B. is business 22:23
  B. is the salt of life 48:9
  Do b. with men... 181:46
  Do no b. with a kinsman 143:8
  Everybody's b.... 147:21
  Every man knows his own b. best 99:19
  Without b., debauchery 48:8
Busy Ever b.... 48:49
  For the b. man... 171:27
  He that is b.... 169:9
  To be too b.... 27:5
  Who is more b.... 95:11
Butter B. is mad twice a year 30:21
  B. is once a year... 30:20
  That which will not be b.... 134:27
Buy Better b. than borrow 14:1
  B. at a fair... 22:30
  B. in the cheapest market... 22:26
  They b. good cheap... 22:47
  To b. dear... 22:44
  When you go to b.... 22:3
Buyer Let the b. beware 22:10
  The b. needs a hundred eyes... 22:12
Buyers There are more foolish b.... 22:13
Buys He that b. and sells... 22:28
  Who b. dear and takes up on credit...
    22:25
Bygones Let b. be bygones 71:17

C

Caesar C.'s wife... 9:14
Cake You cannot have your c.... 20:2
Calamity C. is the touchstone... 37:18
Calf C. love, half love... 109:100
  The c., the goose, the bee... 188:2
  They think a c. a muckle beast... 160:37
Calm In a c. sea... 37:19
Camel It is easier for a c.... 180:36
  The c. never sees its own hump... 34:13
Can He c. who believes he can 13:6
  Man does what he c.... 77:74
  Those who c., do... 54:22

Candlemas If C. Day be fair and bright...
  152:18
  On C. Day, if the sun shines clear...
    181:104
  On C. Day, throw candle... 117:9
  On C. Day, you must have half your
    straw... 117:8
Cap If the c. fits... 34:28
Capon If thou hast not a c.... 28:48
Carcase Where the c. is... 82:23
Cards C. are the devil's books 74:7
  There is no pack of c. without a knave
    97:28
Care A pound of c.... 186:12
  C. and diligence... 48:3
  C. brings grey hair 186:6
  C. is no cure 186:11
  C. killed the cat 186:10
  Hang c. 186:9
  When everyone takes c. of himself...
    153:1
Careless A c. hussy... 33:8
Carl As the c. riches... 180:32
Carpenter The best c.... 158:15
Carrion A c. kite... 18:33
  C. crows... 94:8
Case Well goes the c.... 183:23
Cask A c. of wine... 51:19
  The c. savours of the first fill 18:19
Castle An Englishman's home is his c.
  121:18
  Better a c. of bones... 164:6
Cat A c. has nine lives 111:33
  A c. in gloves... 146:5
  A c. may look... 60:14
  How can the c. help it... 147:33
  Let the c. wink... 63:8
  Never was c. or dog drowned... 91:4
  The c. and dog may kiss... 94:4
  The c. shuts its eyes... 94:9
  The c. would eat fish... 98:4
  When the c.'s away... 1:11
  Woe's to them that have the c.'s dish...
    14:18
Catch First c. your hare 6:8
  Never c. at a falling knife... 88:12
  You cannot c. old birds... 125:12
Cats All c. are grey... 11:17
  C. eat what hussies spare 170:36
  C. hide their claws 7:16
  He who lives with c.... 29:17

Cause Take away the c.... 145:13

Causes That which a man c. to be done...
147:18

Cavil C. will enter at any hole... 141:34

Ceases He that c. to be a friend... 72:28

Censure Every man's c.... 34:6

Ceres Without C. and Bacchus... 53:7

Certain Nothing is c. but death.... 39:6
Nothing is c. but the unforeseen 6:29
Nothing so c. as death 39:7

Certainty He that quits c.... 111:13

Chad Before St C.... 117:28

Chain A c. is no stronger... 164:19

Chamber The c. of sickness... 87:30

Chances It c. in an hour... 111:3

Change A c. is as good... 17:1
A man will never c. his mind... 114:8
C. brings life 17:2
C. of pasture... 17:8
C. of weather... 69:88
C. your dwelling-place often... 17:3
C. your name... 113:145
Don't c. horses... 17:14
It is harder to c. human nature... 18:24
One may c. place... 172:7

Changing C. of works... 17:7

Charges The c. of building... 16:5

Charitable The c. give out at the door...
75:7

Charity C. and pride... 138:14
C. begins at home 143:19
C. construes all doubtful things... 101:4
C. covers a multitude of sins 101:5

Charon C. waits for all 39:4

Chastens He that c. one... 49:8

Chastises He that c. one... 49:9

Chatters Who c. *to* you... 79:36

Cheap Good c. is dear 22:41
He will never have a good thing c....
22:45
Ill ware is never c. 22:43
It is c. enough to say... 101:2
Light c.... 22:38

Cheapen Never c.... 22:8

Cheat He that will c. at play... 40:37

Cheats C. never prosper 40:20

Cheek Turn the other c. 148:17

Cheer When good c. is lacking... 84:39

Cheerful A c. look... 84:76
A c. wife... 113:8

Cheese After c. comes nothing 53:48

C. and money... 30:23

C. digests... 53:49

If you will have a good c.... 30:22

Cherry A c. year, a merry year... 30:44

Cheshire In C. there are Lees... 58:81

Chides He that sharply c.... 71:24

Child A c. may have too much... 49:16
A c.'s service is little... 19:7
Give a c. while he craves... 49:18
Give me a c. for the first seven years...
49:12
Let not a c. sleep... 19:39
Put another man's c. in your bosom...
128:24
The c. is father... 19:41
The c. says nothing... 19:22
When the c. is christened... 88:17

Children Better c. weep... 49:10
C. and chicken... 19:19
C. and fools cannot lie 19:21
C. and fools have merry lives 69:1
C. and fools must not play... 69:7
C. are certain cares... 19:15
C. are poor men's riches 19:4
C. are to be deceived... 19:16
C. learn to creep... 130:40
C. pick up words... 19:24
C. should be seen... 19:37
C. suck the mother... 19:9
C. when they are little... 19:13
He that has c.... 19:8
He that has no c. brings.... 3:61
He that has no c. knows.... 19:1
What c. hear at home... 19:23
When c. stand quiet... 19:38

China In C. are more tutors... 133:6
In C. we have only three religions...
133:5

Chinaman A C. is ill only once... 133:7

Choice A man has c. to begin love...
109:38
No c. amongst stinking fish 20:10
There's small c. in rotten apples 20:9

Choleric From a c. man withdraw a
little... 5:10

Choose C. a wife by your ear... 113:82
C. a wife on a Saturday... 113:83
C. neither women... 20:6
C. not a wife... 113:81
C. thy company... 23:4
C. your neighbour... 121:3

There is nothing to c. between bad
tongues... 79:39
Choosing In c. a wife... 113:63
Christian A complete C.... 144:50
Christmas C. comes but once a year
126:2
Church In c., in an inn... 60:8
The c. is an anvil... 144:60
What the c. takes not... 144:63
Churchyard A piece of c. fits everybody
39:72
Churl A c.'s feast... 80:13
Circumstances C. alter cases 100:16
Cities C. are taken by the ears 178:16
Citizens The c. of Cork... 133:79
City A great c.... 161:18
Civility C. costs nothing 15:6
Clartier The c. the cosier 21:4
Claw C. me... 88:26
Clean C. and whole... 21:3
Cleanliness C. is next to godliness 21:1
Clear A c. conscience fears not... 26:14
A c. conscience is like... 26:23
Preserve a c. conscience... 26:17
Clemency Sometimes c. is cruelty...
101:17
Clent The people of C.... 58:82
Clergymen C.'s sons... 144:74
Clerks The greatest c.... 102:25
Clever A c. man will build a city... 184:97
Client A c. twixt his attorney... 104:37
Climb He who would c. the ladder...
130:45
Climbed He that never c.... 151:7
Cloak Have not thy c. to make... 70:15
It is good to have a c. for the rain
147:39
Clock One cannot put back the c. 17:21
Clogs From c. to clogs... 136:84
Close A c. mouth... 156:5
Clothe C. thee in war... 132:8
C. thee warm... 53:53
Clothes C. do not make the man 50:10
C. make people... 50:1
Good c. open all doors 50:5
Cloud Every c. has a silver lining 127:20
Clouds All c. bring not rain 7:30
If the c. look as if scratched by a hen...
181:82
Cloudy C. mornings... 127:17
Clout Ne'er cast a c.... 117:55

Clown Give a c. your finger... 101:15
Coach A c. and four... 104:11
Coat He who has but one c.... 105:4
It is not the gay c.... 7:7
Cobble They that can c. and clout...
124:4
Cobbler Let the c. stick... 124:22
Cock Every c. will crow... 31:27
If the c. crows on going to bed... 181:1
If the c. moult before the hen... 181:2
There's many a good c.... 7:36
Who eats his c. alone... 153:23
Cockers He that c. his child... 49:17
Coin Much c.... 180:16
Where c. is not common... 136:41
Cold A c. April the barn will fill 181:90
A c. May and a windy... 181:91
C. hands, warm heart 167:20
C. pudding... 109:77
Feed a c.... 87:37
If c. wind reach you through a hole...
87:24
The c. is Russia's cholera 133:59
Coldest In the c. flint... 7:41
Comes Everything c. to him who waits
130:13
He that c. of a hen... 18:5
Coming C. events... 171:53
Command C. your man... 153:33
He is not fit to c. others... 9:19
The c. of custom... 104:59
Commands He c. enough... 183:24
Commits He that c. a fault... 26:12
Commodity Every c.... 98:2
Common C. fame is a liar 79:8
C. fame is seldom to blame 79:1
C. proverb... 140:7
Companion A merry c.... 23:7
There is no c. like the penny 180:7
Company A man is known by the c....
23:11
Good c. upon the road... 23:6
It is good to have c. in trouble 186:15
Keep c. with good men... 23:16
Keep good men c.... 23:3
Keep not ill men c.... 29:13
The c. makes the feast 23:5
Comparison It is c. that makes men...
84:4
Comparisons C. are odious 100:15

Complains He c. wrongfully on the sea... 62:30

Complies He that c. against his will... 182:20

Complimentary One c. letter... 68:11

Confess C. and be hanged 89:14

Confide C. in an aunt... 79:21

Congruity C. is the mother of love 109:68

Conquer Though the left hand c. the right... 178:25

Conquering There is no such c. weapon... 120:3

Conquers He c. who endures 56:1

Conscience A good c. is a continual feast 26:22

A good c. is a soft pillow 26:20

A good c. is the best divinity 26:21

A good c. makes an easy couch 26:19

C. does make cowards... 26:9

C. is a cut-throat 26:2

C. is a thousand witnesses 26:3

Some make a c.... 94:20

Whose c. is cumbered... 26:10

Consciences Men whose c. are clear... 26:15

Consolation Great c. may grow... 140:3

Constancy The c. of the benefit of the year... 77:33

Constant A c. guest... 92:11

C. dripping... 134:18

Consulting Too much c. confounds 3:29

Contempt C. is the sharpest reproof 27:7

C. pierces... 27:10

C. will sooner... 27:6

Contending It is ill c. with the master... 37:46

Content C. is all 28:1

C. is happiness 28:4

C. is more... 28:3

C. is the philosopher's stone... 28:5

C. lodges... 28:10

He who is c. in his poverty... 28:6

Let every man be c.... 28:45

No man is c.... 28:35

Contented A c. mind... 28:8

He may well be c.... 28:11

Who is c.... 28:9

Contention C.'s roots are three... 141:1

Convenience No c.... 98:1

Conversation C. makes one what he is 168:96

C. teaches more... 168:97

Converses He that c. not... 168:99

Cooks Too many c.... 88:9

Cool A c. mouth... 87:11

Cord The c. breaks at last... 56:22

Corn C. and horn go together 30:5

C. him well... 131:5

C. is cleansed with wind... 49:2

If you look at your c.... 117:56

When the c. is in the shock... 30:6

Cornish All C. gentlemen... 58:37

Cornwall C. will bear a shower... 58:39

Corporations C. have neither bodies... 147:23

Corrects He that c. not small faults... 49:3

Corruption C. of the best... 29:23

The c. of one thing... 29:22

Cost The more c.... 187:12

Costs It c. more to do ill... 78:50

Nothing c. so much... 75:39

What c. little... 187:11

Counsel Come not to c. uncalled 3:51

C. is irksome... 3:7

C. is no command 3:10

C. is to be given... 3:35

C. must be followed... 3:20

C. over cups... 3:43

C. will make a man... 3:14

Give neither c. nor salt... 3:50

Good c. has no price 3:1

Good c. never comes amiss 3:3

Good c. never comes too late 3:2

If the c. be good... 3:38

Ill c. mars all 3:15

Take c. only... 3:11

The c. thou wouldst have another keep... 3:55

We have better c. to give... 3:56

Counselled He that will not be c.... 3:19

Counsellor Like c.... 3:31

Counsellors Though thou hast never so many c.... 3:12

Counsels C. in wine... 3:42

Count C. not four... 6:10

Don't c. your chickens... 6:6

Countries All c. stand in need of Britain... 133:65

So many c., so many customs 104:65

Country In the c. of the blind... 81:15
Couple Every c. is not a pair 47:7
Courage A man of c.... 31:16
  C. and perseverance... 31:2
  C. and resolution... 31:1
Course The c. of true love... 109:50
Court At c., every one for himself 149:27
  Far from c., far from care 149:36
  He that lives in c.... 149:33
  Long in c.... 149:37
  Whoso will dwell in c.... 149:28
Courtesy C. is cumbersome... 15:22
  C. is the inseparable companion... 15:8
  Full of c.... 36:8
Courtiers C. are shod... 149:32
Covet All c., all lose 82:17
Covetous C. men live drudges... 115:15
  C. men's chests... 115:8
  Over c. was never good 82:14
  The c. man is good to none... 115:18
  The c. spends more than the liberal 82:24
Covetousness C. breaks the sack 82:13
  C. brings nothing home 82:19
  C. is always filling... 82:4
  C. is the father... 82:8
  C. is the root... 82:12
  C. often starves... 82:10
Cow Bring a c. to the hall... 18:36
  Look to the c.... 30:28
  Many a good c.... 18:16
  The c. knows not... 187:7
  The c. that's first up... 52:3
  Why buy a c.... 113:25
Coward It is better to be a c.... 32:12
  Put a c. to his mettle... 32:20
Cowardice C. is afraid... 32:8
Cowards C. are cruel 32:16
  C. die many times... 32:3
  C. die often 32:2
  C. run the greatest danger... 32:1
  Many would be c.... 32:18
  Of c. no history... 32:10
Cowl The c. does not make the monk 7:8
Crab You cannot make a c. walk straight 18:38
Cradle If you rock the c. empty... 167:27
Craft C. must have clothes... 176:19
  No man is his c.'s master... 130:38
Crafty A c. knave... 36:7
  To a c. man... 36:13

Cranes A thousand c. in the air... 135:3
Crave Nothing c.... 4:5
Cravers Sore c.... 131:28
Creaking A c. gate... 87:31
Credit C. lost... 64:22
  Give c.... 100:14
  He that has lost his c.... 64:21
Creditors C. have better memories... 14:19
Creep First c.... 130:41
Crime C. does not pay 33:20
  What greater c.... 171:31
Crimes C. are made secure... 33:12
Cripple He that dwells next door to a c.... 29:15
Croaking The c. raven... 167:17
Crook There is a c. in the lot... 2:22
Crooked A c. man should sow beans... 30:18
  C. logs... 7:37
Crooks Timely c. the tree... 19:45
Cross Don't c. the bridge... 186:17
  Each c. has its inscription 166:20
  No c., no crown 166:8
Crosses C. are ladders... 166:7
Crow How can a c. sleep soundly... 169:11
Crowd A c. is not company 161:19
Crown A c. is no cure... 149:13
Crowns C. have cares 149:8
Cruelty A man of c.... 35:1
  C. deserves no mercy 35:2
  C. is a tyrant... 35:12
  C. is more cruel... 43:11
  C. is the first attribute... 35:3
  C. is the strength... 35:4
Crust A c. is better than no bread 80:9
Crutch The c. of time... 171:11
Cry Don't c. before you are hurt 186:19
Crying It is no use c.... 142:5
Cuckold Who is a c. and conceals it... 155:12
Cuckoo The c. comes in April... 117:38
  The c. goes to Beaulieu Fair... 117:40
  When the c. comes, he eats... 152:6
  When the c. comes to the bare thorn... 30:35
Cunning C. surpasses strength 36:1
  Too much c. undoes 36:4
Cupar He that will to C.... 182:27
Cure A c. for all sorrows... 162:45

D. is the great leveller 39:71
D. is the only master... 39:65
D. is the poor man's... 39:40
D. keeps no calendar 39:21
D. makes us equal... 39:78
D. pays all debts 39:42
D. rather frees us... 39:41
D.'s day... 39:36
D. sends his challenge... 125:65
D. surprises us... 39:23
Look upon d.... 39:46
The d. of a young wolf... 39:51
The d. of the wolves... 39:52
When d. is on the tongue... 39:61
Debt A man in d.... 14:13
D. is an evil conscience 14:15
D. is the worst poverty 14:4
Out of d.... 14:35
Debtors D. are liars 14:23
Of ill d., men take oats 14:39
Deceive He that will d. the fox... 52:16
To d. a deceiver... 40:25
To d. oneself... 40:33
Who thinks to d. God... 40:32
Deceivers D. have full mouths... 40:39
Deceives He that d. me once... 62:31
He that once d.... 40:16
Deceiving D. those that trust us... 40:21
Deed A good d. is never lost 41:32
An evil d. remains... 41:42
An ill d. cannot bring honour 41:40
Every d. is to be judged... 41:28
One good d. atones... 41:31
The d. comes back... 44:10
To see a man do a good d.... 41:33
Deeds By his d.... 41:4
D. are fruits... 41:8
D. are males... 184:103
D. will show themselves... 41:11
Evil d. are like perfume... 41:47
Deeply They that too d. loved... 86:6
Defects Every man has the d. of his qualities 179:18
Deferred What is d.... 43:17
Delay After a d.... 43:16
D. is the antidote... 43:10
That d. is good... 43:6
Delays D. are dangerous 43:1
D. are not denials 8:18
Delight There is more d. in hope... 91:8
Deliver D. your words... 168:79

Demand Where the d. is a jest... 27:4
Demands He that d. misses not... 8:7
Denial A civil d.... 8:17
Depends He who d. on another... 153:36
Descent The d. to hell... 144:34
Desert D. and reward... 44:5
Deserves He d. not the sweet... 44:22
Desire D. has no rest 4:17
Desires D. are nourished... 43:7
He that d. but little... 28:20
Despair D. gives courage... 31:12
Desperate D. cuts... 145:12
Destiny A man's d.... 45:10
D. has four feet... 45:1
Destroy D. the nests... 145:14
Devil Away goes the d.... 169:15
Better keep the d. at the door... 169:14
Better the d. you know... 17:10
Give the d. his due 100:13
He that has shipped the d.... 147:14
He that takes the d. into his boat...
147:13
He that the d. drives... 46:8
If the d. find a man idle... 95:15
Said the d. when flying... 58:57
The d. always leaves... 46:5
The d. and the dean... 144:85
The d. can cite Scripture... 46:2
The d. dances... 136:62
The d. finds work... 95:14
The d. gets up to the belfry... 29:36
The d. goes shares in gaming 74:1
The d. is a busy bishop... 46:13
The d. is at home 46:14
The d. is busy... 181:23
The d. is God's ape 77:67
The d. is in the dice 74:9
The d. is not so black... 42:14
The d. is subtle... 46:1
The d. knows many things... 46:9
The d. looks after his own 111:43
The d. loves no holy water 46:16
The d. lurks... 46:15
The d. makes his Christmas-pies... 29:42
The d. never assails a man... 96:12
The d.'s children... 111:44
The d. sets his foot... 117:68
The d.'s meal... 33:23
The d.'s mouth... 115:21
The d. sometimes speaks... 46:4
The d. tempts all... 169:10

The d. was sick... 144:40
The d. will not come into Cornwall...
58:38
The d. will play... 46:12
The d. wipes his tail... 136:103
There is a d. in every berry... 51:26
There is no d. so bad... 184:4
What is got over the d.'s back... 112:23
When the d. prays... 46:3
Where the d. cannot come... 46:11
Dicing D., drabbing and drinking... 51:30
Die All men must d. 39:3
A man can d.... 39:43
Better d. with honour... 32:9
Better to d. a beggar... 170:34
He begins to d.... 4:11
Never say d. 134:21
They d. well... 39:86
Dies He d. like a beast... 39:88
Man d. and leave a name... 118:6
Difference The d. is wide... 141:36
There is a d. between 'Will you buy?'...
22:9
There is great d.... 41:19
There is no d. of bloods... 60:11
There's little d. between a feast and a
bellyful 76:19
Difficult All things are d.... 130:39
The d. is done at once... 108:17
Diligence D. is a great teacher 48:5
D. is the mother... 48:2
D. makes an expert workman 48:4
Without d.... 48:34
Diligent A d. scholar... 48:11
D. youth... 19:63
For the d. the week... 48:58
The d. spinner... 48:24
Dimple A d. in the chin, a devil within
167:23
A d. in the chin, your living comes in...
167:22
Ding You may d. the devil... 49:29
Dinner After d. sit awhile... 53:51
Better a d. of herbs... 86:9
If you want your d.... 53:77
Dirt He that deals in d.... 29:10
He that falls into the d.... 42:6
He that flings d. at another... 42:11
Throw d. enough... 42:1
Discontent A man's d.... 28:31
D. is the first step... 28:30

Discontented A d. man... 28:32
Discourse Sweet d.... 168:100
Discreet D. women... 168:91
While the d. advise... 3:16
Discretion D. is the better part of valour
31:32
Disease A d. known... 87:34
Whatsoever was the father of a d....
53:64
When a d. returns... 87:42
Diseases D. are the price... 87:21
Dish No d. pleases all palates alike 47:16
Dishes Many d.... 53:65
Disputants Of two d.... 141:32
Dispute In too much d.... 141:18
Disputing There is no d. a proverb...
140:9
Dissemble Who knows not how to d....
94:1
Distaff On St D.'s Day... 117:5
Distance D. lends enchantment... 7:26
Distrust Wise d.... 175:28
Divide D. and rule 141:24
Divine D. grace... 77:46
Divinity There's a d. that shapes our
ends... 45:9
Do D. as most men do... 25:12
D. not all you can... 116:19
D. right... 26:16
D. what you ought... 45:4
He that may not d. as he would... 28:49
If thou thyself canst d. it... 153:30
It is better to d. well... 41:13
Doctor If the d. cures... 87:50
One d. makes work... 87:51
The d. is often... 87:52
Doctors The best d.... 87:35
Dog A good d.... 44:1
Better to have a d. fawn on you... 27:17
D. does not eat dog 110:6
Every d. has his day 111:41
Every d. is a lion... 31:29
Every d. is allowed... 104:55
Every d. is valiant... 31:28
Give a d. a bad name... 42:7
He that keeps another man's d.... 80:32
If the d. is not at home... 1:13
If you would wish the d. to follow
you... 154:15
It is an ill d.... 44:8
It is a poor d.... 187:16

Never d. barked against the crucifix...
144:18
One d., one bull 100:20
Only a d. and a Frenchman... 133:31
The d. bites the stone... 147:34
The d. that fetches... 79:37
The d. that is idle... 95:13
Why keep a d.... 154:20
Dogged It's d. as does it 134:2
Dogs D. bark as they are bred 15:23
   D. that bark at a distance... 168:40
   D. wag their tails... 68:8
   D. will redd swine 141:37
   If you lie down with d.... 29:16
   Many d. may easily worry... 100:22
Doing D. is better than saying 41:12
   In d. we learn 62:15
Done Do as you would be d. by 61:10
   Whatever man has d.... 108:5
   What's d. cannot be undone @sub-
     line:When a thing is d.... 3:8
Donkey Send a d. to Paris... 172:11
Donkeys Scabby d.... 157:11
Door A d. must either be shut or open
  20:4
   Every d. may be shut... 39:9
   When one d. shuts... 127:2
Double D. charge... 56:13
   He gets a d. victory... 49:34
Doubt D. is the key... 13:21
   When in d.... 146:10
Down He that is d.... 2:15
Dowry A great d.... 113:53
Draught Back to the d.... 87:25
Draw Never d. your dirk... 116:21
Drawn D. wells... 177:5
Dream A d. grants... 159:28
   After a d. of a wedding... 159:21
   D. of a funeral... 159:20
Dreams D. are lies 159:25
   D. go by contraries 159:24
   In d. and in love... 159:29
Dress D. up a stick... 50:7
Dressing Fine d.... 50:8
Dries Nothing d. sooner than tears
  162:26
Drink A good d.... 51:20
   Do not d. between meals 51:63
   D. as much after an egg... 51:64
   D. less... 51:57
   D. only with the duck 51:55

   D. wine, and have the gout... 51:70
   If you d. in your pottage... 51:69
   Those who d. but water... 51:54
   When you d. from the stream... 80:4
Drinking D. water... 51:53
Drinks He that d. not wine... 51:71
   He who d. a little too much... 51:68
Dripping A d. June... 181:56
Drive D. your business... 22:22
Drops Many d.... 160:13
Drought D. never bred dearth... 181:123
Drowning A d. man... 91:14
Drums Where d. beat... 104:13
Drunk Ever d.... 51:77
Drunkard A d.'s purse... 51:13
   Let but the d. alone... 51:12
Drunkards D. and fools... 51:3
   There are more old d.... 51:17
Drunken A d. man is always dry 51:76
   D. days... 51:11
   D. folks seldom take harm 51:16
Drunkenness D. does not produce
  faults... 51:6
   The best cure for d.... 51:15
Dry A d. cough... 87:32
   D. August... 181:122
   D. bread at home... 172:26
   D. feet... 87:12
Dumb D. dogs... 156:35
   D. men get no lands 168:21
Dunder D. do gally the beans 181:73
Dust While the d. is on your feet... 22:17
Dwarf A d. on a giant's shoulders...
  102:19
Dwell Wherever a man d.... 97:35
Dying D. is as natural as living 39:11
   D. men speak true 39:60

E

Eagles E. do not breed doves 18:3
   E. don't catch flies 81:31
Ear What is told in the e. of a man...
  79:18
Early E. master... 163:12
   E. rain and a woman's tears... 184:34
   E. sow... 52:14
   E. to bed... 52:7
   E. wed... 113:90
   The e. bird... 52:1
   The e. man never borrows... 52:13

A right E.... 58:17
It is an E.'s privilege... 58:19
One E. can beat... 58:15
The E. Italianate... 133:34
The E. weeps... 133:67
What an E. cares to invent... 133:54
Enough E. is as good... 28:14
He has e. who is contented... 28:21
More than e.... 28:15
Of e., men leave 28:16
There was never e.... 28:17
Enquire E. not what boils... 99:14
Enter He that will e. into Paradise...
144:27
When you e. into a house... 5:30
Enters Nothing e. into a close hand 115:7
Envied Better be e.... 136:89
Envies He who e. admits his inferiority
59:10
Envious An e. man waxes lean... 59:6
The e. man shall never want woe 59:5
Envy E. and covetousness... 59:4
E. and idleness... 59:7
E. eats nothing... 59:1
E. envies itself 59:9
E. never dies 59:3
E. never enriched any man 59:11
E. shoots at others... 59:2
If e. were a fever... 59:12
Equal If all were e.... 60:3
Ermine In an e. spots are soon discovered
11:45
Err To e. is human 97:4
To e. is human; to forgive, divine 71:7
Errs Who e. and mends... 142:38
Escaped The e. mouse... 62:29
Essex E. stiles... 58:32
Ethiopian When the E. is white... 133:29
Evening E. red and morning grey...
181:21
The e. crowns the day 39:32
Every E. day braw... 50:16
Evil Bear with e.... 91:27
E. communications... 29:1
E. doers are evil dreaders 10:44
For every e. under the sun... 145:5
He that does e.... 10:20
Never do e.... 10:50
Of an e. crow... 18:4
Of e. grain... 18:12
Put off the e. hour... 43:9

The e. that men do lives after them...
41:53
Whoso will no e. do... 41:46
Evils Of two e.... 20:7
Some e. are cured... 27:8
The e. we bring on ourselves... 147:9
Example A good e.... 61:5
E. is better than precept 61:2
Exception The e. proves the rule 173:12
Excess If in e.... 116:29
Exchange Fair e. is no robbery 100:18
Excuse A bad e.... 147:38
Excuses Bad e.... 147:37
He who e. himself... 147:36
Expect We may not e. a good whelp...
18:1
What can you e. from a pig... 18:39
Expectation E. is better than realization
6:1
Expects Blessed is he who e. nothing...
6:26
Experience E. is a precious gift... 62:6
E. is good... 62:3
E. is the best teacher 62:13
E. is the mistress... 62:19
E. is the mother... 62:1
E. keeps a dear school... 62:20
E. must be bought 62:18
E. without learning... 62:4
Experiment Make your e.... 173:9
Extreme E. justice... 100:6
E. law... 116:35
No e. will hold long 116:36
Extremes E. are dangerous 116:40
E. meet 116:37
Extremity Every e.... 116:34
Man's e.... 77:43
Eye An e. for an eye... 148:16
Better e. out... 150:10
Better e. sore... 80:22
Better to have one e.... 80:23
Far from e.... 1:5
If thine e. offend thee... 150:9
One e. of the master... 49:36
The e. is bigger... 53:19
The e. of the master... 49:35
The e. that sees all things... 34:15
What the e. doesn't see... 96:6
Eyes Four e. see more than two 88:7
In the e. of the lover... 109:4
Keep your e. open... 22:11

F. are thick... 109:16
Faulty The f. stands on his guard 26:5
Favour F. will as surely perish... 149:31
Fazarts To f.... 32:4
Fear All f. is bondage 66:10
  F. can keep a man out of danger... 31:4
  F. gives wings 66:4
  F. has a quick ear 66:5
  F. has magnifying eyes 66:6
  F. is a great inventor 66:7
  F. is one part... 66:14
  F. is stronger... 66:16
  F. is the prison... 66:11
  F. nothing but sin 10:31
  F. of death... 39:81
  F. the Greeks... 75:42
  Men f. death... 39:83
  'Twas f. that first... 66:8
  Wise f. begets care 66:15
Fearful Better a f. end... 66:13
Fears He that f. death... 39:82
  He that f. every bush... 66:22
  He that f. every grass... 66:23
  He that f. leaves... 66:24
  He that f. you present... 1:14
  No man f. what he has seen grow 65:8
  Who f. to suffer... 66:9
Feather A f. in hand... 135:6
  F. by feather... 134:13
Feathers Fine f.... 50:6
February If in F. there be no rain... 181:121
Februeer F. doth cut and shear 117:7
Feed F. by measure... 53:54
Feet All f. tread not... 47:3
  The f. of the avenging deities... 77:63
Fellow-ruler He that has a f.... 9:29
Female The f. of the species... 184:102
Fence There's no f. against ill fortune 111:24
Fences Good f.... 121:17
Fern When f. grows red... 152:11
  When the f. is as high as a spoon... 30:53
Fetters No man loves his f.... 154:35
Fewer The f. the words... 144:92
Field A f. requires three things... 30:1
Fields F. have eyes... 79:23
Fight F. fire... 178:19
Fights He that f. and runs away... 32:15
Fill Better f. a man's belly... 53:20

Filth The f. under the white snow... 7:44
Finders F. keepers... 135:17
Finding F.'s keeping 135:18
Fine F. words dress ill deeds 94:10
Fingers F. were made before forks... 53:68
Finland F. is the devil's country 133:20
Fire As f. is kindled by bellows... 5:16
  F. cannot be hidden... 18:42
  F. that's closest kept... 129:15
  Give me f.... 88:27
  He that can make a f. well... 141:38
  One's own f. is pleasant 172:25
  Put not f. to flax 174:12
First F. come... 52:5
  F. impressions... 12:5
  F. things first 130:44
  He that comes f. to the hill... 52:4
  The f. and last frosts... 181:101
  The f. blow... 12:6
  The f. day a guest... 92:14
  The f. degree of folly... 69:48
  The f. dish is aye best eaten 53:23
  The f. dish pleases all 53:24
  The f. faults... 71:26
  What we f. learn... 54:15
Fish All's f. that comes to the net 177:8
  Big f.... 81:43
  F. and guests... 92:13
  F. begins to stink... 29:20
  F. must swim thrice 51:47
  'Had I f.'... 182:38
  That f. will soon be caught... 99:7
  The best f.... 134:12
  There are as good f.... 127:3
Fish-guts Keep your ain f.... 143:21
Fishing It is good f.... 141:23
  It is ill f. before the net 6:12
Fit All things f. not... 47:5
Five F. hours sleeps a traveller... 159:11
Flatterer A f.'s throat... 68:19
  There is no such f.... 24:5
  When the f. pipes... 68:20
Flatters Beware of one who f. unduly... 68:16
Flattery F. sits in the parlour... 68:1
Flax Keep f. from fire... 74:2
Flay No man can f. a stone 108:22
Flea If you kill one f. in March... 117:24
Flee F. never so fast... 45:3
Fleech Better f. the devil... 68:2
Flesh F. is frail 179:16

He that f. all perils, will win no worship 32:11

Forehead In the f. and the eye... 63:2

Foreheets That which one most f.... 123:13

Forenoons You cannot have two f.... 125:58

Forethought F. is easy... 70:11

Foretold Long f., long last... 181:20

Forewarned F. is forearmed 70:8

Forewit One good f.... 70:1

Forget Do not f. little kindnesses... 80:3

Forgive F. all but thyself 71:20
    F. and forget 71:18
    If we are bound to f. an enemy... 175:23

Forgiveness F. from the heart... 71:9
    F. is perfect... 71:19

Forgives He that f. gains the victory 71:4
    He who f. others... 71:8

Forgiving F. the unrepentant... 71:15

Forgotten Seldom seen, soon f. 1:26

Forth F. bridles... 133:73

Fortune F. can take from us... 111:30
    F. favours fools 111:35
    F. favours the bold 31:6
    F. favours those... 111:34
    F. is blind 111:4
    F. is fickle 111:5
    F. is made of glass 111:11
    F. is the mistress... 111:27
    F. is weary... 111:10
    F. knocks once... 111:40
    F., not prudence... 111:28
    F. to one is mother... 111:6
    Great f. brings with it... 111:19
    He that has no ill f.... 186:5
    If f. torments me... 91:10
    When f. smiles... 126:20

Foul A f. morning... 127:16
    He that has to do with what is f.... 29:12

Fouls No man f. his hands... 153:17

Four He that has but f.... 163:34

Fowler The f.'s pipe... 7:25

Fox A f. should not be of the jury... 153:44
    At length the f.... 36:5
    The f. fares best... 42:10
    The f. knows much... 36:12
    The f. may grow grey... 18:29
    The f. preys farthest... 36:11

Though the f. run... 36:6
    When the f. preaches... 36:9

France F. is a meadow... 133:21
    He that will F. win... 133:22
    The day of F.'s ruin... 133:23

Free He is f. of fruit... 75:28
    He is f. of horse... 75:29

Freedom F. is a fair thing 106:3

Freer Nothing f. than a gift 75:40

Freezes He f. who does not burn 129:16

French Every F. soldier... 133:24
    The F. would be the best cooks... 133:25

Frenchman Have the F. for thy friend... 133:26
    The F. is a scoundrel 133:27

Fresh F. fish... 72:25

Friar Do as the f. says... 61:8
    The f. preached against stealing... 94:19

Friday F. and the week... 38:5
    F. night's dream... 38:6
    F.'s hair... 38:7
    F.'s moon... 38:8

Friend A f. in court... 72:2
    A f. in need... 72:39
    A f. in the market... 72:3
    A f. is another self 72:45
    A f. is never known... 72:40
    A f. is not so soon gotten... 72:86
    A f. to everybody... 72:56
    A good f. is my nearest relation 72:46
    A good f. never offends 72:49
    A reconciled f.... 72:18
    Before you make a f.... 72:66
    He is a good f. that speaks well... 72:53
    Make not thy f. thy foe 72:72
    No f. to a bosom friend... 57:7
    No man has a worse f.... 153:38
    Select your f.... 72:65
    When a f. asks... 72:79
    Whensoever you see your f.... 72:31

Friends All are not f.... 72:34
    A man is known by his f. 23:12
    Among f. all things are common 72:47
    F. agree best... 1:7
    F. are made in wine... 72:42
    F. are thieves of time 72:17
    F. tie their purse... 72:11
    Have but few f.... 72:63
    If f. have faith... 72:12
    It is good to have some f.... 72:4
    When f. meet... 72:8

When two f. have a common purse...
72:38

Friendship F. cannot stand always...
72:75

F. increases... 72:76

F. is a plant... 72:82

F., the older it grows... 72:59

Real f.... 72:44

The f. of the French... 133:30

Fright To f. a bird... 101:9

Fristed The thing that's f.... 43:18

Frog The f. cannot out of her bog 18:37

Frost A white f. never lasts... 181:99

F. and fraud... 33:15

Frosts Many f. and many thowes...
181:100

Frugality F. is the mother of virtue 170:11

Fruit He that would have the f.... 48:38

If you would f. have... 30:47

Frying-pan He who has the f.... 9:3

The f. said to the kettle... 34:10

Fuel Take away f.... 174:3

Full A f. belly... 76:4

He that has a f. purse... 180:92

Funeral One f. makes many 39:54

G

Gain G. savours sweetly... 73:9

G. time... 171:10

Great g. makes work easy
Sometimes the best g.... 73:16

Gaining No g.... 73:3

Gains He g. enough... 2:19

The g. will quit the pains 73:4

Gambler If the g. can change... 74:17

Game At the g.'s end... 55:4

Games In all g.... 165:3

Gamester The better g.... 74:15

Gamesters G. and race-horses... 74:16

Gaming G., women, and wine... 51:31

Gangs When it g. up i' sops... 181:85

Gapes He that g. until he be fed... 95:35

Garbage G. in... 55:9

Garden It is in the g. of patience...
130:23

No g. without its weeds 97:25

Garlic G. makes a man wink... 53:40

Garner None says his g. is full 28:36

Gather G. ye rosebuds... 126:6

Gathering Little good comes of g. 115:2

Gaudy A g. morning... 181:106

Gazes He that g. upon the sun... 99:5

Gear G. is easier gained... 180:123

General He is the best g.... 178:15

One bad g.... 141:27

Generation A man lives a g.... 118:1

Generations It takes three g.... 15:44

Genius G. is an infinite capacity...
48:33

The g., wit, and spirit... 140:2

Genoa G. has mountains without
wood... 133:36

Gentility G. is but ancient riches 15:26

G. without ability... 15:27

Gentle He is a g. horse... 97:40

Gentleman A g. ought to travel... 172:33

A g. will do... 15:38

A g. without an estate... 15:39

He is a g.... 15:37

Gentry G. sent to market... 15:28

German The G.'s wit... 133:47

Gets He who g. does much... 135:14

Gift A g. much expected... 75:22

Never look a g. horse... 80:5

Throw no g. again... 80:6

Gifted The gear that is g.... 48:14

Gifts G. blind the eyes 29:34

G. enter everywhere... 29:28

She that takes g.... 75:41

Gimmingham G., Trimmingham... 58:72

Gist The g. of a lady's letter...184:63

Give Better g. a shilling... 75:4

G. and spend... 75:6

G. a thing and take a thing... 75:31

It is more blessed to g.... 75:3

Given Nothing is g. so freely... 3:57

Gives He g. twice... 75:19

He that g. his goods... 75:17

He that g. thee a bone... 75:34

He that g. to be seen... 94:7

He who g. discreetly... 75:8

He who g. to the unworthy... 75:14

Who g. to all... 139:18

Giving G. much to the poor... 75:10

Gladness A man of g.... 84:24

Glass The first g. for thirst... 51:29

Those who live in g. houses... 34:5

Glitters All that g. is not gold 7:3

Glowing G. coals... 129:3

Glow-worm When the g. lights her
lamp... 181:5

Glutton A g. is never generous 76:15

Gluttony G. is the sin of England 76:14
　G. kills more... 76:12
Gnaw G. the bone... 28:46
Goat The g. must browse... 28:50
God All must be as G. will 77:2
　Before G. and the bus-conductor... 60:7
　G., and parents... 77:19
　G. comes at last... 77:29
　G. comes with leaden feet... 77:62
　G. complains not... 77:12
　G. creates dreams 159:30
　G. defend me from my friends... 72:16
　G. forgives sins... 77:59
　G. gives, but he does not lock... 77:40
　G. gives his wrath... 77:57
　G. gives the grain... 77:38
　G. gives the milk... 48:29
　G. heals... 77:56
　G. helps them... 77:34
　G. help the rich... 136:104
　G. himself is the help of the helpless
　　77:42
　G. is above all 77:1
　G. is a good man 77:20
　G. is a good worker... 77:37
　G. is always on the side... 164:9
　G. is a sure paymaster 77:66
　G. is no botcher 77:13
　G. keep me from four houses... 105:22
　G. knows well... 77:14
　G. made the country... 77:73
　G. made the earth... 133:49
　G. makes and apparel shapes 50:2
　G. makes and man shapes 77:72
　G. makes the back... 77:23
　G. moves in a mysterious way 77:54
　G. never sends mouth... 77:32
　G. oft has a great share... 160:32
　G. provides for him that trusts 77:30
　G. reaches us good things... 77:35
　G. save us from a Polish bridge... 133:56
　G. sends cold... 77:24
　G. sends corn... 77:70
　G. sends fortune... 69:4
　G. sends good luck... 111:1
　G. sends meat... 53:78
　G. send you joy... 84:57
　G.'s grace and Pilling Moss... 77:47
　G.'s help is better... 77:44
　G.'s help is nearer... 77:45
　G.'s in his heaven... 127:8

　G.'s lambs will play 19:33
　G. stays long... 77:64
　G. strikes not with both hands... 77:26
　G. strikes with his finger... 77:28
　G. tempers the wind... 77:22
　Have G. and have all 144:5
　If G. does not give us... 77:17
　Not G. above gets all men's love 47:25
　One G., no more... 72:10
　Since G. has not bent... 77:25
　That G. will have see... 77:3
　That which G. will give... 77:71
　The man of G. is better... 144:12
　The most high G., sees... 77:58
　There are G.'s poor... 136:2
　Though G. take the sun out of heaven...
　　130:8
　To whom G. gives the task... 77:16
　What G. will... 77:5
　When G. is made the master... 144:9
　When G. loathes aught... 77:51
　When G. made the world... 133:55
　When G. will... 77:6
　Where G. dwells... 77:69
　Where G. has his church... 77:68
　Where G. will help... 77:4
　Who has G. for his friend... 77:49
　Whom G. loves... 77:50
Gods The g. send nuts... 103:7
　Whom the g. love... 39:63
Goes He g. not out of his way... 51:39
Going A g. foot... 48:20
Gold G. does not belong to the miser...
　115:9
　G. dust blinds all eyes 180:87
　G. goes in at any gate... 180:105
　G. is an orator 180:119
　G. is but muck 180:63
　G. is tried... 173:6
　He that has g.... 180:104
　He who flings g. away... 163:8
　What cannot g. do 180:98
　When we have g.... 180:35
Golden A g. handshake... 29:41
　A g. key... 180:107
　G. dreams... 159:27
　The g. age... 171:46
　We must not look for a g. life... 28:51
Golgotha In G. are skulls... 39:66
Gone When all is g.... 178:26
Good A g. heart cannot lie 78:37

A g. heart conquers ill fortune 78:9
A g. life makes a good death 78:10
A g. man can no more harm... 78:38
All things are g.... 173:4
As g. horses draw in carts... 60:16
Better a g. cow... 15:34
Better g. afar off... 78:49
Bode g., and get it 127:5
Do g.: thou doest it for thyself 41:34
G. and evil... 78:45
G. folks are scarce 78:34
G. for the liver... 78:30
G. is good... 78:33
G. is to be sought out... 78:48
G. men must die... 78:40
G. men suffer much 78:42
G. people walk on... 78:43
G. things are hard 78:31
He is a silly man that can neither do g.
    nor ill 27:16
He who does no g.... 10:5
If one knew how g. it were... 117:3
If you can't be g.... 169:18
It is a g. goose... 75:25
It is a g. horse... 113:117
It is g. to be good in your time... 78:24
No man so g.... 138:26
None so g.... 78:27
Nothing but is g. for something 127:30
Nothing so g.... 97:20
Ten g. turns lie dead... 41:49
That which is g. for the back... 78:28
That which is g. for the head... 78:29
The g. die young 39:64
The g. is the enemy... 78:32
The g. or ill hap... 113:62
The only g. Indian... 57:20
There are two g. men... 78:35
There is a g. time coming 127:13
There is no such thing as g. small beer...
    53:41
There is nothing either g. or bad...
    114:4
They are aye g. that are away 1:31
Goodman As the g. says... 113:110
    When the g. is from home... 113:97
Goodness G. is better than beauty 78:6
    G. is not tied to greatness... 81:13
Goods A man has no more g.... 135:24
    G. are theirs... 135:23
    G. that are much on show... 65:10

Goose He that has a g.... 180:70
Gorse When the g. is out of bloom...
    30:52
Gospel With the g.... 144:48
Gossip A g. speaks ill of all... 79:26
    The g. of two women... 79:12
Gossiping G. and lying... 79:6
Gossips G. are frogs... 79:27
Got So g., so gone 163:11
Gout To the g.... 87:47
Gown Look to a g. of gold... 4:9
    The g. is his that wears it... 135:22
Grace G. will last... 11:33
    The g. of God is enough 77:52
    The g. of God is worth a fair 77:53
Grafting It is good g. on a good stock
    113:68
Grain G. by grain... 134:14
    One g. fills not a sack... 160:9
Grapes One cannot gather g. of thorns...
    18:10
Grasp G. all, lose all 82:16
Grass G. and hay... 39:2
    G. grows not... 112:10
    If g. look green... 117:2
    The g. is always greener... 28:40
    While the g. grows... 43:2
Grateful To a g. man... 80:2
Gratitude G. is the least of virtues...
    80:27
    G. preserves old friendships... 80:1
Graves G. are of all sizes 39:67
Greases Who g. his way... 29:35
Great A g. man and a great river... 81:26
    A g. tree... 81:1
    All things that g. men do... 81:21
    G. businesses... 81:40
    G. engines... 81:41
    G. men have great faults 81:23
    G. men's favours... 81:27
    G. men's sons... 81:25
    G. oaks... 81:35
    G. persons seldom see... 81:22
    G. things are done... 31:5
    G. trees are good... 81:16
    G. trees keep down... 81:45
    G. weights... 81:42
    G. winds... 81:2
    G. wits have short memories 183:73
    If g. men would have care... 81:33
    Some are born g.... 81:14

Great h., great danger 84:49
H. is not a horse... 84:62
With h. comes intelligence... 84:28
Happy Better be h. than wise 84:32
    Call no man h.... 39:35
    H. is he that chastens himself 84:6
    H. is he that is happy... 84:7
    H. is he whose friends... 84:8
    H. is she who marries... 84:10
    H. is that child... 84:9
    H. is the country... 84:11
    H. is the wooing... 109:93
    He is h., that knoweth not... 84:17
    Let him that would be h. for a day...
        84:5
    When a man is h.... 84:29
Hard It is h. to break a hog... 83:4
    It is h. to make an old mare... 83:5
    Things that are h. to come by... 134:10
Hard-fought It's a h. field... 127:22
Hare H. is melancholy meat 53:42
    The h. always returns... 172:23
Hares H. may pull dead lions... 31:25
    If you run after two h.... 48:55
Harry King H. robbed the church...
    144:17
Harvest He that has a good h.... 180:11
Haste H. and wisdom... 69:67
    H. comes not alone 85:15
    H. is from the devil 85:1
    H. is the mother... 85:21
    H. is the sister... 85:4
    H. makes waste 85:16
    H. makes waste, and waste makes
        want... 113:51
    H. trips up... 85:18
    In h. is error 85:20
    Make h. slowly 85:24
    More h., less speed 85:42
    Nothing should be done in h.... 85:26
    Who has no h. in his business... 130:19
Hasty A h. man drinks his tea... 85:44
    A h. man never wants woe 85:9
    Be not too h.... 85:28
    H. climbers... 4:20
    H. work... 85:22
    The h. bitch... 85:14
    The h. leaps over... 85:17
Hatch It is good to have a h. before the
    door 156:6
Hate H. not at the first harm 85:29

He that cannot h.... 86:5
The greatest h.... 86:7
Hated He that is h. of his subjects...
    149:20
Hates One h. not the person... 10:47
Hatred H. blasts the crop... 86:2
    H. is blind... 86:8
    H. is worse than murder 86:1
    H. with friends... 86:3
Have Better to h. than wish 135:8
    H. at it... 134:3
    H. is have 135:10
    What you h., hold 135:15
Hawks H. will not pick out... 110:7
Haws Many h.... 181:16
Hay It is time to cock your h.... 30:4
    Make h. while the sun shines 126:3
Head Better be the h.... 4:27
    The h. and feet keep warm... 87:13
    When the h. aches... 149:24
Heads Two h. are better than one 88:6
Healing It is ill h. of an old sore 52:20
Health H. and gaiety... 87:1
    H. and money... 87:3
    H. and wealth... 87:2
    H. is better than wealth 87:5
    H. is great riches 87:4
    H. is not valued... 87:9
    H. without money... 136:48
    He that wants h.... 87:8
    He who has good h.... 87:7
    The beginning of h.... 159:2
Healthful No man was ever made more
    h.... 172:14
    The h. man... 3:36
Hear H. all parties 100:10
    H. and see... 168:71
    H. much, speak little 168:70
    H. twice... 168:76
Hearers Were there no h.... 79:38
Hearing From h., comes wisdom...
    168:69
    Ill h.... 114:17
Hears He that h. much... 168:72
    Who wrong h.... 114:16
Heart If your h. is in your prayer...
    144:93
    Man's h. is never satisfied... 28:39
    Many a h. is caught... 109:108
    The h.'s letter... 63:3
    Tine h.... 91:9

What the h. thinks... 168:65
When the h. is a fire... 129:4
When the h. is full of lust... 112:7
Who has not a h.... 32:24
Heat If you don't like the h.... 145:15
There is no h. of affection... 129:1
Heaven All of h. and hell... 144:22
Better go to h. in rags... 144:19
H. and hell are within... 144:21
H. takes care of children... 77:27
If h. drops a date... 126:8
No coming to h.... 144:24
There is no going to h.... 144:29
The way to h. is alike... 144:32
The way to h. is as ready... 144:33
Whom H. at his birth... 69:19
Heaviest The h. baggage... 172:36
Heavy A h. purse... 180:3
Hedge A h. between... 121:16
Where the h. is lowest... 179:13
Hedgehogs H. lodge among thorns...
157:12
Heed Good take h. does surely speed 3:4
Take h. is a fair thing 3:5
Take h. of an ox before... 144:84
Take h. of a person marked... 113:156
Take h. of a young wench... 184:10
Take h. of mad fools... 69:9
Take h. of reconciled enemies 57:21
Height It is h. makes Grantham steeple...
81:12
Hell From h., Hull, and Halifax... 58:56
H. hath no fury... 184:13
H. is always open 144:37
H. is wherever... 144:20
The road to h. is paved... 144:35
Help A little h.... 41:14
H., for help in harvest 88:28
One can't h. many... 88:1
Helping Three h. one another... 88:5
Helps Everything h., quoth the wren...
160:8
He h. little... 153:8
He that h. the evil... 88:11
Hen If a h. does not prate... 113:113
Hengsten H. Down... 58:46
Henry H. the Eighth pulled down monks
and their cells... 144:52
Hens H. are free... 75:30
Herb No h. will cure love 109:80
Hercules Not even H.... 164:10

Heresy H. is the school of pride 144:44
H. may be easier kept out... 144:45
Heretic For the same man to be a h....
144:47
Hero No man is a h.... 65:5
To the real h.... 31:21
Herring Every h. must hang... 147:4
Hesitates He who h. is lost 146:6
Hide Don't h. your light... 24:19
H. nothing from thy minister... 176:62
High He who stands h.... 81:11
Hew not too h.... 4:23
H. cedars fall... 81:8
H. places have their precipices 4:21
It is good to be neither too h.... 116:9
Higher The h. the ape goes... 15:21
The h. the hill... 75:26
The h. the mountain... 4:22
Highest The h. branch... 81:4
The h. tree... 81:5
Hill Do on the h.... 15:19
Himself Every man for h., and God...
153:6
Every man for h., and the devil... 153:5
Every man is nearest h. 153:25
He that is ill to h.... 153:7
Hindmost The h. dog... 130:20
History H. repeats itself 171:51
Hitch H. your wagon... 4:12
Hoards He that h. up money... 115:16
Hog A h. that's bemired... 29:9
Better my h. dirty home... 80:25
The h. never looks up... 80:30
Hogs He who does not kill h.... 150:3
Hoist H. your sail... 126:5
Hold H. fast to the words of your ances-
tors 140:6
They that h. the greatest farms...
180:126
Hole A h. in the ice... 151:8
The h. calls the thief 169:5
Holiday Every day is h.... 95:41
Holy A h. habit... 7:47
Holyrood On H. Day... 117:63
Home Better at h.... 172:30
Far from h.... 172:31
H. is home, as the devil said... 29:43
H. is home, though it be... 172:22
H. is where... 172:28
Homer H. sometimes nods 97:16
Homo H. is a common name... 60:6

H. is sharper... 93:17
H. is stronger... 93:18
H. is the best sauce 93:10
H. makes dinners... 76:20
H. makes hard beans sweet 93:11
They must h. in frost... 93:3
Hungry A h. horse... 93:12
  A h. man is an angry man 93:16
  A h. man is glad... 93:23
  A h. man smells meat... 93:19
  H. dogs... 93:22
  Two h. meals... 93:27
Hunting H., hawking, and paramours...
  112:13
Hurry H. bequeaths disappointment
  85:10
Hurts He that h. another... 35:8
Husband A good h. makes a good wife
  113:96
  He is an ill h.... 113:98
  If the h. be not at home... 113:99
Husbands H. are in heaven... 113:115

I

Idle An i. brain... 95:16
  An i. person... 95:17
  An i. youth... 95:27
  I. folks have the least leisure 95:10
  I. folks lack no excuses 95:44
Idleness I. is the key... 95:28
  I. is the root... 95:22
  I. is the shipwreck... 95:4
  I. must thank itself... 95:30
  I. turns the edge... 95:23
  Of i. comes no goodness 95:21
If 'I.' and 'An'... 108:9
Ifs If i. and ans... 108:8
Ignorance I. and incuriosity... 96:2
  I. is the mother of devotion 96:17
  I. is the mother of impudence 96:16
  I. is the night... 96:10
  I. is the peace... 96:1
  I. of the law... 104:50
  Where i. is bliss... 96:5
Ill An i. turn is soon done 41:43
  He that does i.... 10:7
  He that does you an i. turn... 71:22
  He that has done i. once... 10:12
  If you do no i.... 41:45
  If you have done no i. the six days...
    144:70

I. air slays sooner... 87:22
I. comes in by ells... 2:26
I. comes often... 2:30
I. gotten, ill spent 33:24
I. weeds grow apace 10:42
I. will never said well 168:62
Of one i. come many 2:29
Who would do i.... 41:44
Ill-bred It is an i. dog... 15:20
Ill-gotten I. goods... 33:21
Ill-served Who wishes to be i.... 154:5
Imitation I. is the sincerest form of flat-
  tery 68:4
Impatience A little i.... 130:33
Impossibilities No one is bound to do i.
  108:18
Impossible Nothing is i. to a willing heart
  108:15
  Nought's i., as t'auld woman said...
    108:16
Imps No marvel if the i. follow... 61:16
Inch An i. is as good as an ell 160:36
  An i. of gold... 171:8
  Give him an i.... 101:16
Indispensable No man is i. 138:27
Industry I. is fortune's right hand... 48:22
Infallible No man is i. 97:3
Ingenious He was an i. man... 53:14
Ingleborough I., Pendle, and
  Penyghent... 58:47
Injuries I. are written... 41:51
  I. don't use to be written... 41:52
Innocence I. is no protection 26:27
Innocent Every one is held to be i....
  104:52
  I. actions... 26:25
Insatiable Three things are i.... 82:27
Inside There's nothing so good for the i.
  of a man... 87:10
Inspiration Ninety per cent of i.... 48:32
Intention The good i.... 41:27
Intermeddling Little i.... 99:16
Intimacy I. lessens fame 65:4
Irishman An I. before answering... 133:76
  Put an I. on the spit... 133:77
  The I. for a hand... 133:68
  Will any, but an I.... 133:78
Iron An i. anvil... 101:7
  I. not used... 177:3
  I. with use... 177:2
Irons Many i. in the fire... 48:53

Island In settling an i.... 133:15
Isle The I. of Wight... 58:36
Italians The I. are wise... 133:14
Italy A man would live in I.... 133:39

J

Jack If J.'s in love... 109:2
  J. is as good... 60:22
  J. of all trades... 124:15
  J. would be a gentleman if he could
  speak French 15:42
  J. would be a gentleman if he had
  money 15:41
Jackdaw J. always perches... 157:10
James Till St J.'s Day be come and gone...
117:59
Janiveer If J.'s calends... 181:120
  Who in J. sows oats... 117:1
Jest If you give a j.... 44:20
  J. not with the eye... 144:16
Jesting It is ill j. with edged tools 37:45
Jewel None can guess the j.... 7:31
Jews The J. spend at Easter... 144:51
Joan J. is as good... 60:25
Jollity There is no j.... 84:70
Jolly Over j. dow not 84:55
Jove J. laughs... 109:98
Joy J. and sorrow... 84:56
  No j. emanates... 161:12
  No j. without annoy 84:44
  One j. scatters a hundred griefs 84:34
  The j. of the heart... 84:23
Judas Had J. betrayed Christ in Scot-
land... 133:75
Judge A good j. conceives quickly...
104:45
  A j. knows nothing... 104:47
  J. not... 34:3
  Never j. from appearances 7:29
  No one ought to be j.... 153:43
Judgment He has a good j.... 183:41
  He that passes j. as he runs... 85:7
July If the first of J.... 181:60
June If on the eighth of J. it rain...
181:59
Jupiter Far from J.... 149:35
Just A j. war... 100:5
  Be j. before you are generous 75:15
Justice In j. is all virtue... 100:1
  J. will not condemn... 100:2

K

Kail Good k.... 53:29
  K. spares bread 53:30
Keep Better k. now... 135:12
  He that has it and will not k. it... 136:4
  K. something for the sore foot 170:27
  K. some till furthermore come 170:28
  Who will not k. a penny... 163:4
Keeps He k. his road well enough... 23:10
Kent K. and Keer... 58:48
  Some places of K.... 58:33
Kettle The k. calls the pot burnt-arse 34:8
Kick K. an attorney downstairs... 104:43
  The k. of the dam... 49:13
Kid You can't k. a kidder 40:40
Kill K. not the goose... 82:18
Kills He that k. a man... 51:27
Kiln Ill may the k.... 34:9
Kin A man cannot bear all his k....
143:18
  It is a poor k.... 143:12
  It is good to be near of k. to land 143:3
Kind A k. heart loseth nought... 101:1
  K. hearts are more than coronets 15:33
  K. hearts are soonest wronged 101:13
Kindle K. not a fire... 174:10
Kindly A k. aver... 18:40
Kindness K. cannot be bought... 101:18
  K. comes of will 101:19
  K. is lost... 19:17
  K. is the noblest weapon... 101:6
  K. lies not aye... 88:22
  One k. is the price of another 88:21
Kindred Wheresoever you see your k....
143:7
King A k.'s face... 149:16
  A k.'s favour... 149:30
  It is the lot of a k.... 149:12
  K.'s chaff... 149:26
  Like k., like people 149:19
  Nearest the k.... 149:34
  The k. can do no wrong 149:1
  The k. can make a knight... 15:45
  The k. is dead... 149:7
  The k. never dies 149:6
  The k.'s cheese... 149:29
  The k.'s word... 149:15
  What the k. wills... 149:4
  When the k. makes a mistake... 149:23
Kingdoms K. divided... 141:30
Kings K. are out of play 149:18

K. have long arms 149:2
K. have many ears... 149:3
Kinsfolk Many k.... 143:4
Kinsman K. helps kinsman... 143:2
Kirk The k. is aye greedy 144:62
Kiss It is better to k. a knave... 98:8
  Many k. the child... 94:6
  Many k. the hand... 94:5
Kitchen K. physic... 87:36
Knave A k. and a fool... 69:65
  No k. to the learned knave 102:17
  No k. to the old knave 125:15
  Once a k.... 18:28
  The more k.... 111:37
Knavery K. may serve for a turn... 89:4
  There is k. in all trades... 124:35
Knock K. a carle... 35:7
Know He that would k. what shall be...
  171:50
  He who wants to k. himself... 121:10
  If you wish to k. a man... 9:9
  K. thyself 153:48
  One learns to k. oneself... 79:5
  What you don't k.... 96:7
  You never k. what you can do... 48:61
  You should k. a man seven years...
  65:12
Knowledge K. has bitter roots... 54:5
  K. is a wild thing... 102:4
  K. is folly... 102:28
  K. is no burthen 102:10
  K. is power 102:9
  K. is the mother... 102:8
  K. makes one laugh... 102:20
  K. without practice... 102:21
Known Better k. than trusted 175:10
  Every man is best k. to himself 153:49
Knows He k. enough that knows noth-
  ing... 156:13
  He that k. little... 96:18
  He that k. nothing... 96:4
  No man better k. what good is... 2:14
  No man k. when he shall die... 39:25
  None k. what will happen to him...
  171:48
  The more one k.... 13:19
  Who k. himself... 153:50
  Who k. most... 168:81
  Who k. much... 166:2
Kythe K. in your own colours... 94:24

L

Labour A little l.... 48:15
  L. as long lived... 48:28
  L. is light... 109:17
  L. overcomes... 48:10
Labourer The l. is worthy... 44:6
Labours He that l. and thrives... 48:21
Labyrinth If you go into a l.... 70:19
Lack Many men l.... 22:6
Lackey When a l. comes to hell's door...
  68:21
Lacking L. breeds laziness... 34:2
Lad L.'s love's a busk of broom... 109:102
Ladder Go down the l.... 113:79
Lady On L. Day the latter... 117:75
  You a l.... 60:4
Ladybirds Plenty of l.... 30:11
Laird If the l. slight the lady... 27:13
Lame The l. tongue... 168:20
Lament To l. the dead... 39:100
Lammas After L. corn ripens... 117:60
Lancashire He that would take a L.
  man... 58:24
  What L. thinks today... 58:23
Land Every l. has its own law 104:66
  He that buys l.... 51:36
  In the l. of hope... 91:11
  L. was never lost... 180:90
  Many a one for l.... 113:57
  No l. without stones... 97:26
  The l. is never void... 3:58
  There is good l.... 127:24
Lands He that has l.... 180:18
Language That is not good l.... 168:94
  The l. of truth... 176:22
  There were no ill l.... 42:20
Larder No l. but has its mice 97:36
Last He that comes l. to the pot... 103:2
  The l. drop... 56:20
  The l. straw... 56:21
  The l. suitor... 103:13
Late A l. spring... 152:2
  Better l. ripe and bear... 103:9
  Better l. than never 103:8
  It is too l. to call back yesterday 142:2
  It is too l. to grieve... 142:4
  It is too l. to spare... 170:16
  L. children... 128:20
  L. was often lucky 103:10
  Never too l. to learn 103:12
  Never too l. to repent 142:40

Lend L. and lose; so play fools 105:19
  L., and lose the loan... 105:13
  L. money to a bad debtor... 105:15
  L. never that thing... 105:3
  L. only that... 105:2
  L. sitting... 105:5
  L. your horse... 105:21
  L. your money... 105:10
Lending L. is like throwing away...
  105:17
  L. nurses enmity 105:11
Lends He that l., gives 105:16
  He that l. his pot... 105:20
Lent He has but a short L.... 14:32
  When I l., I was a friend... 105:12
Leopard The l. cannot change his spots
  18:31
Lewd A l. bachelor... 112:9
Liar A l. can go round the world... 40:10
  A l. is not believed... 40:15
  A l. is worse... 40:24
  A l. should have a good memory 40:34
  The l. and the murderer... 40:23
  The l. is sooner caught... 40:11
Liars L. begin by imposing... 40:17
Libertine A l. life... 112:11
Liberty L. is a jewel 106:2
  L. is more worth... 106:1
  L. is not licence 106:10
  Too much l.,... 106:9
Lice L. do not bite busy men 48:6
Lie A l. is the curse of God 40:22
  Better a l. that heals... 40:29
  Give a l. twenty-four hours' start...
   79:25
  He that will l.... 40:35
  One l. makes many 40:13
  Tell a l.... 176:39
  Though a l. be swift... 176:10
  Though a l. be well drest... 40:30
  We must not l. down... 77:36
Lies He that l. long abed... 95:31
Life An ill l.... 39:87
  L. and misery... 162:29
  L. begins at forty 107:12
  L. is a pilgrimage 107:14
  L. is a shadow 107:15
  L. is but a span 107:1
  L. is half spent... 107:2
  L. is just a bowl... 107:17
  L. is not all beer... 107:7

L. is short... 107:5
L. is sweet 107:9
L. means strife 107:13
L. without a friend... 72:6
L. would be too smooth... 107:8
Man's l. is like a candle... 107:3
Such a l.... 39:89
The l. of man... 107:10
There is but one way to enter this l....
  39:53
While there's l.... 91:26
Lifeless He is l. that is faultless 97:2
Light A l. purse makes a heavy heart
  136:44
  Every l. has its shadow 97:30
Light-heeled A l. mother... 95:1
Lightning L. never strikes twice... 2:32
Like L. breeds like 157:1
  L. cures like 157:3
  L. to die... 108:10
  L. will to like 157:8
  No l. is the same 157:6
Likeliest Do the l.... 77:11
Likely L. lies in the mire... 108:2
Likeness L. begets love... 138:20
  L. causes liking 157:5
Likes Every man l. his own thing best
  153:40
Lime L. makes a rich father... 30:2
Limerick L. was... 133:80
Lion A man is a l.... 129:2
  Destroy the l.... 52:24
  If the l.'s skin cannot... 164:15
  The l. spares the suppliant 71:14
  Who takes a l. when he is absent...
   31:26
Lip-honour L. costs little... 94:3
Listeners L. never hear good... 99:3
Literature L. is a good staff... 188:10
Litter The l. is like to the sire and dam
  18:7
Little A l. and good... 160:38
  A l. bird... 28:25
  A l. body... 160:2
  A l. child... 19:14
  A l. fire... 160:24
  A l. given seasonably... 75:35
  A l. learning... 102:32
  A l. pot... 160:43
  A l. stone... 160:27
  A l. wind kindles... 160:6

A l. with quiet... 28:12
A l. wit will serve... 183:33
A l. wood... 28:26
Every l. helps 160:7
He that has l. is the less dirty 136:35
He that has l. shall have less 136:49
L. and often fills the purse 160:16
L. can a long tongue lein 168:13
L. fish are sweet 160:4
L. fishes slip through nets... 81:9
L. gear... 136:30
L. Jock... 136:106
L. sticks kindle the fire... 160:5
L. things are great... 28:24
L. things please little minds 69:50
L. wealth... 136:31
Many a l. makes a mickle 160:10
The l. cannot be great... 81:39
Live Everything would fain l. 153:15
He is unworthy to l.... 153:22
He that would l. for aye... 53:61
If you would l. ever... 51:66
If you would not l. to be old... 125:60
Let all l. as they would die 39:90
L. and learn 62:14
L. and let live 34:4
No one can l. on beauty... 11:24
One may l. without father or mother...
   144:3
The longer we l.... 107:19
They that l. longest, must die at last
   125:61
They who l. longest, will see most
   107:18
We can l. without our friends... 121:2
We l. by laws... 104:34
We must l. by the living... 39:99
Lives As long l. a merry man... 84:27
He l. long... 78:39
He that l. ill... 26:6
He that l. in hope... 91:21
He that l. long... 166:18
He that l. not well one year... 10:8
He that l. well... 78:22
He that l. wickedly... 10:19
He who l. by the sword... 178:7
Who l. by hope... 91:20
Living L. well... 148:8
No l. man all things can 97:11
Loan Give a l.... 105:14
Lock No l. will hold... 29:31

London L. Bridge was made... 58:78
Lone The l. sheep... 161:15
Long Be the day never so l.... 127:37
He that is l. a giving... 75:21
It is a l. lane... 127:41
It is not how l.... 78:23
L. beards heartless... 58:21
L. life has long misery 107:6
L. looked for comes at last 130:14
L. mint, little dint 168:44
Not a l. day... 48:59
Longer The l. you look at it... 146:8
Longest The l. at the fire... 180:19
The l. day has an end 127:38
The l. night will have an end 127:39
The l. way round... 85:46
Longing Better go away l.... 116:14
Look L. before you leap 85:33
L. to the end 55:3
L. to thyself... 153:16
Lookers-on L. see most... 153:45
Looks L. breed love 109:70
Loose Better hand l.... 106:6
Lords Many l.... 104:3
Lose A man may l. his goods... 8:2
A man may l. more in an hour... 73:17
Better l. a jest... 72:1
If you l. your time... 171:34
L. a leg... 150:11
L. an hour in the morning... 171:33
What you l. on the swings... 73:18
You cannot l.... 73:24
You must l. a fly... 150:2
Losers Give l. leave to speak 73:28
L. are always in the wrong 73:27
Loses He l. his thanks... 43:14
He l. indeed... 73:22
He l. nothing who keeps God... 144:6
He that l. anything... 73:15
He that l. his wife... 113:126
One never l. by doing a good turn 41:37
Who l. his liberty... 106:11
Loss Better a little l.... 150:7
He that is not sensible of his l.... 73:23
L. embraces shame 73:21
No great l. but some small profit 127:28
One man's l.... 73:20
There's no great l. without some gain
   73:13
Lost All is l. that is put into a riven dish
   80:33

All is not l.... 127:14
For a l. thing... 142:9
He has not l. all... 91:29
There is nothing l. by civility 15:7
What is l. in the hundred... 73:19
Louse Better a l. in the pot... 80:10
Love As good l. comes... 109:107
  Greater l. hath no man than this...
    72:54
  He that does not l. a woman... 109:42
  He that has l. in his breast... 109:19
  If you l. the boll... 109:116
  In l. is no lack 109:21
  In l.'s wars... 109:79
  L. and a cough... 109:41
  L. and business... 109:31
  L. and hate... 86:4
  L. and leprosy... 109:43
  L. and lordship... 109:123
  L. and pease-pottage... 109:58
  L. asks faith... 109:118
  L. begets love 109:71
  L. being jealous... 109:121
  L. cannot be compelled 109:37
  L. conquers all 109:27
  L. covers many infirmities 109:14
  L. delights in praise 109:84
  L. does much... 109:124
  L. is a fair garden... 113:134
  L. is a flower... 113:137
  L. is a game... 109:82
  L. is as strong... 109:40
  L. is a sweet torment 109:54
  L. is blind 109:1
  L. is free 109:20
  L. is full of fear 109:56
  L. is lawless 109:7
  L. is never without jealousy 109:122
  L. is not found... 109:75
  L. is sweet in the beginning... 109:53
  L. is the fruit... 109:76
  L. is the loadstone... 109:72
  L. is the touchstone... 109:25
  L. is the true reward... 109:73
  L. is without reason 109:6
  L. lasts as long... 109:125
  L. laughs at locksmiths 109:34
  L. lives in cottages... 109:128
  L. locks no cupboards 109:22
  L. makes all hard hearts gentle 109:33
  L. makes all men equal 109:30

L. makes a wit... 109:32
L. makes one fit... 109:18
L. makes the world... 109:29
L. me little... 116:13
L. me, love my dog 109:83
L. needs no teaching 109:74
L. not at the first look 85:30
L. of lads... 109:101
L. rules his kingdom... 109:28
L. sees no faults 109:3
L. speaks... 109:64
L. the babe... 109:115
L. will creep... 109:48
L. will find a way 109:35
L. will go through... 109:36
L. without end... 109:49
L. without return... 109:109
L. your friend, but look to yourself
  72:30
L. your friend with his fault 72:74
L. your neighbour... 121:15
Men l. to hear well... 24:1
Next to l., quietness 109:67
No l. is foul... 109:5
No l. like the first love 109:103
No l. to a father's 109:114
One cannot l.... 109:10
One l. expels another 109:105
The l. of money and the love of learn-
  ing... 180:128
The l. of the wicked... 109:59
They l. too much... 109:60
When l. is greatest... 109:65
When l. puts in... 109:57
Where l. fails... 109:15
Where l. is... 109:119
Whom we l. best... 109:66
Loved Men are best l.... 1:2
  'Tis better to have l. and lost... 109:26
Lovers L. are madmen 109:11
  L.' quarrels... 109:96
Loves Every man as he l.... 47:20
  He that l. the tree... 109:117
Low A l. hedge... 179:14
Lower The l. millstone grinds... 60:17
Lowly L. sit... 136:32
Loyalty L. is worth more... 110:1
Luck Good l. reaches further... 111:15
  He that would have good l. in horses...
    167:1
  Ill l. is good for something 2:16

There is l. in leisure 85:25
There is l. in odd numbers 167:2
You never know your l. 111:7
Lucky Better be born l. than wise 111:17
  It is better to be born l. than rich 111:14
  L. at cards... 167:10
  L. at life... 167:11
  L. men need no counsel 111:31
Luke On St L.'s Day... 117:69
  St L. was a saint... 87:46
Lying L. rides upon debt's back 40:6

M

Mackerel M.'s in season... 117:41
  M. sky and mares' tails... 181:83
Mad Every man is m.... 97:10
  For m. words... 69:87
Maid A m. and a virgin... 184:30
  A m. marries... 113:65
  A m. oft seen... 65:9
  A m. that laughs... 184:83
Maiden A m. with many wooers... 20:12
Maidens All are not m.... 7:4
  M. must be mild and meek... 184:61
  M. should be meek... 184:31
  M. should be seen... 184:62
Maids M. say 'Nay'... 184:87
  M. want nothing... 113:15
Main Look to the m. chance 22:21
Malice M. hurts itself most 35:9
Malta M. would be a delightful place...
  133:18
Man A m. at five... 19:46
  A m. at sixteen... 19:54
  A m. can do no more... 164:11
  A m. is as old as he feels... 184:104
  A m. of straw... 184:99
  As a m. is... 23:13
  Every m.'s man had a man... 9:28
  M. is the head... 184:91
  M. punishes the action... 41:30
  M., woman, and devil... 184:100
  Sike a m. as thou wald be... 23:14
  There is no m.... 160:28
  Whatever is made by the hand of m....
  179:19
Manchester What M. says today... 58:55
Manners It is not good m.... 15:15
  M. and money... 15:11
  M. make often fortunes 15:10
  M. maketh man 15:9

Of evil m.... 127:26
Many M. words would have much drink
  51:74
March In M., kill crow... 117:22
  In M., the birds begin to search...
  117:23
  M. borrowed from April... 117:19
  M. comes in like a lion... 117:20
  M. comes in with adder heads... 117:21
  M. dust and May sun... 181:128
  M. in Janiveer... 181:18
  M. whisker... 181:31
  M. wind kindles the adder... 181:30
  M. winds and April showers... 181:29
  On the first of M.... 117:25
  The M. sun causes dust... 181:114
  The M. sun raises... 181:115
Market He that desires to make a m. of
  his ware... 22:20
Markets Good ware makes quick m. 22:48
Marls He who m. sand... 30:3
Marriage An ill m. is a spring... 113:28
  M. halves our griefs... 113:35
  M. is a lottery 113:33
  M. is destiny 113:37
  M. is the tomb... 113:133
  M. makes or mars... 113:34
  M. rides upon the saddle... 113:42
  More belongs to m.... 113:47
  Where there's m. without love...
  113:139
Marriages At m. and funerals... 72:43
  M. are made in heaven 113:36
Married A m. man turns his staff...
  113:13
  A m. woman has nothing... 113:14
  She is well m.... 113:130
  The m. man has many cares... 113:5
Marries He that m. a widow and two chil-
  dren... 113:152
  He that m. a widow, will often have...
  113:153
  He that m. ere he be wise... 113:88
  He that m. for wealth... 113:54
  He that m. late... 113:92
  He who m. might be sorry... 113:4
  The woman who m. many... 113:151
  Who m. for love... 113:136
Marry Before you m.... 113:46
  It is better to m. a shrew... 113:69
  It is good to m. late... 113:91

A m. heart... 84:40
Aye be as m. as be can... 84:38
It is good to be m. and wise 84:66
It is good to be m. at meat 84:72
It is m. in hall... 84:73
It's m. when maltmen meet 84:74
M. is the feast-making... 84:52
M. meet... 84:30
Mettle M. is dangerous... 129:21
Meum M., tuum, suum... 135:19
Michaelmas M. chickens... 117:65
M. rot... 117:67
The M. moon... 117:66
Mickle Many a m. makes a muckle
160:11
M. head... 69:59
M. must a good heart thole 166:19
Might M. is right 164:7
Mile Every m. is two in winter 152:17
Milk M. is white... 53:32
M. says to wine... 51:67
Mill He who goes into a m.... 29:18
The m. cannot grind... 126:18
The m. gets by going 48:19
The m. that is always going... 168:107
Miller Put a m., a weaver... 124:30
The m. is honest... 124:28
Millers M. and bakers... 124:26
M. are the last... 124:25
Mills M. and wives... 113:17
M. will not grind... 131:1
The m. of God... 77:65
Mind A m. enlightened... 114:5
M. other men... 153:10
M. your own business 99:10
The m. is the man 114:1
What is a man but his m. 114:2
Minds Great m. think alike 157:7
If m. were alike... 47:19
Mine What's yours is m.... 135:21
Mirror The best m.... 72:58
Mirth M. is the sugar of life 84:41
M. without measure... 84:65
The m. of the world... 84:54
Mischief Better a m.... 98:6
He that m. hatches... 10:14
M. comes by the pound... 2:25
M. comes without calling for 10:3
No m. but a woman... 10:2
The more m., the better sport 10:21
Miser A rich m. is poorer... 115:17

If a man is a m.... 115:3
Misery He bears m. best... 162:39
It is m. enough... 162:2
M. loves company 162:46
Misfortune M. arrives on horseback...
2:24
M. comes to all men... 2:21
M. is not that which can be avoided...
2:23
M. makes foes... 2:9
Misfortunes M. come of themselves 2:1
M. find their way... 2:20
M. hasten age 2:6
M. never come singly 2:27
M. tell us... 2:13
Our worst m.... 186:21
Miss A m. is as good... 165:13
You never m. the water... 187:8
Mist When the m. comes from the hill...
181:89
Mistakes He who makes no m.... 97:12
If you don't make m.... 97:5
Mistress Where the m. is the master...
113:107
Mistrust M. is an axe... 175:30
Mists So many m. in March... 181:88
Misunderstanding M. brings lies... 114:14
Mix Never m. your liquor 51:61
Moderation M. in all things 116:1
Modesty M. sets off... 24:16
Though m. be a virtue... 24:17
Moist A m. hand... 167:21
Monday M. for wealth... 38:1
M. is Sunday's brother... 38:3
M.'s child... 38:2
Money A man without m.... 136:52
He that has m. has what he wants 180:2
He that has m. in his purse... 183:18
He that has no m.... 136:25
M. answereth all things 180:111
M. governs the world 180:114
M. is a good servant... 180:124
M. isn't everything 180:52
M. is often lost... 180:47
M. is round... 180:26
M. is the ace of trumps 180:115
M. is the only monarch 180:113
M. is the root... 180:29
M. is the sinews of love... 109:126
M. is the sinews of war 180:121

N. are debts 118:3
No n., no pack-drill 79:34
Naples See N. and die 133:37
Narrow N. gathered... 115:4
Natural It is as n. to die... 39:12
Nature He that follows N.... 119:9
N. abhors... 119:10
N. and the sin of Adam... 18:43
N. does nothing... 119:6
N. draws more... 119:1
N. has given us two ears... 168:74
N. hates all sudden changes 119:11
N. is conquered... 119:13
N. is content... 119:12
N. is no botcher 119:7
N. is the true law 119:5
N. passes art 119:15
N. requires five... 159:12
N., time, and patience... 119:8
N. will have her course 119:2
That which N. paints... 119:16
You can drive out n.... 18:25
Naughty N. boys... 19:50
Neapolitan The N. is wide-mouthed...
133:38
Near A n. neighbour... 121:7
N. is my coat... 153:11
N. is my shirt... 153:12
Nearer The n. the church... 144:61
Nearest The n. way... 85:45
Necessity N. and opportunity... 120:8
N. breaks iron 120:4
N. has no holiday 120:5
N. is a powerful weapon 120:2
N. is the mother... 120:7
N. knows no law 120:1
Need He has great n. of a fool... 69:31
N. makes greed 136:69
N. makes the naked man run 136:13
N. makes the old wife trot 136:14
When n. is highest... 88:16
Needles N. and pins... 113:30
Needs N. must... 120:6
Needy He that is n.... 113:1
Neglect N. will kill an injury... 148:6
Neighbour A good n.... 121:5
An ill n.... 121:11
He's an ill n.... 121:14
Our n.'s ground... 28:42
To have a good n.... 121:6
Neighbours He has ill n.... 137:21

Netherlands The N. are the cockpit...
133:48
Nettle Tender-handed stroke a n....
101:12
Nettles If they would drink n. in March...
53:62
New A n. broom... 17:17
Everything n. is fine 17:37
N. grief... 162:16
N. lords... 17:19
N. meat begets... 17:9
N. things are fair 17:36
Of a n. prince... 17:18
The n. love... 109:104
There is nothing n. under the sun 17:40
What is n. cannot be true 176:38
When a n. book appears... 17:26
You can't put n. wine... 17:43
Newer N. is truer 17:42
News Bad n. travels fast 122:3
Good n. may be told... 122:12
Ill n. comes apace 122:4
Ill n. comes often... 122:7
Ill n. comes unsent for 122:5
Ill n. is too often true 122:8
Ill n. never comes too late 122:6
No n. is good news 122:1
Night N. is the mother of counsel 3:33
Nile If the N. knows your secret... 79:22
Nineteen N. nay-says... 184:86
No Don't say 'N.'... 8:19
If you always say 'N.'... 8:20
'N.', thank you... 8:21
Nobility N., without ability... 15:29
Noble He is more n. that deserves...
75:27
He is n. that has noble conditions 15:36
The more n., the more humble 15:32
Noblest The n. vengeance... 148:4
Nod A n. from a lord... 69:74
A n. is as good as a wink... 168:87
Noise The n. of the kettledrum... 79:20
North Out of the n.... 58:43
The n. for greatness... 58:42
The n. of England... 58:41
The n. wind does blow... 181:33
Three ills come from the n.... 58:44
Northampton N. stands on other men's
legs 58:58
The Mayor of N.... 58:59
Northerly N. wind and blubber... 181:35

Northern N. wind brings weather fair 181:34

Nothing By doing n.... 95:20
He has n., that is not contented 28:2
He that does n.... 95:40
He that has n. is not contented 136:51
He that has n. need fear to lose nothing 136:24
If you put n. into your purse... 48:39
N. comes of nothing 108:28
N. have, nothing crave 136:36
N. is to be got... 136:5
Where n. is... 136:21

Nought He that has n.... 136:50

Novelty N. always appears handsome 17:35

November N. take flail... 117:71
On the first of N.... 117:72

Now N. is now... 171:40

Number Look after n. one 153:2
N. one is the first house... 153:3

Nurse The n. is valued... 124:38
The n.'s tongue... 124:39

Nurses N. put one bit... 124:36

Nurture N. and good manners... 15:5
N. is above nature 15:4

Nutmeg If you carry a n.... 113:146

Nutting If you go n. on Sundays... 144:67

O

Oak An o. is not felled... 130:37
Every o. has been an acorn 81:36
If the o.'s before the ash... 181:17

Oaks O. may fall... 81:7

Oats If you cut o. green... 30:7
O. will mow themselves 30:8

Obedience O. is much more seen... 123:5
O. is the first duty... 123:7
O. is the mother... 123:1

Obedient All things are o. to money 180:109
An o. wife... 113:108

Obey He that cannot o.... 123:2

Obstinate O. oxen... 182:24

Occasion An o. lost... 126:17

Occupation An o. is as good... 124:8

Offender The o. never pardons 71:23

Offer To o. much... 139:17

Office Out of o.... 9:6

Offspring The o. of those that are very old... 128:21

Oft O. ettle... 134:25

Often O. and little eating... 53:67

Oil Pouring o. on the fire... 174:13

Old A man must go o. to the court... 144:28
An o. cart well used... 125:23
An o. dog barks not... 125:4
An o. dog bites sore 125:53
An o. fox is not... 125:11
An o. knave... 125:14
An o. man in a house... 125:24
An o. man is a bed... 125:28
An o. man never wants... 125:46
An o. man's sayings... 125:1
An o. man's staff... 125:64
An o. man who weds... 113:74
An o. ox makes... 125:25
An o. ox will find... 125:49
An o. wise man's shadow... 125:18
As the o. cock crows... 125:42
Better be an o. man's darling... 113:71
He that would be o. long... 19:55
If the o. dog bark... 125:3
In the o. of the moon... 181:86
It is best to be off with the o. love... 109:106
Never too o. to learn 125:35
None so o. that he hopes not... 125:72
O. acquaintance... 72:62
O. age comes stealing on 125:57
O. age doesn't protect... 125:32
O. age is a hospital... 125:38
O. age is a malady... 125:40
O. age is sickness... 125:37
O. be... 125:59
O. cattle... 125:27
O. chains... 17:28
O. churches... 125:41
O. customs... 17:33
O. fish, old oil... 72:60
O. foxes want no tutors 125:10
O. friends and old wine... 72:61
O. hate... 86:10
O. love does not rust 109:45
O. love will not be forgotten 109:44
O. men and travellers... 125:47
O. men are twice children 125:36
O. men go to death... 125:69
O. men, when they marry young women... 113:73
O. shoes... 17:29

Things p. cannot be recalled 142:3
Patch P. by patch... 170:50
Patent There is nothing p. in the New
  Testament... 144:101
Pater 'P. noster' built churches... 144:53
Path Every p. has a puddle 97:38
Patience Have p. with a friend... 72:73
  He that has p.... 130:18
  Let p. grow... 130:2
  P. is a flower... 130:3
  P. is a plaster... 130:29
  P. is a remedy for every grief 130:28
  P. is a virtue 130:1
  P. is the best buckler... 130:4
  P. is the key of joy... 130:7
  P. is the knot... 130:6
  P. is the remedy of the world 130:27
  P. provoked... 130:24
  P. surpasses learning 130:5
  P., time, and money... 130:17
  P. under old injuries... 130:26
  P. with poverty... 130:31
  With p. the mulberry leaf... 130:21
Patient Be p. in poverty... 136:115
  P. men win the day 130:11
Paul If St P.'s Day be fair and clear...
  181:125
  P.'s will not always stand 17:22
Pay Better to p. and have little... 14:2
  He must p. with his body... 131:12
  He that cannot p. in purse... 131:13
  He that cannot p., let him pray 131:11
  If you p. not a servant his wages...
    131:14
  If you p. peanuts... 131:26
  P. beforehand and your work... 131:16
  P. beforehand was never well served
    131:15
  P. what you owe... 14:33
  P. with the same dish... 14:34
Payer A good p.... 131:22
Paymaster A good p. may build Paul's
  131:25
  A good p. needs no surety 131:23
  A good p. never wants workmen 131:24
  An ill p. never wants excuse 131:27
Payment P. in advance... 131:17
  The best p.... 131:20
Pays He that p. last... 131:19
  He who p. the piper... 131:30
  Let him that p. the lawing... 131:31

Who p. the physician... 87:39
  You p. your money... 20:11
Peace He that will not have p.... 132:6
  If you want p.... 132:7
  P. in a thatched hut... 84:12
  P. makes plenty 132:3
  Where there is p.... 132:1
Peaceably To live p. with all... 132:2
Peach The p. will have wine... 51:48
Peacock The p. has fair feathers... 11:5
  When the p. loudly bawls... 181:3
Pearls Do not cast your p.... 15:25
Pears Plant p. for your heirs 30:45
Peas Sow p. and beans... 30:17
Pease Every p. has its veaze... 53:44
Peck A p. of March dust... 181:126
Pedigrees In good p.... 143:14
Pedlar Let every p. carry... 147:6
Peeps He who p. through a hole... 99:4
Peerage The P. is the Englishman's Bible
  15:46
Pen P. and ink... 188:3
  The p. is mightier... 188:1
  The p. is the tongue... 188:4
Pence Take care of the p.... 170:21
Pennies Put two p. in a purse... 180:71
Penniless P. souls... 136:59
Penny A p. at a pinch... 187:13
  A p. saved... 170:7
  Every one has a p.... 51:38
  In for a p.... 134:28
  No p., no pardon 29:37
  No p., no paternoster 29:38
  P. and penny... 160:15
  P. in purse... 72:23
  P. wise... 170:40
  That p. is well spent... 163:30
Penny-weight A p. of love... 104:15
Pens P. may blot... 188:6
People Like p.... 144:72
Perfect P. friendship... 72:48
  P. love... 109:39
Permanent There is nothing p. except
  change 17:24
Perseverance P. kills the game 134:1
Persuasion The p. of the fortunate...
  13:23
Petticoats When p. woo... 109:95
Physic If p. do not work... 87:45
Physician A p. is an angel... 87:59
  If you have a p. for your friend... 87:56

Q

R

Race The r. is got by running 48:43
  The r. is not to the swift... 134:6
Ragged A r. colt... 19:51
  Under a r. coat... 136:112
Rain Although it r.... 70:16
  In r. and sunshine... 144:26
  More r., more rest... 181:51
  Near burr, far r. 181:10
  R. before seven... 181:64
  R. from the east... 181:63
  R., rain, go away... 181:67
  Some r., some rest 181:50
  The r. comes scouth... 181:65
  The r. falls on every roof 60:13
  The r. of tears... 54:6
  There is no r.... 144:54
Rainbow A r. at morn... 181:71
  A r. in the morning... 181:72
Rainbows If two r. appear at one time...
  181:70
Rains If it r. on Easter Day... 181:58
  If it r. when the sun is shining... 181:68
  It never r. but it pours 2:28
  It r. by planets 181:66
  Many r., many rowans... 181:52
Rainy After a r. winter... 181:54
  Keep something for a r. day 170:29
Raise It is easier to r. the devil... 174:8
  R. no more devils... 174:9
Rake There is little for the r.... 82:26
Rancour R. sticks long... 86:11
Rape Oft r. rueth 85:5
Rare That thing which is r.... 187:14
Rats R. desert... 110:14
Raw R. leather will stretch 19:26
  R. pulleyn... 53:45
Ready R. money is a ready medicine
  180:4
  R. money will away 180:25
Reason A man without r.... 114:22
  Hearken to r.... 114:21
  One r. is as good as fifty 173:15
  R. binds the man 114:19
  R. governs the wise man... 114:20
  R. lies between... 116:10
  R. rules all things 114:18
Reasons The r. of the poor... 136:109
Receiver The r. is as bad as the thief 33:35
Receivers If there were no r.... 33:36
Receives Who r. a gift... 75:36

Reckless R. youth... 19:57
Reckoning The r. spoils the relish 131:10
Red A r. cow gives good milk 30:24
  If r. the sun begins his race... 181:109
  R. clouds in the east... 181:84
  R. sky at night... 181:22
  R. wood makes gude spindles 30:41
  To a r. man read thy rede... 167:25
Redemption There is no r. from hell
  46:10
Reed-player The r. of your own street...
  65:7
Reeds Where there are r.... 79:3
Reek R. comes aye down again... 18:27
Refuse Never r. a good offer 8:22
  R. a wife... 113:64
  To r. and to give tardily... 75:20
Religion A man without r.... 144:2
  No r. but can boast... 144:56
  R., credit... 144:15
  R. is the rule of life 144:1
Religions He that is of all r.... 144:55
Rely Never r. on love... 109:51
Remarriage Frequent r.... 113:150
Remedy No r. but patience 130:30
  The best r. against an ill man... 10:45
  There is a r. for all things... 145:3
  There is a r. for everything... 145:4
  There is no r. for fear... 66:19
  The r. for injuries... 148:7
  The r. may be worse... 145:16
Remember R. man and keep in mind...
  72:20
  R. to distrust 175:26
  R. you are but a man 138:29
Remembrance The r. of past sorrows...
  162:23
Remorse R. is lust's dessert 142:18
Removals Three r.... 17:13
Remove R. an old tree... 125:51
Repairs He that r. not a part... 52:23
  Who r. not his gutter... 52:22
Repentance R. comes too late 142:13
  R. is a bitter physic 142:16
  R. is a pill... 142:17
  R. is good... 142:37
  R. is not to be measured... 142:36
  R. is the loveliest... 142:35
  R. is the virtue of fools 142:14
Reply No r. is best 156:15
Reputation R. is often got... 64:4

S. is one thing... 41:21

S. 'No' a woman... 184:88

Says He who s. what he likes... 168:8

Many a one s. well... 94:11

What everybody s. must be true 176:36

Scalded A s. cat... 62:28

Scare A good s. is worth more... 3:13

Scathe One does the s.... 147:30

Scatter S. with one hand... 163:32

Scholar Every good s.... 54:24

The s. may waur the master 54:28

Scholars The greatest s.... 102:24

Science Much s.... 102:31

S. has no enemy... 96:13

Scold Who has a s.... 113:120

Scolds S. and infants... 113:111

Score S. twice before you cut once 85:35

Scorn S. at first... 27:9

S. comes commonly... 27:3

Scornful Never was a s. person... 27:12

Scorpion There is a s. under every stone 37:8

Scot A S., a rat... 133:69

The S. will not fight... 133:70

Scotsman A S. is always wise... 133:72

Scottish A S. mist... 133:74

Scratch S. my back... 88:24

S. my breech... 88:25

Scratching By s. and biting... 141:17

Sea Being on s., sail... 172:34

Seaman A s., if he carries a millstone... 124:45

Seamen S. are the nearest to death... 124:44

Season Everything is good in its s. 171:38

Second S. thoughts are best 85:38

The s. word... 141:5

Secret A s. foe... 57:10

He that tells a s.... 79:41

The s. wall of a town... 132:5

Thy s. is thy prisoner... 79:40

Secure He that is s.... 151:10

Seed Everything has its s. 12:2

Seeing S. is believing 63:4

Seek Nothing s.... 4:6

S. and ye shall find 4:7

S. mickle... 4:8

S. that which may be found 4:29

S. till you find... 134:22

Seem Be what you would s. to be 94:23

Things are not always what they s. 7:2

Seill S. comes not... 84:14

Sel S., sel, has half-filled hell 153:21

Seldom S. is a long man wise... 160:40

Self S. do, self have 153:35

Self-praise S. is no recommendation 137:18

Self-preservation S. is the first law of nature 153:14

Sell A man must s. his ware... 22:19

Don't s. the skin... 6:7

If you s. your purse... 113:125

It is no sin to s. dear... 22:35

You cannot s. the cow... 20:3

Separation S. secures manifest friendship 1:8

September S. blow soft... 117:62

Serpent Whom a s. has bitten... 62:27

Servant A good s. must come... 154:11

A good s. must have good wages 154:14

A good s. should have the back of an ass... 154:9

A good s. should never be in the way... 154:8

An ill s. will never be a good master 154:27

A s. and a cock... 154:7

A s. is known... 154:10

A s. that is diligent... 154:12

Choose none for thy s.... 154:1

If you would have a good s.... 154:2

One must be a s.... 154:28

Servants S. make the worst masters 154:25

S. should put on patience... 154:39

S. will not be diligent... 154:17

So many s.... 154:21

Serve As long as you s. the tod... 154:40

No man can s. two masters 110:11

S. a great man... 154:31

S. a noble disposition... 154:30

They also s...: 130:10

You cannot s. God... 20:5

Served He that will be s.... 130:9

He that would be well s., must know... 154:6

If you would be well s., serve yourself 153:29

Serves He that s. a good master... 154:29

He that s. God for money... 131:32

He that s. well... 154:13

He who s. God, serves a good master 77:21

He who s. is not free 154:33

Many a man s.... 154:32

Service No s. to the king's 149:25

S. is no inheritance 154:36

S. without reward... 131:4

The first s. a child does... 19:12

Serving S. one's own passions... 129:23

Serving-man A young s.... 154:37

Set S. good against evil 78:47

Seven Keep a thing s. years... 177:6

S. hours' sleep... 159:14

Severity Sometimes s. is better... 35:5

Severn Fix thy pale in S.... 119:3

Seville He who has not seen S.... 133:43

Shadow Catch not at the s.... 82:15

Shake Better s. out the sack... 170:44

Shaking After s. hands with a Greek... 133:63

Shallow S. streams... 69:77

Shame He that has no s., has no conscience 155:8

He who has no s. before the world... 155:9

He who is without s.... 155:10

Past s.... 155:7

S. fades in the morning... 14:14

S. in a kindred... 143:17

So long as there is s.... 155:6

Shameful S. craving... 8:16

S. leaving... 170:45

Share S. and share alike 100:23

Sharp All that is s. is short 127:35

A s. stomach... 93:6

Sharpens Nothing s. sight... 59:8

Sharper The s. the storm... 127:36

Shaving It is ill s. against the wool 25:5

Sheaf One s. of a stook... 113:70

Shear S. your sheep in May... 117:46

Shearer A bad s.... 147:25

Sheep He that has s.... 30:26

He that makes himself a s.... 56:26

If one s. leap o'er the dyke... 61:15

Let every s. hang... 147:3

One might as well be hanged for a s.... 10:13

One scabbed s.... 29:6

One s. follows another 61:14

Sheffield When S. Park is ploughed and sown... 58:26

Sheltering It is good s.... 125:19

Shift A good s. may serve long... 147:40

Ship A s. and a woman... 184:67

A s. under sail... 11:37

Shipwreck Let another's s.... 62:39

Shitten S. luck... 167:7

Shod S. in the cradle... 19:40

Shoe Every s. fits not... 47:4

Shoemaker The s.'s son... 153:13

Shoots He that s. oft... 134:24

Shop Keep your s.... 48:18

Short A s. prayer... 144:91

S. boughs... 30:48

S. folk are soon angry 160:41

S. folk's heart... 160:42

S. pleasure... 84:46

S. reckonings make long friends 14:37

Shortest The s. answer... 41:17

Should He that does what he s. not... 33:11

Shoulder In a s. of veal... 53:47

One s. of mutton and English beer... 53:21

S. of mutton... 58:6

When the s. of mutton is going... 126:10

Show S. a good man his error... 78:44

S. me a liar... 33:33

S. me the man... 29:46

Shower A s. in July... 181:55

Shrew Every man can rule a s.... 3:62

Shrouds S. have no pockets 180:64

Sick He that is s. of a fever lurden... 95:37

That s. man is not to be pitied... 147:8

Sickness S. shows us... 87:28

S. soaks the purse 87:29

The s. of the body... 87:27

Sides There are two s. to every question 100:11

Sieve A s. will hold water... 184:64

Sight Out of s.... 1:21

The farther the s.... 181:14

Sign It is an ill s.... 36:10

Silence S. and thinking... 156:21

S. catches a mouse 156:18

S. does seldom harm 156:22

S. is a woman's best garment 156:16

S. is golden 156:1

S. is of the gods 156:2

S. is the sweet medicine... 156:3

S. means consent 156:20

S. never makes mistakes 156:11

Silent Beware of a s. man... 156:33
He that is s.... 156:31

Silk You cannot make a s. purse... 18:34

Silks S. and satins... 163:15

Silly It is a s. fish... 62:32
S. child is soon ylered 54:29

Silver A s. key... 180:108
He that has not s. in his purse...
136:119
No s. without its dross 97:27

Simon S. and Jude... 117:70

Sin Every s. brings its punishment...
10:29
It is a s. against hospitality... 92:7
S. is the root... 10:9
S. plucks on sin 10:11

Sing If you s. before breakfast... 84:60
Who can s. so merry a note... 136:29

Single S. long... 113:3

Sings He that s. on Friday... 84:61
Many a man s.... 113:31

Sinner The greater the s.... 10:25

Sins When all s. grow old... 115:23

Sits He s. not sure... 81:6
Where MacGregor s.... 9:12

Six S. hours' sleep... 159:13

Sixpence There is not the thickness of a
s.... 78:46

Skaiths Better two s.... 162:36

Skeer S. your own fire 99:12

Skeleton Every family has a s. in the cupboard 143:10

Skilfullest The s. wanting money...
158:11

Skill All things require s.... 53:18
S. and confidence... 158:1
S. is no burden 158:6
S. will accomplish... 158:2
'Tis s., not strength... 158:3
Try your s. in galt first... 173:10

Skin There is more than one way to s. a
cat 47:27

Skirts Who has s. of straw... 26:7

Sky If the s. falls... 108:12

Slander S. cannot make... 42:5
S. flings stones... 42:12
S. is a shipwreck... 42:4
S. leaves a score... 42:3

Slanderer The s. kills a thousand times...
42:13

Slave Give a s. a rod... 154:22
He is a s. of the greatest slave... 153:19

Slavery Think no labour s.... 170:51

Sleep In s. all passes away 159:5
In s., what difference is there... 159:6
S. is a priceless treasure... 159:3
S. is better than medicine 159:1
S. is the brother... 159:18
S. is the greatest thief... 159:9
S. is the image... 159:19
S. is the poor man's treasure 159:4

Sleeping It is good s. in a whole skin
32:13
Let s. dogs lie 174:5
There will be s. enough... 159:15

Sleeps He who s. all the morning...
159:16
Let him that s. too sound... 14:16

Sleepy A s. master... 49:39
The s. fox... 159:17

Slip There's many a s.... 6:25

Sloe When the s. tree is as white as a
sheet... 30:51

Sloth S. breeds a scab 95:25
S., like rust... 95:24

Slothful The s. is the servant of the counters 95:45
The s. man is the beggar's brother 95:33

Slow S. but sure... 134:4
S. help... 88:18

Sluggard A s. takes an hundred steps...
95:9
The s. must be clad in rags 95:34
The s.'s convenient season... 95:42

Sluggards S. are never great scholars
95:46

Slumber One s.... 159:7

Small A s. leak... 160:26
Better are s. fish... 80:11
From s. beginnings... 81:38
He that gives me s. gifts... 75:33
It's a s. world 185:3
Many s. make a great 160:12
Of a s. spark... 160:25
S. birds must have meat 19:11
S. gifts make friends... 75:32
S. is beautiful 160:3
S. is the seed... 81:37
S. rain allays great winds 160:18
S. rain lays great dust 160:17
S. riches... 136:33

S. sorrows speak... 162:20
The best things come in s. packages 160:1
Smaller The s. the peas... 11:47
Smell The best s. is bread... 53:27
The s. of garlic... 145:11
Smelt One is not s.... 29:25
Smith Often a full dexterous s.... 158:12
Smoke There's no s. without fire 79:2
The s. of a man's own country... 172:27
Snail The s. slides up the tower at last... 134:7
Snails When black s. on the road you see... 181:4
Snake When a s. gets warm on ice... 133:46
Snite The s. need not... 34:11
Snow A s. year... 181:95
S. for a se'nnight... 181:96
Snowdon S. will yield sufficient pasture... 133:83
Sober You cannot make people s.... 51:14
Soberness What s. conceals... 51:5
Soft S. fire... 116:12
S. pace goes far 85:49
S. wax will take any impression 19:27
Softly He that goes s.... 85:52
Ride s.... 85:51
Sold Pleasing ware is half s. 22:49
Soldiers Old s. never die... 124:48
S. fight... 124:51
S. in peace... 124:49
Solitary A s. man... 161:17
Solitude S. dulls the thought... 161:1
S. is often the best society 161:5
S. is the nest... 161:2
Solomon S. was a wise man... 108:24
Something S. is better than nothing 80:26
You don't get s. for nothing 48:36
Son A s. is a son... 19:6
Even the S. of Heaven... 143:11
Every man is the s.... 147:2
It is better to have no s.... 124:52
Soon He that s. deemeth... 85:6
S. enough, if well enough 85:27
S. gotten... 163:10
S. tod... 167:18
Sooner S. begun... 52:15
Sooth S. bourd... 176:56
S. saws... 176:57

Sore As s. fight wrens as cranes 160:44
Sorrow A hundred pounds of s.... 142:10
A s. is an itching place... 162:52
Hang s.... 162:37
Never lay s. to your heart... 162:38
Of thy s. be not too sad... 162:43
One for s.... 167:31
S. and an evil life... 162:19
S. comes unsent for 162:34
S. is at parting... 162:8
S. is born... 162:6
S. is soon enough... 186:22
S. kills not... 162:17
S. makes silence... 162:21
S. makes websters spin 162:22
S. will pay no debt 142:11
When s. is asleep... 162:41
Sorrows The s. of the rich... 136:97
Sorry It is a s. flock... 113:109
Sound It is a s. head... 97:9
S. love... 109:46
S. travelling far and wide... 181:15
Soup Of s. and love... 53:31
Southerly A s. wind and a cloudy sky... 181:42
A s. wind with showers of rain... 181:43
Sow As you s., so you reap 147:11
S. in the slop... 30:13
S. or set beans... 117:10
S. thin and mow thin 115:6
S. with the hand... 163:31
They that s. the wind... 10:15
Sows He that s. thistles... 44:9
He that s., trusts in God... 77:31
Spain In S., the lawyer... 133:17
Nothing ill in S.... 133:40
Spaniard A bad S.... 133:44
The S. is a bad servant... 133:41
Spaniels S. that fawn when beaten... 49:27
Spare Better s. at brim... 170:15
Better s. to have of thine own... 170:4
S. the rod... 49:22
S. to speak... 168:22
S. well... 170:9
S. when you're young... 170:22
Spared Better s. than ill spent 170:14
Sparing S. is the first gaining 170:10
Sparrow Better a s. in the hand... 135:2
Speak Better s. truth rudely... 176:4
He cannot s. well... 168:103

Many s. much... 168:102
Never s. ill of the dead 168:57
S. and speed... 168:23
S. fair and think... 94:2
S. fitly... 156:30
S. not of a dead man... 53:74
S. only what is true of the living... 39:93
S. the truth... 176:52
S. well of your friend... 57:14
S. when you are spoken to 15:16
To s. ill of others... 168:59
To s. of a usurer... 105:26
When all men s.... 168:10
You may s. with your gold... 180:120
Speaks He that s. ill of the mare... 22:7
He that s. lavishly... 79:16
He that s. me fair... 94:13
He that s. sows... 156:26
He that s. the thing he should not...
   79:15
He that s. well... 168:25
He who s. much of others... 79:14
He who s. the truth... 176:53
Of him that s. ill... 168:61
Speech More have repented s.... 156:28
S. is silver... 156:23
S. is the picture... 168:66
Spend If you can s. much... 163:25
Know when to s.... 163:29
Never s. your money... 6:9
S. and be free... 163:28
S., and God will send... 170:37
S. as you get 163:21
S. not where you may save... 163:26
Who more than he is worth does s....
   163:5
Spender To a good s.... 163:27
Spenders Great s.... 163:33
Spends Much s. the traveller... 172:32
Who s. before he thrives... 163:1
Who s. more than he should... 163:3
Spent What we s. we had... 170:32
Spice He that hath the s.... 180:10
Spindle Get thy s. and thy distaff ready...
   77:41
Spins She s. well... 49:15
Spirit The s. is willing... 182:6
Spit S. on a stone... 134:17
Spits Who s. against the wind... 44:13
Spoil Don't s. the ship... 115:10
Spoils Too much s.... 116:11

Spoke The highest s.... 111:9
Spots There are s. even in the sun 97:22
Sprat Every s. now-a-days... 24:3
Throw out a s.... 150:6
Spread Don't s. the cloth... 6:15
S. the table... 53:10
Spring In the s. a young man's fancy...
   152:5
The s. is not always green 152:3
Spur A s. in the head... 51:23
Never s. a willing horse 182:17
S. a jade a question... 99:8
Squeaking The s. wheel... 168:24
Stable It's too late to shut the s. door...
   142:31
Stake Nothing s.... 37:37
Standing S. pools gather filth 95:8
Stands He s. not surely... 97:14
Stay He that can s., obtains 130:16
S. a little... 122:11
Steal He that will s. an egg... 33:27
He that will s. a pin... 33:26
If you s. for others... 33:19
One man may s. a horse... 100:9
Steals He that s. honey... 33:16
Steer S. not after every mariner's direc-
   tion 3:28
Step S. after step... 134:15
The first s.... 12:8
The greatest s.... 12:9
Stepmother Take heed of a s.... 128:23
Steward There is a good s. abroad...
   181:94
Stick It is easy to find a s.... 147:42
The s. is the surest peacemaker 132:16
Sticking S. goes not by strength... 158:4
Sticks S. and stones... 168:56
Stile He that will not go over the s....
   182:31
Still A s. tongue... 156:8
Be s., and have thy will 130:15
S. waters run deep 156:32
The s. sow... 7:17
Sting The s. of a reproach... 176:58
Stinking No man cries s. fish 24:18
Stitch A s. in time... 52:21
Don't s. your seam... 85:36
Stolen S. goods... 33:22
S. waters... 33:14
Stomach Make not thy s.... 87:49
To have a s. and lack meat... 166:3

Stone Never take a s.... 116:20
　　There is a sliddery s.... 81:29
　　The s. that lies not in your gate... 99:13
　　Though s. were changed to gold... 28:37
Stone-dead S. has no fellow 39:28
Stones Who remove s.... 37:28
Stools Between two s.... 146:9
Stoop He that will not s. for a pin...
　　138:30
　　It is no time to s.... 142:33
Store They that have got good s. of but-
　　ter... 180:8
　　Where there is s. of oatmeal... 180:9
Storm After a s. comes a calm 127:19
Stout Put a s. heart... 31:10
Stoutest The s. beggar... 58:73
Straight A s. stick... 7:38
　　S. trees have crooked roots 7:21
Straw Let an ill man lie in thy s.... 101:14
Straws S. show which way... 160:23
Stream The s. stopped... 129:14
Streets The s. of London... 58:77
Strength S. grows stronger... 164:1
Stretch S. your arm... 163:22
Stretches Everyone s. his legs... 163:23
Strife Better s. than solitude 161:11
　　S. never begets... 141:19
Strike S. while the iron is hot 126:4
Strikes He that s. with his tongue... 168:2
　　He that s. with the sword... 178:6
String The s. of a man's sack of pa-
　　tience... 130:25
Strings S. high stretched... 56:18
Striving It is ill s. against the stream 25:6
Strokes Great s.... 158:5
　　Little s. fell great oaks 134:19
Strong A s. town is not won... 130:36
　　The s. man and the waterfall... 164:8
Strumpet Never was s. fair 112:29
Stuarts All S. are not sib... 7:13
Studies A man's s.... 102:6
　　He that s. his content... 28:34
Stuffing S. holds out storm 53:4
Stumble A s. may prevent a fall 98:7
Stumbles He that s. twice... 62:33
Stung It is better to be s. by a nettle...
　　72:15
Style The s. is the man 188:17
Subject The s.'s love... 149:21
Subjects Although there exist many thou-
　　sand s.... 168:93

Sublime From the s. to the ridiculous...
　　116:39
Submit To the man s.... 92:8
Submitting The s. to one wrong... 56:25
Subtlety S. is better than force 164:18
Succeed If at first you don't s.... 134:23
Succeeds Nothing s.... 165:1
Success S. has many friends 165:7
　　S. makes a fool seem wise 165:4
Sudden S. friendship... 72:67
　　S. joy... 84:50
Suffer Better s. ill... 41:41
　　If thou s. a calf... 56:24
　　S. the ill... 98:3
　　We must s. much... 166:17
Sufferance Of s., comes ease 166:13
Suffered He that is s. to do more than is
　　fitting... 33:9
Suffering It is not the s.... 144:58
　　S. does not manifest itself 166:5
　　S. is better than care 166:14
　　S. is bitter... 166:15
Suffers Who s. much... 166:4
Suffices That which s.... 28:18
Sufficient S. unto the day... 186:16
Suffolk S. is the land of churches 58:31
Suit One s. of law... 104:22
Summer Look for s. on the top... 152:8
　　No s., but has its winter 97:33
　　S. in winter... 181:119
　　S. is a seemly time 152:7
Sun Although the s. shine... 70:17
　　If the s. goes pale to bed... 181:110
　　If the s. in red should set... 181:111
　　Let not the s. go down... 5:32
　　No s. without a shadow 97:31
　　The s. has stood still... 171:28
　　The s. is never the worse... 78:41
　　The s. shines upon all alike 60:12
　　When the s. rises... 87:38
　　When the s. sets bright and clear...
　　181:113
　　When the s. sets in a bank... 181:112
　　When the s. sets, the moon rises...
　　127:4
　　Where the s. enters... 87:19
Sunday S.'s wooing... 144:68
　　When S. comes... 144:69
Sundial What is the good of a s.... 24:20
Sup It is better to s. with a cutty... 80:16
　　No man can s.... 108:20

Who gives not t. to men... 80:28

Thatch T. your roof... 70:14

Thatches He that t. his house with turds... 3:59

Thief A t. knows a thief... 33:38
A t. passes for a gentleman... 15:40
One t. robs another 33:37
One t. will not rob another 110:5
Set a t.... 33:29
The t. doth fear... 26:8
The t. is sorry... 33:39

Thieves All are not t.... 7:42
Little t. are hanged... 29:47
T. and rogues... 111:39
T. and whores... 112:17
T.' handsel... 33:40
When t. fall out... 141:22

Think First t.... 85:32
One may t.... 114:12
They that t. none ill... 13:14
T. of ease... 48:44
T. on the end... 55:2
T. with the wise... 168:95

Thinking T. is very far from knowing 13:13

Thinks He t. not well... 85:37

Third The t. is a charm 167:4
The t. time pays for all 167:5
T. time lucky 167:3

Thirsty He is not t.... 51:73
He that goes to bed t.... 51:78

Thomas On St T. the Divine... 117:77
St T. gray... 117:76

Thorn Of a t. springs not a fig 18:9

Thorns He that handles t.... 37:27

Thought The t. has good legs... 188:5
T. is free 114:11

Thousand A t. pounds, and a bottle of hay... 180:66
In a t. pounds of law... 104:16

Thread A t. will tie an honest man... 89:22
He who holds the t.... 9:4
The t. breaks... 179:4

Threatened There are more men t. than stricken 168:42
T. folk live long 168:41

Threatens He t. many... 35:10

Three T. dear years... 124:27
T. may keep a secret... 79:42
T. things are not to be trusted... 175:21

T. things cost dear... 112:18
T. things drive a man out of his house... 113:119

Thrift T. is a great revenue 170:1
T. is the philosopher's stone 170:2

Thrive All things t.... 167:6
First t.... 113:45
He that will t. must ask... 113:101
He that will t., must rise... 52:8
He who would wish to t.... 167:14

Thrives Well t. he... 77:48

Throw Don't t. out your dirty water... 85:39
The best t. of the dice... 74:11

Thunder While the t. lasted... 37:14

Thunders When it t. in March... 181:75
When it t., the thief becomes honest 37:15

Thursday T. come... 38:4

Tide The t. must be taken... 126:12
The t. never goes out so far... 127:42

Tie No t. can oblige... 110:15

Tiger If you do not enter a t.'s den... 37:42

Time He that has t.... 171:9
It is t. to set in... 113:93
It is t. to yoke... 113:94
No t. like the present 43:26
Take t. by the forelock 126:14
Take t. when time comes 126:15
Take t. when time comes, lest time steal away 171:36
There is a t. and place... 171:37
There is a t. to speak... 156:27
The t. to come... 171:47
Those that make the best use of their t.... 48:46
T. and straw... 171:13
T. and tide... 171:29
T. cures all things 171:1
T. devours... 171:14
'T. enough' lost the ducks 43:4
T. flees away... 171:24
T. flies 171:23
T. has wings 171:25
T. is a file... 171:15
T. is a great healer 171:2
T. is money 171:7
T. is the father... 171:21
T. is the rider... 171:17
T. is, time was... 171:26

T. lost... 171:35
T., not the mind... 109:78
T. passes away... 140:20
T. spent in vice... 171:32
T. stays not... 171:30
T. tames... 171:4
T. tries all things 171:18
T. tries truth 171:20
T. undermines us 171:16
T. will tell 171:19
T. works wonders 171:5
Who will in t. present... 84:19
With t. and art... 171:12

Times Every one puts his fault on the t.
147:29
T. change... 17:20

Tine Many t. half-mark whinger... 115:11

Tired When a man is t. of London...
58:75

Tocherless A t. dame... 113:59

Tod The t. never sped better... 153:27
The t.'s bairns... 18:2

Today If t. will not... 43:8
One hour t.... 43:21
One t. is worth two tomorrows 43:22
T. a man... 39:26
T. is the scholar... 171:45

Toll When thou dost hear a t. or knell...
39:17

Tomorrow Never put off till t.... 43:20
T. is another day 91:28
T. never comes 43:23

Tongue A good t. is a good weapon
168:46
A long t.... 139:22
An ill t. may do much 79:13
If you keep your t. prisoner... 156:12
It is a good t. that says no ill... 168:58
Let not thy t. run away... 168:11
Let not your t. run at rover 168:12
One t. is enough... 184:50
That t. does lie... 85:19
The t. breaks bone... 168:48
The t. is more venomous... 168:50
The t. is not steel... 168:52
The t. is the rudder... 168:26
The t. of experience... 62:7
The t. of idle persons... 168:111
The t. stings 168:49
The t. talks... 168:3
Under the t.... 168:47

Too T. much of ought... 116:26
You can have t. much... 116:25

Toom T. bags rattle 69:76
T. pokes... 113:50

Too-too T. will in two 56:14

Tortoise The t. wins the race... 134:5

Tottenham When T. wood... 181:87

Touch T. wood... 167:15

Town He that is in a t.... 117:47
If you see a t. worshipping a calf... 25:2
There was never a good t.... 97:34
The t. for wealth... 180:81

Trade A t. is better... 124:12
Every man to his t. 124:24
He that has no good t.... 124:11
T. is the mother... 124:5
Who has a t.... 124:2
Who hath a good t.... 124:1

Trades A dozen t.... 124:14
A man of many t.... 124:13
Let all t. live 124:17

Tradesmen T. live upon lack 124:18

Train T. up a child... 19:31

Tramp The more you t. on a turd... 42:15
T. on a snail... 35:11

Travel He who does not t.... 172:5
It is better to t. hopefully... 6:5
Much t. is needed... 172:3
The best way to t.... 144:7
To t. through the world... 172:35
T. broadens the mind 172:1
T. makes a wise man better... 172:13

Traveller A t. may lie... 172:16

Travellers Nothing so necessary for t....
172:38
T. and poets... 172:17
T. change climates... 172:6
T. should correct... 172:15

Travelling Much t.... 172:4

Travels He that t. far... 172:2
He t. fastest... 161:9
He who t. not by sea... 37:34

Tre By T., Pol, and Pen... 58:80

Tread When you can t. on nine daisies...
152:1

Treat T. a friend... 72:81

Tree As a t. falls... 17:15
A t. often transplanted... 17:12
He that plants a t.... 30:39
It is a good t. that has neither knap nor
gaw 97:39

Vincent Remember on St V.'s Day...
181:105

Vine Make the v. poor... 30:49
  Take a v. of a good soil... 113:67
  The v. brings forth three grapes... 51:40

Vinegar A v. seller... 124:21

Violent Nothing that is v.... 129:10

Viper No v. so little... 160:29

Virtue He that sows v.... 78:18
  There is no v.... 78:26
  The v. of a coward... 32:23
  V. and a trade... 78:8
  V. and happiness... 78:2
  V. and vice... 78:52
  V. flies from the heart... 131:33
  V. has all things... 78:13
  V. is a jewel... 78:4
  V. is found... 116:7
  V. is its own reward 78:14
  V. is more important... 78:15
  V. is praised by all... 78:36
  V. is the beauty... 78:5
  V. is the only true nobility 78:16
  V. joins man to God 78:1
  V. never grows old 78:17

Visits Long v.... 92:12

Vitus If St V.'s Day be rainy weather...
181:62

Voice The v. is the best music 168:27

Volunteer One v.... 182:18

Vows V. made in storms... 139:6

Voyage That v. never has luck... 9:26

Vulgar The v. will keep no account...
165:12

W

Wage W. will get a page 131:7

Wager A w. is a fool's argument 74:12

Wages The w. of sin... 10:28

Wagon When the w. of fortune... 111:20

Wake W. not a sleeping lion 174:6

Walk We must learn to w. before we can
run 130:42

Walking It is good w. with a horse...
151:15

Wallet We see not what is in the w. behind 34:16

Walls W. have ears 79:24

Walnut-tree He who plants a w.... 30:46

Wame Lay your w.... 163:24

Wand Thraw the w.... 19:30

Wanswell All the maids in W.... 58:74

Want A thing you don't w.... 22:37
  For w. of a nail... 160:22
  If you w. a thing done, go... 153:32
  If you w. a thing well done... 153:31
  W. of money... 136:42

Wanton W. kittens... 19:49

War He that makes a good w.... 132:10
  In w. all suffer defeat... 178:5
  In w., it is not permitted... 178:14
  No w. without a woman 184:6
  W., hunting, and love... 178:11
  W. is death's feast 178:2
  W. is sweet... 178:20
  W. is the sport... 178:21
  W. makes thieves... 132:13
  When w. begins... 178:3

Warm He that is w.... 153:28

Warned W. folks may live 168:43

Warning He was slain that had w.... 3:22

Wars He that is not in the w.... 37:7
  Of all w.... 132:14
  W. bring scars 178:4

Wash Don't w. your dirty linen... 143:23
  W. your hands often... 87:14

Washing For w. his hands... 21:2

Waste W. makes want 170:42
  W. not, want not 170:41

Watched A w. pot... 130:34

Water Don't go near the w.... 37:43
  There was aye some w.... 79:4
  Under w., famine... 181:97
  W. drinkers... 51:56
  W. is a boon in the desert... 177:10
  W. is the king... 51:51

Way Once a w.... 104:56
  The w. to an Englishman's heart... 53:6

Ways There are many w. to fame 64:3
  There are more w. to kill a cat... 47:28
  There are more w. to kill a dog... 47:29
  There are more w. to the wood... 47:26

Weak Every man has his w. side 97:7
  W. men had need be witty 179:10
  W. things united... 179:7

Weaker The w. goes to the pot 179:1
  The w. has the worst 179:3

Weakest The w. goes to the wall 179:2

Weal Be it w. or be it woe... 117:54
  No w. without woe 162:24

Wealth A man's w. is his enemy 180:37
  Bear w.... 136:85

If we have not the world's w.... 136:28

The greatest w.... 180:54

W. infatuates... 180:39

W. is best known by want 136:16

W. is the test... 180:48

W. makes worship 180:88

Where w. is established... 180:28

Weapon The w. of the brave... 31:15

Weapons All the w. of war... 66:17

W. breed peace 132:18

Wear Better to w. out than to rust out 48:12

Better w. out shoes than sheets 48:7

Do not w. out... 92:10

Weary Never be w. of well doing 41:39

Weasel When the w. and the cat... 10:6

Weather No w. is ill... 181:24

Weather-eye Keep your w. open 63:6

Web For a w. begun... 77:39

Wed Better w. over the mixen... 113:75

Wedding As your w. ring wears... 113:11

One w. brings another 113:148

Wedlock W. is a padlock 113:12

Wee Better a w. fire... 136:87

Weed One ill w.... 29:4

Weeds The w. overgrow the corn 10:43

W. want no sowing 10:4

Weel W.'s him and wae's him... 144:86

Weep To w. for joy... 84:33

Weeping We w. come into the world... 162:30

Weigh W. justly... 22:36

Weight W. and measure... 22:34

Welcome Good will and w.... 92:3

He that is w.... 92:4

Such w.... 92:6

They are w. that bring 75:5

W. is the best dish 92:5

Well All is w. with him... 121:8

Do w. and have well 41:35

He that does w.... 41:36

He that would be w.... 172:29

If the lad go to the w.... 182:21

That which is w. done... 48:26

W. is, that well does 41:3

When the w. is full... 56:19

Where men are w. used... 101:11

Well-bred A w. youth... 15:17

Welshman The older the W.... 133:84

The W. had rather see... 181:116

The W. keeps nothing... 133:85

Westminster Who goes to W. for a wife... 58:76

What It is not w. is he... 180:50

Wheat Sow w. in dirt... 30:12

Whip A w. for a fool... 49:23

Whispered W. words... 79:19

Whispering Where there is w.... 79:7

Whistling A w. girl... 167:13

A w. woman... 167:12

White A w. wall... 69:45

He that has a w. horse... 113:87

W. silver draws black lines 11:10

Whole Our w. life... 107:11

Whore A w. in a fine dress... 112:30

A w. repents... 112:28

Once a w.... 112:27

Whoredom W. and grace... 112:31

Whores W. affect not you... 112:19

W. and rogues... 112:32

Whoring W. and bawdry... 112:21

Why Every w. has a wherefore 8:14

Wicked A w. book... 188:15

A w. man is his own hell 10:17

A w. woman and an evil... 184:3

It is a w. world... 10:33

The more w.... 111:38

Wickedness W. with beauty... 10:26

Wide He that has a w. therm... 76:16

Widecombe W. folks are picking their geese... 181:98

Widow Long a w.... 155:4

Widows W. are always rich 180:75

Wife A good w. and health... 113:7

A good w. makes a good husband 113:100

A good w.'s a goodly prize... 113:9

A man without a w.... 113:6

A w. is sought for her virtue... 113:80

He that has a w. has a master 113:105

He that has a w., has strife 113:20

He that has no w.... 3:63

If you make your w. an ass... 113:122

Next to no w.... 113:27

The first w. is matrimony... 113:149

There is one good w. in the country... 24:4

There was a w. that kept her supper... 170:33

The w. is the key... 113:102

Wae's the w. that wants the tongue... 113:116

From the evil w. guard yourself...
184:78

If a w. were as little... 184:16

Let no w.'s painting... 184:79

Tell a w. she is fair... 184:82

The w. that deliberates... 146:7

Who has a w. has an eel... 184:75

W. is the confusion... 184:95

Women All w. are good 184:15

All w. may be won 184:81

Many w., many words... 184:55

The more w. look in their glass... 24:9

Three w. make a market 184:58

Three w., three geese... 184:59

Weal and w. cannot pan... 184:8

Where there are w. and geese... 184:57

W. and dogs... 184:5

W. and hens... 184:70

W. and music... 184:76

W. and sparrows... 184:56

W. and wine... 51:34

W. are as wavering... 184:21

W. are great talkers 184:51

W. are like wasps... 184:12

W. are necessary evils 184:18

W. are saints in church... 184:32

W. are the devil's nets 184:2

W. are the snares of Satan 184:1

W. have long hair... 184:38

W. in mischief... 184:90

W. in state affairs... 184:14

W. laugh when they can... 184:33

W. may blush to hear... 184:29

W. must have their wills while they
live... 184:24

W. naturally deceive... 184:28

W., priests, and poultry... 184:66

W. resist... 184:85

W.'s counsel is cold 184:9

W.'s instinct... 184:89

W. will have their wills 184:25

W. will have the last word 184:54

W. will say anything 184:52

Wonder W. is the daughter of ignorance
96:3

Woo A man may w. where he will...
109:92

To w. is a pleasure... 109:91

Wood It is a sairy w.... 143:13

Once w.... 69:18

W. in a wilderness... 136:110

Wool There is no w. so white... 29:33

Woos He that w. a maid... 109:89

Word A good w. costs no more... 101:24

A w. and a stone let go... 168:17

A w. before... 70:4

A w. spoken... 142:8

A w. to the wise... 168:85

From w. to deed... 41:22

One ill w. asks another 44:19

While the w. is in your mouth... 168:18

Words A man of w.... 41:10

Fair w. and foul deeds... 41:24

Fair w. and foul play... 41:25

Fair w. break no bones 101:21

Fair w. fill not the belly 168:31

Fair w. hurt not the mouth 101:22

Fair w. will not make the pot play
168:32

Few w. are best 168:78

Fine w. butter no parsnips 168:30

Flow of w.... 168:104

Good w. and ill deeds... 41:26

Good w. anoint us... 168:64

Good w. are good cheap 101:23

Good w. cool more... 168:28

Good w. cost nought 101:25

Good w. fill not a sack 168:34

Good w. without deeds... 41:16

Hard w. break no bones 34:1

He who gives fair w.... 168:33

Ill w. are bellows... 168:63

In many w., a lie or two may escape
168:67

In many w., the truth goes by 168:68

Many w., many buffets 168:6

W. and feathers... 139:9

W. are but wind 139:10

W. are but wind, but blows unkind
168:54

W. are mere bubbles of water... 41:9

W. bind men 168:19

W. cut more than swords 168:53

W. fly... 188:8

W. have wings... 168:16

W. may pass... 168:55

Work All w. and no play... 48:50

He who wants the w. badly done...
131:18

If you won't w.... 48:41

It is good to w. wisely... 48:27

It is not w. that kills... 186:7

PENGUIN ONLINE

READ MORE IN PENGUIN

In every corner of the world, on every subject under the sun, Penguin represents quality and variety – the very best in publishing today.

For complete information about books available from Penguin – including Puffins, Penguin Classics and Arkana – and how to order them, write to us at the appropriate address below. Please note that for copyright reasons the selection of books varies from country to country.

In the United Kingdom: Please write to *Dept. EP, Penguin Books Ltd, Bath Road, Harmondsworth, West Drayton, Middlesex UB7 0DA*

In the United States: Please write to *Consumer Sales, Penguin Putnam Inc., P.O. Box 12289 Dept. B, Newark, New Jersey 07101-5289.* VISA and MasterCard holders call 1-800-788-6262 to order Penguin titles

In Canada: Please write to *Penguin Books Canada Ltd, 10 Alcorn Avenue, Suite 300, Toronto, Ontario M4V 3B2*

In Australia: Please write to *Penguin Books Australia Ltd, P.O. Box 257, Ringwood, Victoria 3134*

In New Zealand: Please write to *Penguin Books (NZ) Ltd, Private Bag 102902, North Shore Mail Centre, Auckland 10*

In India: Please write to *Penguin Books India Pvt Ltd, 11 Community Centre, Panchsheel Park, New Delhi 110017*

In the Netherlands: Please write to *Penguin Books Netherlands bv, Postbus 3507, NL-1001 AH Amsterdam*

In Germany: Please write to *Penguin Books Deutschland GmbH, Metzlerstrasse 26, 60594 Frankfurt am Main*

In Spain: Please write to *Penguin Books S. A., Bravo Murillo 19, 1° B, 28015 Madrid*

In Italy: Please write to *Penguin Italia s.r.l., Via Benedetto Croce 2, 20094 Corsico, Milano*

In France: Please write to *Penguin France, Le Carré Wilson, 62 rue Benjamin Baillaud, 31500 Toulouse*

In Japan: Please write to *Penguin Books Japan Ltd, Kaneko Building, 2-3-25 Koraku, Bunkyo-Ku, Tokyo 112*

In South Africa: Please write to *Penguin Books South Africa (Pty) Ltd, Private Bag X14, Parkview, 2122 Johannesburg*

READ MORE IN PENGUIN

LANGUAGE/LINGUISTICS

Language Play David Crystal

We all use language to communicate information, but it is language play which is truly central to our lives. Full of puns, groan-worthy gags and witty repartee, this book restores the fun to the study of language. It also demonstrates why all these things are essential elements of what makes us human.

Swearing Geoffrey Hughes

'A deliciously filthy trawl among taboo words across the ages and the globe' *Observer*. 'Erudite and entertaining' Penelope Lively, *Daily Telegraph*

The Language Instinct Stephen Pinker

'Dazzling ... Pinker's big idea is that language is an instinct, as innate to us as flying is to geese ... Words can hardly do justice to the superlative range and liveliness of Pinker's investigations' *Independent*. 'He does for language what David Attenborough does for animals, explaining difficult scientific concepts so easily that they are indeed absorbed as a transparent stream of words' John Gribbin

Mother Tongue Bill Bryson

'A delightful, amusing and provoking survey, a joyful celebration of our wonderful language, which is packed with curiosities and enlightenment on every page' *Sunday Express*. 'A gold mine of language-anecdote. A surprise on every page ... enthralling' *Observer*

Longman Guide to English Usage
Sidney Greenbaum and Janet Whitcut

Containing 5000 entries compiled by leading authorities on modern English, this invaluable reference work clarifies every kind of usage problem, giving expert advice on points of grammar, meaning, style, spelling, pronunciation and punctuation.

READ MORE IN PENGUIN

REFERENCE

The Penguin Dictionary of the Third Reich
James Taylor and Warren Shaw

This dictionary provides a full background to the rise of Nazism and the role of Germany in the Second World War. Among the areas covered are the major figures from Nazi politics, arts and industry, the German Resistance, the politics of race and the Nuremberg trials.

The Penguin Biographical Dictionary of Women

This stimulating, informative and entirely new Penguin dictionary of women from all over the world, through the ages, contains over 1,600 clear and concise biographies on major figures from politicians, saints and scientists to poets, film stars and writers.

Roget's Thesaurus of English Words and Phrases
Edited by Betty Kirkpatrick

This new edition of Roget's classic work, now brought up to date for the nineties, will increase anyone's command of the English language. Fully cross-referenced, it includes synonyms of every kind (formal or colloquial, idiomatic and figurative) for almost 900 headings. It is a must for writers and utterly fascinating for any English speaker.

The Penguin Dictionary of International Relations
Graham Evans and Jeffrey Newnham

International relations have undergone a revolution since the end of the Cold War. This new world disorder is fully reflected in this new Penguin dictionary, which is extensively cross-referenced with a select bibliography to aid further study.

The Penguin Guide to Synonyms and Related Words
S. I. Hayakawa

'More helpful than a thesaurus, more humane than a dictionary, the *Guide to Synonyms and Related Words* maps linguistic boundaries with precision, sensitivity to nuance and, on occasion, dry wit' *The Times Literary Supplement*

DICTIONARIES

Abbreviations
Ancient History
Archaeology
Architecture
Art and Artists
Astronomy
Biographical Dictionary of
  Women
Biology
Botany
Building
Business
Challenging Words
Chemistry
Civil Engineering
Classical Mythology
Computers
Contemporary American History
Curious and Interesting Geometry
Curious and Interesting Numbers
Curious and Interesting Words
Design and Designers
Economics
Eighteenth-Century History
Electronics
English and European History
English Idioms
Foreign Terms and Phrases
French
Geography
Geology
German
Historical Slang
Human Geography
Information Technology

International Finance
International Relations
Literary Terms and Literary
  Theory
Mathematics
Modern History 1789–1945
Modern Quotations
Music
Musical Performers
Nineteenth-Century World
  History
Philosophy
Physical Geography
Physics
Politics
Proverbs
Psychology
Quotations
Quotations from Shakespeare
Religions
Rhyming Dictionary
Russian
Saints
Science
Sociology
Spanish
Surnames
Symbols
Synonyms and Antonyms
Telecommunications
Theatre
The Third Reich
Third World Terms
Troublesome Words
Twentieth-Century History
Twentieth-Century Quotations